Aquinas, Original Sin, and the Challenge of Evolution

Is original sin compatible with evolution? Many today believe the answer is "No." Engaging Aquinas's revolutionary account of the doctrine, Daniel W. Houck argues that there is not necessarily a conflict between this Christian teaching and mainstream biology. He draws on neglected texts outside the *Summa Theologiae* to show that Aquinas focused on humanity's loss of friendship with God – not the corruption of nature (or personal guilt). Aquinas's account is theologically attractive in its own right. Houck proposes, moreover, a new Thomist view of original sin that is consonant with evolution. This account is developed in dialogue with biblical scholarship on Jewish hamartiology and salient modern thinkers (including Kant, Schleiermacher, Barth, and Schoonenberg), and it is systematically connected to debates over nature, grace, the desire for God, and justification. In addition, the book canvasses a number of neglected premodern approaches to original sin, including those of Anselm, Abelard, and Lombard.

Daniel W. Houck is senior pastor of Calvary Hill Baptist Church (Fairfax) and adjunct professor of theology at the John Leland Center for Theological Studies. A research fellow at Trinity Evangelical Divinity School in 2017–18, his publications have appeared in journals such as *Archa Verbi* and *Nova et Vetera*.

Aquinas, Original Sin, and the Challenge of Evolution

DANIEL W. HOUCK

John Leland Center for Theological Studies

CAMBRIDGE
UNIVERSITY PRESS

CAMBRIDGE
UNIVERSITY PRESS

University Printing House, Cambridge CB2 8BS, United Kingdom

One Liberty Plaza, 20th Floor, New York, NY 10006, USA

477 Williamstown Road, Port Melbourne, VIC 3207, Australia

314-321, 3rd Floor, Plot 3, Splendor Forum, Jasola District Centre, New Delhi - 110025, India

103 Penang Road, #05-06/07, Visioncrest Commercial, Singapore 238467

Cambridge University Press is part of the University of Cambridge.

It furthers the University's mission by disseminating knowledge in the pursuit of education, learning and research at the highest international levels of excellence.

www.cambridge.org
Information on this title: www.cambridge.org/9781108725439
DOI: 10.1017/9781108642927

First published 2020
First paperback edition 2022

A catalogue record for this publication is available from the British Library

Library of Congress Cataloging in Publication data
NAMES: Houck, Daniel W., 1987– author.
TITLE: Aquinas, original sin, and the challenge of evolution / Daniel W. Houck,
John Leland Center for Theological Studies.
DESCRIPTION: Cambridge, United Kingdom ; New York, NY, USA : Cambridge University
Press, 2020. | Includes bibliographical references and index.
IDENTIFIERS: LCCN 2019042219 (print) | LCCN 2019042220 (ebook) |
ISBN 9781108493697 (hardback) | ISBN 9781108725439 (paperback) |
ISBN 9781108642927 (epub)
SUBJECTS: LCSH: Thomas, Aquinas, Saint, 1225?-1274. | Sin, Original–History of
doctrines. | Evolution (Biology)–Religious aspects–Christianity.
CLASSIFICATION: LCC B765.T54 H649 2020 (print) | LCC B765.T54 (ebook) |
DDC 233/.14–dc23
LC record available at https://lccn.loc.gov/2019042219
LC ebook record available at https://lccn.loc.gov/2019042220

ISBN 978-1-108-49369-7 Hardback
ISBN 978-1-108-72543-9 Paperback

To James and Susan

Contents

Acknowledgments

I completed this book at the Henry Center at Trinity Evangelical Divinity School during a fellowship generously funded by the Templeton Religion Trust (TRT). The atmosphere was ideal for interdisciplinary theological research. I am deeply grateful to the TRT, Trinity, and Professor Thomas McCall for affording me this opportunity. Of course, the views expressed here are my own and do not necessarily reflect those of any other person or institution, including the Henry Center or TRT. Significant parts of this project originated in my doctoral thesis at Southern Methodist University. Bruce Marshall, my advisor, offered invaluable feedback, encouragement, and counsel at every stage. Billy Abraham, Jim Lee, and Oliver Crisp read the dissertation and made a number of helpful suggestions.

Other colleagues and friends commented on the manuscript at various stages of its development, including Daniel Simmons, Thomas Joseph White, Ralph Stearley, Jitse M. van der Meer, Clay Carlson, Gavin Ortlund, Joel Chopp, Matthew Vanderpoel, and David Mahfood. I have benefited from discussion of the book's contents with Matthew Levering, Marc Cortez, Stephen Williams, Geoff Fulkerson, Nathan Chambers, Justus Hunter, Adam Van Wart, William Glass, and Dallas Gingles. My sincere thanks also go to Beatrice Rehl and the team at Cambridge University Press for their assistance.

Last but certainly not least, I would like to thank my wife, Katie, for her inexhaustible support during this process. This book is dedicated to my parents, James and Susan Houck.

Introduction

The eponymous protagonist of Thomas Hardy's *Tess of the d'Urbervilles* gave birth to a boy who fell gravely ill. Fearing scandal (Tess was unmarried), her father refused to allow the parish priest to visit their home. As her son, aptly named "Sorrow," approached death, Tess baptized him herself. Yet because the baptism was not administered by a priest, she mistakenly thought it invalid. When Sorrow died, Tess was devastated. Not only had she lost her son, her pain was amplified a thousand-fold because she was certain he was damned:

> She thought of the child consigned to the nethermost corner of hell, as its double doom for lack of baptism and lack of legitimacy; saw the arch-fiend tossing it with his three-pronged fork, like the one they used for heating the oven on baking days; to which picture she added many other quaint and curious details of torment sometimes taught the young in this Christian country.[1]

What gave rise to this superstition? Who taught Tess that children who die unbaptized are damned? Surely no reasonable religion would teach that children are condemned simply because they weren't sprinkled with water. If we had put this objection to Tess or her priest, however, a response would have been ready to hand: "in every person born into this world, it deserveth God's wrath and damnation."[2] The Church teaches that every child *deserves*

---

[1] Thomas Hardy, *Tess of the d'Urbervilles: A Pure Woman* (London: The Folio Society, 1991 [1891]), 97. For an argument that Tess was raped (as opposed to seduced), see William A. Davis Jr., "The Rape of Tess: Hardy, English Law, and the Case for Sexual Assault," *Nineteenth-Century Literature* 52.2 (1997), 221–31.

[2] Article 9 of the Thirty-Nine Articles of Religion, in *The Harmony of the Protestant Confessions: Exhibiting the Faith of the Churches of Christ, Reformed after the Pure*

damnation. Innocent in the eyes of the world, Sorrow was guilty in the eyes of God: he had contracted "original sin" in his mother's womb.

The doctrine of original sin had been taught in the West since the fifth century. According to the Council of Carthage, Adam, the first man, was created without sin and with the possibility of immortality. But he disobeyed God and ate of the forbidden fruit. As a result, he transmitted sin and death to his descendants. Therefore, the Council proclaimed, children must be baptized "for the remission of sins." There is no place "where little children may live blessedly even if they have gone forth from this world without baptism." For "what Catholic could doubt that he who has not deserved to be a co-heir with Christ is going to share the lot of the devil?"[3]

There is no biblical basis for this doctrine. It rests, ultimately, on a grammatical mistake; as one commentator put it, a *"péché originel grammatical."*[4] Augustine, who first used the phrase *"peccatum originale"* and whose teaching decisively influenced Carthage, relied on an "Old Latin" Bible that mistranslated Rom. 5:12. He mistakenly thought Paul explicitly stated that Adam's sin was transmitted to his descendants. The Vulgate did not affirm inherited sin quite so straightforwardly, but it retained the clause *"in quo omnes peccauerunt* (in whom [Adam] all sinned)," which also functioned as a prooftext for the doctrine. This translation is regarded by modern commentators – as it was by Greek-speaking church fathers – as an unlikely construction of *eph' hō.*[5] Paul merely meant that all, or most, human beings follow Adam's example and sin, not that they all inherit Adam's sin.

   and Holy Doctrine of the Gospel, throughout Europe, ed. and trans. Peter Hall (London: John F. Shaw, 1842), 509.

[3] Quotes from the Council of Carthage, Cann. 2–3 (DH 223–4). DH = Heinrich Denzinger, *Enchiridion Symbolorum: A Compendium of Creeds, Definitions, and Declarations of the Catholic Church*, 43rd ed., ed. Peter Hünermann (San Francisco: Ignatius Press, 2012).

[4] Athanase Sage, *"Le péché originel dans la pensée de saint Augustin, de 412 à 430," Revue des Études Augustiniennes* 15 (1969), 81. As Sage explains, Augustine's translation of Rom. 5:12 read as follows: "per unum hominem peccatum intrauit mundum et per peccatum mors et ita in omnes pertransiit in quo omnes peccaverunt." The verb *"pertransiit"* has no clear subject, and Augustine supplied *peccatum*, with the result that he understood Paul to have said, "sin was transmitted to all human beings." The Vulgate, by contrast, indicates that *mors* ("death") is the subject of *pertransiit*.

[5] "The latter interpretation [explaining the antecedent of *in quo* as *in Adamo*] was unknown to the Greek Fathers before John Damascene." Joseph A. Fitzmyer, *Romans: A New Translation with Introduction and Commentary* (New York: Doubleday, 1993), 414. Unless otherwise noted, references to the Greek text of the New Testament are taken from *Novum Testamentum Graece*, 28th revised edition, ed. Barbara Aland and others (Stuttgart: Deutsche Bibelgesellschaft, 2012) and English translations of the Bible from the New Revised Standard Version Bible, copyright 1989, Division of Christian Education of the National Council of the Churches of Christ in the United States of America. Used by permission. All rights reserved.

Not only is the doctrine of original sin *not* taught in Scripture, it is clearly opposed to the teaching of Jesus. "Unless you change and become like children, you will never enter the kingdom of heaven" (Matt. 18:3). "Let the little children come to me, and do not stop them; for it is to such as these that the kingdom of heaven belongs" (Matt. 19:14). Why should adults imitate children if the latter are damnable sinners? How could the kingdom of heaven belong to children if children belong to the devil? The goal of Jesus' ministry was the salvation of the world (John 12:47), not the condemnation of children. Before Augustine, Christians had no difficulty understanding all this.

Take the fourth-century bishop Gregory of Nyssa, for example. At some point between 371 and 395, his friend Hierios wrote him a letter, asking why God allows infants to die. His perplexity, however, didn't stem from anxiety over infant damnation. Gregory and Hierios both assumed that all babies go to heaven. Hierios was confused, rather, about whether infants will receive great rewards *in* heaven. Because God is just, it seems that he will reward the virtuous – especially martyrs – more than infants. But it seems tragic for infants to be eternally deprived of rewards they never had a chance to earn. Gregory resolved the dilemma by arguing that the kingdom of heaven is not the reward of virtue. It is our *natural* end, such that "[w]e may say that the enjoyment of that future life does indeed belong of right to the human being."[6] Infants and martyrs alike will be saved. What if the West had adopted the Nyssan's teaching instead of Augustine's? How much pointless pain would bereaved parents have been spared? If only Tess had Gregory as a priest!

The doctrine of original sin is pernicious. It is not found in Scripture. It was not taught by the earliest church fathers. But these are not the only, or even the most decisive, reasons for rejecting it. Even if we granted *arguendo* that Augustine's view of original sin was both spiritually salutary and a legitimate development of Scripture and tradition, it still wouldn't be credible to the educated person today. It is, after all, wholly incompatible with a scientific view of the world. A large body of interdisciplinary evidence supports the hypothesis that the human condition is the product of a long evolutionary history of random genetic variation and

---

[6] *ΓΡΗΓΟΡΙΟΥ ΕΠΙΣΚΟΠΟΥ ΝΥΣΣΗΣ ΠΡΟΣ ΙΕΠΙΟΝ ΠΕΡΙ ΤΩΝ ΠΡΟ ΩΠΑΣ ΑΝΑΡΠΑΖΟΜΕΝΩΝ ΝΗΠΙΩΝ* [*De infantibus praemature abreptis*], in *Gregorii Nysseni Opera Dogmatica Minora*, ed. Hadwiga Horner (Leiden: E. J. Brill, 1987), vol. 3, part 2: 82; trans. *On Infants' Early Deaths*, in *Nicene and Post-Nicene Fathers*, series 2, ed. Philip Schaff and Henry Wace (Edinburgh: T&T Clark; Grand Rapids, MI: Eerdmans, 1892), 5: 376.

natural selection, not inherited "corruption" caused by a single act at the dawn of history. Moreover, evolutionary pressure has selected for behavior that Christianity considers sinful, such as selfishness. And in any case, we evolved as a group, so one man couldn't have transmitted sin to everyone else. Just as rational people no longer believe that the Sun revolves around the Earth, or that the Earth is six thousand years old, they no longer believe that humanity has been corrupted by Adam's Fall. As Julius Gross put it, in the course of concluding his magisterial history of the doctrine, "modern science killed original sin."[7]

Or so the story goes. So, at any rate, a composite sketch of a number of popular stories of original sin's demise goes. This book tells a different one. The history of the doctrine is far more complex than the foregoing sketch suggests. Original sin was not founded solely on a mistranslation. Nor did Augustine invent it. And, far from blindly following his authority, theologians after Augustine – from the Middle Ages until the present day – have vigorously debated the nature of the doctrine. Yet there is no doubt that confusion surrounds its contemporary meaning.

Many theologians agree with Julius Gross to the effect that evolution has rendered original sin untenable. At the popular level, however, many Christians – and prominent Christian leaders – reject evolution because they believe it is incompatible with original sin.[8] Others believe that original sin is a crucial corollary to the gospel but are loath to reject the mainstream scientific consensus. But it's far from clear how the doctrine of original sin could be reconciled with evolution without unacceptable theological consequences. In light of the difficulties with the state of original justice – for example, the aforementioned problem that we are disposed to sin because of our evolutionary history – a common proposal in modern theology has been to separate original sin from a historical Fall. Perhaps, some have argued, we have always been opposed to God. But how does this square with the doctrine that God created all things

---

[7] "Die moderne Wissenschaft hat die Erbsünde getötet." Julius Gross, *Geschichte des Erbsündendogmas: Ein Beitrag zur Geschichte des Problems vom Ursprung des Übels*, vol. 4, *Entwicklungsgeschichte des Erbsündendogmas seit der Reformation* (München: Ernst Reinhardt, 1972), 352. Translations mine unless noted.

[8] For example, the president of the flagship seminary of the Southern Baptist Convention – the largest Protestant denomination in the United States – argues as follows. "The evolutionary account is ... incompatible with the claim that all humanity is descended from Adam and the claim that in Adam all humanity fell into sin and guilt. The Bible's account of the Fall, and its consequences, is utterly incompatible with evolutionary theory." R. Albert Mohler Jr., "The New Shape of the Debate," *Southern Seminary Magazine* (Winter 2011), 25–6.

good? There are difficulties, it seems, with all the common approaches to the problem. Denying original sin obscures the universal need for redemption. Affirming original sin and the Fall seems incompatible with evolution. And affirming original sin without a Fall seems to compromise the goodness of creation. In light of this, a fresh perspective on original sin, theologically rigorous and in dialogue with salient research in evolutionary biology, is needed.

This book aims to provide one. I argue that Thomas Aquinas can help us reconcile original sin and evolution. His account of original sin, however, has been neglected, and as a result it has been misunderstood. After a discussion of Augustine and his medieval reception, I offer a reading of Thomas's doctrine of original sin and a reformulation of his account, in dialogue with evolutionary theory and salient modern theologians. The book's primary contributions, accordingly, are to historical theology, systematic theology, and theology and science. We can now briefly review salient scholarship in these fields. I begin with literature on Thomas's account of original sin and then turn to the *status quaestionis* in systematic theology and theology and science.

ORIGINAL SIN IN SCHOLARSHIP

In comparison to the extensive treatment other areas of his theology have received in recent decades, Thomas's account of original sin has been neglected. The most in-depth treatment is still J. B. Kors's monograph, published nearly a century ago.[9] There was a large debate over Thomas's view of original justice in the first half of the twentieth century, but the last detailed study of that issue was published in 1955.[10] Histories of original sin more broadly have generally relied on Kors.[11] My book

---

[9] J. B. Kors, *La Justice primitive et le péché originel d'après S. Thomas* (Paris: Le Saulchoir, 1922).

[10] William A. Van Roo, *Grace and Original Justice According to St. Thomas* (Rome: Gregorian University, 1955).

[11] N. P. Williams, *The Ideas of the Fall and of Original Sin: A Historical and Critical Study* (London: Longman, Green and Co., 1927); D. O. Lottin, *Psychologie et morale aux XIIe et XIIIe Siècles*, tome 4, *Problèmes de morale, troisième partie*, vol. 1 (Louvain-Gembloux, 1954); Gross, *Geschichte des Erbsündendogmas*, vol. 3, *Entwicklungsgeschichte des Erbsündendogmas im Zeitalter der Scholastik (12.–15. Jahrh.)* (München: E. Reinhardt, 1971); Henrich M. Köster, *Urstand, Fall und Erbsünde in der Scholastik* (Freiburg: Herder, 1979). Despite being nearly a century old, Williams's study is still the standard English-language reference for medieval views

differs in three major ways. First, I offer original, critical analysis of Thomas's views. These historical studies, by and large, summarize Thomas. Second, they assume that Thomas's account was static – and fully coherent throughout his career. A central argument of this book is that Thomas's account of original justice developed, leading to problems for his view of the transmission and nature of original sin. Third, rather than treating Thomas's account in isolation, I connect it to other areas of his thought, including his view of the need for grace and salient aspects of his account of providence.

Another strand of scholarship is represented by Otto Pesch's influential ecumenical study of Luther and Aquinas.[12] A Dominican at the time, Pesch was indebted to the predominant reading of the Order of Preachers, which prioritizes the treatise on grace and the corruption of human nature (*STh* I–II, qq. 109–14). On this "Augustinian" reading of Thomas, infants with original sin have lost their natural teleological orientation to God and are born with sinful self-love instead. Réginald Garrigou-Lagrange had defended this interpretation earlier in the century.[13] This is still the standard scholarly reading of Aquinas.[14] I argue against it, at length, in Chapter 3. In addition to the foregoing studies, there have been various introductory or partial treatments of Thomas's account.[15] We can now turn to constructive accounts of original sin.

---

of original sin. He also proposed, constructively, that a "World-Soul" rebelled against God and is responsible for evil. This has not been influential.

[12] Otto Hermann Pesch, *Theologie der Rechtfertigung bei Martin Luther und Thomas von Aquin: Versuch eines systematisch-theologischen Dialogs* (Mainz: M. Grünewald, 1967).

[13] Réginald Garrigou-Lagrange, "La mortification et les suites du péché originel," *La vie spirituelle* 12 (1925), 17–31. See also Réginald Garrigou-Lagrange, *De Deo Trino et Creatore: Commentarius in Summam Theologicam S. Thomae (Ia q. xxvii–cxix)* (Taurini: Marietti and Desclée de Brouwer, 1943), 418–51. For a more recent defense of this reading, see J. P. Torrell, "Nature et grâce chez Thomas d'Aquin," *Revue Thomiste* 101 (2001), 167–202.

[14] I challenged this semi-established consensus in "*Natura Humana Relicta est Christo*: Thomas Aquinas on the Effects of Original Sin," *Archa Verbi* 13 (2016), 68–102. J. A. Di Noia, "Not 'Born Bad': The Catholic Truth about Original Sin in a Thomistic Perspective," *The Thomist* 81.3 (2017), 345–59, without engaging the technical aspects of the debate, calls Thomas's account "relatively optimistic" (p. 353).

[15] For example, Gustav Siewerth's posthumously published *Die Christliche Erbsündelehre: Entwickelt auf Grund der Theologie des heiligen Thomas von Aquin* (Einsiedeln: Johannes Verlag, 1964) includes an elegantly written overview of Thomas's account. More recent treatments include Rudi te Velde, "Evil, Sin and Death: Thomas Aquinas on Original Sin," in *The Theology of Thomas Aquinas*, ed. R. Van Nieuwenhove and J. Wawrykow (Notre Dame: University of Notre Dame Press, 2005), 143–66; Mark Johnson, "Augustine and Aquinas on Original Sin: Doctrine, Authority, and

F. R. Tennant was the first to rethink the doctrines of the Fall and original sin in light of Darwin.[16] Evolution rules out a historical Fall, and strictly speaking "original sin" is a misnomer: "sin" means an act of disobedience to a divine command. These doctrines are meaningful, however, insofar as they refer to our evolutionarily derived dispositions to sin. Moreover, Tennant suggested that Irenaeus's theological anthropology was more defensible in an evolutionary context than Augustine's.[17] Since Tennant, there have been various proposals to identify original sin with some *particular* evolved tendency, such as the disposition to violence, or anxiety, or selfishness.[18] Korsmeyer agreed that we were inclined to sin because of evolution, but he added (rightly, to my mind, if somewhat vaguely) that original sin should relate to the need for redemption in Christ.[19]

Piet Schoonenberg influentially proposed that original sin is the "sin of the world": the complex sinful situation into which human beings are

Pedagogy," in *Aquinas the Augustinian*, ed. M. Dauphinais, B. David, and M. Levering (Washington, DC: The Catholic University of America Press, 2007), 145–58; Mark Johnson, "St. Thomas and the 'Law of Sin,'" *Recherches de théologie et philosophie médiévale* 67 (2000), 90–106; Andrew Downing, "Sin and Its Relevance to Human Nature in the '*Summa theologiae*,'" *The Heythrop Journal* 50 (2009), 793–805.

[16] F. R. Tennant, *The Origin and Propagation of Sin* (Cambridge: Cambridge University Press, 1906 [Hulsean Lectures, 1901–2]); *The Sources of the Doctrine of the Fall and Original Sin* (Cambridge: Cambridge University Press, 1903); *The Concept of Sin* (Cambridge: Cambridge University Press, 1912).

[17] A. Verriele, *Le Surnaturel en nous et le péché originel* (Paris: Bloud et Gay, 1932) resourced Irenaeus for Catholic theology. John Hick, *Evil and the God of Love* (New York: Harper and Row, 1966), used Tennant's dichotomy between Irenaean and Augustinian anthropology to construct a similar dichotomy between approaches to theodicy. Recent examples of Irenaean approaches to the Fall include Gregory R. Peterson, "Falling Up: Evolution and Original Sin," in *Evolution and Ethics: Human Morality in Biological and Religious Perspective*, ed. Philip Clayton and Jeffrey Schloss (Grand Rapids, MI: Eerdmans, 2004), 273–86; John J. Bimson, "Doctrines of the Fall and Sin after Darwin," in *Theology after Darwin*, ed. Michael S. Northcott and R. J. Berry (Colorado Springs, CO: Paternoster, 2009); Gerald Hiestand, "A More Modest Adam: An Exploration of Irenaeus' Anthropology in Light of the Darwinian Account of Pre-fall Death," *Bulletin of Ecclesial Theology* 5.1 (2018), 55–72.

[18] Marjorie Hewitt Suchoki, *The Fall to Violence: Original Sin in Relational Theology* (New York: Continuum, 1994); Patricia A. Williams, *Doing without Adam and Eve: Sociobiology and Original Sin* (Minneapolis: Fortress Press, 2001); Tatha Wiley, *Original Sin: Origins, Developments, Contemporary Meanings* (New York: Paulist Press, 2002); Daryl P. Domning and Monika K. Hellwig, *Original Selfishness: Original Sin and Evil in Light of Evolution* (Burlington, VT: Ashgate, 2006).

[19] Jerry D. Korsmeyer, *Evolution and Eden: Balancing Original Sin and Contemporary Science* (New York: Paulist Press, 1998).

born, which includes environmental, social, and personal factors.[20] This idea – which I will suggest is rooted in Schleiermacher's hamartiology – has been modified in various ways. For example, some have dropped the idea that infants are intrinsically disposed to sin and *identified* original sin with birth into a sinful environment.[21] A prominent Thomist and philosopher of religion, Brian Davies, has tentatively suggested that the core of Aquinas's account could be separated from a historical Fall and linked with a proposal, à la Schoonenberg, that emphasizes birth into a sinful world.[22]

[20] Piet Schoonenberg, *Man and Sin: A Theological View*, trans. Joseph Donceel (Notre Dame: University of Notre Dame Press, 1965); *Der Macht der Zonde* (L.C.G. Malmberg: Hertogenbosch, 1962). Stephanus Trooster, *Evolution and the Doctrine of Original Sin*, trans. Jon A. Ter Haar (New York: Newman Press, 1968 [1965]) follows Schoonenberg. Cf. Timothy McDermott, "Original Sin," *New Blackfriars* 49 (January 1968; February 1968), and Hebert McCabe's chapter on original sin in *God Still Matters* (London: Continuum, 2005 [2002]), 166–81. More recently, theologians have drawn on the coevolution of genes and culture to specify the specific forms of cultural sin. See Benno van den Toren, "Human Evolution and a Cultural Evolution of Original Sin," *Perspectives on Science and Christian Faith* 68.1 (2016), 12–21.

[21] John F. Haught, *God after Darwin: A Theology of Evolution* (Boulder, CO: Westview Press, 2008).

[22] Writes Davies, "it is impossible to be sure how his [Aquinas's] theology of Original Sin would read were he alive to develop it now. However, suppose that we think it reasonable to speculate that he would not be pursuing it with the historical approach to Adam and Eve that he presents in the SCG. In that case, how would he present it? Perhaps along the lines that some theologians have done while knowing the writings of Aquinas very well and while greatly respecting them. Here I think in particular of Timothy McDermott and Hebert McCabe. Both of these authors agree that there is no getting away from the idea of human evolution, and both of them agree that we cannot read the account of Adam and Eve in Genesis as historical. On the other hand both of them note that Aquinas thinks of Original Sin as something that infects us just by being born as human beings coming to exist in a world in which there prevails an opposition to what God is all about." Brian Davies, *Thomas Aquinas's* Summa Contra Gentiles: *A Guide and Commentary* (Oxford: Oxford University Press, 2016), 383. Thus, "perhaps his theology of Original Sin can be separated from his historical assumptions concerning Adam and Eve while leaving his notion of human salvation intact" (p. 384). "On this account, we are all infected by sin since all of us came to birth in a world stained by it" (p. 383). Cf. Davies's introduction to *On Evil* by Thomas Aquinas, trans. Richard Regan (Oxford: Oxford University Press, 2003). My view, developed in the coming chapters, is this. Thomas did insist on a historical Fall, for a number of reasons. Chief among them was his commitment to the view that God did not, and does not, cause original sin. If we hadn't fallen into sin, then either we wouldn't have original sin, or God would be its cause. It would be misleading, then, to simply say that *Aquinas's* view does not require a Fall. On the other hand, if original justice really is supernatural – which it is in Aquinas's mature thought – then it never could have been transmitted by Adam, and originating original sin must be at least logically separated from originated original sin (see Chapter 2). In light of this, the direction to take Thomas's account is not Haught's (Christ was born without sin into a

Another common approach is to reinterpret original sin as the universality of "personal" sin. The idea is that we all, in our own way, reenact the scene of disobedience depicted in Genesis 3. I will suggest in Chapter 5 that this proposal stems from a common reading of Kant's account of radical evil. Whatever its precise provenance, a number of theologians – Protestant and Catholic alike – have defended this view. Alfred Vanneste argued that this was the true intention of the Catholic dogmas concerning the Fall and original sin.[23] Karl Barth offered a Christocentric version of this proposal: original sin is the universal, culpable lack of faithfulness to Jesus Christ.[24] Henri Rondet uses Schoonenberg's language – original sin is the sin of the world – but as he unpacks his account it seems close to Vanneste's reduction of sin to actual sin.[25]

In recent years, interest in the doctrine has been increasing. Ian McFarland has written a substantive monograph that retrieves a broadly Augustinian account of the fallen will (though not an Augustinian account of the Fall). To be born in original sin is to be born with a will turned away from God, regardless of whether one ultimately descends from a person created in original justice.[26] In dialogue with Zwingli, Oliver Crisp proposes a "moderate Reformed doctrine" of original sin: we inherit corruption – but not original guilt – from an early population of human beings who were created without corruption.[27] Matthew Levering devotes a chapter of his recent monograph on creation to an

---

sinful world; thus the doctrine of original sin cannot be identified with birth into a sinful world). Rather, the focus of the account developed here is on the human person's need for the redeeming grace of Jesus Christ. Moreover, the question of the Fall's historicity cannot be settled by the logical possibility of separating originated from originating sin. What is needed is (inter alia) further reflection on Paul's use of Adam and the doctrines of creation and providence.

[23] A. Vanneste, *Het dogma van de erfzonde: Zinloze mythe of openbaring van een grondstruktuur van het menselijk bestaan?* (Tielt: Lannoo, 1969); *Le dogme du péché originel* (Louvain: Nauwelaerts, 1971).

[24] Karl Barth, *Church Dogmatics* IV.1, §60.3, ed. G. W. Bromiley and T. F. Torrance (London: T&T Clark; New York: Continuum, 2009), 478–513.

[25] "Le péché originel en nous a pour cause un péché actuel, mais un péché collectif, constitué par l'ensemble des péchés personnels des hommes de tous les temps." Henri Rondet, *Le Péché originel dans la tradition patristique et théologique* (Paris: Librairie Fayard, 1967), 321.

[26] Ian A. McFarland, *In Adam's Fall: A Meditation on the Christian Doctrine of Original Sin* (Oxford: Wiley-Blackwell), 2010.

[27] Oliver D. Crisp, "On Original Sin," *International Journal of Systematic Theology* 17.3 (2015), 252–66. Cf. Henri Blocher's *Original Sin: Illuminating the Riddle* (Grand Rapids, MI: Eerdmans, 1997), which proposes that original sin is an inherited – but somehow culpable – *habitus* of self-love.

ecumenical discussion of Edwards, Aquinas, and original sin.[28] There is a rapidly growing literature on human origins, the Fall, and the book of Genesis, especially (though not exclusively) among broadly evangelical and Catholic theologians.[29] Philosophers of religion have also contributed to the discussion by challenging theologians to address the metaphysical assumptions at play in their accounts of original sin and evolution.[30]

This book's constructive proposal is the first retrieval and revision of Thomas's authentic doctrine of original sin. Unlike modern Irenaean accounts (à la Tennant), original sin is not a mere disposition to sin. Unlike Schoonenbergian accounts, original sin is not being born into a sinful world. Unlike Vanneste's and Barth's accounts, original sin is not reduced to personal sin. Unlike attempts to separate Augustine's account from a historical Fall, original sin is not simply self-love. Original sin is, rather, the lack of sanctifying grace, the deifying grace of the Holy Spirit, sent by the Father to lead us into the knowledge and love of Jesus Christ. This is importantly, if somewhat subtly, different from Thomas's own view, on which original sin is the lack of due original justice.

---

[28] Matthew Levering, *Engaging the Doctrine of Creation: Cosmos, Creatures, and the Wise and Good Creator* (Grand Rapids, MI: Baker Academic), 227–71. Levering focuses on one of Thomas's favorite analogies: original sin is like being born into a disgraced family.

[29] *Darwin, Creation and the Fall: Theological Challenges*, ed. R. J. Berry and T. A. Noble (Nottingham: Apollos, 2009); *Adam, the Fall, and Original Sin: Theological, Biblical, and Scientific Perspectives*, ed. Hans Madueme and Michael Reeves (Grand Rapids, MI: Baker Academic, 2014); John H. Walton, *The Lost World of Adam and Eve: Genesis 2–3 and the Human Origins Debate* (Downers Grove, IL: InterVarsity Press, 2015); Nicanor Pier Giorgio Austriaco, James Brent, Thomas Davenport, and John Baptist Ku, *Thomistic Evolution: A Catholic Approach to Understanding Evolution in the Light of Faith* (Providence, RI: Cluny Media, 2016); Denis R. Venema and Scot McKnight, *Adam and the Genome: Reading Scripture after Genetic Science* (Grand Rapids, MI: Brazos Press, 2017); *Evolution and the Fall*, ed. William T. Cavanaugh and James K. A. Smith (Grand Rapids, MI: Eerdmans, 2017); *Finding Ourselves after Darwin*, ed. Stanley P. Rosenberg, Michael Burdett, Michael Lloyd, and Benno van den Toren (Grand Rapids, MI: Baker Academic, 2018). For an older defense of the compatibility of Catholic theology and evolution from a traditional Thomist perspective, see M. M. Labourdette's *Le Péché originel et les origines de l'homme* (Paris: Alsatia, 1953).

[30] Michael C. Rea, "The Metaphysics of Original Sin," in *Persons: Human and Divine*, ed. Peter van Inwagen and Dean Zimmerman (Oxford: Oxford University Press, 2007), 319–56; Kenneth W. Kemp, "Science, Theology, and Monogenesis," *American Catholic Philosophical Quarterly* 85 (2011), 217–36; Hud Hudson, *The Fall and Hypertime* (Oxford: Oxford University Press, 2014). This last work has convincingly argued that there is a conflict between evolution and a "literal" reading of Genesis only if the hypertime hypothesis is false. My central arguments do not rely on the hypertime hypothesis being a live epistemic option.

OVERVIEW

Chapter 1 puts Thomas's account in its historical context by discussing Augustine and his medieval reception. The first part of the chapter focuses on Augustine's mature account of original sin, drawing on *The City of God* and his anti-Pelagian works. I argue that Augustine's account contained several fruitful ambiguities which would be the basis for medieval reflection. How should we understand the transmission of original sin and the origin of the soul? In what sense are infants guilty of sin? How can we make sense of the claim that human nature has been "corrupted"? The second major part of the chapter discusses Anselm of Canterbury, Peter Abelard, and Peter Lombard. Each of these theologians defended original sin while challenging at least one important aspect of Augustine's teaching. Anselm claimed that concupiscence cannot be sinful. Abelard denied original guilt. The Lombard emphatically denied traducianism and insisted that infants who die unbaptized are guilty only in a highly mitigated sense.

Chapter 2 argues that Thomas's mature view of the formal cause of original justice created an unresolved problem for his doctrine of original sin. Though his early writings sharply distinguished the rectitude of the human will in the state of original justice from supernatural sanctifying grace, by the mid-1260s (e.g., *STh* I, q. 95, a. 1) he implied that the formal cause of original justice is sanctifying grace. The problem is that Thomas also held (1) that Adam should have been the principal cause of original justice in his posterity and (2) that no creature can be the principal cause of sanctifying grace. Thomas's mature view implies that the disposition to original justice never could have been sexually transmitted. This implies that his account of original sin as a whole needed to be modified. Adam's failure to transmit the disposition to original justice rendered the lack of original justice sinful in his posterity: if Adam couldn't have done this in the first place, how could his descendants have original sin?

Chapter 3 argues that Thomas radically reconfigures the relation between original sin and human nature. Whereas Augustine had argued that nature is "corrupted" by the Fall, Thomas draws on Denys the Areopagite to argue that strictly speaking, human nature survives the Fall. For Thomas, there are two senses of the word "nature." In the strict sense, "nature" refers to the *principia naturae* and the *propria* that follow therefrom. The secondary sense of "nature" refers to what is good *for* nature – including communion with God. Thomas regularly uses Augustinian language concerning the corruption of nature by sin (e.g., *STh* I-II,

q. 109), but when he explains this usage he indicates that it is improper (e.g., *De malo* q. 5, a. 2). Nature is "corrupted" only insofar as human beings have lost the good of nature, original justice. The principles and properties of human nature – including the orientation to God – remain. This is why Thomas argues that children who die unbaptized will know and love God in limbo.

Chapter 4 discusses Thomas's account of original guilt. Infants are guilty only in an analogical sense. A human being with the use of reason is guilty in the proper sense when she commits a sinful act of her own volition; an infant is guilty in an analogical sense when she fails to receive original justice by Adam's volition. The infant is in a moral middle ground, between the state of mortal sin and sanctifying grace (*Scriptum* II, d. 35, q. 2, a. 2, ad 2). She has not turned away from God, yet she needs grace nonetheless. Thomas's explanation of infant guilt developed. He initially compared the guilt of original sin to an inherited disease (*Scriptum* II, d. 30, q. 1, a. 2). He later abandons this analogy and compares the infant to a homicidal hand. I defend Thomas's view that the infant's will is positioned between mortal sin and sanctifying grace. But I criticize his view of analogical guilt, arguing that receiving the effect of another's sinful act cannot increase one's own guilt.

Chapter 5 engages proposals that deny the importance of a historical Fall. I begin with Kant's account of radical evil. An influential reading is this. Every human being who reaches the age of reason freely subordin-ates the moral law to self-interest. Next is Karl Barth's "christologized" version of radical evil: the Fall is the universal act of unbelief in Christ. I argue that the reduction of original sin to the universality of actual sin is insufficiently inclusive. Neither infants nor the severely mentally disabled *choose* wrongdoing. Schleiermacher separated original sin from the Fall in a different way. Original sin is the corporate act of humanity. The "force" of sin is present in infants, albeit in germinal form, and when they mature they lack God-consciousness and tend to sinful self-love. Schleier-macher's view leads to one of two problematic conclusions. Either sin is numerically one, or sin is merely environmental, external to the will. Another difficulty with Schleiermacher's account – and also with more recent, similar proposals – is that it implies that God brings about oppos-ition to himself. Schoonenberg defends a view similar to Schleiermacher's but stresses human freedom. It shares Schleiermacher's weaknesses, but I argue that its account of the "situation" of sin could be synthesized with Thomas's hamartiology. McFarland intriguingly proposes a synthesis of Maximus's and Augustine's accounts of the fallen will, while arguing that we can avoid etiological explanations of sin altogether. I argue, however, that we have to choose: we need either to explain *why* original justice is theologically unnecessary or to defend it in some form.

Chapter 6 unpacks salient hypotheses in contemporary evolutionary theory that challenge traditional views of the Fall and original sin. The first challenge comes from the gradual nature of evolutionary change. On the modern synthesis of Mendel's account of particulate inheritance with Darwin's account of natural selection, evolutionary change happens gradually. It is hard to see how a single volition could have corrupted human nature. (This seems to be true even on the "extended evolutionary synthesis.") The second challenge stems from the legacy of our evolutionary history. It appears that the first human beings had evolved dispositions to sinful forms of behavior. How could we have fallen from a righteous state if our desires weren't rightly ordered in the beginning? The question of aggressive violence is explored as a case study. The third challenge stems from the widely supported hypothesis that the human population never dipped below 6,000 individuals. Either some people were created in sin or far more people were created without sin than traditionally assumed.

Chapter 7 proposes a new Thomist view of original sin. Thomas's account of original sin was a brilliant synthesis of Eastern and Western views of the Fall. With Denys, he argues that human nature survives the Fall; with Augustine, he affirms that postlapsarian nature is sinful. The core of Thomas's proposal – original sin has more to do with the lack of a right relation to the Triune God than the inheritance of personal guilt or corruption – is defensible today. His mature teaching stressing the necessity of supernatural grace for original justice, however, implies that he should have denied that original sin has a necessary connection to Adam's failure to sexually transmit justice. In other words, Thomas's account arguably points to the view that originated original sin in infants is logically separable from originating original sin in Adam. I propose a "new Thomist view," on which original sin is the lack of sanctifying grace. Grace is the Father's gift of the Holy Spirit that orients the person to Jesus Christ. Every infant is born with human nature but called to exist in Christ. I construct this account in dialogue with salient biblical scholarship and respond to the challenges posed by evolution. I sketch two possible views of the Fall compatible with the new Thomist view of original sin. One possibility is that there was not a historical Fall; and unlike the modern Augustinian view, this does not involve God creating habitual idolaters. Another possibility is that there was a Fall, understood however not as the corruption of nature or DNA but as the loss of an original gift of supernatural grace.

Chapter 8 responds to potential objections. Against the objection that my proposal is a recrudescence of "two-tier Thomism," I argue that it is deeply congruous with Henri de Lubac's view that nature innately *desires* grace. The second objection is that my view implies that a state of pure nature is impossible. I argue that it is in fact compatible with a wide variety of views of divine providence. Further objections are raised that focus on the nature of sanctifying grace, the ecumenical potential of a Thomist perspective, and Pelagianism. My proposal, I suggest, is compatible with a wide variety of views of justification, and it is not "Pelagian" in any meaningful sense.

I

Augustine and the Long Twelfth Century

"The new conception of original sin developed by St. Augustine when he defended it against the Pelagians has subsisted almost unchanged in later theology."[1] Thus Piet Schoonenberg, Jesuit theologian and influential coauthor of *The Dutch Catechism*, sums up the history of original sin. His view is common today. As evinced by the lack of attention medieval views of the doctrine have received of late, many assume that the crucial question for contemporary theology is whether *Augustine's* account of original sin is salvageable after Darwin. If the medieval doctrine simply consists in repetitions or (at most) minor developments of Augustine's doctrine, why study it, except for antiquarian purposes? This book contends, however, that there are more things in the Middle Ages than are dreamt of in Schoonenberg's theology. The doctor of grace's doctrine of sin did not "subsist unchanged" in the medieval period, as though it were a priceless painting preserved by generations of curators. It was rather, like Plato's oeuvre, an "inexhaustible mine of suggestion" for subsequent generations.[2] Medievals mined the Augustinian corpus for minerals of truth. Equally, they refined what they had extracted from the dross of error. There was debate over, inter alia, whether the concept of inherited guilt was coherent, whether disordered concupiscence should be considered sinful, and whether the Fall had

---

* Portions of this chapter are adapted from Daniel W. Houck, "Original Sin in Abelard's Commentary on Romans," in *Being Saved: Explorations in Soteriology and Human Ontology*, ed. Marc Cortez, Joshua Farris, and S. Mark Hamilton (London: SCM Press, 2018), 54–67, with kind permission of the publisher.
[1] Schoonenberg, *Man and Sin*, 157.
[2] A. N. Whitehead, *Process and Reality: An Essay in Cosmology* (New York: Free Press, 1979 [Gifford Lectures, 1927–8]), 39.

"corrupted" human nature. Eventually, a consensus rejected the theory that would torment Hardy's Tess: that unbaptized babies burn in hell. (When Gregory of Rimini tried to revive it in the fourteenth century, he was mocked as the *"infantium tortor."*) Only when the medievals began to be ignored could the belief that their thought on original sin was a monolith arise.

This chapter discusses Augustine and his reception in the "long twelfth century" (for present purposes, the late 1090s till the 1240s). This productive period of reflection stands out for its influence and originality. It provides an indispensable context for the discussion of Thomas Aquinas that follows. I will suggest, moreover, that three basic theories of original sin's transmission were forged during this time, theories that dominated Catholic and Protestant theology until the twentieth century. They correspond to the respective accounts of Anselm of Canterbury, Peter Abelard, and Peter Lombard, which will be discussed in chronological order, after Augustine.

AUGUSTINE

Why begin with Augustine? Is it because he "invented" the doctrine of original sin? The aforementioned assumption to the effect that the doctrine didn't undergo significant development during the Middle Ages is often linked with the assumption that Augustine was the first to teach it. Both assumptions may rest on the view that the doctrine should be more or less identified with his presentation of it. As the Patristic provenance of the doctrine is not a focus of this study, I will simply mention a few antecedents to Augustine. This should help put his account in context. Moreover, even a brief discussion of the pre-Augustinian period should serve to cast some doubt – at the very least – on the popular notion that Augustine invented the doctrine of original sin whole cloth.

The Origins of Original Sin

I agree with Pier Beatrice – and the majority report of modern scholarship – that the Greek Fathers generally affirmed that infants receive "physical death and moral frailty" from Adam, not sin or guilt.[3] Origen (185–254), however, adapting the *Phaedo*'s doctrine that mortality is a

---

[3] Pier Beatrice, *The Transmission of Sin: Augustine and the Pre-Augustinian Sources*, trans. Adam Kamesar (Oxford: Oxford University Press, 2013 [1978]), 166. He is speaking in particular of the views of Irenaeus, Basil of Caesarea, Gregory of Nazianzus, and John Chrysostom.

"demotion from the heavenly realms" to Christianity, proposed that each infant's embodiment is a penal consequence of her sin in a pre-mortal spiritual life.[4] This hypothesis "had in Origen's eyes the advantage of providing him with an argument against the most difficult objection advanced by the Marcionites against the goodness of the Creator God: the inequality of human conditions at birth."[5] For Origen, then, infants have sin. Unlike Augustine, however, he denies that they are sinners from the beginning of their existence as individuals. Existence, for individual human beings, begins without the body and without sin.

Sharp criticism of pre-mortal existence from a Christian perspective is found as early as Tertullian (c. 160–220).[6] He argued that it contradicts Genesis's account of creation and blasphemously implies that human beings are divine. Tertullian's "traducian" counterhypothesis – roughly, the view that parents generate their children's souls – also attempts to explain infant mortality. Instead of attributing it to a pre-mortal Fall, however, he appears to attribute it to inherited sin. The following claims are found in Tertullian's writings. Adam's sin corrupted human nature.[7] The human being is infected by Adam's seed and transmits condemnation.[8] The human being who is born in Adam is *sinful*.[9] Due to Adam's

---

[4] Terryl L. Givens, *When Souls Had Wings: Pre-mortal Existence in Western Thought* (Oxford: Oxford University Press, 2010), 31; see 91–8 for a discussion of Origen in the context of a monograph on "pre-mortal" existence. For Origen's account of the Fall, see Stephen Bagby, *Sin in Origen's Commentary on Romans* (Lanham, MD: Lexington, 2018).

[5] Henri Crouzel, *Origen: The Life and Times of the First Great Theologian*, trans. A. S. Worrall (San Francisco: Harper & Row, 1989 [1985]), 208–9.

[6] My comments about Tertullian are indebted to Anthony Dupont, "Original Sin in Tertullian and Cyprian: Conceptual Presence and Pre-Augustinian Content?," *Revue d'études augustiniennes et patristiques* 63 (2017), 1–29.

[7] "Besides the evil that mars the soul as a result of the machinations of the Devil, still another evil has previously affected it, and this is in a certain sense natural to it, since it flows from its origin. As we have said, the corruption of nature is a second nature." Tertullian, *Tertullian on the Soul* [*De anima*] c. 41, in *The Fathers of the Church: A New Translation*, vol. 10, trans. E. A. Quain (New York: Fathers of the Church, 1950), 273.

[8] "Through him [Satan], man was deceived from the beginning so that he transgressed the commandment of God and, therefore, having been given unto death, made the whole human race, which was infected by his seed, the transmitter of condemnation." Tertullian, *The Testimony of the Soul* [*De testimonio animae*] c. 3, in *The Fathers of the Church: A New Translation*, vol. 10, trans. Rudolph Arbesmann (New York: Fathers of the Church, 1950), 136.

[9] "Every soul is considered as having been born in Adam until it has been reborn in Christ. Moreover, it is unclean until it has been thus regenerated (Rom. 5, 14; 6, 4). It is sinful, too, because it is unclean, and its shame is shared by the body because of their union." Tertullian, *Tertullian on the Soul* [De anima], c. 40, 271.

sin, human wills are turned against God.[10] Tertullian's views seem to have been influential in Carthage.

Cyprian of Carthage (c. 200–258), in a letter that Augustine would cite as proof that original sin was taught by the fathers of the Church, claimed that infants are born with the "contagion of the ancient death" (*contagium mortis antiquae*). Cyprian had been asked by Fidus – a bishop about whom we know very little – whether infants should be baptized shortly after birth or on the eighth day. Fidus inclined toward waiting, as baptism would thus correspond to circumcision (Gen. 17:12). The question was discussed during a council at Carthage (c. 252). Cyprian sums up the council's decision in his response to Fidus:

> [I]f, in the case of the greatest sinners and those sinning much against God, when afterward they believe, the remission of their sins is granted and no one is prevented from baptism and grace, how much more should an infant not be prohibited, who, recently born, has not sinned at all, except that, born carnally according to Adam, he has contracted the contagion of the first death from the first nativity (*nihil peccauit, nisi quod secundum Adam carnaliter natus contagium mortis antiquae prima natiuitate contraxit*). He approaches more easily from this very fact to receive the remission of sins because those which are remitted are not his own sins, but the sins of another (*non propria sed aliena peccata*).[11]

Baptism should not be delayed. If the worst sinners are given baptism and forgiveness, why should this grace be withheld from infants? The sins of infants are not their own but another's; they are carnally born from Adam and contract the "contagion of the ancient death." Cyprian seems to consider this contagion a sin. He states explicitly that infants receive the "*remissam peccatorum*" through baptism.

The belief that sin should be predicated of infants because they received it from Adam – and not on the basis of their own pre-mortal lapse – arose, at the latest, in the early third century in Carthage. Tertullian's view seems

---

[10] "And if you ask me whence comes this volition of ours by which we set our will against the will of God, I should reply that it comes from our own selves. Nor is this rashly said, if, indeed, Adam, the author of our race and of our fall, willed the sin which he committed; for you yourself must needs be like the father whose seed you are." Tertullian, *An Exhortation to Chastity* [*De exhortatione castitatis*] c. 2, in *Tertullian: Treatises on Marriage and Remarriage* trans. William P. Le Saint (Westminster, MD: Newman Press, 1951), 44.

[11] Cyprian, *Epistle* 64.5, in *S. Thasci Caecili Cypriani Opera Omnia*, ed. W. Hartel, in *Corpus Scriptorum Ecclesiasticorum Latinorum*, vol. 3, part 2, 720–1; trans. *Cyprian and the Bishops at the Council of Carthage to Fidus*, in *The Fathers of the Church: A New Translation*, vol. 51, trans. Rose Donna (Washington, DC: Catholic University of America Press, 1964), 218–19.

to have been adopted by a consensus of bishops in the Roman Province of Africa, including Cyprian, by the mid-third century. Meanwhile various Christian Platonists, including Origen, agreed that sin was predicable of infants but denied that Adam was its ultimate source. Still others, such as Gregory of Nyssa in his work on the premature death of infants, only affirmed that Adam brought mortality and disordered passions to humanity.

Thus by the time of Augustine's birth in 354, the range of live options within the church included a Fall without the affirmation of original sin, a pre-mortal Fall with the affirmation that infants have sin of their own volition, and a Fall with the affirmation that infants have sin from Adam. If either of the last two options counts as an affirmation of original sin avant le lettre – that is, before Augustine coined the phrase *"peccatum originale"* and developed an account of it – it follows that Augustine did not invent the doctrine. My central arguments, however, do not depend on whether the doctrine antedates Augustine. Indeed, this book doesn't defend a precise view of the nature or scope of the *doctrine* of original sin. It constructs, and endeavors to show the salient advantages of, a *theory of* the doctrine.[12] That said, I of course operate with a rough idea of what the doctrine of original sin is, which it may be helpful to mention.

As I understand it, the doctrine of original sin is that the human being's individual, embodied existence normally begins with sin. Why include the qualifications "individual" and "embodied"? Many theologians who clearly affirmed the doctrine – including, as we will see momentarily, Augustine – held that human beings existed in a "seminal," non-individual form in Adam (i.e., they "preexisted" in Adam, to use a common but misleading word). If one tried to claim that the doctrine involved the belief that infants normally have sin at the beginning of their

---

[12] The difference between a doctrine and a theory of a doctrine is not, as I understand it, hard and fast; it is simply, and inevitably roughly, the distinction between a generic account of a teaching and a more specific one. For example, one might hold that the doctrine of the atonement is the teaching that Jesus' death brings about the reconciliation of God and humanity. One could affirm this while acknowledging that there have been various explanations of how his death brings about reconciliation (through satisfaction, for example, or moral influence). These more specific accounts of a doctrine I call "theories." And just as theologians could agree on a given theory of the atonement while disagreeing over the status of another theory they reject – with one holding, for example, that the rejected theory is utterly incompatible with Christianity, and the other holding that it is a perfectly orthodox, understandable mistake – so too readers of this book could opt for a stricter, or looser, definition of the doctrine of original sin than I stipulate, while accepting my proposed theory of the doctrine.

existence simpliciter, this would imply, absurdly, that Augustine's and other similar accounts were not examples of the doctrine of original sin. Given that a sinless "preexistence" in Adam is compatible with affirming the doctrine, it seems to me that a sinless pre-mortal existence is as well. What is central is the affirmation that individual human beings normally come into this world with sin. I say "normally" because it is not necessary to hold that every human being is born in sin in order to affirm the doctrine. The traditional Augustinian view, of course, is that Adam, Eve, and Jesus began to exist without sin. As is well known, the Roman Catholic Church teaches that Mary was conceived without original sin (see Pius IX's *Ineffabilis Deus* [1854]). My definition does not prejudge the question of how many exceptions are compatible with affirming the doctrine. I trust that other aspects of the definition will become clearer as this study progresses.

My stipulated definition implies – to return to the question posed at the outset of this section – that Augustine did not invent the doctrine of original sin. He *was* the first to offer an in-depth, theoretical account of the doctrine of original sin as such, which, in conjunction with his incalculable influence, is why his is the first account we will consider at some length. In what follows, we will focus on his mature account of the doctrine in *The City of God*, while drawing at times on other works from the Pelagian controversy.[13] The discussion will be divided into three sections: his account of Adam and Eve before the Fall, the Fall, and original sin in infants.

Before the Fall

Underlying Augustine's account of the creation of human beings are his views of God and evil. God is good. He creates all things good. There is not anything that creates itself, or that exists alongside God in eternity. From this, it follows that "evil has no nature of its own. Rather, it is the absence of good which has received the name 'evil.'"[14] Human beings

---

[13] For an argument that Augustine affirmed original sin from the *Confessions* on, see Paul Rigby, *Original Sin in Augustine's Confessions* (Ottawa: University of Ottawa Press, 1987).

[14] Augustine, *The City of God against the Pagans*, trans. R. W. Dyson (Cambridge: Cambridge University Press, 1998), XI, c. 9. Translations in this section are Dyson's unless otherwise noted. I have occasionally supplemented the English with Latin from the *Corpus Christianorum Series Latina*.

were created good, and whatever evil is in them is the absence of a good that ought to be present. In order to understand what it means for human beings to be "good," consider the following summary of their created condition:

> Man, however, whose *nature* was to be in a manner intermediate between angels and beasts, God created in such a way that, if he remained subject to his Creator as his true Lord, and if he kept His commandments with pious obedience, He should pass over into the company of the angels and obtain, without suffering death, a blessed immortality without end. But if he offended the Lord his God by using his free will proudly and disobediently, he should live ... subject to death: the slave of his own lust, destined to suffer eternal punishment after death.[15]

Three features of prelapsarian goodness can be gleaned from this quotation. In accordance with human nature, Adam and Eve were created with the possibility of immortality, free from lust, and in a state of subjection to God. It is worth briefly describing each of these conditions.

First is their possible immortality. Their bodies were naturally subject to the withering of age.[16] Yet they were protected from aging by the tree of life, and if they hadn't sinned they would have advanced to perfect immortality – the impossibility of dying.[17] Second is their freedom from lust. Their passions did not rise up against their wills.[18] They were thus free of "concupiscence."[19] They would have had sexual intercourse, but their genitals (or at least Adam's) would have been under their direct voluntary control. Though some scholars have tried to deny this latter

---

[15] Augustine, *The City of God* XII, c. 22, emphasis mine.

[16] Augustine, *The City of God* XIII, c. 23.

[17] For prelapsarian and post-resurrection immortality, see *The City of God* XIII, c. 20, and *The City of God* XIII, c. 22, respectively.

[18] "[T]hose philosophers who have come closer to the truth than others have acknowledged that anger and lust are vicious parts of the soul, in that they are turbulent and disorderly emotions inciting us to acts which wisdom forbids ... But in Paradise, before sin arose, these passions did not, I say, exist in their present vicious form. For they were not then moved to do anything contrary to a righteous will, from which it was necessary to force them to abstain by means of the guiding reins, as it were, of reason." Augustine, *The City of God* XIV, c. 19.

[19] "Together with the verb *concupisco*, it [*concupiscentia*] may be said to be Augustine's standard word stem for evil desire." Timo Nisula, *Augustine and the Functions of Concupiscence* (Boston: Brill, 2012), 35. Augustine also, though less frequently, uses the word to refer to good desire. Insofar as "concupiscence" refers to good desire, one could say Adam and Eve had rightly ordered concupiscence before the Fall; insofar as it refers to evil desire, one must say they were free of it altogether.

point, Augustine clearly affirms it.[20] Third is their subjection to God. It was rooted in love, a love that constitutes the City of God over against the City of Man. "Two cities, then, have been created by two loves: that is, the earthly by love of self extending even to contempt of God, and the heavenly by love of God extending to contempt of self."[21] Though they loved God, they did not love him perfectly; they did not enjoy perfect happiness. Indeed the condition for the possibility of sin was the fact that their happiness was not perfect.[22] The perfectly happy person is not able to sin: perfect happiness is incompatible with even the slightest twinge of anxiety or nescience concerning its loss. They were thus able to sin and able not to sin.[23]

Given Adam's condition, however – the beautiful garden in which he lived; the lack of ignorance or weakness in his intellect and will, respectively;[24] the health of his body – what could have motivated his sin?[25] Put differently – his love was rightly ordered; he loved the plants he ate, the animals he named, and the wife he married. He loved the God whose gifts they were. Why wreck this beautiful order of love? Perfect happiness *for all eternity* was his – if only he continued to enjoy the blessings he already had. What could have motivated his sin? How *could* he have sinned, without a motive?

Peccatum Originale Originans

There was no evil motive *preceding* Adam's sin. His sin consisted in the defection of his will from divine rule. He abandoned humble obedience

---

[20] "[T]he vessel created for this purpose would have sown its seed upon 'the field of generation' as the hand now sows seed upon the ground." Augustine, *The City of God* XIV, c. 24.

[21] Augustine, *The City of God* XIV, c. 28. Whether Augustine implied that Adam and Eve's love of God was "natural" or "supernatural" has been debated. See Henri de Lubac, *Augustinisme et théologie moderne* (Paris: Les Éditions du Cerf, 2008 [1968]), for a discussion of the legitimacy (or lack thereof) of reading medieval and modern distinctions back into Augustine.

[22] Augustine, *The City of God* XI, c. 12.

[23] For Augustine's account of free will more broadly, see Gerald Bonner, *Freedom and Necessity: St. Augustine's Teaching on Divine Power and Human Freedom* (Washington, DC: Catholic University of America Press, 2006).

[24] Augustine, *The City of God* XIV, c. 12.

[25] I have begun to speak of Adam in particular because, as we will see, for Augustine it was his Fall that was decisive for humanity, not Eve's.

for prideful rebellion: "what but pride can have been the beginning of their evil will? – for 'pride is the beginning of sin.' And what is pride but an appetite for a perverse kind of elevation?"[26] His sheer refusal to obey God was an act of pride, and his act of pride consisted in his sheer refusal to obey God. God did not abandon Adam first; it was the other way round. "The soul was not forsaken by God first, and so then forsook Him; rather, it first forsook God, and so was then forsaken by Him. For its own will was the originator of its own evil."[27] Yet having abandoned God, Adam deserved the death God had threatened. *Morte morieris.*

What did God mean by "death"? Augustine distinguishes two kinds of death. The first kind of death has two parts. The death of the soul is its separation from God (this is the first part of the first kind of death). The death of the body is its separation from the soul (the second part of the first kind). The first death itself is the death of the whole human being: it occurs when the soul forsaken by God forsakes the body. The second kind of death is eternal damnation: those who die the first death are punished initially as souls, but those resurrected unto damnation are punished eternally in soul and body. To the question of what was meant by the divine threat of "death" in Genesis 2:17, Augustine answers that it includes every kind.[28]

[T]his threat included not only the first part of the first death, by which the soul is deprived of God; nor only the second part, by which the body is deprived of the soul; nor only the whole of the first death itself, by which the soul is punished by separation from both God and the body. Rather, it included whatever of death there is, even to that final death which is called second, and which is followed by no other.[29]

Adam's pride deserved both deaths. The first part of the first death was automatic: the act of pride is the soul's forsaking of God, by which God forsakes the soul. The second part of the first death was brought about by God cutting Adam off from the Tree of Life in Eden; it was then inevitable that Adam's soul would be separated from his body. He was "dead in spirit by an act of his own will, and doomed, against his will, to die in body also."[30] He deserved the second death, eternal damnation; though, as tradition had it, Adam was forgiven and saved.

---

[26] Augustine, *The City of God* XIV, c. 13.   [27] Augustine, *The City of God* XIII, c. 15.
[28] For Augustine's discussion of death, see all of XIII and c. 12 in particular.
[29] Augustine, *The City of God* XIII, c. 12.   [30] Augustine, *The City of God* XIV, c. 15.

Adam's sin also disordered his passions and made him liable to suffering. Augustine argues that this was a supremely fitting punishment:

[I]n the punishment of that sin, what is the retribution for disobedience if not disobedience itself? For what is man's misery if not simply his own disobedience to himself, so that, because he would not do what he could, he now cannot do what he would? ... For who can count the many things that a man wishes to do but cannot? For he is disobedient to himself: that is, his very mind, and even his lower part, his flesh, do not obey his will.[31]

The punishment for disobedience is disobedience. By his sin, Adam brought it about that his own desires would rise up against him.

Even granting Augustine's view that Adam deserved both kinds of death and the disordering of his passions, why should Adam's children have anything to do with his punishment? Isn't is obvious that it belongs to Adam alone (and Eve, for her part)? In answering this question, Augustine forged his account of originated original sin: original sin in infants.

Peccatum Originale Originatum

Although Augustine did think that Paul explicitly stated in Rom. 5:12 that Adam's sin was passed to his posterity, his deepest argument for the doctrine was, as Ian McFarland puts it, "fundamentally Christological."[32] Jesus Christ is the savior of all kinds of human beings: rich and poor, young and old, Jew and Gentile, male and female. If infants were sinless, however,

then the gospel doesn't apply to them. And if it doesn't apply to infants, then it is hard to see on what basis it can be assumed to apply to all persons of other ages and conditions. In short, the good news is that *Jesus* saves, and if this news is truly *for all* (Luke 2:10–11; cf. Acts 2:39), then it follows that all human beings without distinction *need* saving.[33]

As Augustine put it during the Pelagian controversy, "[i]f we admit that the small and the great, that is, wailing infants and old grey heads, need this savior and that medicine of his, namely, that the Word became flesh in order to dwell among us, the entire question under dispute between us has been resolved."[34]

Augustine goes further than asserting the fact of original sin. Admitting that the doctrine is shrouded in mystery, he claims that we can come to a

---

[31] Augustine, *The City of God* XIV, c. 15.   [32] McFarland, *In Adam's Fall*, 62.

[33] McFarland, *In Adam's Fall*, 33.

[34] Augustine, *Nature and Grace*, trans. Roland Teske (Hyde Park, NY: New City Press, 1997), 60. Cited in McFarland, *In Adam's Fall*, 79.

limited grasp of both the possibility and even the justice of infants being born guilty of sin. It is worth quoting his explanation at length:

For God, who is the author of nature, and certainly not of vices, created man righteous. Man, however, depraved by his own free will, and justly condemned, produced depraved and condemned children. For we were all in that one man, since we all were that one man (*Omnes enim fuimus in illo uno, quando omnes fuimus ille unus*) who fell into sin through the woman who was made from him before they sinned. The particular form in which we were to live as individuals had not yet been created and distributed to us; but the seminal nature from which we were to be propagated already existed (*Nondum erat nobis singillatim creata et distributa forma, in qua singuli uiueremus; sed iam erat natura seminalis, ex qua propagaremur*). And, when this was vitiated by sin and bound by the chain of death and justly condemned, man could not be born of man in any other condition. Thus, from the evil use of free will there arose the whole series of calamities by which the human race is led by a succession of miseries from its depraved origin, as from a corrupt root, even the ruin of second death, which has no end, and from which only those who are redeemed by the grace of God are exempt.[35]

God created humanity in a righteous state. The righteousness in which Adam was created, however, was not only his but also human *nature's*. In what sense? All human beings who would descend from him were seminally present in his loins. Augustine had suggested earlier that God created only two human beings so that all of humanity would be blood kin. Here we see the dark side of monogenesis: Adam's sin damned the entire human race. Having sinned, Adam's depraved and corrupted nature could only produce depraved and condemned children. The same corruption and guilt that were Adam's become his posterity's. As Hans Staffner observed, the consequences of Adam's *originating* original sin correspond precisely to his offspring's *originated* original sin.[36] Every child save Christ deserves the same punishment as Adam: the triple death that leads to hell. Every child save Christ is proud like Adam, a slave to self. Every child save Christ is lustful like Adam, a slave to concupiscence. Every child save Christ is mortal like Adam, destined to die the death of the body even if saved by baptismal waters from the death of the damned.[37]

---

[35] Augustine, *The City of God* XIII, c. 14, emphasis mine. The parenthetical Latin is from the *Corpus Christianorum Series Latina* XLVIII, 395.1–15. Cf. Augustine, *The City of God* XIII, c. 3.

[36] "Die Folgen der Erbsünde entsprechen also genau dem, was Augustinus als Ursache dieser Sünde bezeichnet hat." Hans Staffner, "Die Lehre des hl. Augustinus über das Wesen der Erbsünde." *Zeitschrift für Katholische Theologie* 79 (1957), 398.

[37] I am not concerned here with Augustine's view of Mary. For a famous (and controverted) passage which has been read as implying that she was exempted from original sin, see

There is a subtle yet significant equivocation in Augustine's description. He argues that it is just for God to damn infants because they were *in* Adam (*fuimus in illo uno*), and in the same breath he says it is just because they *were* Adam (*omnes fuimus ille unus*). Which is it? Or is it both? Does our "preexistence" in Adam according to seminal nature also mysteriously ground a metaphysical preexistence, such that we are or were one and the same entity as Adam? If so, is this because our souls were in him, or for some other reason?[38] Or did Augustine mean to say *only* that we were in Adam according to seminal nature physically, such that we have descended from him according to our body? Either way, does God count only Adam's first sin against us? Why or why not?[39] One might suspect Augustine had a divine judgment in mind at this juncture: God decided to impute Adam's sin to his posterity because they preexisted in him, though God did not decide to impute other sins. Augustine, however, ultimately left these questions regarding the precise mode of our union with Adam unanswered. For him, it was enough to assert that we are somehow united to Adam, that we existed in him according to seminal nature and were in him or were him, that God in his unsearchable providence has ordered things such that we inherit Adam's sin.

What is infants' inherited sin, then, given that they are justly damned for it on the basis of their union with Adam? On a verbal level the answer is clear: concupiscence, contracted through sinful, concupiscent sex.[40]

Nature and Grace XXXVI, c. 42, in *Answer to the Pelagians I*, trans. Roland J. Teske (New York: New City Press, 1997).

[38] Augustine never made up his mind on traducianism. See Jesse Couenhoven, "St. Augustine's Doctrine of Original Sin," *Augustinian Studies* 36.2 (2005), 383–5.

[39] We might expect Augustine to have inferred from our unity with Adam that we are accountable for all of Adam's sins. Indeed, why don't we inherit the guilt of all the ancestors in whom we seminally preexisted? Augustine was, in fact, open to the possibility of original *sins* (*peccata originalia*), though he never seems to have explored the idea in depth. See Sage, "Le péché originel dans la pensée de saint Augustin, de 412 à 430," 78–80. Medieval theologians tended to deny the possibility of *peccata originalia*.

[40] "[C]oncupiscence, I say, which is wiped away only by the sacrament of rebirth, certainly transmits the bond of sin to offspring by birth, at least until they themselves are released from it by rebirth. Concupiscence itself, after all, is not a sin in those who have been reborn, provided they do not consent to it for acts that are forbidden and the mind, remaining sovereign, does not hand over the members to it to carry out those acts ... It is called sin by a figure of speech, because it was produced by sin and leads to sin, if it is victorious. Its guilt is present in one who has been born, but by the forgiveness of all sins the grace of Christ does not allow this guilt to be present in one who has been reborn, if we do not obey it when it somehow bids us to do sinful actions." *Marriage and Desire I*, in *Answer to the Pelagians II*, trans. Roland J. Teske (New York: New City Press, 1998), para. 25, 44. "[C]oncupiscence of the flesh is not forgiven in baptism in such a way that it

It would seem that infants deserve grave penalties for their original sin of concupiscence, in correspondence with the gravity of Adam's act of pride. Augustine avers, however, that they will have the lightest penalty (*mitissima poena*) in hell.[41] He does not deny that they will endure the torments of Satan or experience remorse and material hellfire.

What precisely Augustine means by "concupiscence" in the context of original sin is difficult to know. Is it a synecdoche, referring not only to the evil in infants that remains for Christians to battle but also pride, the *mors animae*?[42] In this case, the concupiscence of original sin could be said to implicitly denote a specific mode or type of concupiscence, what we might call "enslaving concupiscence," the concupiscence that is simply removed when we receive the grace of the gospel. Afterward, the evil of "enslaved concupiscence" remains, but it is not imputed as a sin because it is *not* a sin – not in the full sense of the word. On behalf of this "Catholic" reading one could cite the fact that Augustine says that concupiscence in Christians is no longer sin but only an evil to fight (and even anticipates the specific language of Trent by saying that concupiscence inclines to sin and is the effect of sin but is not itself sin unless one consents to it).

Alternatively, one could argue that original sin in infants is concupiscence simpliciter, and pride is the result or punishment of this sin. In this case, it is not concupiscence qua enslaving or concupiscence qua enslaved that is original sin but concupiscence as such. In this case, the "removal" of original sin in baptism is principally God's non-imputation of the sin that remains. Original sin itself, correspondingly, is not so much an ontological feature of infants as much as a relation to God's wrath. Concupiscence is reduced in Christians, but the concupiscence that remains is still, in its intrinsic nature, sinful and damnable. On behalf of this "Protestant" reading one could argue that there is no fundamental opposition, ontologically, between natural and moral evil in rational

---

no longer exists, but in such a way that it is not counted as sin. Although its guilt has been removed, it still remains until all our weakness is healed." *Marriage and Desire* I, para. 28, 46.

[41] "Who has ever doubted that unbaptized little ones who have only original sin and are not burdened by any personal sins will suffer the lightest punishment of all? Though I cannot spell out the kind and degree of this punishment, I still do not dare to say that it would be better for them not to exist than to be in that state." *Answer to Julian*, in *Answer to the Pelagians II*, trans. Roland J. Teske (New York: New City Press, 1998), V, para. 44, 461. Cf. *Enchiridion*, c. 93, for the same point.

[42] This is Staffner's overarching argument in "Die Lehre des hl. Augustinus über das Wesen der Erbsünde."

creatures for Augustine (this is why he was so confident that God made humanity not only in friendship with God but in immortality and freedom from concupiscence).[43] Evil is just evil, though God mercifully doesn't impute concupiscence to Christians as sin. Moreover, Augustine insisted that there is sin even in licit sexual intercourse. But this wouldn't be the case if concupiscence were *only* the effect and disposition to sin, only a "natural evil" as later theologians would use the term.

There is evidence in Augustine's corpus for each of these views. I am inclined to agree with the judgment of Nicolas Merlin, from some time ago, to the effect that it's anachronistic to claim that Augustine even *had* a position on the "essence" of original sin, as though original sin were concupiscence as opposed to the *mors animae*. He did have a "stable and consistent concept" of original sin, but the stability and consistency included the foregoing ambiguities.[44] The most that should be said with confidence is this: original sin is concupiscence contracted from carnal concupiscence, ultimately derived from Adam, in whom we preexisted seminally and from whom we have descended, causing us to have the same type of guilt as Adam, if not the very same guilt, in such a way that damns us (unless we are healed by Christ in Baptism, after which time concupiscence as an evil remains and yet is not counted as sin).

Some of Augustine's teachings, including his affirmation of infant sin and damnation, were adopted during his lifetime by the Council of Carthage.[45] In the sixth century the Council of Orange affirmed original sin, denied what came to be known (much later) as "Semipelagianism,"

---

[43] Cf. *Exsurge Domine*'s 1520 condemnation of Luther's view that "[t]o deny that sin remains in a child after baptism is to disregard both Paul and Christ alike" (DH 1452).

[44] "Si l'on entend par là [a view of the essence of original sin] une dissertation en règle avec arguments, objections et réfutations, il est clair que ce serait un anachronisme de transplanter en Afrique, au commencement du siècle, ce qui n'est guère apparu qu'au treizième et même plus tard, pour le point qui nous occupe. Mais si d'autre part on veut désigner une notion déterminée et constante, bien dégagée de tout ce qui forme seulement l'accessoire et l'accidentel en pareille matière, en un mot, ce qui existe toujours là où le péché originel n'a pas été pardonné, et jamais là où cette même faute a été remise grâce aux mérites du sang rédempteur, alors nous répondons sans hésiter que l'évêque d'Hippone a eu cette notion de l'essence de péché originel." P. Nicolas Merlin, *Saint Augustin et les dogmes du péché originel et de la grâce* (Paris: Letouzey et Ané, 1931), 367–8.

[45] In 418, Carthage taught that Adam was created in conditional immortality (Can. 1, DH 222), that infants contract original sin from Adam (*ex Adam trahere originalis peccati*) and are thus baptized for its remission (Can. 2, DH 223), and that, as we mentioned in the Introduction, there are no rooms in the kingdom of heaven for infants who die unbaptized (Can. 3, DH 224).

and at least appeared to affirm that those with original sin do nothing but sin.[46] Medieval theologians would not be content to repeat Augustine's *expressis verbis*, however. He would have the first word, but he wouldn't always have the last. He left many crucial questions open. As we have seen, the mode of Adam's unity with his posterity was obscure, as was the closely related question of original sin's nature. The boundaries between heresy and orthodoxy were unclear as well. Did one really need to affirm all of the parts of Augustine's teaching that *were* clear – for example, that infants deserve eternal hellfire – in order to avoid Pelagianism? In response to questions such as these, theoretical accounts of the doctrine of original sin proliferated.

I find it helpful to categorize them in accordance with their divergent views of the unity between Adam and his posterity. By the end of the long twelfth century, three basic theories had emerged. Unity with Adam is conceptualized primarily either in physical, metaphysical, or legal terms. Here is a brief description of each of these theories. The "disease theory" of original sin emphasizes humanity's physical unity with Adam. Human beings were created sinless, in a state of health, and if they had refrained from sinning they would have remained healthy through the generations. But they did sin, and as a result they transmitted sin to their children. The transmission of sin is thought to be analogous to the transmission of a contagious physical disease. Disease theories have been attractive because they highlight the justice of God. God is not to blame for infants' original sin, because only Adam corrupted human nature. The "legal theory" of original sin, by contrast, emphasizes humanity's unity with Adam in the eyes of God. Physical unity is held to be inadequate, often on the grounds that one cannot be culpable for what one inherits. Original sin is grounded in a divine decision to count infants as sinful. There are various versions of this theory. An important one is "federalism," on which God appointed Adam as the federal head of humanity and chose to impute his

---

[46] Cann. 1–2 teach that Adam's sin corrupted his body and soul as well as his descendants', such that "[i]f anyone maintains that the fall harmed Adam alone and not his descendants or declares that only bodily death, which is the punishment for sin, but not sin itself, which is the death of the soul (*mors est animae*), was passed on to the whole human race by one man, he ascribes injustice to God and contradicts the words of the apostle [Rom 5:12]" (DH 372). Cann. 3–8 affirm that the grace of God and faith in Jesus Christ come to us not because we seek God but because God seeks us (DH 373–8). Can. 22 states, "No one has anything of his own except lying and sin" (DH 392). The twelfth-century theologians to whom we are about to turn did not have access to the Council of Orange. (And as we will see in Chapter 3, it has been argued that Thomas became familiar with it only later in his career.)

sin to subsequent human beings. Legal theories have been attractive because they have a relatively high degree of intelligibility. They have a more difficult time accounting for God's goodness or justice. The "realist theory" of original sin emphasizes humanity's metaphysical unity with Adam. Original sin is not inherited like a disease, or imputed on the basis of God's decision to count Adam's sin against human beings who didn't otherwise participate in it. Original sin must be the infant's own, real sin; she somehow truly acted in Adam. The realist theory has been attractive because it takes the sinful character of original sin seriously, while maintaining the goodness and justice of God. Its weakness, though, is that it is generally less intelligible than disease theory or legal theory.

ANSELM OF CANTERBURY

Anselm is best known for his satisfaction theory of the atonement and ontological argument for God's existence.[47] He also offered an innovative account of original sin in the mature treatise *De conceptu virginali et de originali peccato*, written during his stay in Lyons between May 1099 and August 1100.[48] This work is a sequel to the celebrated *Cur Deus homo*, in which Anselm promised his student Boso a more detailed explanation of how God could assume a sinless human nature from the sinful mass of humanity.[49] In order to answer that question, *De conceptu virginali* offers a full-fledged account of original sin, heavily indebted to yet at times departing sharply from the Bishop of Hippo's. Here I focus on Anselm's views of what original sin is, how it is transmitted, and the union between humanity and Adam.

Anselm begins with a discussion of the words "nature" and "person." Every human being has a nature, by virtue of which she is human. She shares this nature with all human beings. Every human being also has a person, by virtue of which she is an individual. She does not share her person with any human being.[50] In every human being, then, there is

---

[47] For Anselm's life and works, see the biography by R. W. Southern, *Saint Anselm: A Portrait in a Landscape* (Cambridge: Cambridge University Press, 1990).

[48] Southern, *Saint Anselm*, xxviii.

[49] Anselm describes the purpose of *De conceptu virginali* in the treatise's first chapter: "Ad videndum igitur qualiter deus hominem assumpsit de generis humani massa peccatrice sine peccato, primum de originali peccato necesse est investigare." *De conceptu virginali et de originali peccato* 1, in F. S. Schmitt, ed., *Sancti Anselmi Cantuariensis Archepiscopi Opera Omnia* [hereafter, Schmitt] (Edinburgh: Thomas Nelson, 1946), vol. 2, 140.3–5.

[50] *De conceptu virginali* 1 (Schmitt, vol. 2, 140.18–21).

nature and person. This distinction corresponds to two different sins, the sin committed by the individual person and the sin received or contracted with the reception of human nature. The latter is called "original sin." It is called "original" and "natural" not because human beings originally had it (they were created just), nor because it is part of the essence of human nature (which is good), but because every human being who descends from Adam receives it with human nature at the beginning of her fully human existence. "Personal" sin is committed later.[51] Anselm proceeds to describe how human nature was corrupted and why this corruption counts as sin.

Adam and Eve were created in original justice. Anselm's account of prelapsarian rectitude is very close if not identical to Augustine's: Adam and Eve were conditionally immortal, with rightly ordered concupiscence, and were subject to God.[52] Anselm confidently claims that, considering God's power and goodness, God must give justice to every human being he creates directly (as opposed to human beings who descend from human beings already in existence).[53] He also argues that this justice would have

---

[51] "Illud quidem quod trahitur in ipsa origine vocatur 'originale,' quod potest etiam dici 'naturale,' non quod sit ex essentia naturae, sed quoniam propter eius corruptionem cum illa assumitur. Peccatum autem quod quisque facit postquam persona est, 'personale' potest nominari." *De conceptu virginali* 1 (Schmitt, vol. 2, 140–141.26-1).

[52] *De conceptu virginali* 2 (Schmitt, vol. 2, 141.9–15).

[53] "Nam eadam ipsa ratione, qua non debuit deus ADAM facere nisi iustum nec aliquo debito sive incommodo gravatum: aperte mens rationalis cognoscit eum quem similiter propria voluntate et virtute procreat, alicui malo subditum fieri non debere; quoniam nimis inconveniens est omnipotenti et sapienti dei bonitati talem facere rationalem naturam sola propria voluntate, de materia in qua nullum est peccatum. Quod qui non intelligit, non cognoscit quid deo non conveniat. Quapropter etiam si purum hominem sic faceret deus, ut dictum est: necesse esset eum non minori praeditum iustitia et beatitudine, quam fuit ADAM cum primum factus fuit." *De conceptu virginali* 13 (Schmitt, vol. 2, 155.21–9). See *Cur Deus homo* II, 1 (Schmitt, vol. 2, 97–8) for the same point. Thus although Anselm can call original justice a grace (cf. *De conceptu virginali* 10), this does not show that he thought God could have withheld it; that is, Anselm did not call justice a gracious gift *as opposed* to a natural gift, at least not in the later, Thomist sense. We will see in the next chapter that Thomas argues that God could have withheld original justice. Mainstream historical scholarship since Kors has recognized this: "il faut rappeler d'abord que saint Anselme n'avait pas une conception nette de la distinction entre le naturel et le surnaturel." Kors, *La Justice primitive et le péché originel d'après S. Thomas*, 27. Older scholarship tended to read the distinctions of Aquinas straightforwardly into earlier theologians such as Anselm. R. M. Martin's "La question du péché originel dans Saint Anselme," *Revue des sciences philosophiques et théologiques* 5 (1911), is a good example: "S. Anselme entendait par cette justice, un don surnaturel, une grâce" (p. 739). Some recent authors have characterized Anselm in this way, though without engaging Kors. For example, Jeffrey E. Brower argues that Anselm held Adam's justice was "supernaturally infused," much like Thomas's view of the theological virtues. "Anselm

been passed on to Adam and Eve's children if they had not sinned.[54] The reason this would have been the case is the same reason why all their offspring in fact have original sin: the whole of human nature existed in Adam and Eve, and therefore the whole of human nature was corrupted when they sinned.[55]

Adam's sin put human nature in debt. Nature ought to have maintained justice but did not; now, it has the obligation or debt to have the justice it forfeited, *together* with the obligation to make satisfaction for having abandoned justice.[56] Infants, born with the nature that was in Adam, contract this debt of justice and satisfaction. How can infants have the obligation to make satisfaction or possess justice when they *cannot* make satisfaction or possess justice?[57] The same nature which could have kept justice but did not is in them.[58] The lack of original justice that ought to be present is original sin; or, more briefly, original sin is the lack of due original justice.

---

on Ethics," in *The Cambridge Companion to Anselm*, ed. Brian Davies and Brian Leftow (Cambridge: Cambridge University Press, 2004), 249.

[54] "Ergo ADAM et EVA si iustitiam servassent originalem: qui de illis nascerentur, originaliter sicut illi iusti essent." *De conceptu virginali* 2 (Schmitt, vol. 2, 141.8–9). Anselm assumes a traducian account of the soul's transmission; that is, he assumes at least that human beings have the power to transmit the soul in sexual reproduction. Cf. *De conceptu virginali* 10 (Schmitt, vol. 2, 152.20–1), where Anselm speaks of the grace Adam would have transmitted of his own power if he had not sinned.

[55] "Et quia tota humana natura in illis erat et extra ipsos de illa nihil erat, tota infirmata et corrupta est." *De conceptu virginali* 2 (Schmitt, vol. 2, 141.15–16).

[56] As Kors noted, Anselm applied the same logic to redemption. If Adam had triumphed over the devil, not only would he have propagated children in justice, he would have propagated children confirmed in justice who had defeated the devil: "Anselme conclut-il que si Adam n'avait pas succombé à la séduction du démon, mais en avait triomphé, il eut été confirmé dans la justice, et toute sa postérité avec lui et par lui. Toute la nature humaine aurait en effet triomphé en lui, et par conséquent elle aurait, comme telle, mérité la confirmation dans la justice." *La Justice primitive et le péché originel d'après S. Thomas*, 31. On this point, see *Cur Deus homo* I, 18. For Anselm's Christological use of the concept of satisfaction, see Bruce D. Marshall, "Debt, Punishment, and Payment: A Meditation on the Cross, in Light of St. Anselm," *Nova et Vetera*, English edition, 9.1 (2011), 163–81.

[57] For Anselm's argument that no mere human being can make satisfaction for sin, see *Cur Deus homo* I, 20–3.

[58] "Nec impotentia excusat eam in ipsis infantibus, quia in illis non solvit quod debet, quoniam ipsa sibi eam fecit deserendo iustitiam in primis parentibus in quibus tota erat, et semper debitrix est habere potestatem, quam ad semper servandum iustitiam accepit. *Hoc esse videri potest in infantibus originale peccatum.*" *De conceptu virginali* 2 (Schmitt, vol. 2, 142.1–5), emphasis mine. Anselm does link this debt with guilt (*culpa*) (see, for example, *Cur Deus homo* I, 24); though, as we'll see, infants' original sin and guilt is not as grave as Adam's.

Anselm's theory is realist: infants participated in Adam's sin; they did not merely inherit sin or have God count them as sinners. Despite Kors's argument to the contrary,[59] the Bishop of Hippo may be the major influence here, though Anselm – often "too deeply immersed in Augustine to search for proof texts" – does not cite him.[60] I say this because, as we have seen, one of the reasons Augustine gave in defense of the claim that original sinners are guilty is that they existed in Adam in their seminal nature. Anselm emphasizes the realism he (may have) picked up from Augustine, while rejecting Augustine's definition of original sin as concupiscence. Why did Anselm propose that original sin is the lack of due original justice, as opposed to concupiscence?

The answer lies in Anselm's view of the relation between sin and reason. He argues in chapter 3 that "there is no sin except in the rational will."[61] Sin pertains to rational beings only. We shouldn't attribute sin to infants before they receive rational souls, just as we do not attribute justice or injustice to other beings without reason.[62] Now original sin is an injustice, just as *every* sin must be an injustice. Otherwise, we would be able to say that a completely just human being could have sin – which is absurd.[63] And original sin is an injustice absolutely speaking, just as it is sin absolutely speaking. If it were, by contrast, called "sin" like a painting of a human being is called a "human being," then it would not really be sin, just as a painting of a human being is not a real human being. Infants would be, strictly speaking, free from sin, which implies either that infants are saved or that they are damned without sin (both of which are false).[64]

---

[59] Twentieth-century scholarship tended to follow Kors's argument to the effect that Anselm's views at this point are due to a metaphysical "ultra-realism" found not in Augustine but rather in Eriugena. "Anselme fortement influencé par l'ultra-réalisme de Scot Erigène, n'a pas une idée claire du rapport de la personne et de la nature." Kors, *La Justice primitive et le péché originel d'après S. Thomas*, 27. Kors proceeds to contrast Augustine and Anselm as follows: "Pour le premier [Augustin] le péché originel est dans la concupiscence, et c'est par elle que s'explique sa propagation; pour le second [Anselme], le péché héréditaire est la privation de la justice primitive dans et par la nature humaine, et c'est sur son ultra-réalisme que se fonde la théorie de la propagation" (p. 35).

[60] Southern, *Saint Anselm*, 73.

[61] "[N]on sit peccatum nisi in voluntate rationali." *De conceptu virginali* 3 (Schmitt, vol. 2, 142.12).

[62] "[P]uto nullatenus illud posse asseri esse in infante, antequam habeat animam rationalem." *De conceptu virginali* 3 (Schmitt, vol. 2, 142.11–13). Anselm, in accordance with medieval science, did not think that fully human life begins at conception (cf. *De conceptu virginali* 7).

[63] *De conceptu virginali* 3 (Schmitt, vol. 2, 142.22–4).

[64] *De conceptu virginali* 3 (Schmitt, vol. 2, 142.24–30).

Original sin is therefore true injustice and true sin. This raises the question of what justice is.

Justice is "rectitude of will preserved for its own sake" and can only be found in a rational nature. There cannot be an obligation or debt to have this justice except in a rational nature; thus original sin can only be in a rational nature.[65] Moreover, it follows from justice's definition that justice and injustice can only be in the rational will. Nothing apart from justice and injustice themselves is called just or unjust but the will (or something done on account of a just or unjust will).[66] What does it mean to say that justice and injustice are only "in" the rational will?

Neither the appetites which the apostle calls "flesh," which "lust (*concupiscit*) against the spirit" (Gal. 5:17), nor the "law of sin" which is "in the members," "fighting the law of the mind" (Rom. 7:23), are considered just or unjust per se. They do not make a human being who feels them just or unjust, but they do make a human being unjust when she consents to them when she should not.[67]

The appetites of the flesh which are contrary to the spirit are not sinful in and of themselves. Anselm argues that the urges of the flesh – which may come unbidden to human beings – are not sinful until the will consents to them.

Anselm gives three arguments for the restriction of sin to the rational will. The first is soteriological. Paul states that there is no damnation for those who are in Christ Jesus. Yet if injustice followed from merely feeling the urges of the flesh, damnation would follow. Therefore, the feelings of disordered concupiscence do not make one unjust and are not sins, only consent to them.[68] Anselm's second argument is more philosophical. He notes that if carnal concupiscence were unjust per se, it would always cause injustice. Yet carnal concupiscence is in animals, who are neither just nor unjust.[69] Finally, Anselm offers an argument from baptism. Baptism washes away every sin. But disordered concupiscence is not removed by baptism. Therefore it is not sin.[70]

---

[65] *De conceptu virginali* 3 (Schmitt, vol. 2, 143.7–11).

[66] *De conceptu virginali* 3 (Schmitt, vol. 2, 143.14–21).

[67] "Nec ipsi appetitus, quos apostolus 'carnem' vocat, quae 'concupiscit adversus spiritum,' et 'legem peccati,' quae est 'in membris,' 'repugnantem legi mentis,' iusti vel iniusti sunt per se considerati. Non enim hominem iustum faciunt vel iniustum sentientem, sed iniustum tantum voluntate cum non debet consentientem." *De conceptu virginali* 4 (Schmitt, vol. 2, 144.4–8).

[68] *De conceptu virginali* 4 (Schmitt, vol. 2, 144.8–12).

[69] *De conceptu virginali* 4 (Schmitt, vol. 2, 144.12–14).

[70] *De conceptu virginali* 4 (Schmitt, vol. 2, 144.14–15).

The two theological arguments amount to the same point: the undamned, just Christian has concupiscence. Concupiscence therefore does not damn, is not unjust, and is not sin. Infants' carnal concupiscence is neither the whole nor a part of their original sin.[71] We can now turn to his explanation of original sin's transmission and culpability.

Anselm's discussion of these issues comes in the last seven chapters of the treatise.[72] These final chapters offer a more rigorous explanation and defense of Anselm's position stated in chapter 2: the infant is justly damned by God for original sin because her nature sinned in Adam. Chapter 22 begins this section with a discussion of the gravity of original sin. Anselm argues that we must deny that infants personally committed Adam's sin: "I do not hold that the sin of Adam descends to infants as though they ought to be punished for it in this sense: as though each one of them had personally sinned. This is the case even though it is because of Adam's sin that none of them are able to be born without sin, followed by damnation."[73] Anselm is not denying that infants have original guilt – he is denying that they have *personal* guilt. Recall that we just saw him insist that infants have the debt of justice – a debt which is a guilt (*culpa*) in them because they should have preserved it in the Garden. They should have because they could have: they had the same nature that should have preserved it in the Garden. Here Anselm claims that the punishment infants deserve for their original sin is less than the punishment Adam deserved for his personal sin: in other words, infants' original sin and original guilt is less severe than personal sin and personal guilt.

In order to understand why original sin is less grave in infants, we must understand that infants existed in Adam materially or causally. They did

---

[71] Anselm's view of concupiscence would prove influential in Roman Catholic theology. Cf. §5 of the Council of Trent's decree on original sin (DH 1515).

[72] For the sake of space, we are skipping over Anselm's answer to the Christological question that impelled him to write this treatise. For Anselm's discussion of why the debt of sin cannot apply to Christ, see *De conceptu virginali* 7–21. In brief, Anselm argues that Christ did not contract original sin because Adam never had the power to make Christ just or unjust in the first place. Adam only had the ability to maintain or forfeit justice for those who would descend from him. Even if Jesus were a mere man, he would have been exempt from sin, falling outside the natural order of generation.

[73] "Peccatum ADAE ita in infantes descendere, ut sic pro eo puniri debeant, ac si ipsi illud singuli fecissent personaliter sunt ADAM, non puto, quamvis propter illud factum sit, ut eorum nullus possit nasci sine peccato, quod sequitur damnatio." *De conceptu virginali* 22 (Schmitt, vol. 2, 161.19–22). Anselm then offers an exegetical argument for this conclusion. Paul says that not all human beings sinned after the transgression of Adam. Anselm reads this as a claim that not all human beings sinned personally in Adam. *De conceptu virginali* 22 (Schmitt, vol. 2, 161.24–6).

exist in him but not *as* themselves, for they were not yet individual persons.[74] Anselm is aware of an obvious objection, however: Wouldn't it be more accurate to deny that infants existed in Adam? Properly speaking, don't infants begin to exist when they receive rational souls? Anselm's response is as follows. He argues that if you say infants were not truly in Adam, then Christ wasn't truly in David. Moreover, you might as well admit that God made nothing when he made all things from their seeds.[75] Since these assertions would be ridiculous, we should admit that infants had existence in Adam – just a different sort than the existence with which we're most familiar. "[I]n him they were not other than him, and thus they were quite different than they are in themselves."[76] More precisely, infants were in Adam according to seminal power, the power of propagation.[77] How does this help us understand infants' mitigated culpability?

When Adam sinned and ate the forbidden fruit, his nature sinned and ate the forbidden fruit; when Adam sinned, humanity sinned. Thus the sin of the person (Adam) became the sin of the nature (humanity). With infants, however, the reverse process occurs; the sin of their nature becomes the sin of each of their persons.[78] Anselm concludes from this that Adam's sin is a fundamentally different type of sin than infants'.

[I]nfants do not bear the sin of Adam but their own. For the sin of Adam was one thing, and the sin of the infant is another.... One was the cause, the other is the

---

[74] "Equidem negari nequit infantes in ADAM fuisse cum peccavit. Sed in illo causaliter sive materialiter velut in semine fuerent, in se ipsis personaliter sunt; quia in illo fuerunt ipsum semen, in se sunt singuli diversae personae. In illo non alii ab illo, in se alii quam ille. In illo fuerunt ille, in se sunt ipsi. Fuerunt igitur in illo, sed non ipsi, quoniam nondum erant ipsi." *De conceptu virginali* 23 (Schmitt, vol. 2, 163.1–6).

[75] *De conceptu virginali* 23 (Schmitt, vol. 2, 163.8–18).

[76] "[I]n illo fuerunt non alii ab illo, et ideo longe aliter quam sunt in se ipsis." *De conceptu virginali* 23 (Schmitt, vol. 2, 163.18–19).

[77] "Omnes quippe alii sic fuerunt in illo, ut per naturam propagandi." *De conceptu virginali* 23 (Schmitt, vol. 2, 163.21–2).

[78] "Est peccatum a natura, ut dixi; et est peccatum a persona. Itaque quod est a persona, potest dici 'personale'; quod autem a natura, 'naturale,' quod dicitur 'originale.' Et sicut personale transit ad naturam, ita naturale ad personam, hoc modo: Quod ADAM comedebat, hoc natura exigebat; quia ita ut hoc exigeret creata erat. Quod vero de ligno vetito comedit, non hoc voluntas naturalis, sed personalis, il est propria fecit. Quod tamen egit persona, non fecit sine natura. Persona enim erat quod dicebatur ADAM; natura, quod homo. Fecit igitur persona peccatricem naturam, quia cum ADAM peccavit, homo peccavit. Siquidem non quia homo erat, ut vetitum praesumeret impulsus est; sed propria volunte, quam non exigit natura sed persona concepit, attractus est. Similiter fit in infantibus e converso." *De conceptu virginali* 23 (Schmitt, vol. 2, 165.5–14).

effect. Adam lacked due justice not because of another but because he himself abandoned it; infants lack due justice not of themselves but because another abandoned it. *Therefore, the sin of Adam and the sin of the infant are not the same.*[79]

The sin of Adam and the sin of the infant are different; one is the cause, the other the effect. Infants are damned only for their own sin, not Adam's. Anselm does not clarify precisely what sort of penalties are due to infants in hell. He implies clearly that they will lack all happiness and teaches explicitly that they will not be punished for *any* sins other than their own.[80]

Anselm ends the treatise with an analogy intended to show that God's judgment of infant sin is not as different from human judgment as we might suppose.[81] Adam and Eve are comparable to a man and wife who were given a valuable estate through no merit of their own (*nullo suo merito sed gratia sola*). If the married couple foolishly forfeits such an estate through some crime, who would insist that it be restored to their children? Likewise, who would insist that infants be given the justice Adam forfeited on their behalf? The parable trades on the distinction between what is gracious and what is owed, implying human beings are not owed justice or beatitude. We saw earlier that Anselm held that God – when we consider his goodness – must create human beings with justice. This analogy of the lost estate would seem to imply that justice is not owed to human nature considered in itself. As far as I know, Anselm never makes this latter point. We will see Aquinas, however, pick up Anselm's family disgrace analogy (cf. *STh* I-II, q. 81, a. 1, ad 5) and argue that justice is altogether undue to humanity. Moreover, Aquinas will

---

[79] "[N]on portant infantes peccatum ADAE sed suum. Nam aliud fuit ADAE peccatum, et aliud est peccatum infantum.... Illud enim fuit causa, istud est effectum. ADAM caruit debita iustitia, non quia alius sed quia ipse deseruit; infantes carent, non quoniam ipsi sed quoniam alius dereliquit. *Non est ergo idem peccatum ADAE et infantum.*" *De conceptu virginali* 26 (Schmitt, vol. 2, 169.14–19), emphasis mine. He goes on to say that infants are not damned for Adam's sin. "Quapropter cum damnatur infans pro originali peccato, non damnatur pro peccato ADAE sed pro suo. Nam si ipse non haberet suum peccatum, non damnaretur." *De conceptu virginali* 26 (Schmitt, vol. 2, 169.24–6).

[80] Anselm argues that the lack of happiness follows the lack of justice. "Quam comitatur beatitudinis quoque nuditas, ut sicut sunt sine omni iustitia, ita sint absque omni beatitudine." *De conceptu virginali* 27 (Schmitt, vol. 2, 170.19–21). He argues in chapters 24–5 that no other sins except Adam's act in the Garden are transmitted, though the effects of various sins harm children in diverse ways. Since justice is either possessed or not possessed, all infants equally lack justice and no other sins can be transmitted.

[81] *De conceptu virginali* 28 (Schmitt, vol. 2, 171.9–18).

adopt Anselm's language of the sin of the person and the sin of the nature, as well as (formally) Anselm's definition of original sin as the lack of due justice.

Here is a summary of Anselm's account. Adam ought to have resisted the devil's temptation and transmitted the justice in which he was created to his children, thereby conquering the devil and confirming his children in justice. He did not. When Adam sinned, human nature sinned. Infants have the human nature which acted in Adam. They thus lack justice, have the obligation to possess justice, and have the corresponding obligation to make satisfaction for failing to conserve justice. Sin is only in the rational will; thus concupiscence cannot be a part or the whole of original sin. Original sin is the lack of due original justice. Yet infants do not acquire injustice like Adam, whose personal act redounded to human nature. Human nature redounds to each of their persons. They are thus not guilty for as grave a sin as Adam, and when they are condemned, they are condemned for their own, much lighter sin.

I consider Anselm's account to be one of the first, if not the first, major examples of a "realist" theory of original sin, due to its emphasis on infants' participation in Adam's act and denial that inherited concupiscence is sinful. Although by the mid-thirteenth century *De conceptu virginali* was read by leading theologians such as Thomas, its reception history in the twelfth century is difficult to trace. Neither Peter Abelard nor Peter Lombard appears to have heard of it. The only twelfth-century theologian known to have espoused Anselm's position is Odo of Cambrai in his work *De peccato originali*, and Odo himself had little influence.[82]

PETER ABELARD

Abelard is often thought to have denied original sin outright. Marcia Colish argues that he "dispenses with the need to explain the transmission

---

[82] Dom Lottin suggests that Honorius and the *Ysagoge* were aware of Anselm's views. See his *Psychologie et morale aux XIIe et XIIIe siècles*, tome IV, *Problèmes de morale, troisième partie*, vol. 1 (Louvain-Gembloux: 1954), 169–70. With the important exception of Odo's emphatic rejection of traducianism, his view of original sin is basically identical to Anselm's. Scholarship has generally assumed Odo was Anselm's follower, though Odo's English translator argues that we do not know whether Odo or Anselm's treatise was first. See Irven M. Resnick, "Introduction: Odo of Tournai," in *On Original Sin and a Disputation with the Jew, Leo, Concerning the Advent of Christ, the Son of God* trans. Irven M. Resnick (Philadelphia: University of Pennsylvania Press, 1994).

of original sin by dropping the idea of original sin itself, in effect reducing original sin to actual sin."[83] In his magisterial history of original sin, Julius Gross likewise asserts that "for Master Peter there is no original sin, only an original punishment, or better, a collective punishment."[84] Others have suggested that Abelard was simply incoherent. "[Abelard] talks around original sin as guilt, denying it on the one hand but using similar terms to define it on the other. He also again speaks of the inherited nature of original sin and of the presence of humanity in Adam at the time of his sin."[85] According to Paul Kemeny, for Abelard "original sin is a misnomer."[86] I will argue, however, that Abelard's view was coherent and that his goal was to defend the doctrine of original sin.[87] Like Anselm, he found significant aspects of Augustine's account unacceptable. Unlike Anselm, Abelard had no time for the realism in Augustine's account. He focused instead on divine judgment and pioneered the legal theory of original sin.

As far as I am aware, Abelard's most in-depth treatment of the doctrine of original sin is found in his Romans commentary, probably written in Paris sometime during the 1130s.[88] A treatise on the doctrine is interpolated into the commentary after a brief gloss on Rom. 5:12–19. Abelard comments in the gloss that Rom. 5:12 – "in whom all [Adam] sinned" (*IN QVO OMNES PECCAVERVNT*) – means that all human beings "have incurred the penalty of sin."[89] The discussion of original sin that follows is, in effect, an extended commentary on this verse. Abelard's gloss taken in itself is misleading, however: he does *not* simply take original sin to be the divinely inflicted punishment for Adam's sin. Before

---

[83] Marcia L. Colish, *Peter Lombard*, vol. 1 (Leiden: Brill, 1994), 388.

[84] "[F]ür Magister Petrus gibt es keine Erbsünde, sondern nur eine Erb- oder besser Kollektivstrafe." Gross, *Geschichte des Erbsündendogmas*, 3: 73.

[85] Steven R. Cartwright, "Introduction," in Peter Abelard, *Commentary on the Epistle to the Romans*, trans. Steven R. Cartwright (Washington, DC: Catholic University of America Press, 2011), 54.

[86] Paul C. Kemeny, "Peter Abelard: An Examination of His Doctrine of Original Sin," *The Journal of Religious History* 16.4 (1991), 375.

[87] Parts of this section are found in Daniel W. Houck, "Original Sin in Abelard's Commentary on Romans," *Being Saved: Explorations in Soteriology and Human Ontology*, ed. Marc Cortez, Joshua Farris, and S. Mark Hamilton (London: SCM Press, 2018), 54–67.

[88] John Marenbon, *Abelard in Four Dimensions: A Twelfth-Century Philosopher in His Context and Ours* (Notre Dame, IN: University of Notre Dame Press, 2013), 22.

[89] *Commentaria in epistolam Pavli ad Romanos* II, cap. 5, in E. M. Buytaert, ed., *Petri Abaelardi Opera Theologica* (Turnhout: CCCM XI, 1969), vol. 1 [hereafter, Buytaert], lines 125–6.

he gives his precise account, he raises several objections, frankly admitting that the doctrine is difficult to grasp.

We have difficulty grasping both what original sin is and how it comports with God's nature. Abelard, along with mainstream theology in the West, accepted the teaching of Augustine – which, as we have seen, was taught by the Council of Carthage in 418 – that original sin prevents unbaptized infants from entering the kingdom of heaven. But why would the God who proclaimed that the *regnum caelorum* belonged to little children bar them from entering (Matt. 19:14)? Even *human* courts do not punish children for the sins of their parents. The doctrine, then, seems to imply that God is unjust because it is unjust to children for their parents' sins. Moreover, Christians believe that God is the most merciful. If the exigencies of justice preclude punishing a child for his father's sin, how could mercy even consider it? There is another problem. The doctrine of original sin seems to require that Adam's children are condemned for the same numeric sin that he committed. But that sin was forgiven him. If a sin is not held against the one who committed it, why is it held against those who neither committed nor approved of it? Original sin, in sum, seems unjust and contrary to God's mercy.[90]

Abelard begins his response by noting that Scripture speaks of sin in different ways.[91] First, and properly speaking, sin designates a guilt or fault (*culpa*) of the soul and contempt for God.[92] For example, Adam's act of sin showed contempt for God's command and thereby brought guilt upon his soul. Whatever "properly" (*proprie*) means here – and Abelard does not say – it does not mean that broader usages of the word are unimportant.[93] For Abelard constructs his theory of the doctrine on the basis of sin's *secondary* sense: "sin" said with reference to

---

[90] For Abelard's statement of these objections, see *Ad Romanos* (Buytaert, 341–50) and *Ad Romanos* (Buytaert, 350–3).

[91] "Pluribus autem modis peccati nomen Scriptura sacra accipit." *Ad Romanos* (Buytaert, 354–5).

[92] "[U]no quidem modo et proprie pro ipsa animi culpa et contemptu Dei, id est praua uoluntate nostra qua rei apud Deum statuimur." *Ad Romanos* (Buytaert, 355–7).

[93] Consider Peter King's claim that for Abelard, "the signification of a term is the informational content of the concept that is associated with the term upon hearing it, in the normal course of events." Peter King, "Peter Abelard," in *The Stanford Encyclopedia of Philosophy* (Summer 2015 edition), ed. Edward N. Zalta, https://plato.stanford.edu/archives/sum2015/entries/abelard/. If using a word "properly" is using it in accordance with its signification, we can see why Abelard would claim that sin, properly speaking, is the act of contempt for God. Contempt for God's law would have been strongly associated with the concept of sin, in accordance with biblical texts such as 1 John 3:4.

punishment. An example of this usage is when Christians speak of the "forgiveness of sin." They are clearly talking about the forgiveness or removal of sin's *punishment* (not bringing it about that they had never sinned).[94] Abelard proposes that original sin be spoken of in this second-ary, penal sense: "Because human beings are begotten and born with original sin and contract it from the first parent, it seems that original sin should be referred more to the penalty of sin, for which they are held liable to punishment, than to the guilt of the soul and contempt for God."[95] Human beings are born with original sin, which they contract from the first parent. This original sin should be understood as a punish-ment for Adam's sin – to be precise, as Abelard will clarify, the debt of punishment (*damnationis debitum*) for Adam's sin – that Adam's off-spring contract from Adam's sin, rather than a culpable contempt of God.[96]

Why does Abelard propose that we think of original sin in this way? He holds that "sin" in infants *cannot* refer to their contempt for God. Infants do not – like non-human animals, the mentally disabled, and the insane – have the use of free will by which they could merit or demerit anything, let alone give homage or contempt to God.[97] They are,

---

[94] "[A]ltero autem modo peccatum dicitur ipsa peccati poena quam per ipsum incurrimus, uel cui propter ipsum obnoxii tenemur. Secundum quam quidem significationem dicuntur peccata dimitti, id est poenae peccatorum condonari, et Dominus peccata nostra portasse, id est poenas peccatorum nostrorum sustinuisse. Et cum aliquis dicitur habere peccatum uel cum peccato adhuc esse, qui tamen per uoluntatem malam non peccat sicut est aliquis iniquus dormiens, tale est ac si adhuc eum obnoxium poenae proprii peccati fateamur." *Ad Romanos* (Buytaert, 357–66).

[95] "Cum itaque dicimus homines cum originali peccato procreari et nasci atque hoc ipsum originale peccatum ex primo parente contrahere, magis hoc ad poenam peccati, cui uidelicet poenae obnoxii tenentur, quam ad culpam animi et contemptum Dei referendum uidetur." *Ad Romanos* (Buytaert, 368–72).

[96] "Est igitur originale peccatum cum quo nascimur, ipsum damnationis debitum quo obligamur, cum obnoxii aeternae poenae efficimur propter culpam nostrae originis, id est priorum parentum a quibus nostra cepit origo. In illo enim, ut supra meminit Apostolus, peccauimus, id est peccati eius causa aeternae damnationi ita deputamur, ut, nisi diuinorum sacramentorum nobis remedia subueniant, aeternaliter damnemur." *Ad Romanos* (Buytaert, 594–601).

[97] "Quam quidem facultatem nemo sani capitis paruulis deesse contradicet siue furiosis aut mente captis qui discretionis iudicium non habent, nec in his quae agunt sola uoluntate uel impetu mentis agitati." *Ad Romanos* (Buytaert, 430–3). "Qui enim nondum libero uti arbitrio potest nec ullum adhuc rationis exercitium habet, quasi eum recognoscat auctorem uel obedientiae mereatur praeceptum, nulla est ei transgresssio, nulla negligentia imputanda nec ullum omnino meritum quo praemio uel poena dignus sit magis quam bestiis ipsis quando in aliquo uel nocere uel iuuare uidentur." *Ad Romanos* (Buytaert, 372–8).

however, damned for Adam's sin. It is contracted, in some sense, from the carnal concupiscence of parents (though Abelard does not elaborate on this point).[98] The question Abelard raised in the beginning of the treatise remains, however: How can a good and just God damn infants for an act they had nothing to do with?

Although it would be unjust for a human court to punish the son with flames for the sins of the father – especially with an *eternal* fire – it is not unjust with God.[99] For God can treat his creature any way he pleases without causing injustice.[100] Whatever God does is good, and we have no way to define good or evil apart from his will.[101] Original sin may be difficult to understand, but so are many of God's actions. We need to believe that God orders things in the best possible way, even if we cannot understand his providence.[102] Still, Abelard argues, it is not satisfactory to simply appeal to God's will. We must attempt to commend God's goodness even in this difficult matter. And we can identify several "graces" related to infant damnation.[103]

The first grace, Abelard notes, citing Augustine, is that infants will suffer the lightest penalties in hell. "We know that this is the lightest punishment (*mitissimam poenam*), as the blessed Augustine attests in his *Enchiridion....* In my judgment, this punishment is nothing other

---

[98] Later in the treatise, in the course of explaining why original sin is still passed on by Christian parents to their children, Abelard claims, "Nec mirum uideri debet si quod indulgetur parentibus, exigatur a filiis, cum ipsa uitiosa carnalis concupiscentiae generatio peccatum transfundat et iram mereatur. Vnde Apostolus: *Natura filii irae.*" *Ad Romanos* (Buytaert, 664–67).

[99] "Numquid etiam apud homines iniquissimum iudicaretur si quis innocentem filium pro peccato patris flammis istis transitoriis traderet, nedum perpetuis? Esset utique, inquam, hoc in hominibus iniquum, quibus etiam interdicitur propriae uindicta iniuriae. Sed non ita in Deo qui dicit: *Mihi uindicta, ego retribuam.*" *Ad Romanos* (Buytaert, 486–91). Abelard will soon clarify that he does not think infants are subject to hellfire, only the torment of the loss of the beatific vision.

[100] "Non enim iniuriam creaturae suae Deus fecit quocumque modo eam tractet, siue ad poenam eam deputet siue ad requiem." *Ad Romanos* (Buytaert, 491–3).

[101] "Nec malum aliquomodo potest dici quod iuxta eius uoluntatem fiat. Non enim aliter bonum a malo discernere possumus, nisi quod eius est consentaneum uoluntati et in placito eius consistit." *Ad Romanos* (Buytaert, 505–8).

[102] *Ad Romanos* (Buytaert, 525).

[103] "Sed quia parum est ad diuinae dispensationis commendationem in hac paruulorum damnatione ab iniuria Deum absoluere, nisi etiam aliquam bonitatis eius gratiam ualeamus adstruere, uidetur nobis id quoque agi ex multiplicis gratiae ipsius dispensatione, tam in ipsis uidelicet paruulos quam in alios redundantis." *Ad Romanos* (Buytaert, 536–41).

than to suffer darkness, that is, to lack the vision of the divine majesty without any hope of ever gaining it."[104] Abelard's opinion is that damned infants will suffer only from the deprivation of the beatific vision. As far as I know, Abelard is the first prominent Western theologian after Augustine to clearly deny that infants will suffer the torment of hellfire. Anselm, as we have seen, was unclear (though he seems to lean toward divine leniency). Abelard then claims there are two more graces of God we can see in the damnation of infants. God has most likely damned infants with this lightest penalty because he foresaw that, if they had lived, they would have sinned grievously and merited far worse punishments.[105] Finally, Abelard suggests that Christians now are motivated to avoid sin through consideration of its dire consequences.[106] If God is willing to damn Adam's progeny for a rather ordinary act – eating fruit – how much more should we avoid sin? Abelard also suggests that God may have hidden reasons, known only to himself. Perhaps he uses the death of children to convert their parents, for example.[107] God has good reasons for what, to us, seems

---

[104] "Scimus quippe hanc esse mitissimam poenam, beato in *Enchiridion* Augustino sic attestante … Quam quidem poenam non aliam arbitror quam pati tenebras, id est carere uisione diuinae maiestatis sine omni spe recuperationis." *Ad Romanos* (Buytaert, 541–7).

[105] "Credimus etiam huic mitissimae poenae neminem deputari, morte in infantia praeuentum, nisi quem Deus pessimum futurum, si uiueret, praeuidebat et ob hoc maioribus poenis cruciandum. Vnde nonnullam in hac remissione uel alleuiatione poenae diuinae bonitatis gratiam percipere paruuli non immerito uidentur." *Ad Romanos* (Buytaert, 549–54).

[106] "Bene etiam Deus ad correctionem nostram hac mitissima paruulorum poena utitur, ut uidelicet cautiores efficiamur ad euitandum propria peccata, cum tales et tam innocentes, quibus nec sepultura uel orationes fidelium conceduntur, damnari quotidie credamus propter alina; et ampliores ei gratias referamus cum nos ab illo perpetuo igne post multa etiam perpetrata crimina per gratiam suam liberat, a quo minime illos saluat. Voluit etiam statim ostendere in prima et fortasse modica priorum parentum transgressione quam ita in posteris nihil adhuc merentibus uindicat, quantum omnem abhorret iniquitatem et quam poenam maioribus culpis et frequentibus reseruet, si hoc semel commissum in unius pomi reparabilis esu ita in posteris punire non differat." *Ad Romanos* (Buytaert, 555–67).

[107] "Sunt etiam in singulorum paruulorum damnatione propriae et familiares quaedam causae, licet nobis occultae, quas ille nouit qui nihil nisi optime disponit. Et nos quidem aliquas huiusmodi ex his quae frequenter accidere uidemus, coniicere possumus. Saepe quippe accidit ut talium paruulorum mortem in uitam suorum parentum diuina gratia conuertat, cum ipsi uidelicet maxime de eorum damnatione quaerentes quam eis per concupiscentiam propriam generatis intulerunt, propriae id culpae totum tribuant et sibi adscribant" *Ad Romanos* (Buytaert, 574–82).

like injustice. Toward the end of his discussion Abelard denies that other sins besides original sin are transmitted.[108] He concludes on a note of humility: his view of original sin is put forth as an opinion, not a firm assertion.[109]

Abelard's account is short and (for the most part) clear. Infants are innocent. Their original sin is the divinely imposed debt of damnation for Adam's sin. It is remittable by baptism alone, and those who die without it are condemned. God condemns these infants for their sake and ours. For their sake, because they would have committed grievous sins if they had grown up and suffered horrible punishments in hell; for our sake, because their damnation is a stark reminder to fear God. (Abelard also suggests, less clearly, that original sin is caused by carnal concupiscence.) In these respects, he was closer to Augustine than Pelagius. It's also worth noting that Abelard seems to have thought that everyone who reaches adulthood commits actual sin.[110] His denial of original guilt, however, sharply separates his account from Augustine's.

What led Abelard to deny original guilt? His arguments explicitly appeal to straightforward premises: infants do not have free will, and free will is required for culpability. That explains why he denied that guilt could be transmitted like a disease. Yet Abelard presumably would have been familiar with the realist idea that infants somehow preexisted their life in the womb and freely sinned in Adam. In the text

---

[108] After citing two well-known texts in which Augustine seems to affirm the probability of *peccata originalia*, Abelard suggests Augustine was only speaking of the opinion of others. "Haec tamen beati Augustini dicta magis ad opinionem aliorum, sicut ipsemet innuit, probabilem, quam ad ipsius assertionem referenda uidentur. Quis namque Ieremiam uel Iohannem Baptistam sanctificatos in utero, longe posteriores quam Cain deteriores nasci arbitretur? Denique et Dominus Iesus ex multis peccatoribus patribus originem ducens secundum carnem, longe post Cain natus est ex Virgine, et cum plures quam Cain peccatores haberet antecessores, nihil tamen ei obfuit numerositas talium patrum quorum carnem accepit in Virgine." *Ad Romanos* (Buytaert, 709–18).

[109] "Haec de originali peccato non tam pro assertione quam pro opinione nos ad praesens dixisse sufficiat." *Ad Romanos* (Buytaert, 730–1).

[110] "Although Abailard offers no discussion of inevitability and only occasional remarks on universality, he does affirm, without qualification, that all men commit actual sin, for which they alone are responsible and for which they need redemption through God's saving work in Jesus Christ. The universality of sin is a brute fact to be recognized rather than explained." Richard E. Weingart, *The Logic of Divine Love: A Critical Analysis of the Soteriology of Peter Abailard* (Oxford: Oxford University Press, 1970), 49.

we have considered he does not directly say why he rejects this idea, but it is tempting to speculate that his philosophical views played an important role. For example, Abelard was committed to the view that there is nothing that is not a particular.[111] There is thus no universal human nature that brought it about that particular human beings are sinful. More work would be needed to establish this possible link between his metaphysics and hamartiology. In any case, Abelard was one of the first, if not the first, to propose and defend the legal theory of original sin. And though he denied original guilt, his account is in fact – if not in word – similar to later federalist accounts that admit infants have not *done* anything wrong and yet are judged for Adam's sin.

Abelard's teaching on original sin was condemned at the Council of Sens. It seems, though, that many later medievals either didn't know of the condemnation or didn't take it especially seriously.[112] As Lottin has pointed out, after a brief lull immediately following the Council, several prominent late twelfth-century theologians, such as Alain of Lille and Simon of Tournai (both professors at the University of Paris), openly advocated the Abelardian position.[113] Many critics of Abelard, in both the twelfth and thirteenth centuries, would judge his position not as a heretical denial of original sin but as a mistaken opinion concerning its nature. One such theologian would guarantee that later generations would wrestle with Abelard's position by including it in his celebrated textbook.

---

[111] For Abelard on nominalism and the problem of universals, see John Marenbon, *The Philosophy of Peter Abelard* (Cambridge: Cambridge University Press, 1997), 117–19, 174–201.

[112] The eighth condemned proposition is the following. "Quod non contraximus culpam ex Adam, sed poenam tantum" (DH 728).

[113] "Après l'éclipse momentanée provoquée par la condamnation de 1140, la théorie d'Abélard, durant toute la second moitié du siècle, s'impose aux cercles porrétains, grâce aux *Sententiae divinitatis* dont l'influence fut décisive: le péché originel est une réalité; cette réalité consiste, non point en ce que l'enfant pèche, mais en ce que l'enfant est condamné à la peine éternelle et que, dès cette vie, il subit une certaine faiblesse du corps et de l'âme ... One la retrouve chez Simon de Tournai, chez Alain de Lille ... Fidèlement ils se transmettent la conception abélardienne qui, à en juger par la personne de ses défenseurs, ne dut point leur paraître contraire à l'orthodoxie." Lottin, *Problèmes de morale, troisième partie*, vol. 1, 166–7. See 142–67 of the same work for discussion of Abelard's followers in the twelfth century. The earliest is the anonymous *Sententiae divinitatis*, written circa 1145–50.

PETER LOMBARD

Peter Lombard's reputation is the polar opposite of Abelard's. He is generally known as a rather unimaginative compiler of quotations.[114] Accordingly, many scholars assume he more or less adopted Augustine's view of original sin and rejected any deviation from it as the heresy of Pelagianism. Marcia Colish, for example, argues that

> it is clear to him that Abelard needs to be shown conclusively to be wrong. His opening salvo makes this plain. Adam's sin was actual, Peter observes, because it was something he willed to do, as well as original, as the first sin and the origin of sin in mankind. In the rest of mankind, however, original sin cannot be reduced to actual sin. Under this heading, Peter attacks the "Pelagians" but the Abelardian reference is unmistakable.[115]

I will offer a different reading. The Lombard refused to categorize Abelard as a heretic. Moreover, he adopted a remarkable amount of Abelard's teaching in the course of communicating his own theory of the doctrine.

The Lombard's discussion of original sin comes in Book II of his *Sentences*, "the Lombardian *summa* that emerged out of the course in systematic theology which Peter taught for well-nigh two decades," the final version of which was finished between 1155 and 1157 in Paris.[116] He begins his discussion of original sin by noting what he assumes no one, Pelagian or Catholic, can dispute. According to the Bible, sin and punishment come to Adam's posterity through Adam.[117] The question is whether the sin that comes to his posterity is original (such that it comes to them at the beginning of their existence) or actual (such that Adam's posterity acquire sin by imitating him).[118] Peter announces that the latter view is that of the Pelagian heretics: "Some heretics wrongly hold this view, who are called Pelagians."[119] Immediately after this the Lombard

---

[114] Thankfully, this view is starting to shift; see Marcia L. Colish, *Peter Lombard*, 2 vols. (Leiden: Brill, 1994), and Philipp W. Rosemann, *Peter Lombard* (Oxford: Oxford University Press, 2004), for general studies of the Lombard's theology.

[115] Colish, *Peter Lombard*, 1: 394.   [116] Colish, *Peter Lombard*, 1: 25.

[117] Peter Lombard, *Sententiae* II, d. 30, c. 1, in *Sententiae in IV libris distinctae*, ed. Ignatius Brady, vol. 1 (Grottaferrata: Editiones Collegii S. Bonaventurae Ad Claras Aquas, 1971–81) [hereafter, Brady], 496.1, 6–8.

[118] "Utrum illud peccatum fuerit originale ac actuale." *Sententiae* II, d. 30, c. 2 (Brady, 496.10). See also *Sententiae* II, d. 30, c. 3 (Brady, 496.16–21) and *Sententiae* II, d. 30, c. 4 (Brady, 497.1–5).

[119] "Hoc male senserunt quidam haeretici, qui dicti sunt Pelagiani." *Sententiae* II, d. 30, c. 4 (Brady, 497.6–7).

cites a fairly long quote from Augustine's *De peccatorum meritis*, to the effect that if Paul had meant to say sin comes by imitation and not propagation, he would have said that sin entered the world through Satan. Thus the sin that passes to posterity is not transmitted by imitation alone but by propagation.[120] This is original sin, the sin passed on to all of Adam's children who were begotten from concupiscent sex.[121]

Having established the fact of original sin, the Lombard turns to its nature. He frankly observes that the fathers – clearly including Augustine, the only father heretofore cited in this distinction – have spoken obscurely on the issue and that the doctors currently disagree.[122] He then discusses two opinions, presumably the opinions on which the doctors currently disagree.

The first opinion is Abelard's (though he is not mentioned by name; the Lombard notes only that "some" subscribe to this opinion). According to this view, original sin is the debt of punishment incurred by children for Adam's actual sin.[123] The Lombard responds *not* by arguing that this view is a denial of original sin; he has already dealt with the Pelagian heresy before this section begins. Instead, he argues that the testimonies of the saints imply that original sin should be understood as a fault.[124] He cites Augustine to that effect and concludes, "It is clearly shown by these

---

[120] "Non est igitur accipiendum peccatum Adae transisse in omnes imitationis tantum exemplo, sed propagationis et originis vitio." *Sententiae* II, d. 30, c. 4 (Brady, 497.20–3).

[121] "Hoc aperit illud esse peccatum originale, quod transit in posteros. Et est illud peccatum originale, ut aperte Augustinus testatur, quod per Adam transivit in omnes per eius carnem vitiatam concupiscentialiter generatos." *Sententiae* II, d. 30, c. 5 (Brady, 497.24–7).

[122] Peter Lombard, *Sententiae* II, d. 30, c. 6 (Brady, 498.2–4).

[123] "Quidam enim putant originale peccatum esse reatum poenae pro peccato primi hominis, id est debitum vel obnoxietatem qua obnoxii et addicti sumus poenae temporali et aeternae pro primi hominis actuali peccato: quia pro illo, ut aiunt, omnibus debetur poena aeterna, nisi per gratiam liberentur. – Iuxta horum sententiam oportet dici originale peccatum nec culpam esse nec poenam." *Sententiae* II, d. 30, c. 6 (Brady, 498.5–11). The Lombard's summary of Abelard is precise: as we saw earlier, Abelard does not say that original sin *is* a punishment but rather the debt of punishment.

[124] What was the Pelagian heresy in the Lombard's mind? Denis Janz's summary of the Lombard's "picture of the Pelagian heresy" seems right to me. "(a) the Pelagians taught that free will without the help of grace was sufficient for obtaining righteousness and salvation; (b) the grace of God is given according to merit; (c) man can fulfill all the divine laws through free will alone, and hence he can avoid sin; and (d) infants are born without sin. This then is the understanding of Pelagianism which Lombard bequeathed to the late Middle Ages." Both from *Luther and Late Medieval Thomism* (Ontario: Wilfrid Laurier University Press, 1983), 41. For the Lombard, then, if one is a Pelagian, one will deny that original sin is a *culpa*, but denying that original sin is a *culpa* does not

and other authorities that original sin is a guilt (*culpam*), contracted by all who are begotten through their parents' concupiscence."[125]

Still, given that original sin somehow involves guilt, what precisely is it? It is not actual sin, for it is not an act or movement of the soul or the body.[126] Here is the Lombard's definition. It may help to quote the English and Latin together:

Original sin is called the kindling of sin, namely concupiscence or the capacity for concupiscence, which is the law of the members, or the languor of nature, or the tyrant who is in our members, or the law of the flesh.

Originale peccatum dicitur fomes peccati, scilicet concupiscentia vel concupiscibilitas, quae dicitur lex membrorum, sive languor naturae, sive tyrannus qui est in membris nostris, sive lex carnis.[127]

Original sin is concupiscence. The concupiscence in which original sin consists is not an act; it is the fault or vice which will result in actual concupiscence later.[128] Just as one cannot tell the difference between a blind man and one who sees when it is dark but only when the light appears, so too the vice of concupiscence is not evident until a more advanced age.[129] Concupiscence, then, is the stable, we might say "subconscious" or (with later scholastics) "habitual" condition which will result in disordered desires or "actual concupiscences." It must stem from concupiscent sexual intercourse. Though infants have not acted in a blameworthy or culpable way, they receive the vice of concupiscence for which they are blamed.

How then were infants in Adam, given that they did not act in him? The Lombard quotes the Augustinian phrase "all were that one man" – which by then was part of the ordinary gloss on Romans – and argues that it means that Adam's descendants "were in him materially."[130] Now, as we have seen, Augustine himself was clear that later humans were in

---

make one a Pelagian; one would also need to affirm at least one of these four propositions.

[125] "His aliisque auctoritatibus evidenter ostenditur peccatum originale culpam esse, et in omnibus concupiscentialiter genitis trahi a parentibus." *Sententiae* II, d. 30, c. 7 (Brady, 499.22–4).

[126] "Quod cum non sit actuale, non est actus sive motus animae vel corporis." *Sententiae* II, d. 30, c. 8 (Brady, 500.1).

[127] *Sententiae* II, d. 30, c. 8 (Brady, 500.4–6).

[128] "Vitium utique est, quod parvulum habilem concupiscere facit, adultum etiam concupiscentem reddit." *Sententiae* II, d. 30, c. 9 (Brady, 501.4–5).

[129] *Sententiae* II, d. 30, c. 9 (Brady, 501.6–9).

[130] "Omnes enim ille unus homo fuerant, id est in eo materialiter erant." *Sententiae* II, d. 30, c. 10 (Brady, 501.22).

Adam according to seminal power, or materially, *at least* in the sense that Adam's semen could form the bodies of his children. (Anselm agreed but assumed Adam's semen could form the souls of his children as well.) The Lombard offers a stronger account of this material preexistence.

First, though, he refutes an objection to the Augustinian thesis that we were in Adam materially. The objection is this: it is impossible for all human beings to have literally been in Adam, for the quantitative mass of the whole human race vastly exceeds the size of Adam's body. It is manifestly absurd to claim we were in Adam materially. We wouldn't all fit! The Lombard responds by arguing that this is not a serious objection. Those who make it are quibbling over words (*"verborum sectatores"*).[131] The objectors, in Lombard's mind, insist on a naive rendering of the phrase that all human beings were materially in Adam. We should envisage this unity "materially" and "causally" but not "formally." That is, the body of Adam has multiplied through the generations such that the bodies of Adam's posterity were in Adam, though at that point they had not yet multiplied.[132] Adam's semen is a little bit or portion (*modicum*) of his body, which is used to create the body of his children and continually expands until they are fully grown. When Cain begot his children he did the same thing, and so on, such that every descendant of Adam was at one time a physical part of Adam. The bodies of Adam's children must expand of their own power, without the assimilation of food. Otherwise much of our body would *not* have existed in Adam, and whatever portion did exist in Adam would continually be diluted, perhaps completely so, which would render Paul's teaching that we were in Adam false.[133] The idea that Adam's body continued to multiply down the generations is not only the best way to understand

---

[131] "Ad hoc autem quod diximus, in Adam fuisse omnes homines, quidam verborum sectatores sic obiciunt, dicentes: Non omnis caro quae ab Adam traducta est, in eo simul exsistere potuit quia multo maioris quantitatis est quam fuerit corpus Adae, in quo nec tot etiam atomi fuerent, quot ab eo homines descenderunt. Quocirca verum non esse asserunt, substantiam uniuscuiusque in primo fuisse parente." *Sententiae* II, d. 30, c. 14 (Brady, 503.22–4, 504.1–4).

[132] *Sententiae* II, d. 30, c. 14 (Brady, 504.7–13).

[133] "Transmisit enim Adam modicum quid de substantia sua in corpora filiorum quando eos procreavit, id est aliquid modicum de massa substantiae eius divisum est et indi formatum corpus filii, suique multiplicatione, sine rei extrinsecae adiectione, auctum est. Et de illo ita augmentato aliquid itidem separatur, unde formantur posterorum corpora. Et ita progreditur procreationis ordo lege propagationis usque ad finem humani generis. Itaque diligenter ac perspicue intelligentibus patet omnes secundum corpora in Adam fuisse per seminalem rationem, et ex eo descendisse propagationis lege." *Sententiae* II, d. 30, c. 14 (Brady, 504.14–23).

the Pauline teaching that we sinned in Adam. It is also, the Lombard argues, implied by the teaching of Jesus and the doctrine of the resurrection.[134] This "surprisingly physical"[135] theory – what Philip Reynolds calls "physical traducianism" – sounds bizarre to modern readers.[136] But the Lombard's goal was not to woodenly repeat Augustine: it was to offer an explanation of Paul's teaching that we sinned in Adam. Nor did the Lombard reduce original sin to the body, as later critics would claim.[137] The flesh is the cause but not the seat of original sin. This is clear from a consideration of original sin's transmission.

Distinction 31 asks whether original sin is contracted from the flesh or the soul.[138] Recall that Anselm assumed a traducian account of the soul's transmission, and Augustine waffled on the issue. It seems easier to explain original sin's transmission if traducianism is true, because Adam is straightforwardly to blame for the corruption of his children's bodies and the guilt of their souls. If God infuses the soul, though, how can we avoid blaming him for the soul's initial condition? Yet for the Lombard, traducianism is not a live option. He is convinced that it is a heresy. "The Catholic faith rejects this and condemns it as against the truth. As we said earlier, the faith admits that the flesh alone and not the soul is transmitted. Therefore original sin is contracted from the parents according to the flesh alone and not the soul."[139]

---

[134] *Sententiae* II, d. 30, c. 15 (Brady, 504.26–9; 505.1–4).

[135] Rosemann, *Peter Lombard*, 114.

[136] "Physical traducianism arises when literal-minded scholars in the twelfth century appropriate Augustine's statements and detach them from their rhetorical context." Philip Lyndon Reynolds, *Food & the Body: Some Peculiar Questions in High Medieval Theology* (Leiden: Brill, 1999), 28.

[137] John Calvin, for example, mischaracterizes the Lombard's position on concupiscence as follows. "In quo crassam inscitiam detexit Petrus Lombardus (lib. 2. dist. 3.), qui sedem quaerens et vestigans, dicit in carne esse ... Quasi vero tantum partem animae designet Paulus, ac non totam naturam, quae supernaturali gratiae opponitur." *Institutionis Christianae Religionis* II, c. 1, §9, ed. F. G. Tholuck (Berolini, 1834), 169. Calvin accepts the definition of original sin as concupiscence – as long as we add that "totum hominem non aliud ex se ipso esse quam concupiscentiam" (p. 169.). Calvin was typically concerned with contemporary Catholics' appropriation of medieval scholastic thought; perhaps some sixteenth-century Catholics had distorted the Lombard's view and claimed original sin is purely a fleshly reality.

[138] "Quomodo peccatum originale a patribus transeat ad filio: an secundum animam, an secundum carnem." *Sententiae* II, d. 31, c. 1 (Brady, 505.15–16).

[139] "Hoc autem fides catholica respuit et tanquam veritati adversum damnat, quae non animas, sed carnem solam, sicut superius diximus, ex traduce esse admittit. Non igitur secundum animam, sed secundum carnam solam, peccatum originale trahitur a

How does this work? Original sin transmitted to the soul through corrupted flesh.[140] Adam's sin corrupted the flesh initially; the rest of his posterity are formed from his flesh and are thus corrupt. Moreover, each individual body is formed through concupiscent sex.[141] When the soul is infused, it is stained from contact with the body and becomes guilty of the vice of concupiscence. God is not to blame in any respect: he instituted human nature without vice and it is the flesh, not God, that infects the soul when he infuses it.[142] The flesh sown in concupiscence has neither guilt nor the action of guilt, to be sure. It is, however, the *cause* of original sin, just as a defective vase turns good wine to vinegar.[143]

Baptism cleanses the infant in the sense that concupiscence will not reign in her – she will be able to obey God – and in the sense that God

---

parentibus." *Sententiae* II, d. 31, c. 3 (Brady, 506.6–10). The Lombard refers us to *Sententiae* II, d. 18, where he cites Gennadius's *Liber seu diffinitio ecclesiasticorum dogmatum* to prove that traducianism and Origenism are both heresies. See Leslie Lockett's *Anglo-Saxon Psychologies in the Vernacular and Latin Traditions* (Toronto: University of Toronto Press, 2011), 305–7, for more information on Gennadius's text. Many manuscripts of this text were not attributed to Gennadius but to Augustine. Sometimes they were even thought to be canons of the first Council of Nicaea, though the Lombard doesn't seem to be under this impression.

[140] "Quae dicitur manere in carne, non quin in anima sit, sed quia per corruptionem carnis in anima fit." *Sententiae* II, d. 31, c. 3 (Brady, 506.16–17).

[141] "Caro enim per peccatum corrupta fuit in Adam, adeo ut, cum ante peccatum vir et mulier sine incentivo libidinis et concupiscentiae fervore possent convenire, essetque thorus immaculatus, iam post peccatum non valeat fieri carnalis copula absque libidinosa concupiscentia, quae semper vitium est, et etiam culpa, nisi excusetur per bona coniugii. In concupiscentia igitur et libidine concipitur caro formanda in corpus prolis. Unde caro ipsa, quae concupitur in vitiosa concupiscentia, polluitur et corrumpitur; ex cuius contactu anima, cum infunditur, maculam trahit qua polluitur et fit rea, id est vitium concupiscentiae, quod est originale peccatum." *Sententiae* II, d. 31, c. 4 (Brady, 506.20–8). In order to contract original sin, one must inherit corrupted flesh from Adam and be begotten in concupiscence. Christ was exempt from original sin because he was begotten supernaturally.

[142] "Ipse enim non incongrue humanae conditionis modum quem a principio instituit, licet peccata hominum intercesserint, sine imutatione continue servat, corpora de materia a principio sine vitio facta fingens, animasque de nihilo creans, eorumque coniunctione hominem perficiens. Cum igitur utraque hominis natura a Deo sine vitio sit instituta, licet a se peccato sit vitiata, non ideo immutabilis Deus humanae conditionis primariam legem mutare debuit, sive ab hominum multiplicatione desistere." *Sententiae* II, d. 32, c. 6 (Brady, 516.11–18).

[143] "Ideoque ipsum peccatum dicitur manere in carne. Caro igitur quae in concupiscentia libidinis seminatur, nec culpam habet nec actum culpae, sed causam." *Sententiae* II, d. 31, c. 5 (Brady, 507.3–5). "[S]icut in vase dignoscitur vitium esse, cum vinum infuseum acescit." *Sententiae* II, d. 31, c. 6 (Brady, 508.21–2).

does not impute the concupiscence that remains in her unto damnation.[144] Because concupiscence remains after baptism (as a punishment,
not a guilt), parents who have been cleansed from the guilt of original sin
will continue to pass on concupiscence to their children.[145] Jesus Christ,
however, was not begotten in concupiscence and therefore did not contract original sin.[146]

The Lombard concludes his treatment of original sin by discussing its
eternal punishment (like Anselm and Abelard, the Lombard submits to
the teaching of Carthage that children who die unbaptized are damned).
The first question is whether infants will be punished for any sins in
addition to the concupiscence they inherit. If so, will they inherit all their
ancestors' sins, or only some? He summarizes Augustine's statements on
peccata originalia, concluding that although Augustine spoke ambigu-
ously on the question, his principles imply that infants inherit only one
sin. He taught that infants have the lightest punishment in hell. If infants
were punished for their own original sin *and* their parents' actual sins,
then infants would be punished *more* than their parents – assuming their
parents are also damned – which is patently absurd.[147] Infants will be
punished only for the single sin that they inherit. He describes the punishment as follows.

Infants will be damned for the original sin contracted from their parents, not for
the actual sins of their parents or even the actual sins of the first parent. The *only*
punishment for their original sin will be the perpetual loss of the vision of God:
they will not feel material fire or the worm of conscience. Infants are therefore
bound by one – and not many – sins.[148]

The Lombard has followed Abelard on this crucial point: the loss of the
vision of God, without hellfire and without regret, is the damned infant's
only punishment. Notably, he *drops* Abelard's statement that infants will
suffer some sort of sadness on account of their hopelessness. The

---

[144] *Sententiae* II, d. 32, c. 1 (Brady, 511.21–4).
[145] "Non enim generant parentes filios secundum illam generationem qua denuo sunt nati,
sed potius secundum eam qua carnaliter et ipsi primum sunt generati." *Sententiae* II,
d. 31, c. 6 (Brady, 509.8–10).
[146] *Sententiae* II, d. 31, c. 7 (Brady, 509.17–22).
[147] *Sententiae* II, d. 33, c. 2 (Brady, 520.9–12).
[148] "Non igitur pro peccatis parentum actualibus, nec etiam pro actualibus primi parentis,
sed pro originali quod a parentibus trahitur, parvuli damnabuntur: pro eo nullam aliam
ignis materialis vel conscientiae vermis poenam sensuri, *nisi* quod Dei visione carebunt in
perpetuum. Uno igitur, et non pluribus peccatis, parvuli obligati sunt." *Sententiae* II,
d. 33, c. 2 (Brady, 520.12–17).

Lombard does not speculate further about what the eternal loss of the beatific vision, without hellfire or a guilty conscience, will feel like.

Let's take stock of the Lombard's account. He identifies the Pelagian heresy with the denial of infant sin and the corresponding affirmations that infants who die unbaptized are saved, that Adam's sin is "transmitted" only by imitation, and that free will can merit salvation without grace later in life. Those who deny original guilt are seriously mistaken, as they contradict the fathers; yet the Lombard stops short of saying they contradict the teaching of the Church. (It seems more likely that the Lombard would have condemned Anselm's account of original sin as heretical, if he had known it, as Anselm affirmed traducianism, which the Lombard explicitly claims is contrary to the teaching of the Church.) Original sin is concupiscence, inherited through corrupted flesh and concupiscent sex. It is not an act. The mysterious metaphysical unity with Adam's act of sin that plays such a heavy role in Anselm's account – and that Abelard sharply criticized – is thus absent from the Lombard's account. He enlists a heavy-duty physical union with Adam to do the work of grounding infant culpability. Whether a merely material "pre-existence" was cut out for the job, however, remained to be seen.

We are now in a position to conclude our brief discussion of the twelfth century. None of our theologians was entirely Augustinian. Anselm and Abelard broke with him most radically, denying that concupiscence is sinful and that original sin is culpable, respectively. The Lombard, though, while closest to Augustine verbally, accepted Abelard's denial that human *nature* can act and radicalized Augustine's doctrine of humanity's bodily union with Adam, slamming shut the door of traducianism which Augustine had left cracked open. The Lombard is thus an early, important defender of the "disease theory." Anselm offered a realist theory that focused more on our metaphysical union with Adam. Abelard pioneered a legal theory that focused on our juridical union with Adam. All three of these theologians emphasized Augustine's *mitissima poena* doctrine. For Augustine, and even Abelard, there was no question that God would be just in meting out severe penalties to infants in hell; God in his mercy will – we hope, we pray – only punish them lightly. In the Lombard, we find a confident assertion that the lack of the beatific vision is their only punishment, with no worm of conscience or material fire involved: he even implies that condemned infants might not be sad.

Yet despite their differences from Augustine, these twelfth-century theologians had a significant amount in common with him. They taught that Adam and Eve enjoyed an original righteousness, that Adam's sin resulted in the damnation of the human race, and that God will in fact condemn many children. Moreover, at least Anselm and the Lombard presupposed Augustine's "historical" account of human nature: nature is what God gives to a species at creation. Since God instituted human nature immortality and righteousness, neither sin nor death nor concupiscence attaches to human nature as such, only as corrupted by Adam. Thus they assumed that any human beings created directly by God would have the same basic attributes as prelapsarian Adam and Eve. Anselm even stated explicitly that any directly created human being must have justice.

The *Sentences* was a fantastic success. By the time Thomas Aquinas would comment on it in the 1250s, it had become the standard theological textbook in the university. The Lombard's frank admission that the fathers had not clearly explained original sin, together with the impression he gave that there was wide room for disagreement without falling into heresy, would inspire the greatest theologians of the thirteenth century to offer highly innovative accounts of the doctrine. Thirteenth-century scholastics would agree with the Lombard that Pelagianism and traducianism were out of bounds, but whether original sin consists in concupiscence, punishment, or injustice (or some combination thereof) was open to debate. So too was the mode of our union with Adam. Many would, with the Lombard, focus on our physical unity with Adam, and others would combine different aspects of the twelfth-century accounts. Alexander of Hales, for example – the first thirteenth-century theologian to cite Anselm's *De conceptu virginali* – combined Anselm's definition with many others, calling original sin the lack of due justice as well as concupiscence, punishment, guilt, the law of the flesh, and so on.[149] With this context established, we can now turn to Thomas Aquinas.

---

[149] As Lottin says, speaking of Hales, "C'est ici que l'on voit apparaître pour la première fois, au XIIIe siècle, le nom de saint Anselme, dans les exposés sur le péché originel." Alexander did not appeal to Anselm to reject the traditional formulas; however, he was content to call original sin many names: it is the "*carentia vel nuditas debitae iustitiae,*" but it is also a "*macula, reatus, poena, culpa, iniquitas, fomes, languor, tyrannus, lex membrorum, lex carnis, stimulus carnis, concupiscentia.*" Both from Lottin, *Problèmes de morale, troisième partie*, vol. 1, 171.

2

Aquinas on Original Justice

Thomas Aquinas's account of original sin has been forgotten. His basic *definition* of original sin, to be sure, is still known: a quick glance at any of his discussions of the topic shows that Thomas combined the definitions of Peter Lombard and Anselm of Canterbury. Original sin is the privation of original justice by which the will was subject to God ("formally") and the privation of original justice by which the lower powers of the soul were subject to the higher powers, that is, concupiscence ("materially"). Thomas's immediate influences, too, have been solidly established by scholarship. As Dom Lottin has shown, Thomas's teacher Albert the Great was the first to combine Anselm and the Lombard's definitions.[1] An investigation of *how* Thomas received the distinctive teachings of the twelfth century, however – Anselm's claim that *non est ergo idem peccatum ADAE et infantum*, Abelard's affirmation that human nature does not act, the general emphasis on the *mitissima poena* – reveals that he radically reconfigured the content of the concepts of "justice" and "concupiscence." It is Thomas's new understanding of original sin that has been forgotten.

How could this have happened? I suspect that one of the primary reasons is this: Thomas's treatment of the doctrine in his magnum opus is severely truncated. Seeking to avoid the "multiplication of useless questions, articles and arguments," the *Summa theologiae* devotes a mere

---

[1] Lottin notes that Albert also used Aristotle's matter/form distinction to define original sin. "Mais on peut préciser: la *pronitas*, qui n'est autre que le *fomes* est la matière du péché originel, tandis que la *carentia* en est la forme." Lottin, *Problèmes de morale, troisième partie*, vol. 1, 238.

three questions and 7,700 words to original sin.[2] By contrast, his treatise on original sin in his *Sentences* commentary is more than four times as long (32,000 words). The discussion in *De malo* is more than 25,000 words. Thomas presumably assumed that these works would be read alongside his *Summa* – which was, of course, written for beginners. His readers, however, have all too often assumed that the *Summa* is a sufficient guide to his thought.

The coming chapters contend that it is not. Indeed the hermeneutical key to understanding the *Summa*'s treatment of original sin is found, surprisingly, in the *Scriptum* on Peter Lombard's *Sentences*. It is there, early in Thomas's career, that he explains just what he means by the word "nature," and it is his concept of nature that discloses the radical aspects of his doctrine of original sin. There are two equally legitimate yet distinct senses of the word. One is Augustinian, historical, traditional; the other Aristotelian, Dionysian, and – in Thomas's hands – novel. In the *Summa*, Thomas alternates between these (and several other) senses of the word "nature" without explaining himself at length, assuming that context will clue the reader in to the relevant sense. Detached from the semantic context of the *Scriptum*, the *Summa*'s discussion has been misread, the Augustinian and distinctively Thomist senses of nature confused. My historical argument is also theological. It is impossible to understand the historical question of what Thomas taught without understanding the trajectory of his thought. This latter task requires judgment. The coming chapters thus contain both historically focused material and evaluative or analytical theological argumentation.

This chapter treats the privation of original justice (original sin negatively considered). Chapter 3 discusses the subject of the privation of original justice (the privation positively considered, or as it's sometimes known, the question of the "the effects of original sin"). This chapter and Chapter 3, then, focus on what Thomas calls the evil of original sin (the *ratio mali*). Chapter 4 turns to the guilt of original sin (the *ratio culpae*).

---

[2] *Summa theologiae* (Rome: Ex Typographia Polyglotta S. C. de propaganda Fide, 1888–1906) [hereafter, *STh*], *prologus*. I have used the *corpus thomisticum* to estimate these word counts (www.corpusthomisticum.org/). Thomas's treatment of original sin in other works (e.g., the *Summa contra Gentiles*, *Compendium theologiae*, and Romans commentary) is even briefer than that of the *Summa*. For a helpful collection of Thomas's scattered statements on original sin throughout his Pauline commentaries, see Wieslaw Dabrowski, "La dottrina sul peccato originale nei commenti di san Thommaso d'Aquino alle lettere di san Paolo Apostolo," *Angelicum* 83 (2006), 557–629.

The overarching argument of this chapter and Chapters 3 and 4 is this. Thomas's doctrine of original sin was a brilliant version of disease theory, on which, in a word, original sin involves receiving nature from Adam while needing grace from Christ. Thomas's account was still developing when he stopped writing, however. In particular, his mature view of the grace of original justice was leading him away from thinking of original sin as a sexually transmitted disease. Adam never could have transmitted original justice in the first place.

SCHOLARSHIP ON AQUINAS'S VIEW OF ORIGINAL JUSTICE

Thomas consistently argued that original sin is the lack of due original justice. Thus in order to fully understand his account of original sin, we need to understand his account of original justice. It is not easy to know what Thomas thought original justice is. In particular it is difficult to understand what the "formal cause" of original justice is. For several decades in the first half of the twentieth century, there was a heated debate among Thomists *ad mentem Thomae* on this question (a debate that has gone unresolved to this day). Until 1915, it seems that most Thomists assumed that Thomas, in precise agreement with the Council of Trent, held that the formal cause of original sin is the privation of sanctifying grace – and that baptism removes original sin by conferring grace. On this view, Aquinas thinks that original justice is composed of three essential parts. The first, formal part is sanctifying grace; the other two "material" parts are rightly ordered concupiscence and immortality. Sanctifying grace of a certain intensity is the intrinsic condition sine qua non of the other two parts, and therefore original justice, like grace, is supernatural. When Aquinas says that original sin is formally the lack of original justice whereby the will was subject to God, he *means* that original sin is formally the lack of sanctifying grace whereby the will was subject to God.

In 1915, the Dominican R. M. Martin dropped a bombshell on this Thomistic consensus. He argued that Thomas's conception of original justice was altogether different. Original justice is natural phenomenon, potentially possessed without sanctifying grace and transmissible through sexual intercourse.[3] The formal cause of original justice is preternatural

---

[3] R. M. Martin, "La doctrina sobre el pecado original en la Summa contra Gentiles," *La Ciencia Tomista* 10 (1915), 389–400. Cyril Vollert would claim, twenty-six years later,

rectitude; correspondingly, original sin is formally the lack of the preternatural subjection by which the will was subject to God. Sanctifying grace, by contrast, is supernatural: neither grace nor a disposition thereto could have been transmitted sexually; grace must be given directly by God as a personal gift. For Thomas, original sin *involves* the absence of sanctifying grace (it is, properly speaking, a penalty for original sin), which was all Trent – which didn't intend to settle technical scholastic disputes but rather refute Protestantism's perversion of Augustine – intended to affirm. There is no contradiction between Thomas and Trent. If we are going to speak of *Thomas's* view, however, we need to be precise: original sin is a sin of nature, the privation of the natural gift of original justice.

Martin's article was controversial. Historically minded theologians – including Martin's brother Dominican J. B. Kors, as well as Dom Lottin – agreed with his thesis.[4] Neo-scholastics demurred. Somewhat ironically, given their reputation for ahistoricism, they posited an evolution in Aquinas's thought.[5] Yes, they conceded, Martin was right about Aquinas in his early writings. By the *Summa theologiae*, however, Aquinas thought of original justice as supernatural, anticipating Trent and the truth. But this change didn't require any major shift in Thomistic hamartiology: both the early and late Thomas envisaged Adam as transmitting merely the disposition to original justice, not supernatural grace itself. Original

that "[f]ew theological problems have stirred up such spirited debate thus far in the twentieth century as the problem of this relationship." "Saint Thomas on Sanctifying Grace and Original Justice: A Comparative Study of a Recent Controversy," *Theological Studies* 2 (1941), 369.

[4] The most important initial defense of Martin's thesis was J. B. Kors's monograph *La Justice primitive et le péché originel d'après S. Thomas*. Kors argued, at length, that Martin's thesis applied to Aquinas's entire body of work. D. O. Lottin extended Martin and Kors's thesis to the twelfth and thirteenth centuries, arguing that the entire medieval period tended to view original justice as a natural phenomenon. See his treatment of Albert, Bonaventure, and Aquinas in *"Le péché originel chez Albert le Grand, Bonaventure et Thomas d'Aquin," Recherches de Théologie ancienne et médiévale* 12 (1940), 275–328. For an extensive review of the literature, still useful because the scholarly debate over original justice had more or less died out by the time it was published, see Van Roo, *Grace and Original Justice According to St. Thomas*.

[5] See Reginald Garrigou-Lagrange, "Utrum gratia sanctificans fuerit in Adamo dos naturae an donum personae tantum," *Angelicum* 2 (1925), 133–44. For a further defense of the neo-scholastic view, see Cyril Vollert's aforementioned "Saint Thomas on Sanctifying Grace and Original Justice," 369–87. Vollert argued that early Thomists maintained this teaching as well. See Cyril Vollert, *The Doctrine of Hervaeus Natalis on Primitive Justice and Original Sin: As Developed in the Controversy on Original Sin during the Early Decades 14th Century* (Rome: Gregorian University Press, 1947).

sin, then, is still the sin of nature, despite original justice's supernaturality. Both sides published numerous studies and were able to adduce texts throughout Thomas's corpus for support. It was interrupted by World War II, and other questions took center stage in postwar Catholic theology (not least of which was the question of nature's desire for the supernatural).

This chapter revives the debate. I argue that both sides were right. In the first section, I show that Martin et al. were right that Thomas held to the parallel transmissibility of justice and sin. It is clear in the *Scriptum*, moreover, that original justice and sin must both be natural in Thomas's framework. Yet even in the *Scriptum*, I'll suggest, there was a fundamental instability: Thomas frequently tacitly appeals to original sin to explain the infant's deordination from the beatific vision (when he claims baptism removes original sin by restoring grace, for example), while at the same time in his *ex professo* treatment of original sin's essence he maintains that it consists formally only in the loss of what came to be called "preternatural rectitude." By the time of the *Summa theologiae* – here Garrigou-Lagrange et al. were right – Thomas was teaching that original justice's formal cause is supernatural (which helped him explain how baptism removes sin and linked original sin more closely to the need for salvation). What this implies, however, is that both sides of the debate were also wrong. Neither party recognized that Aquinas's new view of original justice had massive consequences for his doctrine of original sin.

THE FORMAL CAUSE OF ORIGINAL JUSTICE

We will begin with Thomas's commentary (*Scriptum*) on Peter Lombard's *Book of Sentences*. This work stems from Thomas's lectures in Paris from 1252 to 1256, when he was in his late twenties.[6] The title "commentary" can be misleading. Thomas, like other medievals, used the Lombard as a point of departure but felt free to present his own thoughts. Thomas's treatment of original justice in the *Scriptum* is scattered throughout book II, which treats the doctrine of creation more generally. The transmission of original justice (d. 20) is discussed before the state of original justice (d. 29), with various questions on grace coming in between. Much of this

---

[6] For the dating of the *Scriptum*, as well as a helpful overview of this period in Thomas's life, see Jean-Pierre Torrell, *Saint Thomas Aquinas, vol. 1: The Person and His Work*, trans. Robert Royal (Washington, DC: Catholic University of America Press, 1996), 36–53.

material overlaps, however, so for our purposes we can focus on d. 20, q. 2, a. 3. This article, which addresses the question of whether Adam's children would have been born with sanctifying grace if Adam hadn't sinned, tells us precisely what Thomas thinks original justice is.

Before Thomas gives his own opinion, he raises five objections, each concluding that because postlapsarian Adam transmitted original sin, prelapsarian Adam would have transmitted original justice *and* sanctifying grace. As the first objection has it, "the human being corrupted through sin transmitted sin to his posterity. Therefore, the human being with grace and justice would have transmitted them to his posterity."[7] Thomas then raises another objection in the *sed contra* from the opposite point of view: sanctifying grace, like the rational soul, cannot be transmitted; therefore, neither original justice nor grace can be transmitted. "[T]hat which is infused immediately by God, as the rational soul, is not transferred from the parents. But grace is one of these things, as was shown in book I, d. 14. Therefore neither grace nor justice would have been transferred to posterity."[8] Thomas proceeds to give his own view, which adopts neither extreme.

He begins by noting that animal reproduction normally results in a numerically distinct animal which is of the same species as the parents. Various individual accidents of the parents are not necessarily or even normally transmitted, however.[9] Let me give an example. If two shelties reproduce, there is a numerically distinct third sheltie, of the same species

---

[7] "[H]omo corruptus per peccatum transmisit peccatum in posteros. Ergo etiam et gratiam et justitiam quam habuit, in posteros transmisisset." *Scriptum Scriptum super libros sententiarum magistri Petri Lombardi Episcopi Parisensis* (Paris: Lethielleux, 1929) [hereafter, *Scriptum*] II, d. 20, q. 2, a. 3, ob 1.

[8] "[I]llud quod infunditur immediate a Deo, ut anima rationalis, non transfunditur a parentibus. Sed gratia est hujusmodi, ut in 1 libro, dist. XIV, probatum est. Ergo gratiam vel justitiam in posteros non transfudisset." *Scriptum* II, d. 20, q. 2, a. 3, *sed contra*.

[9] "Respondeo dicendum, quod, sicut dicit philosophus in II de *Generat.*, text. 25, in generatione est quaedam circulatio, quae tamen non redit in idem numero, sed ad idem specie: homo enim generat hominem, non Socrates Socratem; et inde est quod generatum generanti assimilatur in omnibus illis quae ad naturam speciei pertinent, nisi adveniat impedimentum, ut in monstris apparet; non autem oportet quod assimiletur in proprietatibus quae consequuntur individuum ratione individui: et si aliquando contingat quod in aliquibus proprietatibus etiam personalibus assimiletur proles patri, hoc tantum accidit in accidentibus corporalibus, sicut quod albus generat album, et podagricus podagricum: non autem in perfectionibus animae generat sibi similem secundum actum, ut grammaticus generat grammaticum; sed forte secundum aptitudinem tantum; secundum quod ex complexione corporis unus est habilior alio ad scientiam vel virtutem." *Scriptum* II, d. 20, q. 2, a. 3.

as her parents, possessing whatever properties are required to be a sheltie, as well as (probably) possessing properties usually found in shelties, such as having four legs. But the pup may have darker hair than her parents – they may not have transmitted the accidental quality of light hair, for shelties can have either dark or light hair. The species is transmitted, but individual accidents are not necessarily transmitted. Thomas then applies this principle to the question of original justice:

The justice befitting the first human being was twofold. One original justice was according to the due order of body under the soul, the inferior powers under the superior powers, and the superior powers under God. This justice was appointed to human nature itself in its commencement from a divine gift. Such justice would have been transferred to children. There is another, gratuitous justice, which elicits meritorious acts, concerning which there are two opinions. Some say that the first human being was created in natural conditions alone and not in grace. On this view, gratuitous justice requires a certain preparation through personal acts. Grace, therefore, is a personal property in the soul, and would in no way be transferred, except according to a certain aptitude. Others, however, say that the human being was created in grace. According to this view, the gift of gratuitous justice was given to human nature itself; thus with the transfusion of nature grace would have been infused simultaneously.[10]

Original justice is twofold; Adam could have received it in one of two ways. The first original justice is "natural original justice," characterized by three conditions. We need to briefly discuss each one.

First, the human being with natural original justice is subjected to God in her "higher powers" of reason (her intellect and will). This means that Adam and Eve followed God's law and did so easily, without being prone to disobey. This was an axiom of medieval theology, though disagreement as to what this rectitude involved abounded. Some argued that the original rectitude required sanctifying grace; others claimed Adam needed to merit sanctifying grace before receiving it. Thomas, at this point in his

---

[10] "Sciendum est ergo quod duplex justitia primo homini poterat convenire. Una originalis, quae erat secundum debitum ordinem corporis sub anima, et inferiorum virium sub superiori, et superioris sub Deo; et haec quidem justitia ipsam naturam humanam ordinabat in sui primordio ex divino munere; et ideo talem justitiam in filios transfudisset. Est etiam alia justitia gratuita quae actus meritorios elicit; et de hac est duplex opinio. Quidam enim dicunt quod primus homo in naturalibus tantum creatus est, et non in gratuitis; et secundum hoc videtur quod ad talem justitiam requirebatur quaedam praeparatio per actus personales; unde secundum hoc talis gratia proprietas personalis erat ex parte animae; et ideo nullo modo transfusa fuisset, nisi secundum aptitudinem tantum. Alii vero dicunt quod homo in gratia creatus est; et secundum hoc videtur quod donum gratuitae justitiae ipsi humanae naturae collatum sit; unde cum transfusione naturae simul etiam infusa fuisset gratia." *Scriptum* II, d. 20, q. 2, a. 3.

career, argues that justice does not require grace, though God could have given justice *and* grace when he created the human being.

The second condition of natural original justice, tightly linked to the first, was that the soul's "lower powers" were subjected to reason. Thomas interchangeably calls these the "sensual powers" or refers to them synecdochically by the name "concupiscence." We don't need to discuss them in-depth at this point.[11] Suffice it to say they enable human beings to desire or resist things in a physical way (to lust for sex, for example, or to sweat in fear). That the lower powers were subjected to reason implied, among other things, that Adam and Eve wouldn't have spontaneously felt any irrational pangs of anger or lust toward each other. Each of them was able to sin only through a fully conscious, deliberate choice. As such, they could not commit venial sin in the state of natural original justice. Finally, the third condition of natural original justice was the subjection of the body to the soul. This meant that Adam and Eve were immortal and free from suffering, as long as they remained obedient to God.

After his summary of these three basic conditions, Aquinas makes a crucial point: God did not give natural original justice to Adam and Eve as individuals only but to human nature, to the human species. Therefore it would have been transmitted to Adam's children (*in filios transfudisset*) along with other features of the species. The other form of justice, "gratuitous original justice," is simply natural original justice plus supernatural sanctifying grace. Sanctifying grace, in contrast to the natural gift of original justice, is properly speaking a personal gift, in just this sense. It cannot under any circumstances be transmitted through natural sexual reproduction, except in the sense that an "aptitude" or disposition to sanctifying grace could be transmitted (*nullo modo transfusa fuisset, nisi secundum aptitudinem tantum*).[12] More on this disposition to grace shortly. Though sanctifying grace is a personal gift, it can also, in a secondary sense, be called a "gift to nature" in the sense that God offers

---

[11] For Thomas's discussion of the passions (the sensual powers in act), see Nicholas Lombardo, *The Logic of Desire: Aquinas on Emotion* (Washington, DC: Catholic University of America Press, 2011).

[12] Thomas's argument against the sexual transmission of grace is Christological. To claim that sanctifying grace is natural, transmissible via intercourse, is to ascribe to Adam a power proper to Christ, the power to save the human race. "[N]on enim unius personae actus toti naturae mereri vel demereri potest, nisi limites humanae naturae transcendat, ut patet in Christo, qui Deus et homo est." *Scriptum* II, d. 20, q. 2, a. 3, ad 3.

it to the whole of human nature, that is, to the total number of individuals possessing that nature.

Natural original justice is possessed by individual persons. Adam had natural original justice, as did Eve. Yet Thomas suggests it should be called a gift to human nature, properly speaking, because Adam was supposed to transmit it to the rest of human nature through the natural reproductive process. There are *two* senses thus far in which natural original justice is natural. First, in the sense that can exist without supernatural sanctifying grace. Second, in the sense that it was to be transmitted through the natural reproductive process.

Original sin corresponds to natural original justice as its privation:

> Original sin is, in the first place and in itself, a sin of nature. Secondarily, it is a sin of the person. Actual sin, however, is properly speaking a sin of the person occurring through a personal act. *Thus, as original sin is transferred and not actual sin, so too natural original justice would have been transferred and not gratuitous original justice.*[13]

Original sin attaches to individual persons, just like original justice. But because it comes to individual persons through the natural reproductive process – again, just as original justice would have if Adam had stayed upright – it is called the sin of nature.

Thomas's position in d. 20 – which officially was concerned with original justice's transmission – is more or less repeated in d. 29, which treats original justice itself. The difference is that in d. 29, Thomas says it is more probable that Adam turned to God and received sanctifying grace immediately upon being created.[14] In both places, however, Thomas

---

[13] "[P]eccatum originale est primo et per se peccatum naturae, et per posterius personae; actuale autem est proprie peccatum personae quod per actum personalem incurritur: et ideo, sicut peccatum originale transfunditur, et non peccatum actuale, *ita etiam justitia originalis naturalis transfusa fuisset, et forte non gratuita.*" *Scriptum* II, d. 20, q. 2, a. 3 ad 1, emphasis mine.

[14] Thomas summarizes three options. (1) Adam was created with natural original justice and never had grace before he sinned; (2) Adam was created first in natural original justice and then given grace before he sinned; (3) Adam was created with natural original justice and received grace in the same instant. The last position "seems to cohere better with the opinion of Augustine" (*satis congruere videtur opinioni Augustini*); however, "it is difficult to prove which of these opinions is better, as they depend solely on the will of God" (*Quae tamen harum opinionum verior sit, multum efficaci ratione probari non potest, sicut nec aliquid eorum quae ex voluntate Dei sola dependent*). Thomas concludes by saying it is probable that "in the first instant of creation [Adam] converted to God, and grace followed" (*in primo instanti creationis ad Deum conversus, gratiam consecutus sit*). All from *Scriptum* II, d. 29, q. 1, a. 2., emphasis mine.

holds that Adam and Eve were certainly at least given natural original justice. Even on the hypothesis that Adam turned to God in the first instant of his creation and received sanctifying grace, it was natural original justice that was to be seminally transmitted to his children.

Why was Thomas unsure whether God gave original justice and sanctifying grace to Adam and Eve right when they were created? Given our discussion thus far it's easy to understand his logic. He doesn't think that sanctifying grace is necessary for the existence of original justice. What this implies, though Thomas doesn't use precisely these terms, is that the formal cause of original justice is "preternatural rectitude" and that sanctifying grace is really distinct from original justice. Preternatural rectitude allows the will to avoid all sin; it is distinct from the will's relation to God that follows from the principles of human nature (to be discussed in depth in the next chapter), as well as the will's relation to God in supernatural sanctifying grace. Now, even if God gave Adam sanctifying grace, preternatural rectitude would still be the formal cause of original justice. But if Adam sinned, he would forfeit both grace and original justice; if he stayed upright, he would maintain both grace and original justice.

The loss of this rectitude is what formally constitutes originated original sin. It's not as though original sin has nothing to do with the lack of sanctifying grace, however. Thomas says that the lack of natural original justice is an "obstacle" to sanctifying grace, that it "redounds" to the lack of grace.[15] But how precisely the absence of a *natural* original justice

---

[15] "[C]arentia visionis divinae potest dupliciter intelligi: vel negative, et sic non est poena, sed defectus naturalis: cuilibet enim naturae creatae convenit ut ex se non habeat unde in Dei visionem ascendere possit; vel privative, et sic est poena, secundum quod importat *quamdam obnoxietatem* ad non videndum Deum." *Scriptum* II d. 20, q. 2, a. 3, ad 4, emphasis mine. The lack of the beatific vision (and the lack of the sanctifying grace which leads to it) is natural to the human being insofar as human nature does not have it of itself. If there is an obstacle in the human being to sanctifying grace, then the lack of grace and the vision can be considered penalties. He repeats this point later, asserting that the lack of natural original justice "redounds" to the privation of grace, in the course of arguing that baptism removes original sin with respect to the person but not with respect to the nature. "[B]aptismus infectionem originalis mundat, *secundum quod infectio naturae in personam redundat*; et ideo per baptismum illa poena tollitur quae personae debetur, scilicet carentia divinae visionis; non autem baptismus removet infectionem naturae, secundum quod ad naturam per se refertur." *Scriptum* II, d. 32, q. 1, a. 2, emphasis mine. When we consider what Baptism restores to the person, however, we find that Thomas's answer is grace. "Per baptismum autem gratia confertur: cujus virtute illa infectio ab homine tollitur quae ex natura in personam devolvebatur." *Scriptum* II, d. 32, q. 1, a. 1. "Quamvis ergo non restituatur originalis justitia quantum ad id quod materiale in ipsa erat, restituitur tamen quantum ad rectitudinem voluntatis, ex cujus privatione

relates to the privation of sanctifying grace Thomas never says. If the presence of a disposition to natural justice in the semen would not have sufficiently transmitted supernatural grace in the first place (but only natural justice, upon reception of the soul), why is the privation of said justice an obstacle to grace?

It is worth pausing to reflect on Thomas's discussion of original justice so far. First, this early Thomist view is an instance of what I have been calling "disease theory." God created human nature in health, and because Adam sinned and corrupted human nature he sexually transmitted original sin. Thomas has clearly distinguished supernatural grace from natural justice. This enabled him to affirm that the grace which orients the human being to the beatific vision is a gift, above nature's power. He agreed with Anselm that concupiscence cannot fully account for original sin; original sin must include injustice in the rational will. Despite the aforementioned vagueness of the relation of original sin to the privation of sanctifying grace in his discussion of baptism, Thomas's emphasis is clear. Adam was to be the principal cause of his posterity's natural justice, but instead he was the principal cause of original sin.

By the time Thomas wrote the *Prima pars* in the mid-1260s in Rome, it seems he had reversed his position. Thomas now argues that Adam and Eve's original justice requires sanctifying grace, implying that grace is original justice's formal cause. He discusses original justice in the context of the creation of the first human beings in qq. 90–102, after he treats the nature of the human being in qq. 75–89. Thomas's treatment of the condition of Adam and Eve beings begins in q. 94.[16] We'll begin in question 95, where he discusses original justice. Article 1 asks whether the first human beings were created in sanctifying grace. After noting the history of disagreement on the question, Thomas confidently argues that they were created in grace.

But that Adam was ornamented in grace, as others say, seems to be required by the rectitude of the first state in which God made the human being. For according to Eccle. VII, *God made the human being right*. This rectitude consisted in the following. Reason was subject to God, the inferior powers to reason, and the

ratio culpae inerat: et propter hoc id quod culpae est, tollitur per baptismum." *Scriptum* II, d. 32, q. 1, a. 1, ad 1. Is original sin formally the obstacle to the reception of grace, or is it the privation of grace itself? Generally, when Thomas considers original justice and original sin's transmission he assumes the former, when he treats baptism and (as we'll see in the next chapter) when he treats the intrinsic, formal *ratio mali* of original sin, he assumes the latter.

[16] See *STh* I, q. 94, *prooemium*.

body to the soul. Now the first subjection was the cause of the second and the third, for as long as the reason remained subject to God, the inferior powers remained subjected to reason, as Augustine says. Now it is manifest that the subjection of the body to the soul and the inferior powers to reason was not natural, otherwise it would have remained after sin. This is because even in demons the natural gifts remain after sin, as Dionysius says in cap. IV of the *Divine Names*. Hence it is manifest that the first subjection, by which the reason was subject to God, was not only according to nature but according to a supernatural gift of grace: for an effect cannot be stronger than its cause.[17]

Thomas argues, first, that the subjection of reason to God was the cause of the subjection of the lower powers to reason and of the subjection of the body to the soul, such that the loss of the subjection of reason to God by disobedience caused the disorder of the lower powers and the body. Second, Thomas argues that the subjection of the lower powers and body was not natural because sin didn't destroy the natural gifts.[18] Original justice thus has the same basic features as it did in the *Scriptum* – it enables the human being to obey God, have ordered concupiscence, and live forever. Yet Thomas's conclusion concerning the nature of the subjection to God has changed drastically.

The third premise, which Thomas states immediately after concluding that Adam had grace, is that an effect cannot be stronger than its cause. That is, a supernatural effect cannot have a natural cause. Thomas concludes that the cause of reason's subjection to God is supernatural, namely, sanctifying grace. We could rephrase his argument as follows. Every supernatural effect requires a supernatural cause. Rightly ordered concupiscence is a supernatural effect. Rightly ordered concupiscence requires a supernatural cause, namely sanctifying grace. Thomas would not have accepted this argument in the 1250s. He would have

---

[17] "Sed quod etiam fuerit conditus in gratia, ut alii dicunt, videtur requirere ipsa rectitudo primi status, in qua Deus hominem fecit, secundum illud *Eccle*. VII, *Deus fecit hominem rectum*. Erat enim haec rectitudo secundum hoc, quod ratio subdebatur Deo, rationi vero inferiores vires, et animae corpus. Prima autem subiectio erat causa et secundae et tertiae: quandiu enim ratio manebat Deo subiecta, inferiora ei subdebantur, ut Augustinus dicit. Manifestum est autem quod illa subiectio corporis ad animam, et inferiorum virium ad rationem, non erat naturalis: alioquin post peccatum mansisset, cum etiam in Daemonibus data naturalia post peccatum permanserint, ut Dionysius dicit cap. IV *de Div. Nom.* Unde manifestum est quod et illa prima subiectio, qua ratio Deo subdebatur, non erat solum secundum naturam, sed secundum supernaturale donum gratiae: non enim potest esse quod effectus sit potior quam causa." *STh* I, q. 95, a. 1.

[18] This, in a nutshell, is Thomas's position on the effects of original sin. The human being with original sin retains everything that follows from the principles of human nature and loses *only* the undue gift of justice.

distinguished the minor premise. Rightly ordered concupiscence is a preternatural phenomenon, only requiring as its cause a preternatural subjection to God. Sanctifying grace is not needed. Here Thomas argues that the effect is not from nature; *therefore* the cause is supernatural. This implies that Thomas did not think a preternatural subjection to God could keep sensuality in check. Why not? Perhaps he reasoned from the fact that sanctifying grace doesn't necessarily fully regulate concupiscence. (Christians in grace still fight concupiscence.) If supernatural grace isn't strong enough, of itself, to regulate concupiscence, how could a preternatural subjection to God do the job? Whatever his underlying reasons, Thomas's conclusion is clear: there is no original justice without grace.

Was this Thomas's consistent mature position? It is hard to say. There are several texts from his mature period that appear to contradict it, several that appear to support it. One place in particular, in Thomas's disputed question on evil, is notoriously vexing. Thomas appears to claim within the same article that original justice's formal cause is both preternatural and supernatural. The blatant character of the apparent contradiction, I'll suggest, offers us a crucial clue regarding Thomas's developing position on this issue.

The article in question is the first of the fifth question of *De malo*, which was written shortly after the *Prima pars*, during Thomas's second regency in Paris.[19] It's unlikely, then, that the article represents a transitional period in between the *Scriptum* and the *Prima pars*. The topic is the punishment of original sin (q. 4 treated original sin itself). Is the loss of the beatific vision the sole eternal punishment for original sin? Agreeing with the growing medieval consensus, Thomas answers yes. In the *corpus*, he endeavors to explain this punishment by making the following argument. It is better to be capable of a great good, even if one cannot reach it without exterior help, than it is to be capable of a lesser good that one can reach on one's own. Rational creatures are capable of the great good of the beatific vision, but they can't reach it without the help of grace. They are still better than subrational creatures who can reach their good yet inferior ends without exterior help.[20] Thomas then turns to the help they

---

[19] Torrell, *Saint Thomas Aquinas*, 328.

[20] "Creatura ergo rationalis in hoc praeeminet omni creature, quod capax est summi boni per diuinam uisionem et fruitionem, licet ad hoc consequendum nature proprie principia non sufficiant, set ad hoc indigeat auxilio diuine gratie." *Quaestiones disputatae de malo* (Rome: Commissio Leonina; Paris: Librairie Philosophique J. Vrin, 1982) [hereafter, *De malo*], q. 5, a. 1.

need. Human beings need sanctifying grace in addition to their natural principles; there is no way to reach the beatific vision without it.[21] But that's not all they need:

In addition to this help [sanctifying grace] the human being needed *another* supernatural help. This is because of the human being's composition: the human being is a composite of soul and body, of intellectual and sensible nature. If these natures are left to themselves, they in a sense aggravate and impede the intellect, preventing it from reaching the peak of its contemplation. This help was original justice, through which the mind of the human being was subdued to God, and the inferior powers and the body were subject to the mind (so long as the mind was subdued to God). Thus neither body nor soul would impede the quest for contemplation. Because the body is for the soul, and the sense is for the intellect, the help by which the body is under the soul and the sensitive powers are under the intellectual mind *is a certain disposition to that help by which the mind is ordained to seeing and enjoying God*. This help of original justice was lost through original sin, as we said earlier. Indeed, one who by sinning loses that through which she was disposed to acquire some good, deserves to lose the good to which she was disposed; the loss of that good to which she was disposed is a fitting penalty for losing that which disposed her that good. Accordingly, the penalty of original sin is the loss of grace, and as a result the loss of that which grace ordains the human being, the vision of the divine.[22]

In addition to sanctifying grace, the human being needs original justice. Thomas appears to imply his position from the *Scriptum*, to the effect that original justice is a formally distinct gift from sanctifying grace. The loss

---

[21] "Set circa hoc considerandum est quod aliquod diuinum auxilium necessarium est communiter omni creature rationali, scilicet auxilium gratie gratum facientis, qua quelibet creatura rationalis indiget ut possit peruenire ad beatitudinem perfectam, secundum illud Apostoli Ro VI[:23]: gratia Dei uita aeterna." *De malo* q. 5, a. 1.

[22] "Sed preter hoc auxilium necessarium fuit homini *aliud* supernaturale auxilium ratione sue compositionis. Est enim homo compositus ex anima et corpore et ex natura intellectuali et sensibili: que quodammodo si sue nature relinquantur, intellectum aggrauant et impediunt ne libere ad summum fastigium contemplationis peruenire possit. Hoc autem auxilium fuit originalis iustitia, per quam mens hominis sic subderetur Deo ei subderentur totaliter inferiores uires et ipsum corpus, neque ratio impediretur quo minus posset in Deum tendere. Et sicut corpus est propter animam et sensus propter intellectum, ita hoc auxilium quo continetur corpus sub anima, et uires sensitiue sub mente intellectuali, est *quasi dispositio quedam ad illud auxilium quo mens humana ordinatur ad uidendum Deum et ad fruendum ipso*. Hoc autem auxilium originalis iustitie subtrahitur per peccatum originale, ut supra ostensum est. Cum autem aliquis peccando abiicit a se illud per quod disponebatur ad aliquod bonum acquirendum, meretur ut ei subtrahatur illud bonum ad quod obtinendum disponebatur, et ipsa subtractio illius boni est conueniens pena eius. Et ideo conueniens pena peccati originalis est subtractio gratie, et per consequens uisionis diuine, ad quam homo per gratiam ordinatur." *De malo* q. 5, a. 1, emphasis mine.

of original justice is the loss of the disposition to sanctifying grace. The lack of sanctifying grace and the beatific vision are together the fitting punishment for original sin, because when one sins and loses the disposition to some good X, the loss of X is a fitting penalty for that sin. It would seem, though, that if sanctifying grace were the formal cause of original justice, then by losing original justice the human being would lose sanctifying grace, and the loss of sanctifying grace wouldn't properly be called the penalty for original sin but a part *of* original sin. Perhaps, then, the passage we discussed from the *Summa theologiae* a moment ago is an aberration, and Thomas didn't change his mind after all.

Many have cited the *corpus* of *De malo* q. 5, a. 1, as proof of Thomas's lifelong consistency. Kors, citing this text (and only this text), while acknowledging the difficulty in light of *STh* I, q. 95, writes, "In any case, they [original justice and sanctifying grace] are formally distinguished."[23] Lottin argues that the body of this article proves without a doubt that Thomas never changed his mind. "[M]oreover, the real distinction between original justice and grace is made very sharply in the *De Malo*."[24] We could add others who cite this text to the same effect. Kors and Lottin explain the fact that Thomas says sanctifying grace is required for original justice in the *Summa* by suggesting that Thomas conceived of sanctifying grace as a necessary condition for original justice later in life, but that nevertheless the true essence of original justice can be defined without sanctifying grace. This must be the case, they add, because otherwise Thomas's view of original sin as a sexually transmissible sin of nature would collapse. Not everyone was convinced by this line of argumentation. Indeed, Thomas himself seems to refute it only a few lines later.

The thirteenth objection of the same article argues that the lack of the beatific vision cannot be the penalty for original sin, because original sin is the lack of original justice, and neither sanctifying grace nor the beatific vision is owed to the one who *has* original justice.[25] Here is Thomas's reply.

---

[23] "En tout cas il les distingue formellement." Kors, *La Justice primitive et le péché originel d'après S. Thomas*, 93.

[24] "[D]ans le *De Malo*, où, de plus, s'accuse très nettement la distinction réelle entre la justice originelle et la grâce." Lottin, "Le péché originel chez Albert le Grand, Bonaventure et Thomas d'Aquin," 305.

[25] "[P]eccatum originale est priuatio originalis iustitie, ut Anselmus dicit. Set habenti originalem iustitiam, cum possit habere <sine> gratia, non debetur uisio diuina. Ergo neque peccato originali respondet carentia uisionis divine." *De malo* q. 5, a. 1, ob 13.

[T]hat argument is based upon the opinion that sanctifying grace is not included in the concept (*in ratione*) of original justice. Yet I believe that opinion is false, because original justice consists primordially in the subjection of the human mind to God, *which cannot be firm without grace. Original justice therefore could not have existed without grace.* And thus the one with original justice was owed the divine vision. But even supposing the previous opinion were true, the conclusion does not follow. Even if original justice did not include grace, it was nevertheless a certain disposition which preexacted (*preexigebatur*) grace. Accordingly, that which is contrary to original justice is contrary to grace, as that which is contrary to natural justice (as theft, murder, and things like this) is contrary to grace.[26]

The objection assumes what Thomas holds is false: that the concept of original justice itself does not include sanctifying grace. Why? Because the human will *cannot* hold firmly to God without sanctifying grace. For that reason any objection that severs the link between sanctifying grace and original justice will not affect Thomas's argument that the lack of the beatific vision is original sin's eternal punishment. Even if original justice were natural, it would have involved a certain disposition to or exigency for grace, such that the lack of the disposition is contrary to grace. Garrigou-Lagrange and other neo-Thomists have accordingly adduced this article to refute Martin et al.[27] Garrigou-Lagrange argues that if sanctifying grace is included in the *ratio* of original justice, it cannot be merely an extrinsically necessary condition (as Kors proposed). The concept or *ratio* of a given thing refers to its intrinsic conditions, not the various external conditions necessary for its existence. For example, Adam was necessarily sustained by God, but God is not part of Adam's *ratio*. Moreover, the reason Thomas gives for holding that grace is included in the *ratio* of original justice is not simply the fact that human

---

[26] "[Q]uod ratio illa procedit secundum opinionem ponentium quod gratia gratum faciens non includatur in ratione originalis iustitiae. Quod tamen credo esse falsum: quia cum originalis iustitia primordialiter consisteret in subiectione humane mentis ad Deum, *que firma esse non potest nisi per gratiam, iustitia originalis sine gratia esse non potuit*; et ideo habenti originalem iustitiam debebatur uisio divina. Set tamen praedicta opinione supposita, adhuc ratio non concludit, quia, licet originalis iustitia gratiam non includeret, tamen erat quedam dispositio que preexigebatur ad gratiam. Et ideo quod contrariatur originali iustitie contrariatur etiam gratie, sicut quod contrariatur iustitie naturali, contrariatur gratie, ut furtum, homicidium et alia huiusmodi." *De malo* q. 5, a. 1, ad 13, emphasis mine.

[27] "Unde juxta S. Thomam *gratiam gratum faciens includitur in ratione justitiae originalis*. Atqui id quod includitur in ratione alicujus, non est causa efficiens extrinseca, alioquin Deus includeretur in ratione creaturae, nec est solum extrinseca conditio sine qua non, ut patet ex ipso textu S. Thomae, quia subjectio mentis ad Deum *firma esse non potest nisi per gratiam*." Garrigou-Lagrange, "Utrum gratia sanctificans fuerit in Adamo dos naturae an donum personae tantum," 140.

nature was instituted in grace; it is that the human mind *cannot* submit to God in the way original justice requires – that is, without being distracted by concupiscence and mortality – without grace.

I agree with Garrigou-Lagrange here (though unfortunately he didn't attempt to take the body of the article into account and merely cited ad 13 as a prooftext). Just as he did in the *Prima pars*, Thomas argues in the *De malo* that the firm subjection of the human being to God requires sanctifying grace. It is impossible to harmonize this with Thomas's early teaching, in which God could have created Adam in natural or supernatural original justice.[28] If a human being needs sanctifying grace to have original justice, then there is no such thing as natural original justice, actually or possibly. The difficulty of the incongruity between the body of this article and the reply to thirteenth objection remains, however.[29] It seems that Thomas flatly contradicts himself, holding that original justice is really distinct from sanctifying grace and that the *ratio* of original justice includes sanctifying grace.

I would venture the following hypothesis. In Thomas's mature treatments of humanity's prelapsarian state (beginning with the *Prima pars*), he argued that personal original justice – the justice that Adam and Eve enjoyed in their historical existence as individuals – required sanctifying grace. This is in contrast to his earlier works, such as the *Scriptum*, which explicitly argued that God may well have created Adam and Eve in a state of original justice without sanctifying grace. Thomas did not, however, consistently apply this new view of personal original justice to other areas of his thought. For example, because his doctrine of original sin required a parallel transmissibility of justice and sin, Thomas continued to assume that natural original justice – the justice Adam was to transmit to his

---

[28] An anonymous reviewer asked whether Thomas might have consistently held that natural original justice is possible, while holding that only sanctifying grace gives the person with original justice moral *stability*. This would allow us to avoid attributing a contradiction to Thomas here: natural original justice is mentioned in the *corpus*, and the reply to the thirteenth objection merely says that original justice requires sanctifying grace for stability. I would say, in response, that Thomas argues in ad 13 that sanctifying grace is part of the *ratio* of original justice, such that "*iustitia originalis sine gratia esse non potuit.*" Moreover, the whole point of natural original justice, as I hope the discussion of Thomas's early works made clear, is that it *did* provide "moral stability" to Adam and Eve. It allowed them to obey God without "wobbling" due to disordered concupiscence, or fear of death.

[29] We could add various other texts to highlight the incongruity. For example, there is Thomas's assumption in the treatise on grace (*STh* I-II, q. 109, a. 4, passim) – to be discussed in the next chapter in a different context – that Adam's integral nature, without grace, sufficed to regulate concupiscence.

children through sexual intercourse – did not require sanctifying grace. Adam's own justice required grace; the justice Abel was to receive from Adam did not. This hypothesis explains *De malo* q. 5, a. 1. The context of the *corpus* shows natural original justice is under discussion; the context of ad 13 clearly indicates Thomas is speaking of personal original justice. The hypothesis is confirmed when we turn to Thomas's treatment of original justice's transmission in q. 100 of the *Prima pars*.

Thomas argues in the *corpus* that original justice would have been transmitted if Adam hadn't sinned.

The human being generates his like according to his species. Thus it is necessary that children are like their parents in whatever accidents follow from the nature of the species, unless there is an error in the operation of nature (which would not have happened in the state of innocence). In individual accidents, however, it is not necessary that children are like the parents. Now original justice, in which the first human was made, was an accident of the nature of the species, not as though it were caused by the principles of the species, but as a gift divinely given to the whole nature. This is clear if we consider the fact that opposites are of the same genus, and original sin, which is opposed to justice, is said to be the sin of nature as it is transmitted from parent to posterity. By the same token, children would have been made like their parents as far as original justice goes.[30]

Faced with the question of the transmission of natural original justice, Thomas gives the view he first defended in the *Scriptum*: original justice was a gift to human nature, to be transmitted by Adam to his children. This is clear from the fact that opposites are of the same genus, and the opposite of original justice, namely, original sin, was transmitted by Adam to his children. But what about sanctifying grace? Could Adam have transmitted sanctifying grace, the formal cause of original justice?

In the *Scriptum*, Thomas had a consistent answer: sanctifying grace would not have been transmitted, properly speaking, only original justice. Adam could transmit various things *in linea naturae*, including natural justice, but a personal gift of God beyond soul infusion would be required for supernatural grace. At that point, Thomas didn't think sanctifying

---

[30] "[N]aturaliter homo generat sibi simile secundum speciem. Unde quaecumque accidentia consequuntur naturam speciei, in his necesse est quod filii parentibus similentur, nisi sit error in operatione naturae, qui in statu innocentiae non fuisset. In accidentibus autem individualibus non est necesse quod filii parentibus similentur. Iustitia autem originalis, in qua primus homo conditus fuit, fuit accidens naturae speciei, non quasi ex principiis speciei causatum, sed sicut quoddam donum divinitus datum toti naturae. Et hoc apparet, quia opposita sunt unius generis: peccatum autem originale, quod opponitur illi iustitiae, dicitur esse peccatum naturae; unde traducitur a parente in posteros. Et propter hoc etiam filii parentibus assimilati fuissent quantum ad originalem iustitiam." *STh* I, q. 100, a. 1.

grace was the formal cause of original justice. But by *STh* I, q. 95, this has changed. Shouldn't Thomas now deny that Adam could have transmitted original justice, given that it is supernatural?

The second objection in q. 100 shows that Thomas is aware of the tension. The objection argues, "justice is through grace ... [b]ut grace is not transferred, for then it would be natural. Grace is infused by God alone."[31] Thomas replies,

[S]ome say that children would not have been born with gratuitous justice, which is the principle of merit, but with original justice. But because the root of original justice, in which rectitude the human being was made, consists in the supernatural subjection of reason to God – which is through grace, as was said earlier – it is necessary to say that if children were born with original justice, they would be born with grace. (This is what we said about the first human beings earlier: if they were to be made with justice they would need grace.) Now, it does not follow from this that grace would have been natural. This is because it could not have been transferred by the power of semen. Instead, it would have been given to the human being immediately upon reception of the rational soul. Likewise, the rational soul is not transmitted by seminal power, but God infuses it as soon as the body is disposed to receive it.[32]

Now, faced with the question of personal original justice, original justice as it would exist in Adam's children, Thomas asserts that it requires grace. Sanctifying grace is the formal cause (the root, *radix*) of original justice. Therefore, because Adam's children will be born with original justice, they must be born with sanctifying grace. Just as in the *De malo*, here in the *Summa* Thomas speaks of a natural original justice when considering its transmission and a supernatural original justice when considering its actual existence in persons. Just as the rational soul is not transmitted but the disposition thereto, so too sanctifying grace is not transmitted but the disposition or exigency thereto.

---

[31] *STh* I, q. 100, a. 1, ob 2.

[32] "[Q]uidam dicunt quod pueri non fuissent nati cum iustitia gratuita, quae est merendi principium, sed cum iustitia originali. Sed cum radix originalis iustitiae, in cuius rectitudine factus est homo, consistat in subiectione supernaturali rationis ad Deum, quae est per gratiam gratum facientem, ut supra dictum est; necesse est dicere quod, si pueri nati fuissent in originali iustitia, quod etiam nati fuissent cum gratia; sicut et de primo homine supra diximus quod fuit cum gratia conditus. Non tamen fuisset propter hoc gratia naturalis: quia non fuisset transfusa per virtutem seminis, sed fuisset collata homini statim cum habuisset animam rationalem. Sicut etiam statim cum corpus est dispositum, infunditur a Deo anima rationalis, quae tamen non est ex traduce." *STh* I, q. 100, a. 1, ad. 2.

Does Thomas's account of original sin still work if original justice is formally supernatural? I will argue that it does not. To get a handle on the issues, we first need to discuss Thomas's understanding of human reproduction, as well as the precise nature of the parallel dispositions to original sin and original justice.

THE TRANSMISSION OF ORIGINAL JUSTICE

Thomas agrees with the Lombard that traducianism is false. God must directly infuse the rational soul to create a new human being, because parents cannot produce a rational soul of their own power.[33] There are several steps in the natural reproductive process before the soul is infused. The male produces semen through excess food, then inseminates the woman through sexual intercourse.[34] The man's semen, the active principle or form, combines with female menstrual blood, the passive principle or matter, producing a brand new vegetative being with its own act of existence. This vegetative being eventually is corrupted and a sensitive being replaces it. The body of this sensitive, "pre-human" being – which Thomas frequently calls simply a human body or flesh – continues to develop until it is disposed to become fully human, that is, until it is disposed to receive the rational soul by a creative act of God.[35] Now,

---

[33] *STh* I, q. 90, aa. 2–3. Thomas rejects both the view that Adam's soul multiplies, such that each of his descendants has a part of his soul, as well as the view that Adam and Eve have the power to cause a new rational soul.

[34] *STh* I, q. 119, a. 2. The topic of this article seems bizarre – why should a theologian care whether semen is produced from excess food? – until we recall that the Lombard emphatically denied it for theological reasons. We saw the Lombard insist that the bodies of Adam's posterity multiply of their own intrinsic power, without excess food, in order to explain our unity with Adam. We were all literally part of Adam's body. Thomas, presumably thinking that this is false from a scientific perspective, argued that we only needed to "preexist" in Adam by power of physical propagation, that is, descend from him.

[35] Cf. *STh* I, q. 118, for an explanation of this process. Article 1 argues that the sensitive soul is transmitted by Adam's seminal power. Article 2 describes the three stages in this process in more depth, from the vegetative being to the sensitive being to the rational being. "[D]icendum est quod anima praeexistit in embryone a principio quidem nutritiva, postmodum autem sensitiva, et tandem intellectiva." "[C]um generatio unius semper sit corruptio alterius, necesse est dicere quod tam in homine quam in animalibus aliis, quando perfectior forma advenit, fit corruptio prioris: ita tamen quod sequens forma habet quidquid habebat prima, et adhuc amplius. Et sic per multas generationes et corruptiones pervenitur ad ultimam formam substantialem, tam in homine quam in aliis animalibus. Et hoc ad sensum apparet in animalibus ex putrefactione generatis. Sic igitur dicendum est quod anima intellectiva creatur a Deo in fine generationis

every stage of this process until the infusion of the rational soul is within human power (though obviously as sustained by God as the *primum movens*). Indeed, Thomas thinks that despite the fact that humans cannot cause their children to exist, they contribute so much to the process that they can be said to generate their offspring. "The human being generates his like, insofar as through the power of his semen matter is disposed to the reception of such a form [the rational soul]."[36] What does it mean, precisely, for a human body to be disposed to receive the rational soul?

One aspect of the answer is easy to understand. For the body to be proximately disposed to receive the rational soul it must be the right *sort* of body, namely, an animal body. This is because the human being is a rational animal. The dust from which God made Adam, by contrast, was not proximately disposed to receive Adam's rational soul. Thus Thomas asserts that God produced Adam's body and soul immediately, that is, without the mediation of proximately disposed matter.[37]

There is another sense in which the body is disposed, however, that it is crucial to grasp. The very same moment that God infuses the rational soul, the body receives its ultimate (or "due") disposition to the form. The *same* body that was proximately disposed to receive the soul is now actually receiving the soul. The sensitive soul has been corrupted and a brand new substance, a brand new human being, exists. What was the body of the pre-human is now the body of the full human, its material cause. Though God can create a human being without proximately disposed matter (as he did in the case of Adam), even God cannot make a human being without ultimately disposed matter, without matter in act, individuating and limiting the form, materially causing the composite.[38] For every human being has a body.

An important implication of this, for our purposes, is that the body's proximate disposition to X and ultimate disposition to X have the same

---

humanae, quae simul est et sensitiva et nutritiva, corruptis formis praeexistentibus." Both from a. 2, ad 2.

[36] "[H]omo generat sibi simile, inquantum per virtutem seminis eius disponitur materia ad susceptionem talis formae." *STh* I, q. 118, a. 2, ad 4.

[37] *STh* I, q. 91, aa. 1–2.

[38] Thomas appeals to this principle in many places, including his discussion of sanctifying grace: "agens infinitae virtutis non exigit materiam, vel dispositionem materiae, quasi praesuppositam ex alterius causae actione. Sed tamen oportet quod, secundum conditionem rei causandae, in ipsa re causet et materiam et *dispositionem debitam* ad formam." *STh* I-II, q. 112, a. 2, ad 3, emphasis mine. Just as God can create a human being without proximately disposed matter, he can infuse grace without a proximately disposed soul.

object. In the case of the soul, the body's proximate disposition to receive the soul becomes ultimate when the body actually receives the soul. The proximate disposition is in potency, the ultimate disposition in act. Matter is always in act through form, but matter has an essential role to play in the act of human existence: it actively limits or receives form. By analogy, if John is ready for Jane to hug him, he is proximately disposed to the hug; once she is hugging him, he is ultimately disposed to the hug by actually receiving it.[39]

The qualities of the pre-human body, accordingly, are very important for the fully human being's existence. If the pre-human being is missing a hand, the fully human being will (*sans* a miracle) miss a hand. If the pre-human being's brain is damaged, the fully human being's brain will be damaged, and so on.[40] The pre-human body can do more than affect the mental and physical operations of the human being. As we mentioned in the first section of this chapter, the pre-human body carries moral power: it has the power to cause original justice and original sin. Indeed, *only* a pre-human body with the proximate disposition to original sin can cause original sin. God is not – and cannot be – the cause of original sin in any respect.

This is true of originating original sin, first of all. God is the sustaining cause of all being, including the being of Adam's originating original sin, insofar as it had being. But insofar as it receded from being through pride, God was not the cause. He was not the cause positively, as though he coerced Adam internally or externally. He was not the cause negatively, as though he withdrew *esse* and Adam fell of a logical necessity.[41] God permitted Adam to fall, which simply means he left Adam to his own counsel to obey him or not, instead of instantly annihilating him before he sinned or miraculously confirming him in the good the instant before he fell. "As God knew that the human being would fall into sin through temptation, he also knew that through free will the human being was able

---

[39] For the Trinitarian background of Thomas's view of the activity of reception, see Norris Clarke's "Person, Being, and St. Thomas," *Communio* 19 (1992), 601–18.

[40] For Thomas, human beings use their brains to understand things despite the essential immateriality of intellection. Cf. *STh* I, q. 84, a. 7, and q. 91, a. 3, ad 1.

[41] See Bernard Lonergan's *Grace and Freedom: Operative Grace in the Thought of St. Thomas Aquinas* (Toronto: University of Toronto Press, 2000 [1971]) for a classic treatment of Thomas's view of free will in relation to God's causality. I suspect that my arguments regarding original justice do not depend on Lonergan's reading.

to resist temptation."[42] The whole point of original justice was for Adam to *succeed* in resisting the devil. "From the special gift of grace that was given to him [Adam], no other creature was able to harm him against his own will, through which he was able to resist even the temptation of the devil."[43] Thomas goes so far as to deny that God's decision to let Satan tempt Adam and Eve was a punishment, because it would have been so easy for them to resist. "The human being in the state of innocence was able to resist temptation *with no difficulty* at all."[44]

God is not the cause of originated original sin either. Thomas follows the Lombard's logic on this point consistently from the *Scriptum* on. The following is his argument in *Summa*.

[T]he infection of original sin is *in no respect* caused by God. It is caused only from the sin of the first parent through carnal generation. And thus, because creation implies a relation of the soul to God alone, it cannot be said that the soul is polluted by its creation. But infusion implies a relation to God infusing and to the flesh into which the soul is infused. Thus, with respect to God infusing, the soul cannot be said to be stained through the infusion; but the soul can only be said to be stained with respect to the body into which it is infused.[45]

The flesh (i.e., the body) alone causes original sin, despite the fact that God directly infuses the rational soul. It's not the flesh as such that causes original sin, only the flesh as moved by Adam's seminal power. The cause of original sin is the flesh not causing original justice as it *ought* to, precisely because it didn't receive the proximate disposition to original justice it *should* have. Instead, the flesh received the proximate disposition to original sin, such that the flesh, upon receiving its ultimate disposition

---

[42] "[S]icut Deus sciebat quod homo per tentationem in peccatum esset deiiciendus, ita etiam sciebat quod per liberum arbitrium resistere poterat tentatori." *STh* II-II, q. 165, a. 1, ad 2.

[43] "Ex speciali autem beneficio gratiae hoc erat ei collatum, ut nulla creatura exterior ei posset nocere contra propriam voluntatem, per quam etiam tentationi Daemonis resistere poterat." *STh* II-II, q. 165, a. 1.

[44] "[H]omo in statu innocentiae poterat absque omni difficultate tentationi resistere. Et ideo impugnatio tentatoris poenalis ei non fuit." *STh* II-II, q. 165, a. 1, ad 3, emphasis mine.

[45] "[I]nfectio originalis peccati nullo modo causatur a Deo, sed ex solo peccato primi parentis per carnalem generationem. Et ideo, cum creatio importet respectum animae ad solum Deum, non potest dici quod anima ex sua creatione inquinetur. Sed infusio importat respectum et ad Deum infundentem, et ad carnem cui infunditur anima. Et ideo, habito respectu ad Deum infundentem, non potest dici quod anima per infusionem maculetur; sed solum habito respectu ad corpus cui infunditur." *STh* I-II, q. 83, a. 1, ad 4. Cf. *Scriptum* II, d. 30, q. 1, a. 2, ad 3. Thomas agrees with the Lombard that the body alone is the cause of original sin; he disagrees with the *magister* by denying that the body causing original sin needed to have been formed through an act of carnal concupiscence.

to be the material cause of the composite (i.e., upon God infusing the rational soul), was ultimately disposed to be the sufficient cause of original sin. As Thomas puts it in the *De malo*, "flesh is not the sufficient cause of actual sin, but flesh is the sufficient cause of original sin, just as the transmission of the flesh is, materially, the sufficient cause of human nature."[46]

What Thomas's teaching about the transmission of original sin entails is that there is a twofold sense in which a body can be proximately/ultimately disposed to original justice. The first sense is what I will call a "purely passive" disposition to justice. This purely passive disposition comes automatically with the proximate disposition to the soul. That is, when a pre-human animal body is proximately disposed to receive the soul, it is also capable of receiving whatever gifts God chooses to bestow along with the soul (like grace or justice). A pre-human being who has descended from two human beings created directly by God without original justice would have the purely passive disposition to justice. Yet Adam needed the ability to pass on something more than a purely passive disposition to original justice in order to pass on original sin. He needed the ability to pass on what I will call an "effectual disposition" to original justice. When Cain's body was proximately disposed to receive the rational soul, his body also should have had a proximate disposition to original justice, such that when God infused the soul, Cain's *body* would at that moment be the sufficient cause of original justice. For it is precisely Cain's body's failure to be the sufficient cause of original justice that is Cain's original sin, not God's decision to infuse the soul without justice. (This is the case despite the fact that God's decision to infuse Cain's soul without justice is a condition sine qua non of Cain contracting original sin; for obviously God could have overridden Cain's flesh, as it were, and given him original justice anyway.) If Adam had been created without original justice, then Cain's failure to be the sufficient cause of original justice would not be original sin; it would simply be a natural defect. In sum, then, the body was supposed to have an effectual disposition sufficient to cause original justice upon soul infusion; instead, the body had an effectual disposition to cause original sin upon soul infusion.

---

[46] "[C]laro non est sufficiens causa peccati actualis, set peccati originalis est sufficiens causa; sicut et traductio carnis est sufficiens causa, materialiter tamen, humane nature." *De Malo* q. 4, a. 1, ad 3.

The body's power to sufficiently cause original sin is instrumental, derived from Adam, the principal cause of original sin.[47] In order to exert principal causality, a being must have the power, of its own nature, to cause an effect. In order to exert instrumental causality, by contrast, a being receives its causal power from another (ultimately a principal cause). As such, the instrument doesn't need to be able to cause a given effect of its own natural power. The classic example of principal and instrumental causality is a carpenter and her saw: the instrument, the saw, can cut only insofar as moved by the principal, the carpenter. Adam is to the carpenter what the pre-human body is to the carpenter's saw. Adam is the principal cause of original sin and the pre-human body of his offspring is Adam's instrumental cause. Ultimately, then, the question of what the pre-human body can do hinges on the question of what Adam can do.

That said, we are now in a position to return to our earlier question. If sanctifying grace is the formal cause of original justice, could Adam have been its principal cause? Or does affirming this blasphemously ascribe to Adam a power proper to Jesus Christ, the power to deify humanity?[48] If

---

[47] "Causa autem est duplex, scilicet instrumentalis et principalis. In principali quidem causa est aliquid secundum similitudinem forme, uel eiusdem speciei si sit causa uniuoca, puta cum homo generat hominem, uel ignis ignem; uel secundum aliquam excellentiorem formam, si sit agens non uniuocum; sicut sol generat hominem. In causa autem instrumentali est aliquis effectus secundum uirtutem quam recipit instrumentum a causa principali in quantum ab ea mouetur: aliter enim est forma domus in lapidibus et lignis, tamquam in proprio subiecto, et aliter in anima artificis tamquam in causa principali, et aliter in serra et securi quasi in causa instrumentali. Manifestum est autem quod esse susceptiuum peccati est proprium hominis, unde oportet quod proprium subiectum peccati cuiuscumque sit id quod est proprium hominis, scilicet anima rationalis, secundum quam homo est homo. Et sic peccatum originale est in anima rationali tamquam in proprio subiecto. *Semen autem carnale sicut est instrumentalis causa traductionis humane nature in prole, ita est instrumentalis causa traductionis peccati originalis. Et ita peccatum originale est in carne, id est in carnali semine, uirtute sicut in causa instrumentali.*" *De malo* q. 4, a. 3, emphasis mine. Cf. the *corpus* of *STh* I-II, q. 83, a. 1.

[48] Thomas denied that Adam or any creature could be the principal cause of sanctifying grace. This seems to have been his lifelong perspective. See *STh* I-II, q. 112, a. 1, which argues that God alone is the principal cause of grace. Even Jesus Christ dispenses grace only instrumentally according to his human nature (*STh* I-II, q. 112, a. 1, ad 1; cf. *STh* III, q. 64, a. 3). See also *STh* III q. 8, a. 5, ad 1, which insists that Adam transmitted original sin but could not have transmitted grace ("gratia non derivatur a Christo in nos mediante natura humana, sed per solam personalem actionem ipsius Christi"), as well as *STh* III, q. 62, a. 1, where Thomas argues that the sacraments cause grace not only as signs but as instruments of God.

we *deny* that original justice is supernatural, however – as the early Thomas did – can we still claim that its absence helps us understand infants' need for the gospel?

A DILEMMA FOR DISEASE THEORY

In this section I will criticize Thomas's disease theory of original sin. It entails commitment to one of two deeply problematic conclusions: either human beings can deify themselves or original sin's link to the gospel is unclear. The argument will proceed in three stages. First, I will argue, against Thomas, that if creatures cannot be the principal cause of grace, then neither supernatural justice nor an effectual disposition thereto can be sexually transmitted. Second, I will argue that even if we grant that natural justice is transmissible, its absence cannot account for original sin. Since Thomas must choose – justice is either natural or supernatural – and both options lead to absurdity within the parameters of disease theory, we need to either abandon his account completely or reconfigure it without disease theory. In conclusion, I will suggest that all disease theories face the same dilemma.

First, let's assume that original justice has sanctifying grace as its formal cause. If Thomas wanted to maintain his early view of original sin's transmission, on which Adam is original sin's principal cause and the body of his posterity his instrumental cause, then Adam couldn't have transmitted the sort of disposition to original justice Thomas needed him to: namely, an effectual disposition to original justice as opposed to a purely passive disposition to original justice. For if we assume that Adam's seminal power could have produced a pre-human body with an effectual proximate disposition to original justice, we thereby assume that this body, upon receiving the rational soul, would have been the sufficient cause of original justice. Given that sanctifying grace is original justice's formal cause, this means that the body would have been the sufficient cause of sanctifying grace. Since this body would have been Adam's instrument, Adam would be the principal cause of sanctifying grace.

Assuming, as we are for the moment, that original justice without sanctifying grace cannot exist in any person (assuming, that is, that natural original justice is impossible), it follows that it is impossible for Adam to have transmitted a disposition of *any* sort to natural original justice. If X is impossible, there cannot be a proximate or ultimate disposition to X. Adam could not have transmitted a disposition to drawing square circles to Cain, because square circles aren't the sort of thing that can be drawn. Thus the body's failure to cause natural original justice, on the assumption there is no possible natural original justice, cannot explain original sin.

Thomas's mature view of original justice, then, absurdly implies that Adam had the power to be the principal cause of sanctifying grace. Here I will anticipate and respond to some potential objections to my argument.

The first objection is this. There is no need to distinguish "purely passive" proximate dispositions from "effectual" proximate dispositions; indeed, this distinction is foreign to Thomas. Because Adam could have transmitted a proximate disposition to the reception of grace, just as he could have transmitted a proximate disposition to the reception of the soul, Thomas's view does not imply Adam could have been the principal cause of grace. All that follows is that he could have been the principal cause of the disposition to grace, just as he was the principal cause of the disposition to the reception of the rational soul. Since he sinned, he did not transmit the disposition to grace: he transmitted an obstacle to grace.

In response, I argue that this objection is founded on at least one of the following assumptions, the first of which is false, the second of which implicitly concedes the point I am making. First, it could be based on the assumption that Adam transmitted an "obstacle" to grace in a strong sense, that is, something in the pre-human that prevented God from infusing grace along with the soul. That assumption, however, is false, because God can infuse grace into any soul he creates, regardless of the proximate disposition of the matter. Second, one could attempt to respond by admitting that it was only an obstacle in a weaker sense: there was some vicious moral property in the pre-human that made it unfitting for God to infuse grace. Yet what would the body have caused if this vicious moral property had not been present? If the objector grants that without the vicious moral property, the body would have caused grace, my point is proven (namely, that Thomas's view absurdly implies that the creature could have been the principal cause of grace). What if the objector claimed that without the vicious moral property, the body would have been (a) neutral with respect to grace or (b) in a position to cause some natural or preternatural moral property making it more fitting for God to infuse grace?

Nothing changes. In either case, it will be God's decision to infuse grace or not that causes grace. That is, the body was not able to cause grace without the vicious moral property in a neutral state, and it was not able to cause grace with a positive natural or preternatural moral property. As we've seen, though, Thomas's logic requires that it is not ultimately God's decision to withhold original justice that causes the infant to lack original justice and have original sin; it was, rather, the body's failure to cause the original justice it should have caused. The body itself should be causing the original justice that God hasn't given on the side of the soul. Recall the Lombardian analogy underlying Thomas's logic: God is like a man who pours wine into a vase. The condition of the vase (the body) will determine whether the wine (the soul) will be good or turn to vinegar (contract original sin or not). The condition of wine being poured is the same in either case, just as the condition of the soul being infused is the same qua its divine source.

Another objection comes from a different angle. One might grant that Thomas's mature position required Adam to be the principal cause of sanctifying grace but wonder why such a conclusion is absurd. One might argue that Thomas's mature, rich account of sacramental causality supersedes his early concern that Adam cannot cause grace.[49] Why couldn't Adam function as a sacramental cause of original justice, such that the whole process – producing semen disposed to original justice, a prehuman body proximately disposed to original justice, and the ultimate disposition causing original justice with sanctifying grace – is understood within the orbit of sacramental causality?

This would be consistent with some of Thomas's principles, as long as one understood Adam as the instrumental cause of original justice in his posterity and God as the principal cause. Sacraments in general are, for Thomas, instrumental causes of grace. However, if one took this route, one would need to bite the bullet and admit (here against Thomas's principles) that God is also the principal cause of originated original sin, even if he wasn't the cause of Adam's primal sin. It would be God's decision to grant grace to each of Adam's descendants on the basis of Adam's obedience that caused their grace, *not* Adam by his seminal power. It would equally be God's decision to withhold original justice from Adam's posterity on the basis of Adam's disobedience that caused their lack of grace and thus their original sin, for Adam couldn't have transmitted grace of his own power even if he had obeyed. If one tried to claim that Adam was the principal sacramental cause, however, this

---

[49] For Thomas's development on the precise nature of the instrumental causality at work in the sacraments, see Bernhard Blankenhorn, "The Instrumental Causality of the Sacraments: Thomas Aquinas and Louis-Marie Chauvet," *Nova et Vetera*, English edition, 4.2 (2006), 255–94.

would contradict Thomas's consistent teaching that no creature can be the principal cause of grace.

One might object, moreover, that Adam could be the principal cause of grace in a different, unproblematic sense. For every creaturely cause is instrumental in relation to God. We call Adam the principal cause because he's the first, chronologically speaking, in a series of creaturely causes. If Adam had stayed upright, he would have been the principal cause of grace just as he is now the principal cause of sin. But in neither case is he *really* a principal cause; thus nothing theologically problematic follows (e.g., it doesn't follow that Adam could have created grace).

In response, I would argue that Thomas distinguishes two senses of principal causality. In one sense, God is the principal cause, the *causa causorum*, of all created being, insofar as he sustains and directs all being. In this sense, every creature is an "instrumental" cause of God. But in another, more proper sense, creatures have their own principal causal powers; they can, in accordance with their natures, be the principal causes of effects. In this latter sense, they also have *limits*, effects to which their powers simply cannot extend. No creature can create anything *ex nihilo*, for example, and as we've seen, no creature can be the principal cause of the rational soul or sanctifying grace. Adam's being the first in the causal chain is only a necessary condition for his being the principal cause of original justice; it is not sufficient. Original justice must also exist *in linea naturae* if Adam is to be its principal cause.

Let's review the argument of this section. Thomas's mature view of original justice required a change somewhere in his theology. He needed to admit either that Adam could have been the principal cause of grace or that God could have been the principal cause of originated original sin. He didn't make either of those moves. Instead, he assumed that Adam's ability to transmit a purely passive disposition to receive grace was enough. What Thomas really needed, though, was for Adam to have had the ability to transmit an effectual disposition to natural original justice, and such a disposition is only possible if original justice is preternatural.

Some readers may disagree with my thesis that Thomas's view of original sin's formal cause shifted, preferring to interpret texts like *STh* I.95.1 along Kors's lines. Others may admit that his view changed but suspect that it was a change for the worse. Both sets of readers will rightly ask: What was so bad about Thomas's early view of original justice? The early Thomas can easily avoid the problems we have focused on thus far. If original sin is formally the lack of preternatural rectitude Adam ought to have passed on and materially the lack of preternaturally ordered concupiscence, then Adam never needed to transmit supernatural grace in the first place.

The problem with Thomas's early view, however, is that defining original sin as the lack of natural original justice leaves the infant's basic relation to God obscure. The person who receives the grace of the gospel is rightly related to God, oriented to the beatific vision. Yet she still lacks natural justice and as a result inevitably sins.[50] If original sin is the lack of natural justice, and we don't receive natural justice when we receive grace, then the infant with original sin may *already* have the grace of the gospel. Defining original sin as the lack of natural justice has, in other words, the strange implication that an infant could be created with the grace of the gospel and original sin simultaneously.

If a chief desideratum of a doctrine of original sin is to help us understand the infant's need for the gospel – and I would submit that it is – then obscurity at this point is unacceptable. The grace of the gospel does not give us preternatural rectitude or rightly ordered concupiscence (not initially, anyway); it gives us the Holy Spirit. It seems, then, that original sin must involve the lack of the Holy Spirit, the lack of the supernatural grace of the gospel. Indeed, as we've seen, Thomas himself reasoned this way when he considered baptism. He assumed that when we receive sanctifying grace we receive what we lacked by virtue of our original sin. He had difficulty squaring this with his view that God is not the one who brings about our lack of the Spirit and thus assumed, when treating original sin's transmission, that our sin is only to lack natural justice.

But Thomas needed to choose, and so do we. Original justice is either supernatural or natural. From within Thomas's disease framework, I've argued, each of these choices leads to an unacceptable conclusion. Either creatures can transmit supernatural grace, "autodeifying" themselves, so to speak, or they could have transmitted natural justice, the lack of which has nothing to do with the lack of the grace of the gospel. Thomas is not the only theologian who has this problem. I would suggest that anyone

---

[50] People who receive grace lack preternatural rectitude on two levels. In the first place, they lack the fullness of natural original justice, because they don't have the ability to pass natural justice on to their children. That much was obvious to Thomas, so he concluded that they receive original justice as it redounds to the person. Yet on the assumption of original justice's preternatural status, grace does not restore justice as it affects the person either, because preternatural rectitude *ex hypothesi* allows the avoidance of all sin, and Christians, Thomas holds, normally inevitably sin (at least venially).

who envisages salvation as deification and wants to defend a disease theory of original sin has it too.

I don't have space to sketch a soteriology here, but consider what follows from Eastern Orthodoxy, as well as a "growing number of Western theological minds" if our salvation involves deification.[51] We are called to an intimate knowledge and love of God, a communion with the Holy Trinity, such that we, as 2 Pet. 1:4 says, participate in the divine nature. Perhaps salvation is more than deification, but let's assume that it isn't less.[52] If this is the case, though, surely creatures don't have it within their power to deify each other (except instrumentally); surely it is principally the Father's to give. This can be, for now, merely a suggestion.

On the assumption that salvation involves a supernatural deification, we are now in a position to restate the dilemma of disease theory more broadly. First I need to tighten my working definition of disease theory. A disease theory of original sin has two essential conditions. God is not the cause of originated original sin because he created humanity in a "healthy" state, without original sin. Adam is the cause of originated original sin because he transmitted the "sickness" of original sin instead of "health."[53]

The dilemma for disease theory is this. If health is supernatural, then creatures could have deified themselves; if health is natural, then its absence has nothing to do with the absence of the grace of the gospel, our need for deification. The first horn of the dilemma follows because if creatures couldn't have transmitted health, then God would be the ultimate cause of their sickness. But God cannot cause sin on disease theory. The second horn of the dilemma follows because, as I've suggested,

[51] Paul L. Gavrilyuk, "The Retrieval of Deification: How a Once-Despised Archaism Became an Ecumenical Desideratum," *Modern Theology* 25.4 (2009), 648. A good deal has been written recently on Thomas's view of deification. See especially Bruce D. Marshall, "*Ex Occidente Lux?* Aquinas and Eastern Orthodox Theology," *Modern Theology* 20.1 (2004), 23–50. For deification in the context of Aquinas's soteriology, see Daria Spezzano, *The Glory of God's Grace: Deification According to St. Thomas Aquinas* (Ave Maria, FL: Sapientia Press, 2015). For an ecumenical study, see A. N. Williams, *The Ground of Union: Deification in Aquinas and Palamas* (New York: Oxford University Press, 1999).

[52] Germain Grisez's "The True Ultimate End of Human Beings: The Kingdom, Not God Alone," *Theological Studies* 69 (2008), 38–61, as the title suggests, argues that our end involves but is not limited to the beatific vision.

[53] Two clarifications. "Adam" here could refer to a literal Adam, or Adam and Eve together, or an Adam-and-Eve-like-pair, or an Adam-and-Eve-like-community. The point is that the first human beings didn't have original sin. "Transmit" here means communicate, give to, implant, sexually or otherwise.

deification is supernatural, and whatever natural defect we might have fails to capture our deepest need.

Many disease theories of original sin do not clarify whether original righteousness was natural or supernatural. Oliver Crisp, a Reformed theologian, has recently defended a version of disease theory. Crisp argues that his theory is indebted to the account of Huldrych Zwingli and calls it the "moderate Reformed doctrine of original sin." After arguing that original guilt is not mandated by several important Reformed confessions, Crisp turns to articulating his own account:

> suppose original sin is a moral corruption that is inherited. It arises early in the development of a first human population, and is passed down by both parents to each successive generation. How does this happen? Here we may turn to the story of Eden as a template. Early in human development, in (say) a first human community, there is some moral breach with God, some primal act of dereliction that introduces a moral corruption to human beings that is inheritable. Call this action the primal sin. On this way of thinking, inheriting a state of sin is not a condition for which the person born in this morally vitiated condition is culpable because (we suppose) a person cannot be held morally responsible for a condition with which he or she is born. It is not the fault of individuals that live diachronically downstream of the first human community that they are generated in a state of moral corruption. It should be fairly obvious that what obtains with respect to the corruption with which fallen human beings are generated also obtains, *mutatis mutandis*, with original guilt. That is, fallen humans can be no more guilty of the sin of a putative human pair or aboriginal human community than they can be culpable for inheriting a state of sin.[54]

Early in the first human population there is a breach with God. This assumes, I presume, some state of "justice" or "righteousness" or "grace" before the breach. The person with original sin is not responsible or culpable for the primal sin or her inherited corruption. Yet she will eventually sin personally: it is "inevitable that all fallen human beings will actually sin on at least one occasion *if they live long enough and are the proper subject of moral states and properties*."[55] Original sin alone leads to "death and separation from God irrespective of actual sin," though Crisp notes that he finds the view that God actually condemns infants or the mentally disabled "morally repulsive."[56]

That last point concerning the reality of infant damnation excepted, Crisp's account (and thus Zwingli's) is quite close to medieval disease

---

[54] Oliver D. Crisp, "On Original Sin," *International Journal of Systematic Theology* 17.3 (2015), 9.
[55] Crisp, "On Original Sin," 10, emphasis his.   [56] Crisp, "On Original Sin," 13, 12.

theory. But it seems to face the same dilemma. What, exactly, would the absence of the heritable moral corruption have consisted in? Natural or supernatural righteousness? Crisp could argue that our original justice is natural. Whether or not our salvation involves deification (it could be argued), God must have created us with the fullness of the goodness of human nature. Adam's sin corrupted that nature, and the gospel begins to bring us back to the fullness of nature, which will be fully restored only in the eschaton. Gospel grace is supernatural now, above postlapsarian humanity's power, but this is so only with reference to nature's corruption, not human nature itself. Thus there's no problem hypothesizing that prelapsarian Adam could have transmitted justice; this is a natural gift. I will address this perspective in Chapter 8.

3

Aquinas on the Effects of Original Sin

Martin Luther regarded the claim that human nature remains intact after
the Fall as a paradigmatic scholastic error.[1] It was linked, in his view, to a
whole series of errors, including the heresy that we can merit saving grace
if we do what is in ourselves. An older generation of textbooks taught that
what Luther criticized was standard medieval Catholic soteriology,
rooted in the teaching of Thomas. Today, however, swaths of specialists
claim that the view that nature remains intact after the Fall has no basis in
the thought of Thomas Aquinas himself. Indeed, a semi-established consensus of contemporary scholars, from neo-Thomists who argue that pure
nature would be stronger than nature now, to *nouvelle* theologians who
deny Thomas even had a concept of pure nature, to ecumenists emphasizing the thirteenth-century's Augustinian bona fides, agree: for Thomas,
original sin has damaged human nature.[2]

Thomas, after all, like Augustine, conceived of original sin as a corruption of nature, akin to a disease. Adam and Eve were created in justice, in
health – nature in the Christian sense – but after sin and the consequent
corruption of Adam's seed, nature is sick with sin. Poisoned by concupiscence, *incuruatus in se*, we now need grace to love God. Thomas says this,
quite explicitly, in q. 109, a. 3, of the *Prima secundae*. How could any

---

[*] Portions of this chapter are adapted from Daniel W. Houck, "*Natura Humana Relicta est
Christo*: Thomas Aquinas on the Effects of Original Sin," *Archa Verbi* 13 (2016): 68–102,
with kind permission of the publisher.

[1] "Quare ii, qui dicunt naturalia post lapsum remansisse integra, impii philosophantur
contra theologiam," *Lutherstudien* II, *Disputatio de Homine*, thesis 26, ed. Gerhard
Ebeling (Tübingen, 1977), cited in Janz, *Luther and Late Medieval Thomism*, 29.

[2] See the Introduction for a list of salient studies.

competent, fair-minded reader fail to grasp this historical point? Moreover, isn't it obvious that, if Thomas had taught that nature is unharmed by the Fall, he would have at least been a semi-, if not a full-blown, Pelagian?

This chapter argues against the current consensus. Thomas did think that nature remains intact after the Fall, but his view of original sin was not "Pelagian" in any meaningful sense. Indeed, there is no necessary connection between the idea that human nature remains intact after the Fall and the claim that postlapsarian human beings can merit salvation.[3] The consensus view, I argue, is not so much wrong as confused: there is one sense in which nature is corrupted, for Thomas, but there is another, more basic sense in which it is not. I show in the first two sections of this chapter that Thomas held – in both his early commentary on the *Sentences* and his later writings – that "nature" in the strict sense refers to the principles of nature (the rational soul and animal body) and the properties that follow from these principles. The infant with original sin has human nature in this strict sense, just as a human being created without original justice and without original sin would.[4] But there is another sense of the word "nature": it can also refer to what is good for the human being, even if this goodness is, strictly speaking, not due to nature. And in this sense, an infant's "nature" is "corrupted" because she no longer has the good gift of original justice.

This reading of Thomas's account on the effects of original sin on human nature is not new, though it has been out of scholarly favor for at least two generations.[5] What is new is this chapter's reading of the treatise on grace (*STh* I-II, qq. 109–14) in conversation with Thomas's

---

[3] The concept of Pelagianism is discussed further in Chapter 8.

[4] Thomas's focus was not on the hypothetical powers a human being created in the "state of pure nature" would have. But he did argue that if God created a human being without original justice and without original sin, then this human would have the principles and properties of human nature, just as postlapsarian human persons do. In either case, the human being is mortal, lacks sanctifying grace, lacks preternatural rectitude, and lacks rightly ordered concupiscence. Moreover, in either case, the teleological orientation to God remains. The argument of this chapter is not that everyone who has original sin is in precisely the same condition. Thomas thinks that habitual concupiscence varies from person to person, for example. I am likewise not claiming that any given individual created in pure nature would have precisely the same sort of body as any given individual with original sin. One might argue, for example, that God wouldn't directly create someone in pure nature with a disability. Thus I am not principally concerned with what a hypothetical state of pure nature would consist in, considered as a totality and compared with our fallen world, so much as with Thomas's view that human beings now do in fact retain the principles and properties of nature.

[5] J. B. Kors defended the view that human beings with original sin have the same moral powers they would have in pure nature in his *La Justice primitive et le péché originel d'après S. Thomas*. His study was approvingly cited by A. Gaudel, "Péché originel," in

broader hamartiology and doctrine of providence. Recent scholarship has typically adduced statements from the treatise on grace as evidence that Thomas held that nature was corrupted by sin in a strong sense. But read in the context of Thomas's semantics of *"natura"* (established in the first two sections of the chapter), as well as salient features of his doctrine of providence (discussed in the third section), the treatise on grace does not demonstrate that Thomas's mature account of the effects of original sin on human nature was different from his early account.

ORIGINAL SIN AND HUMAN NATURE IN THE *SCRIPTUM*

Aristotle was absent from Chapter 2 of this study. This was for the very good reason that he'd never heard of original justice. But in Thomas's account of original sin, the Stagirite (along with Seneca and other philosophers) plays a prominent role. Recall that in our treatment of Thomas's account of original justice in the *Scriptum*, we saw that original justice is "natural" in at least two senses for the early Thomas. It does not require sanctifying grace, and it is transmissible through natural sexual intercourse. This left open the vital question of original justice's relation to what the philosophers had said about human nature. Aristotle famously opposed Plato by arguing that universals exist only in particulars and that, as such, human nature is all around us. We see human nature every time we see a human being, as we see redness every time we see something red. From a Christian point of view, was Aristotle simply wrong? Was human nature fully present only in Eden, remaining now only in corrupted form? If this is the case, in what sense are human beings still *human*? Alternatively, since human beings evidently *do* still exist, should we say that nature remains after the Fall, without the divinely bestowed gifts of grace? If nature remains, though, can we truly say it suffered any penalty for sin? This cluster of questions is, at the most basic

---

Dictionnaire de Théologie Catholique 12 (1933), 275–606; Lottin, *Problèmes de morale, troisième partie*, 1: 245–71; T. C. O'Brien, "Fallen Nature," in appendix 9 to vol. 26 of the *Summa theologiae* Ia2æ, 81–5, ed. T. C. O'Brien (New York: McGraw-Hill, 1965), 154–61; Oswin Magrath, *St. Thomas's Theory of Original Sin* 16.2 (1953), 161–89. I am indebted to Kors's work, but its scope only allowed him to treat original justice and original sin in themselves. He did not discuss the apparent tension between Thomas's hamartiology and the treatise on grace. This may have been one of the reasons why his work has not convinced many Thomists to abandon the consensus reading.

level, the question of the relation between the effects of original sin and human nature. And it is this question with which Thomas begins the *Scriptum*'s treatise on original sin (b. II, dd. 30–3). Are "the defects which we feel penalties in us for the sin of the first human being"?[6]

Thomas begins with Aristotle. As the philosopher says, whatever is ordained to a given end must be disposed to that end. The end to which humanity is ordained, the beatific vision, requires supernatural help.[7] Thus, humanity needed to be given something beyond its natural power, beyond that which follows from the principles of human nature, in order to reach this end. This was the gift of original justice. What are those basic principles of human nature, the principles to which original justice was *added* as a gift?

They are precisely what remain when we subtract the gift of original justice that ordered them rightly. Adam forfeited the gift of original justice on humanity's behalf; he passed on bare human nature instead. Humanity in its fallen state is humanity in its natural state, shorn of the gift of original justice: "Deordained from the end through sin ... the human being is left with only those goods following from the principles of human nature."[8]

How can these natural principles be penalties for sin? Aren't the principles of human nature (the animal body and rational soul) and what follows these principles (such as the powers of the soul) intrinsically good? Here is Thomas's answer:

These defects can be compared to human nature in two ways. First, they can be compared to human nature in its natural principles alone. In this respect, such defects are certainly not penalties but natural defects.... Alternatively, they can be compared to human nature as it was first instituted. In this respect, they are without doubt penalties.[9]

---

[6] "Utrum defectus quos sentimus sint nobis quasi poena pro peccato primi hominis." *Scriptum* II, d. 30, q. 1, a. 1.

[7] "Respondeo dicendum, quod ea quae sunt ad finem, disponuntur secundum necessitatem finis, ut ex II *Physicor.*, tex. 78, patet. Finis autem ad quem homo ordinatus est, est ultra facultatem naturae creatae, scilicet beatitudo, quae in visione Dei consistit; soli enim Deo hoc connaturale est ... Unde oportuit naturam humanam taliter institui ut non solum haberet illud quod sibi ex principiis naturalibus debebatur, sed etiam aliquid ultra, per quod facile in finem perveniret." *Scriptum* II, d. 30, q. 1, a. 1.

[8] "[F]acta deordinatione a fine per peccatum ... relictus est homo in illis tantum bonis quae eum ex naturalibus principiis consequuntur." *Scriptum* II, d. 30, q. 1, a. 1.

[9] "[I]sti defectus possunt ad naturam humanam dupliciter comparari: vel ad eam, secundum quod in principiis naturalibus suis tantum consideratur, et sic proculdubio non sunt poenae ejus, sed naturales defectus ... vel ad eam, prout instituta est, et sic proculdubio poena sunt." *Scriptum* II, d. 30, q. 1, a 1.

The defects of human beings – their lack of subjection to God, disordered concupiscence, and mortality – are natural. In what sense? They flow from human nature, which has these defects when left to itself. If we consider our first parents, who had the gift of original justice added to their nature, we realize that the lack of these gifts is a penalty for sin. Thomas must have known that many would perceive his position as paradoxical. Shouldn't we say that the original gifts were gracious *as opposed* to natural?[10] Isn't simultaneously calling original justice natural, claiming that we lose nothing natural from sin, and claiming that we lose original justice unnecessarily confusing?

Thomas defends his multipronged use of the word "natural" by arguing that we can speak of natural goods either in terms of the principles of nature or in terms of their ordination to the ultimate end.[11] Considered in themselves, the natural principles due to human beings have not been forfeited by sin. Thomas goes so far as to say that the natural gifts in human beings have not been lost or even diminished in *any* respect, appealing to Denys's claim that the "natural gifts remain even in sinful angels."[12] Yet we can also speak of natural principles vis-à-vis their ordination to the ultimate end. In this sense they can be diminished, insofar as original justice is forfeited. This is how Thomas explains the statement on nature's wounds from the *glossa ordinaria* (generally attributed to Bede). The human being is *in naturalibus uulneratus* in the sense that she lost the good *of* her nature that helped her reach the ultimate end; but ultimately, with Denys, he affirms that the natural gifts have neither been lost nor even diminished. We now have a third sense in which

---

[10] Cf. *Scriptum* II, d. 30, q. 1, a. 1, ob 3.

[11] "Bona naturalia dicuntur dupliciter. Vel prout sunt in se considerata, secundum quod naturae debentur ex propriis principiis; *et sic nec homo nec angelus per peccatum aliquid naturalium amisit; vel in aliquo diminutus est: quia Dionysius etiam integra data naturalia in angelis peccantibus permanere dicit* ... Vel secundum quod ordinantur in finem ultimum; et hoc modo in utroque bona naturalia diminuta sunt quidem, non penitus amissa, inquantum uterque factus est minus habilis et magis distans a finis consecutione: et propter hoc etiam *homo gratuitis spoliatus dicitur et in naturalibus vulneratus*, Luc., X, in Glossa." *Scriptum* II, d. 30, q. 1, a 1, ad 3, emphasis mine.

[12] See Richard Schenk's brief but penetrating discussion on the origins (and appropriation, by Thomas and Bonaventure) of Dionysius's saying that nature is "saved" by providence despite sin. "Analogy as the *discrimen naturae et gratiae*: Thomism and Ecumenical Learning," in *The Analogy of Being: Invention of the Antichrist or the Wisdom of God?*, ed. Thomas Joseph White (Grand Rapids, MI: Eerdmans, 2011), 184–90. Though Schenk does not discuss original sin, the essay rightfully stresses that the possession of nature is not for the sake of independence from God but deepening our conviction that we are "anything but self-sufficient" (p. 190).

original justice can be called natural. In addition to the fact that God can give it without sanctifying grace and in addition to the fact that it is transmissible through sexual intercourse, original justice is natural because it's *good* for human nature. It is bad to lose it, then, even though it does not follow from the principles of nature.

How serious is Thomas? Does original sin really leave human nature with its principles and all that follows from them? Would a human being created by God without original justice and without original sin (in "pure nature") be as morally weak as a human being with original sin in corrupt nature?[13] Thomas anticipates this question, answering it in the context of discussing whether original sin passes to all human beings. It does (Christ excepted), even though God has the power to make a human being without original sin and without original justice. What would such a human being be like?

If, by divine power, someone were formed from a finger, she would not have original sin. Nevertheless, *she would have all the defects of those born in original sin*, without the character of guilt. This is clear from the following. When God created humanity in the beginning, he could have formed a different human being from the mud of the earth – left to the condition of her nature, mortal and passible, feeling concupiscence rage against her reason. In this state nothing would be subtracted from human nature, because these defects follow the principles of human nature. Still, as this defect would not be caused through [human] will, it would not have had the character of guilt or penalty.[14]

If God were to make a human being without original justice and without original sin – either from the body of a human being in corrupt nature or

---

[13] As J. P. Torrell observes, the thirteenth-century concept of humanity "*in puris naturalibus*" is not equivalent to the modern "*status naturae purae.*" "Nature et grâce chez Thomas d'Aquin," 180–1. I would add, however, that the reason this is the case is not because Thomas had no concept of human nature without justice, sanctifying grace, and sin; this is precisely what Thomas discusses here and elsewhere. The reason is rather, as de Lubac forcefully argued in many places, that modern theologians came to think that human beings in this "purely natural" state would have far greater power than Thomas ever dreamed. See, for example, the sixth chapter of Henri de Lubac, *Augustinisme et théologie moderne*, 183–223.

[14] "[S]i aliquis divina virtute ex digito formaretur, originale non haberet; *haberet nihilominus omnes defectus quos habent qui in originali nascuntur*, tamen sine ratione culpae: quod sic patet. Poterat Deus a principio quando hominem condidit, etiam alium hominem ex limo terrae formare, quem in conditione naturae suae relinqueret, ut scilicet mortalis et passibilis esset, et pugnam concupiscentiae ad rationem sentiens; in quo nihil humanae naturae derogaretur, quia hoc ex principiis naturae consequitur. Non tamen iste defectus in eo rationem culpae et poenae habuisset; quia non per voluntatem iste defectus causatus esset." *Scriptum* II, d. 31, q. 1, a. 2, ad 3, emphasis mine.

from the dust – this human being would have everything that follows from human nature, including the defects of original sin. She simply wouldn't have original sin. She would lack original sin because she would not have received the lack of original justice from Adam's sinful will. Original sin just *is* the due lack of original justice, the lack of justice that ought to be present by Adam's will. In itself, lacking original justice and having disordered concupiscence is not sinful, because the principles of nature are not sinful.

It would be difficult to overstate Thomas's boldness. His predecessors (not to mention his thirteenth-century critics) rejected the idea that God could create human beings without justice, with sickness and death and concupiscence.[15] Why would Thomas claim God could do this? To answer this question we need to understand Thomas's view of human nature's relation to God. Without justice, is the human being by nature hostile to God, an idolater, full of the *amor sui* over the *amor Dei*? If not, then how can Thomas deny that justice is from nature? It would seem that if nature implies a right relation to God, nature implies justice; conversely, that if nature does not imply right relation to God, nature implies injustice. The clearest way to see Thomas's answer to this question is to move to the final distinction of the treatise, on original sin's punishment.

Although God permits infants to suffer certain temporal, bodily punishments in this life, they do not deserve any spiritual punishment on the part of their souls, which are immediately created by God.[16] Because the "crime" of original sin is merely receiving a nature deprived of original justice, and we know from scripture that God is just, we can infer that he would not unjustly punish infants by depriving them of anything belonging to their nature.[17] Therefore, Thomas argues, their punishment

---

[15] For a discussion of Peckham's and Olivi's criticisms of Aquinas, see Julian Kaup, "Die Begründung des Schuldcharakters der Erbsünde bei Thomas von Aquin und ihre Kritik durch Johannes Peckham und Petrus Johannis Olivi," in *Wahrheit und Verkündigung: Michael Schmaus zum 70. Geburtstag*, vol. 1, ed. L. Scheffczyk, W. Dettloff, and Richard Heinzmann (München: Schöningh, 1967), 851–76.

[16] "Sed quantum ad animam, quae immediate a Deo creatur, non est res parentis, sed ipsius Dei ... Sciendum est ergo quod ... hujusmodi poena [animae] nunquam filius pro peccato patris punitur, quia ista poena non attingit ipsum secundum quod est res patris." *Scriptum* II, d. 33, q. 1, a. 2.

[17] "[P]oena debet esse proportionata culpae, ut dicitur Isa., XXVII, 8: *In mensura contra mensuram, cum abjecta fuerit judicabis eam*. Defectus autem qui per originem traducitur, rationem culpae habens, *non est per subtractionem vel corruptionem alicujus boni quod naturam humanam consequitur ex principiis suis*, sed per subtractionem vel corruptionem alicujus quod naturae superadditum erat." *Scriptum* II, d. 33, q. 2, a. 1, emphasis of Thomas's words mine.

cannot consist of any sense pain; it can only be the loss of the end to which the gift of justice ordained them, the beatific vision.[18] So far, Thomas has followed the Lombard. Yet Thomas will delve deeper into what *follows* from the loss of the beatific vision than the twelfth century had.

In the first place, Thomas argues that because infants did not lose the beatific vision through any action of their own, they will not be sad.[19] Infants who die unbaptized will be "joined to God through participation in natural goods; they will even be able to enjoy him by natural knowledge and love."[20] "Hell" for them is a place of happiness.[21] We do not have time to explore the tension between Thomas's affirmation of a natural happiness in limbo and his teaching that there is a natural desire for the beatific vision.[22] Suffice it to say that, although limbo is not a

---

[18] "[N]ulla alia poena sibi debetur nisi privatio illius finis ad quem donum subtractum ordinabat; ad quod per se natura humana attingere non potest. Hoc autem est divina visio; et ideo carentia hujus visionis est propria et sola poena originalis peccati post mortem." *Scriptum* II, d. 33, q. 2, a. 1.

[19] "Pueri autem nunquam fuerunt proportionati ad hoc quod vitam aeternam haberent: quia nec eis debebatur ex principiis naturae, cum omnem facultatem naturae excedat, nec actus proprios habere potuerunt quibus tantum bonum consequerentur; et ideo nihil omnino dolebunt de carentia visionis divinae." *Scriptum* II, d. 33, q. 2, a. 2.

[20] "[S]ibi [Deo] conjunguntur per participationem naturalium bonorum; et ita etiam de ipso guadere potuerunt naturali cognitione et dilectione." *Scriptum* II, d. 33, q. 2, a. 2, ad 5.

[21] It may be better to avoid calling limbo a part of "hell," because the word "hell" strongly connotes hellfire and a place of abject misery. On the other hand, Thomas does at times speak of limbo as an "*infernus*": "pueri cum originali decedentes gratiam non habuerint, non fuerunt ab Inferno liberati." *STh* III, q. 57, a. 7.

[22] On the reading I am offering, there is no need to choose between affirming that Thomas held (1) there is both a penultimate natural end (enjoyed in limbo) and an ultimate supernatural end; (2) there is a natural desire for the ultimate end; and (3) in God's providence all human beings *in uia* with the use of reason are in a state of sanctifying grace or mortal sin. Readers who deny (1) in light of (2) or (3) have a difficult time understanding Thomas's account of original sin. Denis Bradley, for example, claims that "[i]nsofar as no natural end – including a life combining contemplation and action – adequately satisfies man's desire for beatitude, man is *naturally* endless." *Aquinas on the Twofold Human Good: Reason and Human Happiness in Aquinas's Moral Science* (Washington, DC: Catholic University of America Press, 1999), 512. He leaves limbo unexplained, only noting that it is a "restricted category" (p. 479). Bradley leaves us with the impression that limbo was a purely ad hoc hypothesis, arising perhaps from Thomas's compassionate personality, as opposed to what it was: a theologoumenon stemming directly from his views of divine justice, the analogical character of original sin, and the intelligibility of human nature without sanctifying grace. I am not affirming that (1) and (2) are ultimately coherent, however. How can happiness worthy of the name leave any desire unfulfilled? As Lawrence Feingold argues in *The Natural Desire to See God According to St. Thomas and His Interpreters* (Naples: Sapientia, 2010), it is this dilemma that led Thomists to speculate about what a "wish" (*velleity*) for the beatific

purely natural state, Thomas's view that the infant deserves to know and love God there according to her natural principles shows that he thought infants with original sin are oriented to God by nature.[23] I will call this natural relation to God, which Thomas thinks follows from the principles of nature and is distinct from the preternatural rectitude of justice as well as sanctifying grace, the "natural orientation" to God. We will discuss it in more depth in the following chapters. Is this Pelagianism? I will address this question in more depth in Chapter 8. For now, suffice it to say that Thomas says infants are damned and deprived of their ultimate end, true happiness in God, for all eternity. For now, we can summarize Thomas's view here in the *Scriptum* and move on to the mature texts.

Human beings were created in original justice, with wills subjected to God, rightly ordered concupiscence, and an immortality contingent upon continued obedience. The gift of original justice was natural in three senses: it was transmissible through sexual intercourse; it did not require supernatural grace; and it was good for nature, a natural good. Nevertheless, original justice was above nature considered in its intrinsic principles. When Adam forfeited original justice for humanity, he passed on bare human nature instead, which is to say he passed on original sin. Thomas, accordingly, defines original sin the lack of due justice by which the will was subjected to God; materially, it is the lack of due justice by which concupiscence was rightly ordered.[24] All the defects of original sin would be present if God were to create a human being without original justice, without sanctifying grace, and without original sin; yet all the goodness of human nature would also be present, including the orientation to God.

---

vision, compatible with natural happiness, might be. As we will see later, however, inattention to (3) has caused modern Thomists to miss Thomas's doctrine of original sin.

[23] Thomas held that the human being's destiny is sealed at death; thus the infant who dies unbaptized is immediately confirmed in her default natural goodness and cannot personally sin. If Thomas speculated about the fate of infants not so confirmed, perhaps he would have argued that the will of the separate soul would be like the angel's first moment of existence: possessing natural happiness yet still able to sin (see *STh* I, q. 62, a. 1). In any case, Thomas's view of limbo is a helpful example of his teaching that human beings do not lose their natural orientation to God by original sin. If Thomas didn't think this, he would have affirmed the common medieval view that infants will be sad because they don't have the *uisio Dei*.

[24] "[I]psae vires deordinatae, vel deordinatio virium sint sicut materiale in peccato originali, et ipsa deordinatio a fine sit ibi sicut formale." *Scriptum* II, d. 30, q. 1, a. 3.

ORIGINAL SIN AND HUMAN NATURE IN THE LATER WORKS

Thomas would never again discuss original sin in the detail he did in the *Scriptum*. This choice, as I suggested earlier, would prove pedagogically unfortunate. Misreadings have proliferated. One mistake is to assume that because Thomas claims that Adam's sin is transmitted to his posterity, his posterity contract the same type of sin that Adam committed. Otto Pesch, for example, argued in an influential ecumenical study of Thomas and Luther that because Adam's act of sin was pride, and infants inherit Adam's sin, Thomas *must* have believed that infants begin in a state of pride (even though Thomas never said so explicitly).[25] The problem with this argument is that infants have not committed the act of pride. Pesch's reasoning here was faulty, but he also offered stronger arguments for the same conclusion. Indeed, there is another set of reasons and texts that has led even the most scrupulous of readers to suppose Thomas held a different view by the end of his life.

A large body of scholarship has argued that Thomas underwent an Augustinian transformation midway through his career. Henri Bouillard, for example, influentially claimed that after Thomas's encounter with the late Augustine and the Council of Orange, he repudiated the overly optimistic account of human nature's power held in his youth. In the *Scriptum*, the human being with original sin not only retains the orientation to God; she can avoid all mortal sin, fulfill the natural law, and even merit God's grace if she tries hard enough. Thomas appears to completely reverse himself in the *Summa*, emphasizing instead "the divine initiative

---

[25] "Ein Zweites muß bedacht werden, was Thomas zwar nicht mehr ausdrücklich formuliert, was aber in seinen Überlegungen unabweislich eingeschlossen ist. Wenn es ernst gemeint ist, daß wir keine andere Sünde als die Sünde *Adams* 'erben,' wenn also unsere *Natur*sünde seine *Tat*sünde ist und nur als von ihr beingte überhaupt Sündigkeit und Schuldhaftigkeit hat, dann ist die *carentia iustitae originalis*, die formell das Wesen der Erbsünde ausmacht, nicht nur die allgemeine Wirklichkeit einer Privation, sondern sie trägt die spezifischen Züge der Tatsünde Adams und der Art, wie sich in ihr das Wesen der Sünde als *aversio* und *conversio* realisierte. Nun hat sich aber Thomas über die erste Sünde Adams präzise Gedanken gemacht. Sie war – aus theologischen und ontologisch-anthropologischen Gründen ist gar nichts anderes möglich – ein Akt reinen Stolzes. Der erste Mensch sündigte, indem er seine Stellung als Geschöpf nicht annehmen, sondern Gott ähnlich sein wollte, in der Erkenntnis, die sich selber zum Maßstab von Gut und Böse setzte, und in der Macht, die sich aus eigener Kraft die endgültige Glückseligkeit verschaffen wollte. Dieser Stolz Adams ist also die Natursünde, mit der wir geboren werden." Otto Hermann Pesch, *Theologie der Rechtfertigung bei Martin Luther und Thomas von Aquin: Versuch eines systematisch-theologischen Dialogs* (Mainz: Matthias-Grünewald), 493.

and the intimate dependence of the will on divine help."[26] Scholars, accordingly, tend to regard claims of continuity between the anthropologies of the *Scriptum* and the *Summa* with suspicion, especially when such claims could be taken to imply that Thomas was some sort of "optimist" or "Semipelagian." Surely for the mature Thomas, at least, nature itself is harmed by sin?

We can be more precise. As Garrigou-Lagrange argued, doesn't the clearest proof come from Thomas's argument that the human being in corrupt nature has lost the natural powers to love God and fulfill the natural law (*STh* I-II, q. 109, aa. 3–4)?[27] Don't these powers belong *by definition* to human nature? Moreover, doesn't Thomas argue that the wounds of original sin affect all parts of the human being, causing an unnatural concupiscence and wounding even the natural inclination to virtue (*STh* I-II, q. 85)? Otto Pesch – here making a stronger argument than the one we mentioned a moment ago – argues that the disordered concupiscence of original sin *explains* the human will's idolatrous aversion from God.[28] Both of these theologians hold that at least for the

---

[26] Henri Bouillard, *Conversion et grâce chez s. Thomas d'Aquin* (Paris: Aubier, 1944), 92. See pp. 92–121, the first chapter of the second part of the book, for Bouillard's discussion of Thomas's discovery of Semipelagianism. Bouillard argues that in the *Scriptum* II, d. 28, aa. 2–4, Thomas teaches that the human being with original sin can, without sanctifying grace, avoid all mortal sin, fulfill the natural law, and prepare herself for grace by doing what is in herself. As M. G. Lawler noted, however, Thomas only admits that those who do what is in themselves can be said to merit their grace *de congruo* in a certain sense ("*quoddamodo*"); namely, it is not *unfitting* for God to give them grace (*Scriptum* II, d. 27, a. 4, ad 4). "Grace and Free Will in Justification," *The Thomist* 35 (1971), 607.

[27] "[L]'homme, dans l'état de déchéance non réparée, a moins de forces pour faire le bien moral naturel qu'il n'en aurait eu dans l'état de nature pure." Garrigou-Lagrange, "La mortification et les suites du péché originel," 24. "[O]n peut s'en rendre compte surtout par ce qu'il enseigne sur la nécessité de la grâce pour aimer Dieu par-dessus tout et pour observer la loi naturelle. La saint Docteur, parlant de l'état purement naturel où l'homme aurait pu être créé, dit: 'L'homme par ses seules forces naturelles peut aimer Dieu (auteur de sa nature) plus que soi et par-dessus tout.' Mais dans l'état de nature corrumpue, ajoute-t-il, l'homme ne le peut pas, car, *par suite de la corruption de la nature, la volonté se porte vers son bien propre, à moins qu'elle ne soit guérie par la grâce de Dieu.* Pour la même raison l'homme, dans l'état de déchéance, ne peut observer toute la loi naturelle" (pp. 25–6).

[28] "Daß der Wille, das Ich-Zentrum, durch die Erbsünde Gott nicht unterworfen ist, sich der Hinordnung auf Gott entzieht, ist sachlich nichts anderes als die Abkehr von Gott, das formelle Moment jeder Sünde. Daß die niederen Kräfte gegen die Vernunft rebellieren und auseinanderstrebend nur noch ihre Eigenziele zu verfolgen suchen, ist nichts anderes als die ungeordnete, das heißt nicht auf Gott bezogene Hinkehr zum geschaffenen Gut. Diese doppelte Identifikation ist aber nicht nur sachlich zwingend, sondern wird von Thomas auch *expressis verbis* mehrfach vollzogen, indem er die Wesenskonstituentinen der Erbsünde mit den aus der allgemeinen Sündenlehre bekannten Begriffen erklärt."

mature Thomas, both the higher and lower powers of the soul are worse in corrupt nature than pure nature. Others, like J. P. Torrell, focus on the higher powers, such as the will's loss of love of God.[29]

To clear this tangled web of issues, we need to begin with Thomas's discussion of original sin in the *Summa*. Thomas announces his plan for discussing original sin early in the *Prima Secundae*: "As will be explained later, through the sin of the first parent the supernatural gift divinely given to humanity was subtracted, and nature was left to itself (*natura est sibi relicta*). Thus we need to consider the natural reason why the motion of these members especially does not obey reason."[30] In other words, Thomas promises to explain later in the *Summa* how original sin can leave human beings with the natural disorders of human nature, including disordered concupiscence (the disobedience of the genitals being an example). He keeps his promise near the end of the *Prima secundae*, in the midst of a treatise on sin and vice more generally (qq. 71–89). Only the thirteen articles of questions 81–3 are devoted to original sin itself.

Thomas defines original sin, just as he did in the *Scriptum*, as the loss of original justice by which the will was subject to God (formally) and disordered concupiscence (materially).[31] Thomas also maintains his biological explanation of original sin's transmission, which grounds the

---

Pesch, *Theologie der Rechtfertigung bei Martin Luther und Thomas von Aquin*, 492. Pesch cites *De malo* q. 4, a. 2 and *STh* I-II, q. 82, a. 3, as the *expressis verbis* proving that the disordered concupiscence of original sin is what causes the will to be turned away from God to the mutable good.

[29] "[L]a perte de l'état d'innocence n'a pas ramené la premier homme à un chimérique état de nature pure qu'il n'a jamais connu. La nature qui demeure après le péché est celle d'un homme qui, dès son premier instant, avait Dieu pour seule fin dernière, qui était donc capable de le connaître et de l'aimer au plan surnaturel, et qui était appelé à vivre en sa communion la plus intime dans la beatitude. La fait d'être privé de la possibilité même de rejoindre sa fin le laisse dans un douloureux état d'incomplétude auquel seul le don renouvelé de la grâce pourra porter remède, comme seule elle pourra rétablir l'équilibre interne que le péché a rompu." Torrell, "Nature et grâce chez Thomas d'Aquin," 192. Torrell is cited frequently in this connection (e.g., David Decosimo, *Ethics as a Work of Charity: Thomas Aquinas and Pagan Virtue* [Stanford: Stanford University Press, 2014], 247).

[30] "[P]er peccatum primi parentis, ut infra dicetur, natura est sibi relicta, subtracto supernaturali dono quod homini divinitus erat collatum; ideo consideranda est ratio naturalis quare motus huiusmodi membrorum specialiter rationi non obedit." *STh* I-II, q. 17, a. 9, ad 3.

[31] See *STh* I-II, q. 82, a. 3. Thomas frequently calls original sin simply the lack of original justice (see *STh* I-II, q. 81, a. 5, ad 2). This is somewhat imprecise, however, because conditional immortality is part of original justice, whereas mortality and the death that inevitably follows are original sin's penalties.

distinction between original sin, the inherited sin of nature, and actual sin, the committed sin of the person. Adam ought not to have sinned and thus he ought to have transmitted original justice. Because he sinned, he passed on human nature deprived of original justice, which caused original sin when God infused the rational soul.[32] It is important not to confuse this biological explanation of original sin's transmission – which Thomas always assumes – with the question of whether Thomas thought that the guilt of original sin is best explained by comparison to a hereditary disease. We'll turn to original sin's transmission in the next section; for now it's sufficient to say that despite his denial that disease analogies *explain* the guilt of original sin, the very point of the article is that original sin must be sexually transmitted. "According to the Catholic faith, it must be held that the first sin of the first man is transmitted by way of origin to his posterity."[33] "[T]hrough the power of semen human nature is transferred from parent to child, and with nature the infection of nature."[34]

Thomas, accordingly, continued to think that original justice is a good of nature, nature's health, and that, correspondingly, the lack of original justice is bad for nature, nature's sickness and defect. The defect, however, follows from the principles of human nature. Thus Thomas reaffirms, in the *Summa theologiae* and many other places, that habitual disordered concupiscence is natural and requires the gift of original justice to restrain it.[35] There is no indication that the disordered concupiscence of original sin is somehow more severe in Thomas's mature works. It is not an act. It's more aptly called a "disposition" than a vice.[36] It does not

---

[32] "Unde sicut illa originalis iustitia traducta fuisset in posteros simul cum natura, ita etiam inordinatio opposita." *STh* I-II, q. 81, a. 2.

[33] "[S]ecundum fidem catholicam est tenendum quod primum peccatum primi hominis originaliter transit in posteros." *STh* I-II, q. 81, a. 1.

[34] *STh* I-II, q. 81, a. 1, ad 2.

[35] See *STh* I, q. 95, a. 1, discussed in the previous chapter. Thomas regularly states that disordered concupiscence is natural in his mature writings: in addition to the aforementioned *STh* I-II, q. 17, a. 9, ad 3, see *De malo* q. 5, a. 1; *Compendium theologiae* (Rome: Editori di San Tommaso, 1979), I, c. 186; and *Quaestiones disputatae de anima* (Rome: Commissio Leonina; Paris: Éditions Du Cerf, 1996), a. 8, *corpus* and ad 8.

[36] "[D]uplex est habitus. *Unus quidem quo inclinatur potentia ad agendum: sicut scientiae et virtutes habitus dicuntur. Et hoc modo peccatum originale non est habitus.* Alio modo dicitur habitus *dispositio* alicuius naturae ex multis compositae, secundum quam bene se habet vel male ad aliquid, et praecipue cum talis dispositio versa fuerit quasi in naturam: ut patet de aegritudine et sanitate. Et hoc modo peccatum originale est habitus. Est enim quaedam inordinata dispositio proveniens ex dissolutione illius harmoniae in qua consistebat ratio originalis iustitiae: sicut etiam aegritudo corporalis est quaedam inordinata dispositio corporis, secundum quam solvitur aequalitas in qua consistit ratio

directly incline one to act badly, only indirectly, insofar as original justice is removed.[37] Concupiscence is equal in every human being qua privation – one either has the perfectly ordered concupiscence of original justice or not – though different human beings will be disposed to different degrees of concupiscence later on, in accordance with their different bodies.[38] Concupiscence also varies from group to group, in that humanity's concupiscence grows worse and worse over time.[39]

What does Thomas mean, then, when he says that concupiscence is natural to the human being only insofar as it is regulated by reason?[40] The objection to which Thomas is responding argues that concupiscence could not be part of original sin because it is natural to the human being. Thomas responds by arguing that concupiscence, insofar as it is regulated by reason, is a natural good. Insofar as concupiscence is not regulated by reason, it is against nature, a natural evil. Thus, precisely because it is a natural defect, it *can* be the material cause of original sin. As we saw in the *Scriptum*, however, the natural evil of disordered concupiscence is not a moral evil per se, not the material cause of original sin, unless it is inherited from Adam. Thomas sometimes makes the same basic point by distinguishing what is natural to the human being qua animal from

---

sanitatis. Unde peccatum originale *languor naturae* dicitur." *STh* I-II, q. 82, a. 1, emphasis mine. The disposition of a complex nature is not called a habit in the way a virtue is called a habit. Thomas thus implies that original sin is likewise not called a habit the way a vice is.

[37] "[E]x peccato originali sequatur aliqua inclinatio in actum inordinatum, *non directe, sed indirecte*, scilicet per remotionem prohibentis, idest originalis iustitiae, quae prohibebat inordinatos motus: sicut etiam aegritudine corporali indirecte sequitur inclinatio ad motus corporales inordinatos. Nec debet dici quod peccatum originale sit habitus infusus; aut acquisitus per actum nisi primi parentis, non autem huius personae; sed per vitiatam originem innatus." *STh* I-II, q. 82, a. 1, ad 3, emphasis mine.

[38] "Contingit autem vires aliquas animae esse fortiores in uno quam in alio, propter diversas corporis complexiones. Quod ergo unus homo sit pronior ad concupiscendum quam alter, non est ratione peccati originalis, cum in omnibus aequaliter solvatur vinculum originalis iustitiae, et aequaliter in omnibus partes inferiores animae sibi relinquantur: sed accidit hoc ex diversa dispositione potentiarum, sicut dictum est." *STh* I-II, q. 82, a. 4, ad 1.

[39] Cf. *STh* III, q. 70, a. 2, ad 1, where Thomas argues that the gift of circumcision was not given to humanity right after the Fall because reason was still, despite original sin, fairly strong. (Salvation would still have been through the graced "doctrinam Adae," not natural faith.) By the time of Abraham, however, the "augmentum carnalis concupiscentiae" made the institution of circumcision necessary.

[40] "[Q]uia in homine concupiscibilis naturaliter regitur ratione, intantum concupiscere est homini naturale, inquantum est secundum rationis ordinem: concupiscentia autem quae transcendit limites rationis, est homini contra naturam. Et talis est concupiscentia originalis peccati." *STh* I-II, q. 82, a. 3, ad 1. See also *STh* I-II, q. 85, a. 3, ad 3.

what is natural to the human being qua rational (cf. *De malo* q. 4, a. 2, ad 1). Concupiscence is natural qua animal and unnatural qua rational; the reason concupiscence is unnatural qua rational is because it is bad for the human being considered as a whole, a natural evil, even though it follows from the principles of human nature left to themselves.

Thomas comes close to explicitly repeating this point of original sin's material identity with the principles of human nature left to themselves by posing the same question from the *Scriptum*: Would a human being created directly by God from the flesh of a human being with original sin contract original sin? His answer is the same – "No" – but here all Thomas notes is that such a human being would not be moved by Adam's generative power.[41] He does not spell out what he did in the *Scriptum*: the material defects of original sin would be present but not the sin. It would take a very strained interpretation of this passage, however, to deny that the earlier teaching is implied. Why else would Thomas raise this question? Obviously if God created a human being with original justice she would not have original sin (even the dullest of Dominicans for whom the *Summa* was written would have known *that*). And there is no evidence Thomas ever thought something less powerful than natural original justice would prevent the material defects of original sin. It seems he declined to elaborate for the sake of space.

We can now turn to question 85, on the effects of sin. It is imperative to remember, however, that the treatise on original sin ends in question 83.[42] What this means is that question 85 is not a discussion of the effects of original sin. It is a discussion of the effects of sin in general – mortal, venial, and original. When Thomas asks in a. 1 of q. 85, then, whether sin diminishes the good of nature, he is not asking about the effects of original sin. This becomes clear when we read the article carefully.

Thomas notes that the phrase "good of human nature" can refer to three things: the principles of nature and that which flows therefrom, the natural inclination to virtue, and the gift of original justice to human nature.[43] He then explains that sin relates to each good of nature in a different way.

---

[41] *STh* I-II, q. 81, a. 4. Cf. *De malo* q. 4, a. 8, *corpus*.

[42] "Unde de peccato originali dicendum est. Circa quod tria consideranda occurrunt, primo, de eius traductione [q. 81]; secundo, de eius essentia [q. 82]; tertio, de eius subiecto [q. 83]." *STh* I-II, q. 81, *prooemium*.

[43] "Respondeo dicendum quod bonum naturae humanae potest tripliciter dici. Primo, ipsa principia naturae, ex quibus natura constituitur, et proprietates ex his causatae, sicut potentiae animae et alia huiusmodi. Secundo, quia homo a natura habet inclinationem ad

The first good of nature is neither destroyed nor diminished through sin. The third good of nature was entirely destroyed by the sin of the first parent. But the middle good of nature, namely the natural inclination to virtue, is diminished by sin. The reason for this is that through human acts a certain inclination to like acts is formed (as we said earlier). When someone is inclined to one of two contraries, her inclination to the other is diminished. Therefore, because sin is contrary to virtue, it follows from the fact that the human being sins that her good of nature that is her inclination to virtue is diminished.[44]

The third good of nature, original justice, is destroyed by original sin. What about the first two goods? Neither original sin nor actual sin affects the first good, the principles of human nature, at a root level. The reason is that these principles are necessary for human existence. What about the second good of human nature, the natural inclination to virtue? This good is *diminished* by sin. Does Thomas mean that it is diminished by original sin? Context is crucial. Thomas is not speaking about the effects of original sin but of sin in general. He states that the natural inclination to virtue is diminished *because* human acts produce an inclination to like acts. This implies that the natural inclination is affected by personal, actual sin. He does not state that the natural inclination to virtue is diminished by original sin. In the reply to the second objection, he emphasizes that the diminution of the natural inclination to virtue is damaged by the variation of voluntary action.[45]

Article 2 clarifies the sense in which the natural inclination to virtue is founded in the principles of nature. Thomas argues that the inclination to virtue can be understood in respect to the end or in respect to the root. Nature is at root (*in radice*), radically speaking, unaffected by sin but is

---

virtutem, ut supra habitum est, ipsa inclinatio ad virtutem est quoddam bonum naturae. Tertio modo potest dici bonum naturae donum originalis iustitiae, quod fuit in primo homine collatum toti humanae naturae." *STh* I-II, q. 85, a. 1.

[44] "Primum igitur bonum naturae nec tollitur nec diminuitur per peccatum. Tertium vero bonum naturae totaliter est ablatum per peccatum primi parentis. Sed medium bonum naturae, scilicet ipsa naturalis inclinatio ad virtutem, diminuitur per peccatum. Per actus enim humanos fit quaedam inclinatio ad similes actus, ut supra habitum est. Oportet autem quod ex hoc quod aliquid inclinatur ad unum contrariorum, diminuatur inclinatio eius ad aliud. Unde cum peccatum sit contrarium virtuti, ex hoc ipso quod homo peccat, diminuitur bonum naturae quod est inclinatio ad virtutem." *STh* I-II, q. 85, a. 1.

[45] "[N]atura, esti sit prior quam voluntaria actio, tamen habet inclinationem ad quandam voluntariam actionem. Unde ipsa natura secundum se non variatur propter variationem voluntariae actionis: sed ipsa inclinatio variatur ex illa parte qua ordinatur ad terminum." *STh* I-II, q. 85, a. 1, ad 2.

diminished on the part of the end (*ex parte termini*), teleologically speaking.[46] Actual sin hampers *ex parte termini*, because human beings can turn away from the end and sin. Even when one has already turned from the end, one can continue to sin and place further obstacles between oneself and the end. The radical inclination to virtue remains after one has damaged it *ex parte termini*, even in the lowest levels of hell, just as a blind man's inclination to vision remains.[47] There is no indication whatsoever that original sin affects the natural inclination to virtue, either radically or *ex parte termini*. In article 3, however, we see a different sense in which the human being's relation to virtue *is* affected by original sin.

Thomas argues that the natural *ordination* to virtue is damaged when the third good of nature from article 1, original justice, is destroyed. The question of article 3 is whether weakness, ignorance, malice, and concupiscence are suitably called the wounds of nature following sin. Here is the first part of Thomas's answer:

Through original justice reason perfectly restrained the soul's lower powers, and reason itself was perfected by God and subjected to him. But this original justice was subtracted through the sin of the first parent, as was already said. And therefore all the powers of the soul were, in a sense, destitute of their proper order, by which they are naturally *ordained* to virtue, and this destitution is called a wound of nature.[48]

---

[46] "[I]nclinatio intelligitur ut media inter duo: fundatur enim sicut in radice in natura rationali, et tendit in bonum virtutis sicut in terminum et finem. Dupliciter igitur potest intelligi eius diminutio, uno modo, ex parte radicis; alio modo, ex parte termini. Primo quidem modo non diminuitur per peccatum: eo quod peccatum non diminuit ipsam naturam, ut supra dictum est." *STh* I-II, q. 85, a. 2.

[47] *STh* I-II, q. 85, a. 2, ad 3.

[48] "[P]er iustitiam originalem perfecte ratio continebat inferiores animae vires, et ipsa ratio a Deo perficiebatur, ei subiecta. Haec autem originalis iustitia subtracta est per peccatum primi parentis, sicut iam dictum est. Et ideo omnes vires animae remanent quodammodo destitutae proprio ordine, quo naturaliter *ordinantur* ad virtutem, et ipsa destitutio vulneratio naturae dicitur. Sunt autem quatuor potentiae animae quae possunt esse subiecta virtutum, ut supra dictum est: scilicet ratio, in qua est prudentia; voluntas, in qua est iustitia; irascibilis, in qua est fortitudo; concupiscibilis, in qua est temperantia. Inquantum ergo ratio destituitur suo ordine ad verum, est vulnus ignorantiae; inquantum vero voluntas destituitur ordine ad bonum, est vulnus malitiae; inquantum vero irascibilis destituitur suo ordine ad arduum, est vulnus infirmitatis; inquantum vero concupiscentia destituitur ordine ad delectabile moderatum ratione, est vulnus concupiscentiae. Sic igitur ita quatuor sunt vulnera inflicta toti humanae naturae ex peccato primi parentis." *STh* I-II, q. 85, a. 3, emphasis mine.

Original justice subjected the lower powers of the soul to the higher powers and reason to God. It was also that by human beings are naturally ordained (*ordinantur*) – Thomas does not say "inclined" (*inclinantur*) – to virtue. By the sin of the first parent, original justice was destroyed. All the powers of the soul were wounded, because original justice rightly ordered all the powers of the soul. They are destitute of the proper order in which original justice consisted, the proper order that naturally ordained them to virtue. Thomas is not claiming that nature is wounded with reference to a purely natural state; he has already stated that the principles of nature are at root unaffected by original and actual sin and implied that, *ex parte termini*, they are only affected by actual sin. Original sin wounds nature with reference to the gracious state of original justice, by destroying the graced ordination to virtue.

Thomas then argues, again, that because the natural inclination to virtue is diminished by actual sin, the same wounds of nature from original sin can also be caused by actual sins.[49] For example, concupiscence is a wound of nature from original sin, aggravated by actual sin, thus wounding the inclination to virtue. Thomas uses the word "*ordinatio*" to describe the effect original sin has on human virtue, as opposed to "*inclinatio*," because he denies original sin has any effect on the inclination to virtue, either radically or teleologically.[50] It is also worth noting that Thomas would claim Job had both original sin and the natural inclination to virtue in the womb.[51]

Question 85 ends with Thomas arguing that although death is natural to the human being on the part of matter, God fixed the defects of nature

---

[49] "Sed quia *inclinatio* ad bonum virtutis in unoquoque diminuitur per *peccatum actuale*, ut ex dictis patet, et ista sunt quatuor vulnera ex aliis peccatis consequentia: inquantum scilicet per peccatum et ratio hebetatur, praecipue in agendis; et voluntas induratur ad bonum; et maior difficultas bene agendi accrescit; et concupiscentia magis exardescit." *STh* I-II, q. 85, a. 3, emphasis mine.

[50] J. B. Kors rightly argued that q. 85 does not imply that original sin causes a diminution of the inclination to virtue that would be present in pure nature. Kors's argument was stronger than he knew, however: he didn't notice that Thomas refused to speak of original sin harming the inclination to virtue. Kors thus posited a "double inclination naturelle à la vertu, l'une résultant de la pure nature, l'autre qui provient d'un don surajouté," arguing that only the latter is harmed by original sin. Kors, *La Justice primitive et le péché originel d'après S. Thomas*, 161.

[51] "[M]iseratio de qua Iob loquitur, non significat virtutem infusam: sed quandum *inclinationem naturalem* ad actum huius virtutis." *STh* III, q. 27, a. 6, ad 3, emphasis mine. The objection claimed that because Job speaks of receiving mercy in the womb (Job 31:18 in the Vulgate), we should say he was sanctified there. Thomas denies that Job was sanctified but affirms his possession of the inclination to virtue.

at nature's institution by giving the gift of justice.[52] Since Thomas retired from theology before writing the eschatology of the *Summa*, he didn't address original sin's punishment in infants. Still, there is noteworthy material in two later works.[53] In the *Compendium theologiae*, Thomas argues that it is just for God to permit Adam's children to suffer for his sin because he has only allowed them to suffer the loss of supernatural gifts.[54] Any stricter punishment, Thomas implies, would be contrary to the order of justice. The effect of Adam's sin on his posterity is only their loss of the supernatural gift of original justice, which results in their original sin. In the *De malo*, Thomas argues that the eternal punishment of this inherited privation should correspond to the privation itself.

The eternal punishment of original sin is the lightest of all punishments, the loss of what original justice disposed the human being to receive: the supernatural beatific vision.[55] There are three reasons, moreover, why infants do not deserve any pains of sense for original sin. Because original sin is only the sin of nature, infants lose nothing that is theirs by nature; they lose only things that are above their nature, like grace.[56] The second reason Thomas gives is especially illuminating:

The punishment is proportioned to the crime. Actual mortal sin, in which is found an aversion from the immutable good and conversion to the mutable good, deserves both the punishment of condemnation (namely the loss of the divine vision corresponding to the aversion) and the punishment of sense (corresponding to the conversion). *But in original sin there is no conversion*, only aversion, or rather something like aversion, namely the soul's loss of original justice.[57]

---

[52] *STh* I-II, q. 85, a. 6.

[53] Jean-Pierre Torrell, *Initiation à saint Thomas d'Aquin: Sa personne et son oeuvre* (Fribourg: Cerf, 2002), 293–8, discusses the difficulty of dating the *De malo* exactly but argues that the first fifteen questions were published in 1270, stemming from questions Thomas disputed in Paris starting in 1269. The *Compendium theologiae* is also difficult to date; Torrell suggests (p. 240) that the mid-1260s is most likely.

[54] "Nec hoc est contra ordinem iustitie, quasi Deo puniente in filiis quod primus parens deliquit, quia ista pena non est nisi subtractio eorum que supernaturaliter primo homini divinitus sunt concessa." *Compendium theologiae* I, c. 195.

[55] *De malo* q. 5, a. 1. Original sin's penalty is the "mitissima omnium penarum sola carentia uisionis diuine, in quantum uisio diuine essentie est quoddam bonum omnino supernaturale." *De malo* q. 5, a. 1, ad 3.

[56] "Quod igitur detrimentum aliquod patiatur aliqua persona in his que sunt supra naturam, potest contingere uel ex uitio nature uel etiam ex uitio persone; quod autem detrimentum patiatur in his que sunt nature, hoc non uidetur posse contingere nisi propter uitium proprium persone." *De malo* q. 5, a. 2.

[57] "[P]ena proportionatur culpe; et ideo peccato actuali mortali, in quo inuenitur auersio ab incommutabili bono et conuersio ad bonum commutabile, debetur et pena dampni, scilicet carentia uisionis diuine respondens auersioni, et pena sensus respondens

In original sin, unlike actual mortal sin, there is no act of aversion from God and conversion to the mutable good. There is something *like* or analogous to aversion, namely the loss of original justice, by which the will was subjected to God and ordered to the beatific vision. But there is no conversion to the mutable good; the natural orientation to God remains.[58] Thomas proceeds to repeat roughly the same account of infants' natural happiness in hell as he did in the *Scriptum*. With a natural knowledge of God, infants will not be sad at all; they will instead enjoy beatitude in general.[59] The principal difference is that now Thomas argues infants will not know they lack the *lumen gloriae*.[60]

Those who die without sanctifying grace are not the only human beings with original sin to avoid actual sin. Thomas's view of Mary in

conuersioni. *Set in peccato originali non est conuersio*, set sola auersio, uel aliquid auersioni respondens, scilicet destitutio anime a iustitia originali." *De malo* q. 5, a. 2, emphasis mine.

[58] Thus although it is true, as Pesch claimed, that Thomas speaks at times of the disordered concupiscence of original sin "converting" the human being to the mutable good, such statements should be understood in light of Thomas's analogy between original and actual sin (which we will discuss in more depth in the next chapter). The act of mortal sin involves prioritizing a created good over God, which "formally" is turning away from God and "materially" is turning to the created good itself. There is something similar in original sin: the will lacks rectitude and grace; the lower powers are not subject to the will. The lack of rectitude and grace is, as it were, the form; the habitual disordered concupiscence is, as it were, the matter. The matter of original sin is said to "convert" to the mutable good because habitual concupiscence is a disposition to later acts of concupiscence, which will pull the sinner toward conversion to the mutable good prior to the sinner's consent.

[59] "[A]nime puerorum naturali quidem cognitione non carent, qualis debetur anime separate secundum suam naturam, sed carent supernaturali cognitione que hic in hobis per fidem plantatur, eo quod nec hic fidem habuerunt in actu, nec sacramentum fidei susceperunt. Pertinet autem ad naturalem cognitionem quod anima sciat se propter beatitudinem creatam, et quod beatitudo consistit in adeptione perfecti boni. Sed quod illud bonum perfectum ad quod homo factus est, sit illa gloria quam sancti possident, est supra cognitionem naturalem ... Que quidem reuelatio ad fidem pertinet. Et ideo se priuari tali bono anime puerorum non cognoscunt, et propter hoc non dolent; set hoc quod per naturam habent, absque dolore possident." *De malo* q. 5, a. 3. "[A]nime puerorum in peccato originali decedentium cognoscunt quidem beatitudinem in generali secundum communem rationem, non autem in speciali. Et ideo de eius amissione non dolent." *De malo* q. 5, a. 3, ad 1.

[60] They are separated from God "quantum ad amissionem glorie quem ignorant, non tamen quantum ad participationem naturalium bonorum que cognoscunt." *De malo* q. 5, a. 3, ad 4. For helpful account of Thomas's development on this point, see Christopher Beiting, "The Idea of Limbo in Thomas Aquinas," *The Thomist* 62 (1998), 217–44. For a discussion of Thomas's view of limbo in its thirteenth-century context, see Serge-Thomas Bonino, "La théorie des limbes et le mystère du surnaturel chez saint Thomas d'Aquin," *Revue Thomiste* 101 (2001), 131–66.

the *Tertia pars* is also perhaps worth noting. Mary must have contracted original sin, Thomas argues, but she was sanctified in the womb. Just like those sanctified by baptism, the personal effects of her original sin were removed by the bestowal of grace, while the corruption of her nature remained. Until Christ's conception Mary's concupiscence was "bound" by God so that she had no actual sin or impulse toward it.[61] Even late in life, then, Thomas denied any necessary link between original and actual sin.[62] If Thomas's mature treatment implies the same view of original sin's effects as the *Scriptum*, why does Thomas seem to assume a different account in the treatise on grace?

GRACE AND ORIGINAL SIN

Thomas devotes nineteen questions to law after finishing his discussion of sin. The treatise on law ends with the new law of the gospel, written on the hearts of believers by the Holy Spirit.[63] The treatise on grace (109–14) is a deeper exploration of the grace of the new law, sanctifying grace (*gratia gratum faciens*). The primary sense of the word "grace" in this treatise is sanctifying grace; Thomas defines it as such.[64] The treatise begins with a question on the need for grace. Thomas frequently adverts to the distinction between the prelapsarian powers human beings had in the state of integral nature (*statu naturae integrae*) and their vitiated powers in the state of corrupt nature (*statu naturae corruptae*). As a result, many commentators have assumed that the question is a discussion, in greater detail, of the effects of original sin. The powers in integral

---

[61] For Thomas's argument that Mary was sanctified in the womb after having contracted original sin, see *STh* III, q. 27, aa. 1–2. He goes on to argue that it would be somewhat derogatory to the dignity of Christ for Mary's nature to be healed before the incarnation; thus Mary's nature was corrupt until Christ's conception. She lacked original justice: she still had materially disordered concupiscence, the *fomes peccati*. Her concupiscence was "bound" (*ligatus*) by a special divine gift, so that she had neither actual sin nor any disordered impulse toward sin (*STh* III, q. 27, a. 3).

[62] If the natural love for God is lost, then the state of mortal sin follows. There is no moment of existence when one could stand teleologically aloof, deliberating between ultimate ends without acting for one. To exist is to act for an end. "Every agent acts for an end," as Thomas says in q. 109, a. 6 (and throughout his work). The end is the proper object of the will (*STh* I-II, q. 8, a. 2); the end is always presupposed in choice, which is of the means (*STh* I-II, q. 13, a. 3). For Thomas, there are no demigods between God and creature: the end must be either God (by nature or grace) or a creature.

[63] The treatise on law presupposes that only gracious gifts have been forfeited by original sin. See *STh* I-II, q. 98, a. 4, ad 3.

[64] *STh* I-II, q. 110, a. 2.

nature are thought to be "purely natural," though forfeited by original sin, whereas the moral ability in corrupt nature is thought to be what remains after original sin in the unbaptized. This assumption is doubly wrong.

Integral nature is not pure nature and corrupt nature is not nature with original sin. To understand this, we need to establish a more fundamental point, frequently ignored by commentators on the treatise on grace, perhaps because it comes in the treatise on sin. In the latter's last article, Thomas asks whether a human being can have original sin and venial sin without mortal sin. His concern is eschatological: we know that infants who die unbaptized will be excluded from heaven, though they will enjoy a natural happiness in limbo. But what of the unbaptized who reach the age of reason? If they do their best, can they too have a happy stay in hell? Or, given their disordered concupiscence, will they commit (at least) venial sin and suffer sensibly in the inferno? Despite his belief that venial sins deserve sense punishment, Thomas argues no one in hell suffers for venial sin without mortal sin. But this is not due to nature. Grace intervenes.

Human beings with only original sin will not commit any venial sins.[65] Before the use of reason no one commits sin properly speaking, even if she commits a generically sinful act (as a toddler tells a lie, for example). Then the situation changes:

When the human being begins to have the use of reason, she is no longer excused from the guilt of mortal and venial sin. At that time, the first thing that occurs to the thinking human being is self-deliberation. If she orders herself to her due end, through grace the remission of original sin follows. If she does not order herself to her due end when she reaches the age of reason, however, she sins mortally, not doing what is in herself (*faciens quod in se est*).[66]

Upon reaching the age of reason, the human being is at a crossroads: she either pursues her due end or not. It is so obvious to Thomas that the due end is God that he doesn't bother to state it in the corpus, but he does in

---

[65] The human being with sanctifying grace but without original justice is able to commit venial sin (*STh* I-II, q. 88, a. 1), though in original justice venial sin was impossible (*STh* I-II, q. 89, a. 3).

[66] "Cum vero usum rationis habere inceperit, non omnino excusatur a culpa venialis et mortalis peccati. Sed primum quod tunc homini cogitandum occurrit, est deliberare de seipso. Et si quidem seipsum ordinaverit ad debitum finem, per gratiam consequetur remissionem originalis peccati. Si vero non ordinet seipsum ad debitum finem, secundum quod in illa aetate est capax discretionis, peccabit mortaliter, non faciens quod in se est." *STh* I-II, q. 89, a. 6. See also *Scriptum* II, d. 42, q. 1, a. 5, ad 7.

the reply to the third objection.[67] If she follows God, she will be given sanctifying grace. If not, she sins mortally. Other than claiming they ought to order their lives to God, Thomas doesn't say precisely what human beings with reason are supposed to do. Commentators, however, have proposed a wide variety of proposals, corresponding to their diverse views of Thomas's take on original sin and the possibility (or lack thereof) of congruous merit and natural theology. For the purposes of this chapter, it matters little whether the ability of *faciens quod in se est* is from nature or sanctifying grace,[68] whether it involves a conscious knowledge of God, or indeed any "natural theology" properly so-called.[69] Also

---

[67] "[A]b aliis peccatis mortalibus potest puer incipiens habere usum rationis, per aliquod tempus abstinere: sed a peccato omissionis praedictae non liberatur, nisi quam cito potest, se convertat ad Deum. Primum enim quod occurrit homini discretionem habenti est quod de seipso cogitet, ad quem alia ordinet sicut ad finem: finis enim est prior in intentione. Et ideo hoc est tempus pro quo obligatur ex Dei praecepto affirmativo." *STh* I-II, q. 89, 6, ad 3. Cf. *De malo* q. 5, a. 2, ad 8. Readers who assume there is no sense in which God is the natural end or that original sin has ruptured the orientation to God tend to miss this. For example, Brian Shanley, "Aquinas on Pagan Virtue," *The Thomist* 63 (1999), 572–7, argues that Thomas thinks the civic good is the due end. Thomas, though, states that it is God.

[68] Adriano Oliva attributes it to nature. "La contemplation des philosophes selon Thomas d'Aquin," *Revue des sciences philosophiques et théologiques* 96 (2012), 610–11. Joseph Wawrykow, *God's Grace and Human Action: "Merit" in the Theology of Thomas Aquinas* (Notre Dame: University of Notre Dame Press, 1995), 199 and passim, argues that Thomas, in his mature period, attributes the whole *ordo salutis* to grace, including the *faciens quod in se est* and the preparation for grace.

[69] Lawrence Dewan, in dialogue with Cajetan and Maritain, suggests that this obligation to follow God stems from a conscious, explicit knowledge of God, because Thomas "envisages the young human mind as capable of knowing God in a conscious way, and of considering God as a source of law." "Natural Law and the First Act of Freedom: Maritain Revisited," in *Wisdom, Law, and Virtue: Essays in Thomistic Ethics* (New York: Fordham University Press, 2008), 241. Yet he indecisively admits that in the first act of freedom, "such a person is doing *not only* what is natural but also what is supernatural" (p. 489, n. 97). Bruce Marshall has argued that for Thomas, strictly speaking, there is no natural knowledge of God apart from faith *in uia*. See his "*Quod Scit Una Uetula*: Aquinas on the Nature of Theology," in *The Theology of Thomas Aquinas*, 1–35; "Faith and Reason Reconsidered: Aquinas and Luther on Deciding What Is True," *The Thomist* 63.1 (1999), 1–48; "Aquinas as Postliberal Theologian," *The Thomist* 53.3 (1989), 353–402. It seems to me that Marshall's view is compatible with the reading of Thomas I am offering, though perhaps Marshall's reading (as well as "thin" views of the obligations generated by natural law, like that of John Bowlin, "Nature's Grace: Aquinas and Wittgenstein on Natural Law and Moral Knowledge," in *Grammar and Grace: Reformulations of Aquinas and Wittgenstein*, ed. Jeffrey Stout and Robert MacSwain [London: SCM, 2004]) would require viewing the offer of grace coming immediately to the one who reaches reason. Alternatively, perhaps one could agree with Marshall, hold that the obligation does come from nature, yet deny that the "knowledge" required to fulfill it meets the bar required for a genuine natural theology.

irrelevant is whether the faith resulting from such grace is implicit or explicit, or how many people Thomas thinks receive grace.[70] What matters for us is the assumption this passage reveals.

No one *in uia* has only original sin for long. No one who reaches the age of reason remains without mortal sin or sanctifying grace. This is not because of some metaphysical impossibility stemming from the effects of original sin, as if original sin rendered mortal sin necessary, or venial sin without mortal sin impossible. No, first and foremost it follows from God's global providential care: the effects of original sin are curtailed by grace. This is why Thomas, despite his belief that original sin does not rupture the natural orientation to God, is profoundly uninterested in speculating about original sinners following him by *nature*. De facto, the population enjoying the natural but not supernatural end is limited to limbo: those who die with only original sin. De facto, the population pursuing the natural end without mortal sin is limited to unbaptized infants and – if the *faciens quod in se est* is natural – to whoever has reached the age of reason and is in the process of "self-deliberation." Alternatively, if the *faciens quod in se est* is from supernatural grace, then no human with reason ever acts for the natural end alone, for grace can be freely received instantaneously.[71] Either way, Thomas's theology assumes for all practical purposes that the population pursuing the natural end is *zero*.

This assumption underlies Thomas's entire moral theology, which treats distinctively human action, action with reason, and "free choice."[72] His account of unbelievers' imperfect happiness and acquired virtue, for example, assumes their imperfection arises not only from lacking supernatural gifts; they have turned to mortal sin, damaging their natural inclination to virtue.[73] This assumption is also essential to understanding the treatise on grace. Because grace providentially restricts sin's effects,

---

[70] Citing *STh* II-II, q. 2, a. 7, ad 3, Thomas O'Meara argues that Thomas thinks those who have never explicitly heard the gospel or received a special revelation can be saved through an implicit faith in Christ. *Thomas Aquinas, Theologian* (Notre Dame: University of Notre Dame Press, 1997), 235. See also *STh* II-II, q. 10, a. 4, ad 3, where Thomas claims Cornelius exemplifies implicit faith in Acts 10.

[71] See *Scriptum* II d. 29, q. 1, a. 2; *STh* I, q. 62, a. 3; and *STh* I, q. 95, a. 1.

[72] *STh* I-II, prologus. "[A]ctionum quae ab homine aguntur, illae solae proprie dicuntur *humanae*, quae sunt propriae hominis inquantum est homo." *STh* I-II, q. 1, a. 1.

[73] For Thomas's discussion of imperfect happiness, see *STh* I-II, q. 3, a. 2 and 4. See also *STh* I-II, q. 5, a. 5, where Thomas links imperfect happiness to the achievement of virtue. Thomas's account of the virtues assumes that unbelievers have turned to mortal sin: the imperfection of natural virtue is not only due to original sin. In Thomas's discussion of

we won't find Thomas speaking of human beings with only original sin. Indeed, the treatise on grace has nothing to do with the effects of original sin. It has everything to do with human nature *before* and *after* original sin.

"Human nature can be considered in two ways. In one way, in its integrity, as it was in the first parent before sin. In another way, as it is corrupted in us after the sin of the first parent."[74] Integral nature refers to human nature as it was in our first parents. Since their nature had the gift of original justice, it's clear that integral nature is not equivalent to pure nature.[75] Moreover, in integral nature, due to the right regulation of concupiscence, all mortal and venial sin could be avoided.[76] In pure nature, however, concupiscence would not be rightly regulated. Is the state of integral nature identical to original justice, then? No, Adam and Eve received sanctifying grace as the root cause of their original justice. What does Thomas mean by integral nature, then, if not Adam and Eve's original justice or pure nature?

Integral nature probably refers to human nature with the powers of natural original justice. Because he is now confident that the historical state of original justice included sanctifying grace – natural original justice was never a reality – Thomas calls nature with rightly ordered concupiscence and subjection to God but without sanctifying grace "integral nature."[77] He speculates about the powers of such a state because it

---

prudence, for example, the imperfect prudence in sinners can be directed to particular goods only, not the common good of the universe, God. See *STh* II-II, q. 47, a. 13.

[74] "[N]atura hominis dupliciter potest considerari: uno modo, in sui integritate, sicut fuit in primo parente ante peccatum; alio modo, secundum quod est corrupta in nobis post peccatum primi parentis." *STh* I-II, q. 109, a. 2.

[75] Assuming, that is, that a state of pure nature is one in which human beings only have the principles of nature and that which follows from them – and not any preter- or supernatural gifts. See Chapter 8, section on "The Communal Distinction," for further discussion of the concept of pure nature.

[76] "Secundum statum quidem naturae integrae, etiam sine gratia habituali, poterat homo non peccare mortaliter nec venialiter." *STh* I-II, q. 109, a. 8. Thomas consistently taught that disordered concupiscence and the (ordinary) necessity of venial sin are on a par; the latter follows the former necessarily unless God intervenes, as he did with Mary. This is clear from a. 8 and numerous other places. See *De veritate*, q. 25, a. 7, *sed contra*.

[77] This coheres with my hypothesis from Chapter 2 concerning the (inconsistent) development of Thomas's account of original justice. Thomas changed his view of personal original justice's formal cause without applying it to other areas of his theology, such as the disposition to justice that was supposed to be transmitted, or, in this case, the need for grace in moral theology. It seems that if personal original justice requires sanctifying grace because concupiscence cannot be rightly ordered without grace, then integral nature would also require sanctifying grace. Regardless of how one

allows him to give an account of the precise need for sanctifying grace. Thus articles 2, 4, and 8 argue that the human being in integral nature, without sanctifying grace, can do the proportionate good, fulfill the law, and avoid all sin. To do these things *in charity* requires sanctifying grace. Since integral nature (as natural justice) does not follow from the principles of human nature, Thomas has not claimed that original sin causes human beings to lose any goods following the principles of human nature.

Still, however, there is a difficulty. Article 3 seems to argue that the natural love for God following nature's principles *has* been forfeited by original sin. The question of q. 109, a. 3, is whether the human being without sanctifying grace can love God above all things by her natural powers. The answer is yes: the human being can love God above all things *ex solis naturalibus*.[78] In the *corpus* Thomas explains how nature's corruption interferes with this love. Thomas begins by referring us to his discussion of love in his angelology: angels and human beings can love God above all by nature, without sanctifying grace. Otherwise, natural love would be perverse and charity would not perfect but destroy nature.[79] Indeed, every created nature naturally loves its partial good for the sake of the common good, God. At this point, Thomas is speaking

interprets Thomas's view of the formal cause of original justice, however, it is clear that he denied that rightly ordered concupiscence follows from the principles of nature, and thus it is clear that integral nature cannot be identified with pure nature.

[78] "[P]rimus homo in solis naturalibus constitutus fuit, ut a quibusdam ponitur. In quo statu manifestum est quod aliqualiter Deum dilexit. Sed non dilexit Deum aequaliter sibi, vel minus se: quia secundum hoc peccasset. Ergo dilexit Deum supra se. Ergo homo ex solis naturalibus potest Deum diligere plus quam se, et super omnia." *STh* I-II, q. 109, a. 3, *sed contra*. Here in the *sed contra*, Thomas argues from a view that is not his own: Adam was made *in solis naturalibus*. Thomas himself holds that Adam was created in grace. His point is that regardless of one's position on the debated question of whether Adam had sanctifying grace at the very beginning of his existence, the human being by nature loves God above all.

[79] "[S]icut supra dictum est ... circa naturalem dilectionem angelorum diversae opiniones sunt positae; homo in statu naturae integrae poterat operari virtute suae naturae bonum quod est sibi connaturale, absque superadditione gratuiti doni, licet non absque auxilio Dei moventis. Diligere autem Deum super omnia est quiddam connaturale homini; et etiam cuilibet creaturae non solum rationali, sed irrationali et etiam inanimatae, secundum modum amoris qui unicuique creaturae competere potest. Cuius ratio est quia unicuique naturale est quod appetat et amet aliquid, secundum quod aptum natum est esse: sic enim *agit unumquodque prout aptum natum est* ... Manifestum est autem quod bonum partis est propter bonum totius. Unde etiam naturali appetitu vel amore unaquaeque res particularis amat bonum suum proprium propter bonum commune totius universi, quod est Deus. Unde et Dionysius dicit ... quod *Deus convertit omnia ad amorem sui ipsius*." *STh* I-II, q. 109, a. 3. See *STh* I, q. 60, a. 5, for Thomas's discussion of angelic love.

of a natural power to love God. He then, however, changes the terms of the discussion and refers us to integral nature:

The human being in the state of integral nature referred the love of self and all other things to the love of God as end. In this way she loved God more than herself and above all. But in the state of corrupt nature the human being recedes from this love according to the appetite of her rational will, which, because of the corruption of her nature, follows its private good, unless it is healed by the grace of God. And thus the human being in the state of integral nature did not need the gift of grace superadded to her natural goods to love God naturally above all (though she needed the help of God moving her to this natural love). But in the state of corrupt nature, the human being needs the help of grace healing her nature to do even this.[80]

The human being in integral nature did love God above all; the human being in corrupt nature does not – *unless* she is healed by grace. Is Thomas implying that because of original sin, the natural orientation to God is lost and every human being begins existence following her private good, in a state of mortal sin? Reading Thomas this way is not impossible. He does state that in corrupt nature the human being needs sanctifying grace to love God with a natural love. The first difficulty with this reading should be clear from this chapter's argument thus far: if Thomas had taught this, as Adriano Oliva observes, "his entire doctrine of original sin would have been subverted."[81] I would argue, moreover, that the context we've

---

[80] "[H]omo in statu naturae integrae dilectionem sui ipsius referebat ad amorem Dei sicut ad finem, et similiter dilectionem omnium aliarum rerum. Et ita Deum diligebat plus quam seipsum, et super omnia. Sed in statu naturae corruptae homo ab hoc deficit secundum appetitum voluntatis rationalis, quae propter corruptionem naturae sequitur bonum privatum, nisi sanetur per gratiam Dei. Et ideo dicendum est quod homo in statu naturae integrae non indigebat dono gratiae superadditae naturalibus bonis ad diligendum Deum naturaliter super omnia; licet indigeret auxilio Dei ad hoc eum moventis. Sed in statu naturae corruptae indiget homo etiam ad hoc auxilio gratiae naturam sanantis." *STh* I-II, q. 109, a. 3.

[81] I agree that the natural love for God remains in those with only original sin. It seems to me, however, that Oliva's explanation muddies the waters a bit. He suggests that for Thomas, human beings with original sin normally ("normalement") do not love God by nature, though they still can with difficulty ("bien que difficilement"). As such, Thomas thinks the exercise ("l'exercise") of loving God naturally is rare but possible, because the root capacity ("capacité radicale") remains. All from Oliva, "La contemplation des philosophes selon Thomas d'Aquin," 609. The problem with this suggestion is that Thomas argues that everyone either sins mortally or receives grace before they have a chance to sin venially, implying a quick, if not immediate division between adults in mortal sin and sanctifying grace. The numerical percentage of those who turn to God in the first act of freedom is not at issue (why would Thomas have claimed to know such a thing?). Moreover, it is not enough to say the radical capacity to love God remains in

established in this section allows us to see that this article is not concerned with the effects of original sin.

The *Secunda pars* is concerned not with infant action but with human action with reason. As we have seen, only twenty questions earlier Thomas claimed that all the unbaptized with the use of reason either turn to God, receiving sanctifying grace, or commit mortal sin. Here, Thomas speaks of human beings with reason in corrupt nature: each one has turned away from God by *personal* mortal sin, unless she is healed by grace (*nisi sanetur*). Thomas's wording implies he is speaking of personal sin: the will recedes (*deficit*) from God to follow its private good. If the will in corrupt nature were automatically following its private good by virtue of original sin, there would be no need to recede from God; it would already be following its private good. Moreover, the healing Thomas speaks of need not only refer to the human being who has already sunk into mortal sin. As we have seen, Thomas frequently speaks of original sin itself as analogous to a sickness (*STh* I-II, q. 82, a. 1). Thomas has not argued that loving God in corrupt nature is metaphysically impossible, as though infants with original sin already follow their private good in mortal sin. No, loving God without grace is providentially impossible for those with reason *in uia*: whoever lacks grace has committed mortal sin.

This reading helps make sense of the rest of the treatise, which assumes that all with reason in this life are either in mortal sin or sanctifying grace and that those in mortal sin are there by *personal* fault. Thomas's discussion of whether grace is necessary to avoid sin is instructive. In integral nature all sin could be avoided. In corrupt nature before grace, each individual mortal sin can be avoided, but it is impossible to avoid every mortal sin for a long time. Why? As the first objection has it, it seems that mortal sin must be

---

original sin. Garrigou-Lagrange et al. would agree, despite their exaggerated view of the effects of original sin. The question is whether the capacity remains *ex parte termini*. Another possible interpretation of this article compatible with my view of original sin's effects was suggested by Cajetan: we need to distinguish "having God as the ultimate end of an act" from "loving God above all things" (see his commentary on *STh* I-II, q. 109, a. 3). Infants retain the former, as the ultimate end of their being is God qua penultimate end, but (says Cajetan) Thomas doesn't think this suffices to say they love God above all things. This interpretation has the advantage of avoiding the absurdities of attributing pride to infants, as well as the advantage of appearing to take what Thomas says in the *corpus* quite literally: there is no one in corrupt nature, not even the infant, who loves God above all things. The difficulty, though, is that Thomas's principles imply that having God as the ultimate end of an action *just is* what it means to love God above all things; this is why loving God above all things extends "etiam … irrationali et etiam inanimatae," like rocks.

avoidable. Thomas, in the *corpus*, assumes that the human being without grace is in a state of mortal sin, though she can avoid individual mortal sins. In the reply to the first objection, though, he argues that it is the personal fault of the one who has not received grace for not preparing for grace.[82] The implication is that the first free act need not have been a mortal sin – even after turning to mortal sin, the sinner can avoid individual mortal sins – but that those who do not commit mortal sin receive grace.

If the reading I am offering here is broadly correct, Thomas's teaching was destined to be controversial. The claim that the subject of original sin is oriented to God is debatable, as is his view of providence. If Thomas held that the connection between doing what is in oneself and the reception of sanctifying grace is itself from grace and applies globally, there is the controversial implication that sanctifying grace is at work outside the sacraments. If, however, Thomas held that grace comes to those who do what is in themselves by nature, the question of Semipelagianism also looms. (Thomas himself seems to have been motivated by problems he saw in the traditional Augustinian doctrine of hell. It would be unjust for God, Thomas argues, to condemn children to an eternity of sadness, and it makes no sense to claim that the God who made satisfaction for the sins of the world damns pagans without giving them an opportunity for faith.[83]) In any case, there is no necessary leap from the view that nature

---

[82] "[A]ntequam hominis ratio, in qua est peccatum mortale, reparetur per gratiam iustificantem, potest singula peccata mortalia vitare, et secundum aliquod tempus: quia non est necesse quod continuo peccet in actu. Sed quod diu maneat absque peccato mortali, esse non potest." *STh* I-II, q. 109, a. 8. "[H]omo potest vitare singulos actus peccati: non tamen omnes, nisi per gratiam, ut dictum est. Et tamen quia ex eius defectu est quod homo se ad gratiam habendam non praeparet, per hoc a peccato non excusatur, quod sine gratia peccatum vitare non potest." *STh* I-II, q. 109, a. 8, ad 1. What was said about the *faciens quod in se est* (see n. 65) applies, *mutatis mutandis*, to the preparation for grace. Regardless of whether the preparation itself is from sanctifying grace, it is personal, not original fault that leads to mortal sin.

[83] More work is needed on Aquinas's reception history. In a brief discussion of post-Tridentine Catholic views of original sin (including the Salmanticenses and Billuart), Gross notes with surprise that they abandoned Thomas's view that infants know and love God in limbo. "Erstaunlicherweise hat sich von den hier befragten Thomisten nur Suarez des Aquinaten optimistische Beurteilung des Loses ungetauft verstorbener Kinder einigermaßen zu eigen gemacht. Die übrigen sprechen den kindern eine natürliche Seligkeit ab, weil sie für unvereinbar halten mit dem Zustand der Gottesferne jener Kinder. Diese bleiben nach ihnen für immer, auch nach der Auferstehung, im unterirdischen finsteren Limbus, ohne dort jedoch Sinnesstrafe zu erdulden noch große Traurigkeit zu empfinden." Gross, *Geschichte des Erbsündendogmas*, v. 4, 151–2. Might this signify a rejection of his doctrine of original sin? When exactly did this Augustinian turn among Thomists begin?

survives to the view that nature can merit salvation. Moreover, nature cannot avoid sin. As Richard Shenk notes, "The nature that is not destroyed by grace, far from being the self-glorifying nature that the critics of analogy feared, was the nature that would experience its own failings."[84] And as Bruce Marshall has recently argued, in the context of explicating the irreducibly supernatural character of the virtue of religion in Aquinas, "[h]uman nature is made for a good that it cannot achieve on its own, but only with the constant help of the good it seeks, the triune God himself."[85] All this, in turn, raises further thorny questions about whether nature has any integrity of its own (some of which will be addressed in Chapter 8). For now, we need to move on to our final chapter focused on Thomas. What did he think about original guilt?

---

[84] Schenk, "Analogy as the *discrimen naturae et gratiae*," 188.
[85] Bruce D. Marshall, "Religion and Election: Aquinas on Natural Law, Judaism, and Salvation in Christ," *Nova et Vetera*, English edition, 14.1 (2016), 95.

4

Aquinas on Original Guilt

Contemporary discussions of original sin often separate the concepts of original sin and original guilt. Oliver Crisp, for example, suggests that the doctrine of original sin does not necessarily include original guilt, the view that "the guilt incurred by Adam (and Eve) for their primal sin is imputed or otherwise transferred to all their descendants."[1] One can affirm that infants are born with sin and need Christ's saving grace to avoid perishing, but this is not necessarily to affirm that infants are guilty or stand condemned by God. Be that as it may, most medieval theologians – with the exception of Peter Abelard and his followers – held that there was a tight link between original sin and original guilt, even as they denied that infants are guilty in the same sense as Adam. This was, as we saw in Chapter 1, the view of Anselm of Canterbury and Peter Lombard. Thomas agreed. Original guilt is necessary for original sin, but infants are not guilty of Adam's act of sin.

This chapter focuses, first, on Thomas's arguments to that effect. We will see that he has a thin account of original guilt. Infants are guilty because Adam should have transmitted original justice to them. Adam's failure to do so renders their lack of justice "partially voluntary" (a phrase that is mine but which is intended to capture a concept of Thomas's). Second, I will discuss Thomas's account of the analogical character of the predication of the word "sin." Third, we turn to the concrete analogies Thomas deployed to render his view of original guilt intelligible. Thomas struggled to come up with an adequate analogy to illustrate this

[1] Crisp, "On Original Sin," 6.

peculiar form of guilt. Fourth, I will argue that Thomas's account of original guilt is inadequate, because the moral status of a habit cannot depend on the moral status of its efficient cause. Thus even if my argument from Chapter 2 regarding the transmission of grace is unsound, we still have good reason to reject the precise way Thomas formulated his account of original sin. Original sin cannot be the lack of due original justice in the way Thomas argued it was. That is, it cannot be the lack of original justice that is partially voluntary by Adam's will.

GUILT AND ORIGINAL SIN

Augustine's well-known definition of sin as a word, deed, or desire (*dictum, vel factum, vel concupitum*) against God's law posed serious problems for Peter Lombard and those who thought of sin as a disease. *Ex hypothesi*, original sin is *not* actual sin but received by way of origin. But words, deeds, and desires against God's law – as opposed to inherited concupiscence – are acts. It would seem, then, that original sin is simply not sin. The Lombard found in Augustine's own writings at least part of the solution: original sin in infants is voluntary by the will of Adam (*Retractions* I, c. 13, n. 5).[2] In one sense, then, infants' original sin *is* an action; it is the action of Adam as they receive it.

Thomas agreed with the Lombard. We can begin with his account in the *Scriptum*, which is found immediately after his argument that the defects of original sin are, strictly speaking, natural. Having made that claim, Thomas explains why these defects, despite being natural in themselves, are culpable when they are received from Adam. He follows the Lombard's account of what is required by the Catholic faith closely.[3]

---

[2] "Et voluntarium non incongrue appellatur, quia ex voluntate primi hominis processit, ut I libro [c. 13, n. 5] *Retractationum* ostendit dicens: 'Illud quod in parvulis dicitur originale peccatum, cum adhuc non utantur libero arbitrio voluntatis, non absurde vocatur voluntarium, quia ex prima hominis mala voluntate contractum, factum est quodam modo hereditarium.'" Peter Lombard, *Sententiae* II, d. 32, c. 5 (Brady, 515.18–21; 516.1–4).

[3] "Respondeo dicendum, quod circa hanc materiam duplex error tangitur in Littera. Unus est eorum qui simpliciter peccatum originale negabant, sicut error Juliani et Pelagii; et hic error veritati fidei non consonat, quia sacramentorum necessitatem et redemptionis tollit, quae contra servitutem peccati, in qua nascimur, ordinata sunt. Alius est error eorum qui peccatum originale nomine tenus concedentes, secundum rem negabant, dicentes, in puero nato nullam culpam esse, sed solum obligationem ad poenam; et hoc manifeste justitiae divinae repugnat, ut scilicet aliquis obligetur ad poenam qui culpam non habet, cum poena juste non nisi culpae debeatur." *Scriptum* II, d. 30, q. 1, a. 2. I'm inclined to think the

There is the grave heresy of Pelagianism, which must be avoided at all costs: *hic error veritati fidei non consonat*. Then there is Abelard's error. This is to concede the name "original sin" but claim that it consists in the debt to undergo punishment for Adam's sin, without any guilt. "Having avoided these errors, it should be conceded simpliciter that guilt is transmitted through origin from vitiated parents to their children."[4]

To understand this, Thomas argues, we must distinguish three concepts: defect, evil, and guilt.[5] A defect is a lack of any sort. A stone lacks wings, for example; this is a defect of the stone. An evil is the lack of something that should belong to that thing, the lack of something that is in some sense "due" to it. It is evil for a fly to lack wings, for example. Flies ought to fly; it is not the case that stones ought to fly. Lacking wings is a mere defect in a stone, an evil in the fly. In order for something to have guilt or sin, it must have more than a defect or evil. What must it have? It's worth quoting Thomas's answer at length here:

The concept of guilt adds to "defect" and "evil" the concept of the voluntary. Indeed, we blame the one who fails in that which she could have done through her will. Thus if something is to have the concept of guilt, the concept of the voluntary is necessarily found in it. Now just as there is a good with respect to nature and a good with respect to the person, there is a guilt with respect to nature and a guilt with respect to the person. The guilt of the person requires the will of the person,

---

phrases "denied original sin simpliciter" (*simpliciter peccatum originale negabant*) and "denied original sin according to the thing" (*secundum rem negabant*) refer, respectively, to a heresy and a not-necessarily-heretical error with respect to original sin. I'm inclined to think, that is, that Thomas followed the Lombard's map of the logical space of the doctrine: the heresy is to say that sin comes from Adam to us by imitation alone, the error to say that sin comes by imputation alone. Consider Thomas's reason for rejecting Abelard: he does not, as we might have expected, claim that the denial of guilt implies the denial of sin *ad rem* because guilt is essential to the doctrine as such. Instead, he argues that the denial of guilt implies that God is unjust and *therefore* implies a denial of original sin. Perhaps Thomas thinks it is more obvious that Abelard's God is unjust than that Abelard's conception of original sin is wrong in itself. That is, perhaps Thomas thinks that on the supposition that it would be just to impute Adam's sin to his posterity without his posterity having intrinsic guilt, there's no denial of original sin, and, given that this is what Abelard supposes, adopting Abelard's position does not entail a willful denial of original sin as Pelagianism does.

4   "Et ideo, his evitatis, simpliciter concedendum est, etiam culpam per originem trahi ex parentibus vitiatis in pueris natis." *Scriptum* II, d. 30, q. 1, a. 2.

5   "Sciendum est igitur, quod haec tria, defectus, malum, et culpa, ex superadditione se habent. Defectus enim simplicem negationem alicujus boni importat. Sed malum nomen privationis est; unde carentia alicujus, etiam si non sit natum haberi, defectus potest dici; sed non potest dici malum, nisi sit defectus ejus boni quod natum est haberi; unde carentia vitae in lapide potest dici defectus, sed non malum: homini vero mors est et defectus et malum." *Scriptum* II, d. 30, q. 1, a. 2.

as is clear in actual guilt, which through the act of the person is committed. The guilt of nature, however, only requires a will in that nature. Therefore, just as the loss of that original justice which was given to the human being in creation was caused by the will of the human being (and as that gift of nature was to be propagated into the whole nature, assuming the human being's persistence in justice), so too the privation of that good followed into the whole nature, as a privation and vice of that nature. Privation and habit are referred to the same genus, and there is the concept of guilt in every human being who is led to this defect from the will of the first human being.[6]

Guilt is a narrower concept than evil, just as evil is narrower than defect. Guilt requires voluntareity; evil does not. There is a distinction between the good of a nature and the good of a person. There is a corresponding distinction between the guilt of a nature and the guilt of a person. The guilt of a person, or personal guilt, belongs only to the person who commits a blameworthy act. By contrast, the guilt of a nature, or natural guilt, can belong to persons who have committed no acts whatsoever but have a will in that nature. This is the case with human beings who inherit the loss of original justice from Adam. Their guilt is precisely to not have the justice they ought to have by Adam's will.

Thomas has, in effect, synthesized the Lombard, Anselm, and Abelard on the question of original sin's culpability. From the Lombard he picks up the Augustinian saying that original sin was voluntary in the infant by the will of Adam. We saw earlier that Thomas adopted Anselm's vocabulary of the sin of nature and personal (= actual) sin. Thomas agrees with Anselm that there was a power in human nature, Adam's will, that should have conserved justice; that Adam's failure to conserve justice causes all the wills in that nature to sinfully lack justice.[7] Here, however, we see that

---

[6] "Culpa autem super hoc addit rationem voluntarii: ex hoc enim aliquis culpatur quod deficit in eo quod per suam voluntatem habere potuit. Unde oportet quod secundum hoc quod aliquid rationem culpae habet, secundum hoc ratio voluntarii in ipso reperiatur. Sicut autem est quoddam bonum quod respicit naturam, et quoddam quod respicit personam; ita etiam est quaedam culpa naturae et quaedam personae. Unde ad culpam personae, requiritur voluntas personae sicut patet in culpa actuali, quae per actum personae committitur; ad culpam vero naturae non requiritur nisi voluntas in natura illa. Sic ergo dicendum est, quod defectus illius originalis justitiae quae homini in sua creatione collata est, ex voluntate hominis accidit; et sicut illud naturae donum fuit et fuisset in totam naturam propagatum, homine in justitia persistente; ita etiam et privatio illius boni in totam naturam perducitur, quasi privatio et vitium naturae; ad idem enim genus privatio et habitus referuntur; et in quolibet homine rationem culpae habet ex hoc quod per voluntatem principii naturae, id est primi hominis, inductus est talis defectus." *Scriptum* II, d. 30, q. 1, a. 2.

[7] Thomas echoes Anselm a bit later in the treatise: "In potestate ergo naturae erat ut talis justitia semper in ea conservaretur: sed per voluntatem personae existentis in natura

Thomas's "sin of nature" is conceptually quite different: Anselm's emphasis on the action of human nature is gone. For Anselm, one can say of an infant, "*she* ought to have conserved justice, because she has a nature which preexisted her conception and animation that ought to have conserved justice." For Thomas, however, "acts are attributed to individuals, as the philosopher [Aristotle] says."[8] There is thus no failure of a universal human nature to act, properly speaking, because universal human nature does not act.[9] The individual Adam acted, and his individual children are actors. One *can* say of an infant, "her body ought to have caused justice upon animation because Adam ought to have given her body that power." One cannot say that "she ought to have conserved justice" – if "conserved" refers to some act she should have committed in the past. As an individual, she never had justice to conserve.

The difference between Thomas and Anselm with respect to original sin's culpability is highlighted when we recall that Anselm thought Adam's obedience would have enabled him to propagate children confirmed in justice, children who had, by virtue of their nature, resisted the devil's temptation and thereby defeated him: children who were no longer

---

factum est ut hoc perderetur; et ideo hic defectus comparatus ad naturam, rationem culpae habet in omnibus in quibus invenitur communis natura accepta a persona peccante." *Scriptum* II, d. 31, q. 1, a. 1.

[8] "[A]ctus individuorum sunt, ut philosophus dicit." *Scriptum* II, d. 32, q. 1, a. 2, *corpus*. Cf. *De malo* q. 4, a. 4, *sed contra* 2: "actus enim sunt indiuiduorum, secundum philosophum."

[9] Commenting on c. 2 of *De ente et essentia*, Gyula Klima writes that "a common nature or essence according to its absolute consideration abstracts from all existence, both in the singulars and in the mind. Yet, and this is the important point, it is *the same* nature that informs both the singulars that have this nature and the minds conceiving of them in terms of this nature. To be sure, this sameness is not numerical sameness, and thus it does not yield numerically one nature. On the contrary, it is the sameness of several, numerically distinct realizations of the same information-content, just like the sameness of a book in its several copies. Just as there is no such a thing as a universal book over and above the singular copies of the same book, so there is no such a thing as a universal nature existing over and above the singular things of the same nature; still, just as it is true to say that the singular copies are the copies of *the same book*, so it is true to say that these singulars are of *the same nature*." "The Medieval Problem of Universals," in *The Stanford Encyclopedia of Philosophy* (Fall 2013 edition), ed. Edward N. Zalta, http://plato .stanford.edu/entries/universals-medieval/. Just as there is no universal book existing over and above its singular copies, there is no universal human being or universal human nature that exists over and above individual human beings. A fortiori, there is no such universal human being or nature that acts. For our purposes, the crucial point is that whatever differences there are between Abelard and Thomas regarding universals, they agreed – against Anselm – that actions are of individuals.

able to sin. For Thomas, however, Adam never could have propagated children confirmed in justice; they would be just but still able to sin.[10]

Although he rejects Abelard's debt-of-punishment account of original sin because infants must be guilty, Thomas has in fact accepted one of Abelard's primary arguments: infants are not personally guilty of anything. Put differently, Thomas agrees with Abelard that infants have not done anything for which they could be blamed; only their ancestor Adam did. Abelard reasoned that infants cannot be guilty, therefore God must punish the innocent; Thomas reasoned that God cannot punish the innocent, therefore infants must be guilty. Yet because Thomas agrees with Abelard that infants have not personally acted in a blameworthy or culpable way, he defines their guilt in a new way, exclusively in relation to Adam's will. For Thomas, infants are guilty *only* in the sense that Adam failed to pass on justice to them; they are punished only in the sense that they lose undue gifts by the consequences of Adam's act.

It would be wrong to conclude from this, though, that Thomas didn't *really* believe in original guilt, as though he, in bad faith, intentionally equivocated to hide his Abelardian sympathies. It would be wrong to conclude (along those lines) that Thomas held that infants are really in pure nature, but we can *consider* their lack of justice sinful when we realize it comes from a sinful will, as if the difference between pure nature and original sin were only logical. No, Thomas maintained that the soul of the infant really has guilt from Adam's will. It's just that this guilt is *nothing other* than the "from Adam-ness" of the otherwise natural evil of lacking original justice. In other words, in Thomas's view, the mystery of original sin is located in the thin metaphysical unity between Adam and his posterity: greater than a purely physical relation of descendance, lesser than participation in the action of a universal nature. This "thin" unity explains why originated original sin is voluntary and culpable in the infant and why it is less voluntary and less culpable than originating original sin. Originated original sin, Thomas declares, is even less

---

[10] "Si tamen concedatur quod Adam confirmatus fuisset statim post victoriam tentationis, adhuc non sequitur quod filios confirmatos in justitia genuisset: quia hoc sequebatur actus personales ejus, et ita erat perfectio ad personam pertinens, quam non oportet in filios propagari; sicut si Adam donum philosophiae habuit, vel miracula faciendi, non oporteret quod filii ejus hoc habuissent." *Scriptum* II, d. 20, q. 2, a. 3, ad 5. Cf. *STh* I, q. 100, a. 2: "etiam si primi homines non peccassent, aliqui ex eorum stirpe potuissent iniquitatem committere. Non ergo nascerentur in iustitia confirmati." Thomas claims that Anselm was only opining, not confidently asserting, that Adam would have propagated children confirmed in justice.

culpable than venial sin. "[A]mong all sins, original sin is the least, for it is the least voluntary."[11] It deserves no further punishment than the punishments that automatically follow from its presence: mortality (and ultimately death) and gracelessness (and ultimately the eternal deprivation of the beatific vision).[12]

I will call originated original sin's minimal level of voluntareity "partial voluntareity," as opposed to the "full voluntareity" of originating original sin. In a moment, we will turn to the analogies Thomas offered in an attempt to render partial voluntareity intelligible. Before that, it is important to briefly discuss the role analogy itself plays in Thomas's hamartiology.

THE ANALOGY OF SIN

What role did analogy play in Thomas's view of original sin? One might argue that Thomas's insight into the analogical nature of original sin is the key to his hamartiology. That is, Thomas recognized a relation of similitude-in-difference between original sin, mortal sin, and venial sin, allowing him to avoid the trap of univocity in which Augustine was unfortunately ensnared. There are a couple of difficulties with this way of thinking, however. The first is that Augustine himself recognized that there were differences between infants' sin and Adam's sin. Thomas and Augustine disagreed over what *precisely* those differences were. It is not clear to me that it was Thomas's view of sin and analogy that led to his disagreements with Augustine. It doesn't seem that Thomas's hamartiology in general was driven by a *theory* of the "analogy of sin," still less a theory of analogy in general, as opposed to, say, his view of grace's supernatural status, the justice of God, or the One and the Many. Indeed, it is not clear that a theory of analogy drove *anything* in Thomas's thinking. As Joshua Hochschild observes, "although Aquinas often

---

[11] "[I]nter omnia peccata minimum est originale, eo quod minimum habet de voluntario." *Scriptum* II, 33, q. 2, a. 1, ad 2. Thomas also says this in a passage we'll treat in more depth in a moment: "originale est voluntarium voluntate alterius; unde deficit ex parte illa ex qua peccatum habet rationem culpae." *Scriptum* II, d. 35, q. 1, a. 2, ad 2.

[12] Keep in mind the ambiguities discussed in Chapter 2 regarding original justice's formal cause. The way I've phrased the relation of the sin to its penalty here assumes the early view. When justice is supernatural, though, the penalty is still mortality (and ultimately death), but the initial lack of grace is (or ought to be, if Thomas is to be coherent) the formal cause of original sin itself, its penalty being the automatic result of this sin, namely, to lack the beatific vision for eternity.

discussed analogy, he never did so systematically and wrote no work dedicated to the subject."[13] Thomas likewise never wrote a treatise *De analogia peccati*. He was clear, however, that the word "sin" is said analogically.

What this meant for Thomas can be gleaned from a couple of especially helpful remarks early in Thomas's discussion of personal sin in the *Scriptum*. Here is Thomas's response to an objection claiming, in effect, that Augustine's aforementioned definition of sin as a violation of God's law does not apply to all sins:

> "Sin" is not said univocally of all kinds of sins. In the first place, it is said of actual mortal sin. Venial sin recedes from mortal sin because it does not altogether deordain from the end. But while saving the ordination to the end, it in some way hampers one's progress toward the end. Thus it recedes from that by which sin formally has the nature of evil. Original sin, however, recedes from mortal sin on the part of the substance of the act itself. Actual mortal sin is voluntary by the proper will of the one in whom it is, but original sin is voluntary by the will of another. It recedes from that by which sin has the nature of guilt.[14]

Sin is not said univocally of all types of sin. Instead, Thomas implies here what he states explicitly a bit later: sin is said analogically, according to a "community through analogy" (*commune per analogiam*).[15] This is

---

[13] Joshua P. Hochschild, *The Semantics of Analogy: Rereading Cajetan's* De Nominum Analogia (Notre Dame: University of Notre Dame Press, 2010), xiv. My understanding of Cajetan's view of analogy and the scattered remarks I make about it are indebted to Hochschild's reading. As per Hochschild's overarching argument, I don't assume Cajetan intended to represent Thomas's views on analogy. For a discussion of *Thomas's* own view of analogy, as well as his oft-neglected view of univocal predication of God, see Bruce Marshall, "Christ the End of Analogy," in *The Analogy of Being*, 280–313. Marshall's own treatment interacts with Ralph McInerny, *Aquinas and Analogy* (Washington, DC: Catholic University of America Press, 1996). For Scotus, see Richard Cross, *Duns Scotus* (Oxford: Oxford University Press, 1999), 31–42.

[14] "[P]eccatum non dicitur univoce de omnibus generibus peccatorum, sed per prius de peccato actuali mortali, a quo peccatum veniale deficit ex hoc quod non omnino a fine deordinat. Sed aliquo modo a fine retardat, ordine ad finem salvato; unde deficit ex parte illa ex qua peccatum formaliter rationem mali habet. Originale autem deficit ab eo ex parte ipsius substantiae actus; actuale enim mortale est voluntarium voluntate propria illius in quo est; sed originale est voluntarium voluntate alterius; unde deficit ex parte illa ex qua peccatum habet rationem culpae." *Scriptum* II, d. 35, q. 1, a. 2, ad 2.

[15] In *Scriptum* II, d. 42, q. 1, a. 3, Thomas explains why "sin" is said of venial sin neither equivocally nor univocally. It is predicated analogically. It's worth considering the whole *corpus*: "Respondeo dicendum, quod est duplex modus dividendi commune in ea quae sub ipso sunt, sicut est duplex communitatis modus. Est enim quaedam divisio univoci in species per differentias quibus aequaliter natura generis in speciebus participatur, sicut animal dividitur in hominem et equum, et hujusmodi; alia vero divisio est ejus quod est *commune per analogiam*, quod quidem secundum *perfectam rationem praedicatur de*

different from the division of a genus into species because the univocal *ratio* or concept of the genus is not found in all the species. For example, the univocal *ratio* of animal – a substance with a sensitive nature – is said univocally of Socrates and his dog. They are both animals in the exact same sense, despite the fact that Socrates is a higher or more perfect instance of animal than his dog. Why doesn't Thomas apply this logic to sin? Why doesn't he say that the *ratio* of sin is said equally of the infant and the murderer, though the murderer is a "higher" (or "lower," if you like) instance of sinner than the infant? That is, why does Thomas claim that there is not one genus of sin but rather many genera of sins (*generibus peccatorum*)?

At least on a basic level, the answer is that sin in the first place (*per prius*), sin said with respect to its perfect nature (*perfectam rationem*) – namely, mortal sin – is found only imperfectly in the other kinds of sin. Mortal sin agrees partially with venial sin and partially with original sin, and original sin almost completely disagrees with venial sin. The *rationes* of the genera of sin are each individually comparable to the *ratio* of animal, because each individual *ratio* of sin is a genus. For example, the *ratio* of venial sin is found in every species of venial sin, as the *ratio* of animal is found in every animal. The same goes for original sin. The *ratio* of mortal sin, in Thomas's mind, is more like the *ratio* of animal than the *ratio* of sin. The *ratio* of sin is more like the *ratio* of life or the *ratio entis*. The *ratio propria* of life is found more perfectly in angels than plants.[16] The *ratio propria* of being is found perfectly in substance and imperfectly in accidents. "Sin" is predicated analogically of the different fundamental classes of sin, not univocally, because the *ratio propria* of "sin" is found perfectly in only one class, mortal sin, and imperfectly in the other classes, venial and original sin. What this amounts to is that sin is a

---

uno dividentium, et de altero imperfecte et secundum quid, sicut ens dividitur in substantiam et accidens, et in ens actu et in ens potentia: *et haec divisio est quasi media inter aequivocum et univocum*; et talis divisio est peccati in mortale et veniale: quia *ratio peccati perfecte in mortali invenitur*; in veniali vero non nisi imperfecte et secundum quid; unde minimum quod potest esse de ratione peccati in aliquo actu est in veniali; sicut minimum quod potest esse de natura entis est in ente in potentia et in ente per accidens, et hoc ipsa nomina ostendunt: quia venia non debetur peccato nisi secundum quod aliquam imperfectionem peccati habet; mors autem debetur peccato inquantum peccatum est; et ideo mortale peccatum perfectum quid in genere peccati dicit, veniale autem imperfectum." Emphasis mine. Cf. *Scriptum* I, d. 19, a. 2, ad 1.

[16] For Thomas's concept of life, see *STh* I, q. 18. The more perfectly a being has its own source of operations, the more perfect its life is. Yet life is not a genus, as it is predicated of God and grass.

"supergeneric" concept: wider in scope than a given genus because it is predicated of multiple genera, yet not itself a genus because the genera of which it is predicated participate unequally in the supergeneric or analogical concept. It is supergeneric in that it is more general than a genus, but it is not a supergenus, as though it were predicable of its species as a genus is. Here is an analogy. Life : Sin :: Animal : Mortal Sin. As the analogical concept life is to the analogical concept sin, the genus animal is to the genus mortal sin. As the *ratio* of life as found in (say) plant, animal, and the angel Gabriel, agrees with each because they are all the source of their own movement, despite the fact they do not fall under the same genus but are each their own genus and participate in the *ratio* of life unequally, so too the *ratio* of sin, as found in mortal, venial, and original sin, agrees with all because all are evil and culpable in some respect with respect to the ultimate end, despite the fact that none of them falls under the same genus.[17]

ANALOGIES OF ORIGINAL SIN

In light of his thin conception of infant guilt, it's not surprising that Thomas initially likened original sin to an inherited disease, an analogy which tends to elicit sympathy for the afflicted party.[18] As a leprous man

---

[17] Why can't analogical concepts be predicated univocally of their genera, as genera are predicated univocally of their species? In the case of sin, Thomas seems to deny that this is possible ("sin is not said univocally of all genera of sin"), but as we can see, in explaining himself he immediately moves from "sin" to its *ratio propria*, mortal sin. He doesn't explain why "sin" qua related to all three genera of sin (that is, sin qua "evil and culpable with respect to the ultimate end," which concept is found in mortal, venial, and original sin) should not be predicated univocally of each of the genera. The imperfect *rationes* are imperfect with respect to the *ratio propria*, mortal sin, but they are apparently not imperfect with respect to the analogical concept. (How could they be? For if the *ratio* of sin is "evil and culpable with respect to the ultimate end," then to claim one of the genera of sin was imperfect with respect to that *ratio*, either one would need to deny, *pace* Thomas, that this *ratio* is found in venial, original, or mortal sin – recall that even venial sin only *recedes* from the *ratio mali*, and original sin only *recedes* from the *ratio culpae*, but neither altogether escape from either – or one would need to, again *pace* Thomas, claim that because X and Y are more or less perfect in their intrinsic being or non-being, X and Y cannot be species of the same genus.) Affirming that the analogical concept is univocally predicable of the genera would take us more in a Scotistic direction, and exploring the implications of this would take us too far afield for our present purposes. I admit, though, that I don't see how acknowledging the possibility of "sin" as a supergenus would controvert anything Thomas says about the nature of sin.

[18] "Ad quartum dicendum, quod licet semen non habeat in se infectionem culpae in actu, habet tamen in virtute; sicut etiam patet quod ex semine leprosi generatur filius leprosus,

begets a leprous son, so too Adam without original justice begets children without original justice. Still, this analogy doesn't explain the guilt of a nature very well; for in many cases diseases are involuntary *simpliciter*. Who wants leprosy, after all? Does the son's leprosy necessarily stem from the father's sin? It seems that most diseases arise from natural causes. Of course, one could claim that every case of leprosy ultimately stems from Adam's sin. At this point, though, one would simply be repeating the *explicandum*, not illuminating it through analogy. And while Thomas presumably could have shifted the analogy to make his point – for example, by imagining a man who intentionally contracted leprosy in order to spread it to his enemy – diseases as such are not voluntary in this way. A disease need not arise from a proximate voluntary cause. It would have been preferable for Thomas to have an analogy that rendered the guilt of original sin more intelligible.

Later in his career, Thomas thought he had found one. In *STh* I-II, q. 81, a. 1, Thomas notes that different theologians have explained original sin's transmission differently. Some argue that the rational soul is transmitted along with the body, while others maintain that the defects of the body redound to the soul when God infuses it, as a leper begets lepers.[19] This latter analogy is the one we just saw in the *Scriptum*. Here in the *Summa* Thomas rejects his earlier reasoning.[20] Whether or not the

---

quamvis in ipso semine non sit lepra in actu: est enim in semine virtus aliqua deficiens, per cujus defectum contingit defectus leprae in prole. Similiter etiam ex hoc ipso quod in semine est talis dispositio, quae privatur illa impassibilitate et ordinabilitate ad animam, quam in primo statu corpus humanum habebat, sequitur quod in prole, quae est susceptiva originalis peccati, efficiatur originale peccatum in actu." *Scriptum* II, d. 30, q. 1, a. 2, ad 4.

[19] "Quidam enim, considerantes quod peccati subiectum est anima rationalis, posuerunt quod cum semine rationalis anima traducatur, ut sic ex infecta anima animae infectae derivari videantur. Alii vero, hoc repudiantes tanquam erroneum, conati sunt ostendere quomodo culpa animae parentis traducitur in prolem, etiam si anima non traducatur, per hoc quod corporis defectus traducuntur a parente in prolem: sicut si leprosus generat leprosum, et podagricus podagricum, propter aliquam corruptionem seminis, licet talis corruptio non dicatur lepra vel podagra. Cum autem corpus sit proportionatum animae, et defectus animae redundent in corpus, et e converso; simili modo dicunt quod culpabilis defectus animae per traductionem seminis in prolem derivatur, quamvis semen actualiter non sit culpae subiectum." *STh* I-II, q. 81, a. 1.

[20] "Sed omnes huiusmodi viae insufficientes sunt. Quia dato quod aliqui defectus corporales a parente transeant in prolem per originem; et etiam aliqui defectus animae ex consequenti, propter corporis indispositionem, sicut interdum ex fatuis fatui generantur: tamen hoc ipsum quod est ex origine aliquem defectum habere, videtur excludere rationem culpae, de cuius ratione est quod sit voluntaria. Unde etiam posito quod anima rationalis traduceretur, ex hoc ipso quod infectio animae prolis non esset in

rational soul is transmitted through sexual intercourse, the fact that a child receives a defect in her soul in the manner of a disease does not explain its culpability. Indeed, Thomas claims that having a defect by way of origin excludes the concept of guilt, which must include voluntareity. Thomas offers another explanation, worth quoting at length.

All who are born from Adam are able to be considered as one human being, as they agree in nature which they received from the first parent. Consider the fact that in politics, members of the community are often judged as one body, and the whole community is judged as one human being. Indeed, as Porphyry says, by participation in the species many human beings are one human being.

Likewise, the many human beings derived from Adam are as many members of one body. The act of one member of the body, say the hand, is not voluntary by the will of the hand itself but by the will of the soul, which first moves the members. Hence a murder which the hand commits is not imputed to the hand as sin if the hand is considered in itself as diverse from the body. Yet it is imputed to it as the man is moved from the first motive principle of the human being. The disorder which is in this human being generated from Adam is similar. It is not voluntary by her own will but by the will of the first parent. By the motion of generation, this will moves all who are derived from it by origin, as the will of the soul moves all members to act. Hence the sin which is derived from the first parent into posterity is called original, as the sin which from the soul is derived to the members of the body is called actual. Just as actual sin committed by some member of the body is not a sin of that member except insofar as it is something of that man (because of which it is called human sin), so too original sin is not a sin of the person except insofar as the person receives nature from the first parent. Hence it is called the sin of nature. As Ephesians 2[:3] says, we were by nature sons of wrath.[21]

eius voluntate, amitteret rationem culpae obligantis ad poenam: quia, ut philosophus dicit in III *Ethic.*, nullus improperabit caeco nato, sed magis miserebitur." *STh* I-II, q. 81, a. 1.

[21] "[D]icendo quod omnes homines qui nascuntur ex Adam, possunt considerari ut unus homo, inquantum conveniunt in natura, quam a primo parente accipiunt; secundum quod in civilibus omnes qui sunt unius communitatis, reputantur quasi unum corpus, et tota communitas quasi unus homo. Porphyrius etiam dicit quod participatione speciei plures homines sunt unus homo. Sic igitur multi homines ex Adam derivati, sunt tamquam multa membra unius corporis. Actus autem unius membri corporalis, puta manus, non est voluntarius voluntate ipsius manus, sed voluntate animae, quae primo movet membra. Unde homicidium quod manus committit, non imputaretur manui ad peccatum, si consideraretur manus secundum se ut divisa a corpore: sed imputatur ei inquantum est aliquid hominis quod movetur a primo principio motivo hominis. Sic inordinatio quae est in isto homine ex Adam generato, non est voluntaria voluntate ipsius, sed voluntate primi parentis, qui movet motione generationis omnes qui ex eius origine derivantur, sicut voluntas animae moves omnia membra ad actum. Unde peccatum quod sic a primo parente in posteros derivatur, dicitur originale: sicut peccatum quod ab anima derivatur ad membra corporis, dicitur actuale. Et sicut peccatum actuale quod per membrum aliquod committiur, non est peccatum illius

All who descend from Adam can be considered as one human being, just as in political affairs the nation is considered one human being, or as many through participation in the same species are one human being. Thus many from Adam are as many members of one body. But the act of a bodily member, say, a hand committing murder, is not voluntary by that hand in isolation from the whole; rather, guilt is imputed to the hand as moved by the will. Likewise, the human being moved by Adam's generative power is not considered guilty in isolation; she is considered guilty as moved to this lack by Adam, the first mover.

Commentators have debated the significance of the homicidal hand analogy. Does it imply a new view of original sin altogether, a Thomist realism of some sort? Or is it merely a new illustration of the same concept from the *Scriptum*? The evidence for the latter position is quite strong.[22] It's highly likely that Thomas continued to assume that original sin is partially voluntary in the infant and fully voluntary in Adam. But because he realized that diseases are often involuntary *simpliciter*, he needed a better analogy to render partial voluntareity intelligible. The new analogy works like this:

Murderer's Will : Murderer's Hand :: Adam's Will : Infant's Soul

The idea is not that the infant and Adam are literally one and the same being, or that they are guilty in the same sense for Adam's act. The idea is that the infant's habit of lacking original justice cannot be considered as sinful in isolation from Adam's act, just as the murderer's hand cannot be

---

membri nisi inquantum illud membrum est aliquid ipsius hominis, propter quod vocatur peccatum humanum; ita peccatum originale non est peccatum huius personae; nisi inquantum haec persona recipit naturam a primo parente. Unde et vocatur peccatum naturae, secundum illud *Ephes.* II[:3]: Eramus natura filii irae." *STh* I-II, q. 81, a. 1. Thomas appeals to the same murderous hand analogy whenever he explains original sin's transmission in his mature works. Cf. *De malo* q. 4, a. 1.

22 Kors argued that Thomas's mature view of unity with Adam was primarily physical, the unity of origin: "C'est en vertu de l'unité de la nature humaine qu'on peut considérer tous les hommes comme un seul individu. Cette unité n'est pas d'ordre logique, mais bien d'ordre physique à cause du lien réel de la génération." Kors, *La Justice primitive et le péché originel d'après S. Thomas*, 149. See also the Blackfriars commentary: "there must be a real connection between the disordered nature in every man and the will act that makes the defect sinful . . . The taking of all men as one man is not intended as a fiction or a figure of speech. All men can be considered as one man because they are one in that the nature which each has is de facto derived from the one source; in this sense the unity of men is a real, physical unity." T. C. O'Brien, appendix 9 to vol. 26 of the *Summa Theologiae* Ia2æ, 81–5, 139. O'Brien says the unity is "real" but defines it in physical terms.

considered sinful in isolation from the act of murder. This was at the core of Thomas's account in the *Scriptum*: the infant without original justice simply has natural defects when considered in isolation; when we recognize that she has these defects from Adam's sinful will, we recognize that these defects are culpable.

Moreover, continuity is likely because Thomas continues to argue in the *Summa* that original sin is biologically inherited and sexually transmitted. Keep in mind that this is the first article in the mini-treatise on original sin, and the very question at issue is whether sin can be sexually transmitted. Thomas claims that the affirmative answer is *de fide*.[23] In question 82, he turns to the essence of original sin, which is the habit of lacking due justice. Also worth noting is that Thomas says that Adam and his posterity are able to be *considered* as one man – not "are one man" – because by the motion of generation (*motione generationis*) Adam moves his posterity to guilt.[24] But each descendant can be considered as an individual, as a person, in which case she is not guilty. Considered in isolation from Adam's sinful will, each of his descendants simply has the natural defect of lacking original justice (*STh* I-II, q. 81, a. 4; q. 82, a. 3). Considered as one who receives human nature without original justice from Adam – *peccatum originale non est peccatum huius personae; nisi inquantum haec persona recipit naturam a primo parente* – she has original sin.

The biological character of original is highlighted when we recognize that there was no need for the whole of humanity to be united in original sin. If Eve alone had sinned, original sin would not have been transmitted, and if Adam alone had sinned, it still would have been transmitted (*STh* I-II, q. 81, a. 5). Adam's children would not have been born confirmed in justice even if he had avoided sin (*STh* I, q. 100, a. 2); thus there could have been, in theory, a subgroup of humanity with original sin living side-by-side another group without it (if Cain sinned and Abel didn't, Cain's children would have sin and Abel's justice). Thomas continues to teach that original sin is specifically the same but numerically distinct in every infant, just as every infant is a numerically distinct human

---

[23] "[S]ecundum fidem Catholicam est tenendum quod primum peccatum primi hominis originaliter transit in posteros." *STh* I-II, q. 81, a. 1.

[24] It is true that, as Thomas's quote from Porphyry states, human beings "are one human being" by participation in the species. But *this* sense of specific unity, in Thomas's view, is not a unity of action; the human being must receive designated matter and the act of existence (*esse*) in order to be and to act. The universal "human being" (*homo*), considered absolutely, is immobile.

being and specifically the same according to human nature (*STh* I-II, q. 82, a. 2). If Thomas wanted us to take the homicidal hand literally – that is, as an expression of a strong metaphysical unity infants have with Adam's act – it seems he would have said that original sin is one numerically, just as a murderer and his hand have the same substantial form and commit one action, the murder.

It also seems that a strong realism would have required Thomas to abandon or at least modify his view that infants are minimally guilty. If the infant is an integral part of Adam's act the way a hand is an integral part of sin, then infants would be guilty of the act in the same sense as a murderer's hand. A murderer's hand, of course, is subjected to the same sorts of penalties as the murderer: jail, execution, and so forth. The judge doesn't say, "I sentence William to fifty years in prison. His homicidal hand, however, only gets five." But infants are not subjected to the same penalties as adults. As we saw in Chapter 3, Thomas did not complete the *Tertia pars*, which is why the *Summa theologiae* has no extended treatment of the children's limbo. But in the *De malo*, a work from his mature period, Thomas deployed the homicidal hand analogy to explain original guilt while continuing to insist on the minimal guilt and punishment of infants. If Thomas had been thinking in realist terms, he also would have needed a different argument for his view that only one sin is inherited. His argument for that view (*STh* I-II, q. 81, a. 2) is that personal actions are not transmissible, but the one sin that is transmissible is the sin of *nature*: the infant's non-reception of the sexually transmissible disposition to the gift of original justice.

That said, it might be the case that Thomas's shift away from the disease analogy indicates that he was growing uncomfortable, as it were, with the idea that original sin is sexually transmitted. Recall the reason Thomas gave for rejecting the disease analogy: "having some defect by way of origin seems to exclude the concept of guilt, which must be voluntary." One could take this in two ways. First, it might mean merely that disease analogies don't adequately *illustrate* the guilt of original sin. But he seems to be saying something stronger: one *cannot* be guilty for something qua inheriting it. If that is what Thomas means, then it is hard to see how the homicidal hand analogy – understood as an attempt to render partial voluntareity intelligible – helps either. For original sin is partially voluntary precisely because one inherits the lack of original justice, ultimately from Adam's sinful will. Might Thomas have been driving at a stronger metaphysical union with Adam than I have suggested? It is possible. In that case, Thomas would be arguing that since

one cannot inherit guilt, properly speaking, humanity must really participate in Adam's act in such a way that infants do not inherit but rather
commit sin. But it strikes me that the balance of evidence weighs against
this hypothesis, for the reasons mentioned earlier. What is decisive is
Thomas's continued insistence that infants are minimally guilty, together
with his clear affirmation that original sin is merely a *habitus*. Let's
assume for the moment that the homicidal hand analogy was intended
to be an improvement on the disease analogy, a better explanation of
partial voluntareity. I will now argue that neither analogy is adequate.

THE PROBLEM WITH PARTIAL VOLUNTAREITY

The first premise of my argument is that the moral quality of a given
habit cannot depend upon the moral quality of its efficient cause. The
second premise is that the lack of original justice is a habit. Therefore,
the moral quality of the lack of original justice cannot depend upon the
moral quality of its efficient cause. Thomas, though, claims that the moral
quality of lacking original justice does depend on the moral quality of its
efficient cause: when the lack of original justice comes from God's good
will, it is not a sin or a guilt but merely a natural evil; when the lack of
original justice comes from Adam's bad will, it is original sin.

The first premise, in other words, is that the goodness or badness of a
habit or disposition pertains to the sort of action to which the disposition
disposes, not the goodness or badness of the cause or source that led to
the disposition in the first place.[25] Take the disposition to alcoholism, for
example. This disposition is bad because the behavior to which it inclines,
excessive drinking, is harmful. Whether one is disposed to alcoholism due
to genetic, epigenetic, or cultural factors (or some combination thereof)
makes no difference to the disposition's moral status. If an evil scientist
brought about a disposition to alcoholism in me, the disposition would be
bad. If a virtuous scientist accidentally brought it about that I was disposed to alcoholism in the course of medical research, the disposition
would be equally bad. It seems clear that the disposition to alcoholism is
bad, in me, regardless of its source. And it seems that this principle can be
extended to virtues and vices (and their sources) in general. Even if an

---

[25] I will interchangeably use "habit" and "disposition" in this section in a broad sense,
including inborn habits which are merely dispositions to later actions, like the
concupiscence in original sin according to Thomas, as well as acquired or infused
habits properly speaking, which more strongly incline to actions.

angel or a demon were to infuse a vice or virtue, the vice would be vicious and the virtue virtuous. Indeed, if God were to infuse a vice or virtue the same principle holds: the moral quality of the disposition will depend on the behavior to which it disposes.

I am not claiming that culpability for one's habits has nothing to do with the efficient cause of these habits. One might think that if I was born with a disposition to alcoholism, I am innocent with respect to that disposition, whereas I would have been guilty for having the disposition if I had acquired it through excessive drinking. The point is that regardless of whether an agent is responsible for having a habit, or the actions to which the habit inclines, the habit's goodness or badness is determined by whether it inclines to good or bad acts. It strikes me that this principle is evident on reflection. Admittedly, though, it is not immediately obvious without such reflection, because good and bad habits often follow good and bad actions, respectively. We are tempted to assume that the common link between the moral quality of a habit and its efficient cause is a necessary one, but it is not.

This is crucial for our purposes because Thomas admits that God can cause the bad habit of lacking original justice. The lack of original justice can be caused by God's good will or Adam's sinful will. Thomas argues, as we have seen, that this habit's ultimate origin in Adam's sinful will alters the moral quality of the habit, transforming what would be a natural amoral evil into a voluntary sinful evil. Yet if the foregoing argument is sound, this is impossible. We must choose: either the habit of lacking original justice is sinful or not. If it is, it will be sinful regardless of whether God or Adam caused it; if it is not, it will not be sinful regardless of whether God or Adam caused it. If one holds both that the lack of justice is a sinful habit and that God cannot cause sinful habits, one should deny that God could have created any human being de novo without original justice (Anselm's view). If one insists that God could have created human beings without original justice but agrees that God cannot cause sinful habits, then one should deny that the lack of justice constitutes original sin. Alternatively, one could break with Thomas and admit that the lack of justice per se is sinful, while admitting with Thomas that God could cause this lack. None of these options is without problems.

Before we move on, let's consider an influential defense of Thomas's account. Cajetan, commenting on the homicidal hand analogy, notes that it seems that "the proportional similarity of the sin of a member and the will moving it, and of a human being and the first parent generating her, is inadequate (*inconsona est*)."[26] The problem is that the hand is moved to the execution of a blameworthy deed, whereas the movement of generation terminates in penalties or defects alone. Cajetan replies to the objection he has posed by arguing that when an agent uses an instrument for some work, if that instrument is capable of guilt, that instrumental agent participates in the guilt.[27] This allows Cajetan to avoid the most obvious absurdities that one might suspect follow from partial voluntareity. Inanimate objects used to commit crimes are not guilty because they are not capable of guilt, and rational agents who are simply victims are not guilty because they have not participated in the crime. A stabbing knife cannot participate in the guilt of a murder; a battered wife cannot participate in the guilt of an assault. Postlapsarian persons, however, *membrum Adae ut capitis*, are capable of guilt and do participate in Adam's act of sin; thus Adam's act is partially voluntary in them. Cajetan's response has been influential in the Thomist tradition.[28] It was hinted at by Thomas himself, though Cajetan seems to imply a stronger metaphysical unity between Adam and us than Thomas himself claimed. In any case, it seems to me that Cajetan's reply is inadequate, at least as an attempt to illuminate the concept of *partial* voluntareity.

The reason is because a rational agent's participation in a sinful act does not render that agent partially guilty of that act. Consider the following example. An evil king uses his prisoners of war as weapons, catapulting them against their will from his castle to kill invaders. These prisoners are capable of guilt by nature (they are human) and of being

---

[26] "Proportionalis namque similitudo de peccato membri ac voluntatis moventis illud, et huius hominis ad primum parentem generantem ipsum, inconsona est." Cajetan, *Commentaria in STh* I-II, q. 81, a. 1 (Leonine edition), 88.

[27] "Ad hoc dicitur quod similitudo consonat, et optime declarat intentum, si attendimus ad illud quod est per se. In motione enim membri a voluntate, per se fit quod membrum constituitur in hoc quod est esse instrumentum voluntatis ad tale opus: et ex hoc ipso, supposito quod sit capax culpae, instrumentum illud culpae fit particeps. Et similiter in generatione huius hominis ab Adam, per se fit quod hic homo constituitur in hoc quod est esse membrum Adae ut capitis: ex hoc namque quod per semen ab ipso generatur, eius membrum fit; adeo quod, si aliter generaretur aut fieret, non esset eius membrum. Ex hoc autem quod eius membrum est, suppositio quod susceptivum culpae, particeps fit culpae, et non solum poenae. Generativa ergo motio respondet motioni imperativae in hoc quod est utramque constituere motum in hoc quod est esse aliquid moventis, ut sic possit ei imputari ad culpam, praesupposita eius capacitate." Cajetan, *Commentaria in STh* I-II, q. 81, a. 1 (Leonine edition), 88.

[28] Jacobus Ramírez, for example, cites Cajetan's solution approvingly and a number of commentators who followed him. *De Vitiis et Peccatis, In I–II Summae Theologiae Divi Thomae Expositio* VIII (Salamanca: San Esteban, 1990), §394, 559.

used as instrumental causes of a sinful action (the evil king's war is unjust). But it seems clear that they are not partially guilty of this sinful action. Insofar as they are involuntarily catapulted, they are innocent. Examples are easy to multiply. If John grabs Jane's hand without Jane's consent and uses it to smack Ray, Ray would be right to blame John and wrong to blame Jane. He wouldn't even be justified in partially blaming Jane, even if he were tempted to because Jane's hand was harming him. We need to distinguish active participation from passive participation. If one is merely a passive, unconsenting participant in an action, one cannot be rightly blamed for one's participation. But those who actively consent to participate in crimes can be rightly blamed for those crimes.

One possible response to this criticism would be to reply that the foregoing analogies beg the question by positing numerically distinct, independent agents, when the homicidal hand analogy refers to numerically one action, a homicide, with numerically one substantial form, the soul which moves the hand to homicide. The participation of the infant in Adam's sin is like *that*, not like one agent moving another distinct agent against her will. This response, however, can be formulated coherently only from a thoroughgoing realist perspective. For either Adam and his posterity are united in one substantial form and one action or not. If not, then the criticism holds. If so, then they are guilty of the same action. Infants would deserve the same grave penalties as Adam, and Thomas's view of original sin would be ruptured. It seems that Cajetan wanted to push Thomas in a realist direction because he was concerned with the externality of Thomas's own conception of guilt.[29]

---

[29] Consider his description of the difference between the *Scriptum* and *Summa* accounts: only the latter, he claims, implies that original sin is *not* voluntary by an alien will: "In eodem articulo, adverte quod Auctor positionem quam in II Sent., dist. xxx, secutus est, licet non totaliter, arguere videatur: si tamen diligentius consideretur littera, dum arguitur insufficientiae secunda via, positio illa olim sua reprehenditur. Nam ibi tenuit peccatum originale contrahi per originem sicut podagram vel stoliditatem, redundante in formam conditione materiae; et habere rationem culpae propter voluntatem parentis. Hic autem licet de isto voluntario non fiat mentio referendo illam opinionem, subintelligitur tamen, ut puto, tamquam commune confessum ab omnibus, quod hoc est voluntarium aliena voluntate. *Reprehenditur autem haec positio tanquam insufficiens, quia non salvat rationem voluntarii etiam aliena voluntate*, sic quod sufficiat ad rationem culpae in hoc genito. Quoniam totum hoc quod illa positio dicit acceptatum, verificatur de Socrate secundum se: est namque secundum se habens conditiones formae coaptatas materiae conditionibus, voluntarie Adae voluntate contractas ab eo. Et tamen defectus iste non est culpa Socratis secundum se. Quia ergo oportet ad salvandum voluntarium requisitum ad culpam huius absque propria voluntate, ponere hunc hominem esse aliquid alienae voluntatis, ut sic sit voluntarius defectus voluntate propria non secundum se, sed

It was understandable that Thomas adopted the thesis that original sin is voluntary by the will of another. It was a traditional solution, ready-to-hand in the *Sentences*, which allowed him to avoid major difficulties. It allowed him to deny that nature is sinful per se, a conclusion which his view of nature veers quite close to; correspondingly, it allowed him to deny in principle that God could be the cause of original sin. But partial voluntareity, or so I have argued, is a confused concept. The dispositions we inherit may be good or bad, but their goodness or badness does not depend on the goodness or badness of their source. Original sin is certainly voluntary in that it is *in* the infant's will which is the subject of sin, and it is voluntary in that it is ultimately caused by a voluntary agent; but the sheer fact of the latter does nothing to change the voluntareity of the former. Even if Adam could have been the principal cause of supernatural original justice, Adam's failure to pass it on adds nothing to its culpability in infants. The same thing goes if one holds that original sin is the absence of a preternatural habit. Either the formal evil has an analogical culpability of itself or it simply has no guilt whatsoever.

secundum quod membrum alterius, a quo inchoat haec culpa; et hoc non positum est a praedictis positionibus: ideo arguuntur. *Et ponitur alia via, qua salvatur sufficienter ratio voluntarii per hoc quod ponitur in Socrate hoc peccatum ut est membrum Adae, et ex consequenti in ipso secundum se.*" Cajetan, *Commentaria in STh* I-II, q. 81, a. 1, 89, emphasis mine.

5

Original Sin and Some Modern Theologians

In 1313, thirty-nine years after Thomas's death in Fossanova, anti-Thomist teaching was banned in the Dominican Order.[1] In 1323, he was sainted. As one would expect, his account of original sin was influential in the Order of Preachers and beyond. Yet debate continued. The Dominican Durandus of Saint-Pourçain (1275–1334) defended Abelard's account (on which, the reader recalls, original sin is the inculpable debt of damnation).[2] Another Dominican, Ambrogio Catarino (1484–1553), proposed that infants *are* guilty of original sin *because* God imputes Adam's sin to them.[3] Despite their different views of infant guilt, Catarino's and Abelard's accounts belong in the same genus, namely, the legal. For both, it is the divine decision to hold Adam's sin against his posterity that brings about original sin, not infants' inheritance of sin or participation in Adam's act. The magisterial Reformers initially presupposed the common medieval view that original sin is

---

[1] "The general chapter convened at Metz in early June of 1313 outlawed any dissenting voice within the order outright. Dominican friars were forbidden henceforth to hold any opinion contrary to the teachings of Thomas." M. Michèle Mulchahey, *"First the Bow is Bent in Study ...": Dominican Education before 1350* (Toronto: Pontifical Institute of Mediaeval Studies, 1998), 154.

[2] See Vollert, *The Doctrine of Hervaeus Natalis on Primitive Justice and Original Sin*, for Durandus's debate with the Thomist Hervaeus Natalis.

[3] See Aaron C. Denlinger, Omnes in Adam ex pacto Dei: *Ambrogio Catarino's Doctrine of Covenantal Solidarity and Its Influence on Post-Reformation Reformed Theologians* (Göttingen: Vandenhoeck & Ruprecht, 2011), for an argument that Catarino influenced Protestant covenant theology.

transmitted like a disease.[4] Controversy arose from their claim, which they attributed to Augustine, that original sin is not (completely) removed when one receives saving faith or baptism (the Christian is *"simul iustus et peccator"*).[5] Catholics argued contrariwise that baptism removes sin altogether, and post-baptismal concupiscence is sin's punishment.[6] Intra-Protestant debate continued through the centuries. Many would defend federalism, a legal theory akin to Catarino's, while others forged realist theories.[7] Well into the "modern" era, then, the legal, disease, and realist theories of original sin constructed in the twelfth century continued to be developed. I will not attempt to further narrate the history of the traditional doctrine in the modern period.

This chapter focuses, instead, on the *uniquely* modern interpretation of original sin, which I understand as follows. A historical Fall from original justice is theologically insignificant, such that the true meaning of the doctrine of original sin can be grasped without it. I distinguish the modern

---

[4] John Calvin, for example, writes that original sin "seems to be a hereditary depravity and corruption of our nature, diffused into all parts of the soul, which first makes us liable to God's wrath, then also brings forth in us those works which Scripture calls works of the flesh [Gal. 5:19]." *Institutes* II, ed. Battles (Philadelphia: Westminster, 1960), b. 1, c. 8.

[5] This claim was affirmed by Luther, Calvin, and the major Protestant confessions (see, for example, c. 6, §5, of the 1689 Baptist Confession of Faith).

[6] This teaching was codified at the Council of Trent. The fifth paragraph of Trent's decree on original sin uses two of Anselm's key arguments to defend this position: "If anyone denies that the guilt of original sin (*reatum originalis peccati*) is remitted by the grace of our Lord Jesus Christ given in baptism or asserts that all that is sin in the true and proper sense (*veram et propriam peccati rationem*) is not taken away but only brushed over or not imputed, let him be anathema. For, in those who are reborn God hates nothing, because 'there is no condemnation' [Rom. 8:1] for those [in grace].... The holy council, however, professes and thinks that concupiscence or the tinder of sin (*fomitem*) remains in the baptized. Since it is left for us to wrestle with, it cannot harm those who do not consent but manfully resist it by the grace of Jesus Christ.... Of this concupiscence, which the apostle occasionally calls 'sin,' the holy council declares: The Catholic Church has never understood that it is called sin because it would be sin in the true and proper sense in those who have been reborn, but because it comes from sin and inclines to sin (*ex peccato est et ad peccatum inclinat*). If anyone thinks to the contrary, let him be anathema" (DH 1515).

[7] For discussion of an influential Protestant federalist, see Mark Noll, "Charles Hodge," in *Reading Romans through the Centuries: From the Early Church to Karl Barth*, ed. Jeffrey Greenman and Timothy Larsen (Grand Rapids, MI: Brazos, 2005), 169–86. The following monographs by Oliver D. Crisp discuss two important realists: *Jonathan Edwards and the Metaphysics of Sin* (Ashgate, 2005) and *An American Augustinian: Sin and Salvation in the Dogmatic Theology of William G. T. Shedd* (Milton Keynes: Paternoster, 2007).

denial of the importance of a historical Fall from the denial of original sin
per se; the affirmation of a historical Fall without a strictly monogenetic
account of human origins; and, to borrow a phrase from Jamie Smith, the
"secularization of the Fall."[8] An example of a secularized approach is
Rousseau's view that humanity has been corrupted by society.[9] Other
examples can arguably be found in Nietzsche, Heidegger, and Wittgenstein.[10] As important as various secularized readings of the Fall have been
for modern philosophy, political theory, and culture, they are beyond the
scope of this work, an assumption of which is that a Christian understanding of original sin should focus on the human relation to God. It
may also be worth recalling one of the implications of the first four
chapters of this study: the denial or mitigation of original guilt was a
medieval move.

We need to discuss the modern perspective on the doctrine at this
juncture for two reasons. First, if it is sufficient, there is no need to retrieve
Thomas's account. In the second place, even if it is not, there may be
aspects of it worth preserving. I will argue that even the most promising
and influential modern accounts are ultimately inadequate. I will also
suggest that there are ideas that have been raised in the course of modern
reflection on the doctrine that could be fruitfully integrated with a broadly
Thomist perspective. We will focus on five thinkers: Kant, Barth, Schleiermacher, Schoonenberg, and McFarland (in that order).

---

[8] James K. A. Smith, "Lost in Translation? On the Secularization of the Fall," in *The Devil
Reads Derrida: And Other Essays on the University, Church, Politics, and the Arts*
(Grand Rapids, MI: Eerdmans, 2009), 62–7. In this review essay of Mulhall's book
(cited below), Smith warns that secularized "translations" of the Fall often give up the
doctrine's meaning altogether. Although there are similarities between secularized and
(what I am calling) "modern" interpretations of original sin – neither affirm the
importance of a historical Fall, for example – there is nevertheless a crucial difference
between them. Only modern accounts are at least plausibly read as addressing humanity's
relation to God.

[9] "Even Jean-Jacques Rousseau (1712–1778), who famously rejected original sin (the
Archbishop of Paris condemned his influential tract *Émile* specifically because of this),
believed in both an original innocence *and* a historical fall, which he linked to the
introduction of private property." James Boyce, *Born Bad: Original Sin and the
Making of the Western World* (Berkeley: Counterpoint, 2015), 107. For a helpful
overview of the theological background to the philosophes' views of original sin, see
Anselm Schubert, *Das Ende der Sünde: Anthropologie und Erbsünde zwischen
Reformation und Aufklärung* (Göttingen: Vandenhoeck & Ruprecht, 2002).

[10] Stephen Mulhall, *Philosophical Myths of the Fall* (Princeton: Princeton University
Press, 2005).

IMMANUEL KANT

To the dismay of his more optimistic contemporaries, Kant claimed in *Religion within the Boundaries of Mere Reason* (henceforth *Religion*) that humanity is radically evil. No one who has reached the age of reason is morally good, or even neutral. Everyone is evil. He even called this radical evil "original sin." Kant's affirmation of radical evil has come as a surprise to many of his readers. For he consistently affirms – in the *Religion* and in other major works, including the *Critique of Practical Reason* and *Metaphysics of Morals* – that human beings are obligated to follow the moral law for its own sake and that they are capable of so doing. If human beings can follow the law, however, shouldn't we expect that at least a few of them *do*?

In Kant's works that don't address the question of religion in as much depth, such as the *Metaphysics of Morals*, radical evil is not discussed. This has led many to assume that Kant's affirmation of radical evil in the *Religion* wasn't serious. He mentioned it simply to ward off charges of impiety or heresy. Goethe, for example, wrote that although Kant had attempted to keep his "philosopher's coat" free from the stain of dogmatic prejudice, he unfortunately "slobbered on it with the blot of radical evil so that even Christians would be enticed to kiss its hem."[11]

Recent scholarship has challenged this dismissive attitude.[12] Still, there is a great deal of debate about what Kant meant by "radical evil" and why he affirmed it. The following seems clear. When Kant asserted that evil is universal, he meant at least this: no human being, upon reaching the age of reason, adopts obedience to the law as a sufficient incentive for her

---

[11] Johann Wolfgang von Goethe, *Goethes Briefe*, 4 vols. (Hamburg: Christian Wegner Verlag, 1964), 536:5. Cited in Chris L. Firestone and Nathan Jacobs, *In Defense of Kant's Religion* (Bloomington: Indiana University Press, 2008), 79.

[12] These recent studies contain extensive discussion of radical evil: Chris L. Firestone and Nathan Jacobs, *In Defense of Kant's Religion* (Bloomington: Indiana University Press, 2008); James J. DiCenso, *Kant's Religion within the Boundaries of Mere Reason: A Commentary* (Cambridge: Cambridge University Press, 2012); Lawrence R. Pasternack, *Kant on Religion within the Boundaries of Mere Reason* (London: Routledge, 2014); Eddis N. Miller, *Kant's "Religion within the Boundaries of Mere Reason": A Reader's Guide* (New York: Bloomsbury, 2015); Stephen R. Palmquist, *Comprehensive Commentary on Kant's Religion within the Bounds of Bare Reason* (West Sussex: Wiley-Blackwell, 2016). See also John Hare, *The Moral Gap: Kantian Ethics, Human Limits and God's Assistance* (Oxford: Clarendon, 1996), and Stephen R. Grimm, "Kant's Argument for Radical Evil," *European Journal of Philosophy* 10.2 (2002), 160–77. For a reading on which, à la Rousseau, human beings become evil only through their social contact with other human beings, see Allen Wood, *Kant's Ethical Thought* (New York: Cambridge University Press, 1999).

action. When Kant asserted that evil is freely chosen, he meant at least this: every human being, upon reaching the age of reason, could have adopted obedience to the law as a sufficient incentive for her action.

Now, if evil is universal, then how could Kant insist that it is freely chosen? How could billions of human beings have freely chosen evil without exception? Shouldn't Kant admit either that some human beings might be good – even if he hasn't personally met any of them – or hypothesize that we are bent toward evil of necessity? These questions have led to three common interpretations of radical evil. Some have argued that radical evil is only an empirical hypothesis. Kant doesn't claim to know that all are evil, but it seems to be the case from historical investigation.[13] Others have argued that Kant tried to prove that there is one noumenal act of freedom committed by humanity as such, by which all human beings who exist in space and time are evil.[14] Finally, perhaps Kant is translating the doctrine of original sin into philosophical terms. On (one version of) this reading, the traditional Christian dogma is absurd, taken literally, but the deeper meaning is that everyone freely disobeys the moral law. I won't attempt to weigh in on this debate here, though it seems to me that the last option – radical evil is a philosophical translation of original sin – has been the most influential in modern theology. In any case, however precisely Kant intended his account of radical evil to relate to philosophy and theology, it raises interesting questions for Christian theologians. Here I will briefly discuss the salient aspects of Kant's account. I evaluate Kant's account, together with Barth's, at the end of the section below on Karl Barth.

Kant published *Religion* in 1793. It is not easy to say with confidence what precisely his goals were in writing it. The difficulty stems, in part at least, from the fact that he announces in the preface to the second edition that the work contains two different "experiments." But Kant does not clarify where one ends and the other begins. The first experiment is to examine religion in general from a purely philosophical point of view. The second experiment is to examine a *particular* religion's alleged revelation and see whether, or to what extent, it harmonizes with philosophy.[15] The ambiguity becomes apparent when we examine the first book,

---

[13] Grimm, "Kant's Argument for Radical Evil."

[14] This is the position of Firestone and Jacobs in *In Defense of Kant's Religion*.

[15] "From this standpoint [of philosophy] I can also make a second experiment, namely, to start from some alleged revelation or other and, leaving out of consideration the pure religion of reason (so far as it constitutes a self-sufficient system), to examine in a fragmentary manner this revelation, as an *historical system*, in the light of moral

which, as its title clearly states, concerns radical evil: "Concerning the Indwelling of the Evil Principle with the Good, Or, on the Radical Evil in Human Nature."[16] Is Kant attempting to examine a religious (Christian?) perspective on human evil and harmonize it with reason? Or is he offering an argument from reason (moral philosophy? empirical anthropology?) to the effect that human beings are evil?

Kant begins by contrasting two diametrically opposed views of human nature: ancient religious pessimism and modern philosophical optimism. Priests, poets, and historians have traditionally affirmed that "the world began in a good estate, whether in a Golden Age, a life in Eden, or a yet more happy community with celestial beings." They claim, however, that "a Fall into evil (moral evil, with which physical evil ever went hand in hand) presently hurried mankind from bad to worse with accelerated descent, so that now (this "now" is also as old as history), we live in the final age, with the Last Day and the destruction of the world at hand." Recently, Kant notes, philosophers have been more optimistic, believing that "the world steadily (though almost imperceptibly) forges in the other direction, to wit, from bad to better." Yet this optimism is naive; "the history of all times cries too loudly against it."[17]

What does it mean to say that human nature is good or evil? Kant notes that in the forthcoming discussion, he will not oppose "nature" to "freedom." That is, to say that "human nature" is good or evil, for Kant, is to say that the subjective ground of freedom in human nature is either good or evil. When human beings exercise their freedom in a particular act, is their underlying moral *character* good or evil? Whether human nature is itself good or evil, Kant argues, it must have become good or evil through the exercise of freedom. Otherwise, its moral character couldn't rightly be evaluated in moral terms. The source of evil lies in a rule made by the will – what Kant calls a "maxim."[18] The claim that the human

concepts; and then to see whether it does not lead back to the very same pure *rational system* of religion." Kant, Preface to the Second Edition of *Religion within the Limits of Reason Alone* [hereafter, *Religion*], trans. Theodore M. Green and Hoyt H. Hudson (New York: Harper and Brothers, 1960), 11. Also noteworthy is Kant's recommendation in the preface to the first edition that students, after they have studied biblical theology, take "a special course of lectures on the purely *philosophical* theory of religion (which avails itself of everything, including the Bible), with such a book as this perhaps, as the text." Kant, Preface to the First Edition of *Religion*, 10.

[16] Kant, *Religion*, 15.   [17] All from Kant, *Religion*, 15.

[18] "[T]his subjective ground, again, must itself always be an expression of freedom (for otherwise the use or abuse of man's power of choice in respect of the moral law could not be imputed to him nor could the good or bad in him be called moral). Hence the source of

being is morally evil, then, entails the claim that there is some ultimate, inscrutable ground of the adoption of particular evil maxims. Unfortunately, Kant does not clarify here exactly what he means by "human being." He does not say, for example, whether "human being" refers to the collection of all individual human beings or a universal, predicable of each actually existing human being or something else. It is clear that he is interested in the human being's moral nature insofar as it is the innate, yet freely chosen ground of individual acts of good or evil.

Why think that we are either good *or* evil? Why couldn't a given person be partially good and partially evil? Kant rejects the idea that the human being could be morally neutral (indifferent to the law) in favor of an approach he calls moral "rigorism." Rigorism is the view that the human being must be good or evil. It is true because the moral law is either the supreme incentive for one's actions or it is not. If it is, then one is good; if it is not, then one has *rejected* the law and made something evil the supreme incentive of her action.[19] For example, imagine two politicians who haven't taken any bribes. The first has rejected every bribe because she knows it is her duty. The second has rejected every bribe because the bribes weren't high enough. Which one is morally upright? The first politician clearly is. Her action is in accordance with – and motivated by – duty. The second politician, by contrast, even though her conduct is *in accordance* with the law – she hasn't taken any bribes – is not *sufficiently* motivated by the law. If someone had offered her a high enough bribe, she would have accepted it. And since *ex hypothesi* this choice would have been free, she must have prioritized the incentive of love for money over the incentive of obedience to the law.

(As an aside, it may be worth noting that Kant held that we can consider obedience to the moral law *to be* obedience to the divine law.[20] This strikes me as congruous with Thomas's view that every

---

evil cannot lie in an object *determining* the will through inclination, nor yet in a natural impulse; it can lie only in a rule made by the will for the use of its freedom, that is, in a maxim." Kant, *Religion*, 16–17.

[19] "[T]he moral law, in the judgment of reason, is in itself an incentive, and whoever makes it his maxim is *morally* good. If, now, this law does not determine a person's will in the case of an action which has reference to the law, an incentive contrary to it must influence his choice; and since, by hypothesis, this can only happen when a man adopts this incentive (and thereby deviation from the moral law) into his maxim (in which case he is an evil man) it follows that his disposition in respect to the moral law is never indifferent, never neither good nor evil." Kant, *Religion*, 19–20.

[20] This point is made in the *Religion* but is expressed perhaps more clearly in the *Metaphysics of Morals*: "A law that binds us a priori and unconditionally by our own

human being acts for an ultimate end which is either God or a creature. For Thomas, if the human being is not acting ultimately for God, then her action cannot be truly good, even at the natural level. And if she is acting for God, she cannot be committing a mortal sin.)

Kant argues that this fundamental moral disposition has not been chosen in time.[21] It is not clear to me what this means. He might mean that each human being, because her will can be considered free only insofar as it is not determined by the conditions of space and time, must be considered to have chosen evil in the noumenal realm.

A moral act can consist either in the adoption of a supreme maxim or the exercise of freedom in accordance with the adopted maxim.[22] Kant identifies the adoption of the supreme evil maxim with originating original sin. Particular acts that are motivated by this originating sin are originated sins:

The propensity to evil, then, is an act in the first sense (*peccatum originarium*), and at the same time the formal ground of all unlawful conduct in the second sense, which latter, considered materially, violates the law and is termed vice (*peccatum derivatum*); and the first offense remains, even though the second (from incentives which do not subsist in the law itself) may be repeatedly avoided.[23]

If a human being's supreme maxim has been perverted by sin, then she cannot eradicate it by her own power. For any attempt to reverse the incentives would itself be grounded in a corrupt incentive.

Kant unpacks the proposition "man is evil by nature" in light of the foregoing. It means "that from what we know of man through experience we cannot judge otherwise of him, or, that we may presuppose evil to be subjectively necessary to every man, even to the best."[24] This propensity to evil must itself be morally evil, that is, freely chosen. But the universality of evil is hard to understand, unless

the ultimate subjective ground of all maxims somehow or other is entwined with and, as it were, rooted in humanity itself. Hence we can call this a natural propensity to evil, and as we must, after all, ever hold man himself responsible

---

reason can also be expressed as proceeding from the will of a supreme lawgiver." Immanuel Kant, *Metaphysics of Morals*, in *Practical Philosophy*, trans. and ed. Mary J. Gregor (Cambridge: Cambridge University Press, 1996), 6:227.

[21] "To have a good or evil disposition as an inborn natural constitution does not here mean that it has not been acquired by the man who harbors it, that he is not author of it, but rather, that it has not been acquired in time (that he has *always* been good, or evil, *from his youth up*)." Kant, *Religion*, 20.

[22] Kant, *Religion*, 26.   [23] Kant, *Religion*, 26.   [24] Kant, *Religion*, 27.

for it, we can further call it a *radical* innate *evil* in human nature (and yet none the less brought upon us by ourselves).[25]

Unfortunately, Kant does not clarify just what it would mean for the ultimate subjective ground of all maxims to be rooted in *humanity* – as opposed to the ultimate subjective ground of each human being corrupted by virtue of a series of individual evil choices. If all he meant to affirm was the latter, it is unclear why he adds the possibility of the subjective ground of all maxims being corrupted as a satisfactory explanation of evil's universality.

There is no need for a formal proof that there is such a corrupt propensity in us, because our historical record testifies loudly and clearly.[26] We cannot blame sensuality for evil, for we are not responsible for being sensual creatures. Nor can evil be blamed on the corruption of morally legislative reason. That is, one cannot claim that we are somehow not obligated to follow the moral law (or that we are obligated but unable to follow it). If this were the case, we would be non-moral, neither good nor evil. How then does a person become evil?

[M]an (even the best) is evil only in that he reverses the moral order of the incentives when he adopts them into his maxim. He adopts, indeed, the moral law along with the law of self-love; yet when he becomes aware that they cannot remain on a par with each other but that one must be subordinated to the other as its supreme condition, he makes the incentive of self-love and its inclinations the condition of obedience to the moral law.[27]

There is nothing wrong with self-love, but it is wrong to subordinate the moral law to it. One who has reversed the order of the incentives may *appear* to be good, but that doesn't mean that she is. Her actions might be in conformity with the law but not done out of obedience to the law. We can call this radical evil "perversity" of heart. It could be found in someone who didn't want to be evil. It is also found in many people who believe that they are righteous simply because they act in conformity with the law. For Kant, however, the very fact that so many people think

---

[25] Kant, *Religion*, 27–8.
[26] "That such a corrupt propensity must indeed be rooted in man need not be formally proved in view of the multitude of crying examples which experience *of the actions* of men puts before our eyes." Kant, *Religion*, 28. Kant argues that it is naive to believe that "primitive" human beings are less violent than "civilized" human beings; anthropological studies have proven that violence is ubiquitous. Equally, it would be naive to believe that civilized humans are morally better than primitive humans. As far as duty goes, we're all in the same (evil) situation.
[27] Kant, *Religion*, 31–2.

they are righteous because they don't commit external acts of vice is itself evidence of our radical evil. For a morally good species would not pretend that acting in conformity with the law suffices for morality.

Kant then turns to the origin of evil. He explicitly criticizes the traditional Christian doctrine of original sin (as he understands it):

However the origin of moral evil in man is constituted, surely of all the explanations of the spread and propagation of this evil through all members and generations of our race, the most inept is that which describes it as descending to us as an *inheritance* from our first parents; for one can say of moral evil precisely what the poet said of good: *genus et proavos, et quae non fecimus ipsi, vis ea norta puto* [race and ancestors, and those things which we ourselves have not made, I scarcely account our own].[28]

Instead of thinking of evil as inherited from our ancestors, "every such action must be regarded as though the individual had fallen into it directly from a state of innocence."[29] This is because however strong one's inclinations toward a given action may have been, if we assume that the person who committed it is responsible for it, then she must have been able to refrain. No one is so evil that she doesn't have the obligation to do good, to better herself as best she can.[30]

Kant claims that the foregoing account is in agreement with the book of Genesis. Genesis depicts evil as having a temporal beginning. What is essentially timeless, for Kant, is depicted in Genesis as occurring in time. The temporal origin of evil in Genesis does not have a propensity to evil as its basis. If it did, evil would not have come from a free transgression of a divine command. Instead of treating the law as an adequate incentive, Adam and Eve looked for other incentives; they thereby made it their maxim to follow the law conditionally, only insofar as it suited them. *This* was their inner fall, manifested externally in the eating the forbidden fruit. We, like Adam, do this every day. The difference is that we must presuppose an innate propensity to transgression in ourselves, but the Bible doesn't presuppose this propensity in Adam.

The origin of the propensity to evil cannot be understood as an event in time. If we tried to understand the biblical story historically, as though it

---

[28] Kant, *Religion*, 35.   [29] Both from Kant, *Religion*, 35, 36.

[30] "However evil a man has been up to the very moment of an impending free act (so that evil has become custom or second nature) it was not only his duty to have been better [in the past], it is *now* still his duty to better himself. To do so must be within his power, and if he does not do so, he is susceptible of, and subjected to, imputability in the very moment of that action." Kant, *Religion*, 36.

really occurred in time, we would have to believe that the evil propensity was present *ab initio* – which contradicts the story and the idea of responsibility. Ultimately, we cannot, strictly speaking, understand the origin of evil.[31] The Genesis narrative also gives us hope of our redemption, because it depicts Adam as originally good and not "basically" (i.e., essentially) corrupt. "For man, therefore, who despite a corrupted heart yet possesses a good will, there remains hope of a return to the good from which he has strayed."[32] The rest of *Religion* takes up the possibility of man's redemption.

For Kant, evil is universal because no one has made obedience to the law the sufficient ground of all her maxims. It is innate because there is no moment in time when anyone was innocent. It is freely chosen because it could have been avoided. Kant has difficulty explaining the universality and culpability of evil simultaneously. If each individual is free to do duty for duty's sake, then Kant's assertion that evil is universal seems empty – at least from a philosophical point of view. It seems that he isn't in a position to know whether everyone has chosen evil unless he knows that it is necessary. But if it is necessary, then it cannot be free.

Perhaps, however, the answer to the problem generated by Kant's simultaneous affirmation of evil's freedom and universality is that the philosopher cannot know the latter as a philosopher, but she can have faith in it as a believer. If this was Kant's intention, then the first book of *Religion* is part of the "second experiment" of examining religious doctrine in terms of rational concepts. The doctrine of original sin involves the affirmation of universal evil. The philosopher argues that this universal evil is possible, because it is possible that every human being freely chooses evil. This is not a causal explanation of evil's universality, but if evil is freely committed, then we arguably should not be looking for such as causal explanation of evil's universality in the first place.

Ultimately, however, what is most important for present purposes is not whether that interpretation gets Kant exactly right.[33] What matters is

---

[31] Kant, *Religion*, 38.   [32] Kant, *Religion*, 39.

[33] The other readings of Kant on offer don't differentiate his account, in any significant way, from premodern views of human nature. For example, if all he meant was that most people do evil, his view would not have been substantively different from Pelagius's. For it was precisely Pelagius's teaching that most people sin. In the context of commenting on Paul's words "and through sin death," Pelagius said the following. "By example or by pattern. Just as through Adam sin came at a time when it did not yet exist, so in the same way through Christ righteousness was recovered at a time when it survived in almost no one." *Pelagius's Commentary on Saint Paul's Epistle to the Romans*, trans. Theodore de

that this reading, or something close to it, would be influential. Kant would be read, that is, as though he had rendered the dogma of the Fall intelligible by equating it with "radical evil": the universal yet free subordination of duty to self-love. Theologians glommed onto the concept themselves and retranslated it into theological terms. Alfred Vanneste, for example, explicitly "presents his reinterpretation as involving the reduction of the doctrine of original sin to the universality of actual sins."[34] Vanneste was clear that the first free act of every human being is a sin against God. There are no human beings who reach the age of reason who are not sinners, yet no one is determined to sin. Infants are "virtual" or "potential" sinners, because they will sin if they reach the age of reason, but they don't *really* sin until they freely choose to sin. There is no Adam of Genesis 2 in time; each of us is the Adam of Genesis 3.[35] Vanneste seems to have assumed that those who reached the age of reason without grace violate the natural law. The most important Protestant theologian of the twentieth century would receive Kant's account differently. For Karl Barth, sin must be understood in light of Jesus Christ.

KARL BARTH

Karl Barth's mature view of the doctrines of the Fall and original sin is found in *The Fall of Man*.[36] In what follows, I will summarize his account. I will then evaluate it, together with the general prospect of a theological appropriation of radical evil. We will see that, in critical conversation with Kant, Barth interpreted the doctrine of original sin as the universal act of unbelief in – and the lack of faithfulness to – Jesus

---

Bruyn (Oxford: Oxford University Press, 2002), 92. That is, spiritual death came to human beings after Adam because they followed his bad example. But he is clear that not all do this. Commenting on the second part of 5:12: "As long as they sin in the same way, they likewise die. For death did not pass on to Abraham and Isaac [and Jacob], concerning whom the Lord says: 'Truly they are all living' [Luke 20:38]. But here he says all are dead because in a multitude of sinners no exception is made for a few righteous.... Or: Death passed on to all who lived in a human, [and] not a heavenly, fashion" (pp. 92–3).

[34] George Vandervelde, *Original Sin: Two Major Trends in Contemporary Catholic Reinterpretation* (Washington, DC: University Press of America, 1981), 262.

[35] "The myth or symbol of Adam gives expression to the fact that the first free and conscious act of every human being (from the moment of the hominization of the species) is a sinful one." Vandervelde, *Original Sin*, 266.

[36] Karl Barth, *Church Dogmatics* [hereafter, *CD*], ed. G. W. Bromiley and T. F. Torrance (London: T&T Clark; New York: Continuum, 2009), §60.3.

Christ. Just as Kant proposed that the violation of the moral law is universal yet freely chosen, Barth argued that the lack of fidelity to Jesus Christ is universal yet freely chosen. We first need to begin by putting Barth's account in its immediate context, which requires a brief discussion of the knowledge (§60.1) and nature (§60.2) of sin.

Barth argues that Christian theologians have often made the egregious mistake of assuming that the knowledge of sin precedes the knowledge of Jesus Christ. What mistake did he have in mind? What exactly does it mean for the knowledge of sin to "precede" the knowledge of Jesus Christ?

> [I]n the *locus de peccato* which precedes the doctrine of reconciliation the agreement of older and more recent theology consists concretely in the view that by the knowledge of God, which makes possible and actual the knowledge of sin, we mean the knowledge of God in His basic relationship with man – as distinct from His presence, action and revelation in Jesus Christ.[37]

Barth is criticizing the view that human beings are able to understand sin (i.e., disobedience to God) without knowledge of Jesus Christ. It is reflected in the order of systematic theologies that treat hamartiology before Christology, as well as sermons that preach damnation before salvation. For Barth, sin is the "negative presupposition" of reconciliation; as such, sin can be known *only* in light of Christ.[38] "Within the sphere of the self-knowledge not enlightened and instructed by the Word of God there is no place for anything worthy of the name of a 'knowledge of sin.'"[39]

This should come as no surprise to readers familiar with Barth's broader theological project. He vigorously and consistently rejected "natural theology": the attempt to ground the knowledge of God in anything apart from Jesus Christ. (Recall his famous claim that the "analogy of being" – which he thought was the basis of natural theology – was the "invention of the Antichrist."[40]) This epistemology of sin follows directly from the rejection of natural theology. Since sin is disobedience to God, the one who knows sin must know God. Since God cannot be known except through Jesus Christ, neither can sin.

---

[37] *CD* IV.1, 5.   [38] *CD* IV.1, 2.   [39] *CD* IV.1, 3.

[40] *CD* I.1, xiii. For a contextualization of this claim and treatment of Barth's account of the "analogy of faith," see Bruce L. McCormack, "Karl Barth's Version of an "Analogy of Being": A Dialectical No and Yes to Roman Catholicism," in *The Analogy of Being*, 88–144.

After making that fundamental point, Barth offers a genealogy of hamartiology within Protestantism, from Calvin to liberalism (pp. 9–41). Calvin held that postlapsarian humanity retains a *divinitatis sensum*, a sense of God including a sense of his law. Insofar as God's law is imprinted on the hearts of human beings who don't know Christ, it is called the "natural law." For Barth, the natural law was a disastrous idea. It functioned like a cancerous tumor in Protestantism's theology of grace. Barely detectable in Calvin's own thought, the tumor metastasized in Protestant liberalism. Liberalism denied that humanity stands under the judgment of a wrathful God and reduced "sin" to underdeveloped God-consciousness. In turn, it reduced Jesus to a moral exemplar, an exemplar which reason can provide for itself.[41] By Barth's lights, the inner logic of the "natural law" leads to the denial of Jesus Christ. Once we "begin to toy with the *lex naturae*" we are on our way to contentment with "the hope and peace which we can have and know without the resurrection of Jesus Christ."[42]

What would a hamartiology that *followed* Christology consist in? In the first place, the concept of "sin" must be understood with reference to Jesus Christ. Though there are different words which can rightly be used to describe our sin against Christ (disobedience, transgression, pride, etc.), Barth argues that sin's paradigmatic form is *unbelief* in Jesus Christ.[43] We all, like the Pharisees, pridefully refuse to believe in him. But what of those who have never heard the Gospel, who never have the opportunity to believe in, or conform their lives to, Jesus Christ? By Barth's lights, it seems that in some important sense, there *are* no such people: divine law commands belief in Jesus Christ, and this "law of faith" is objectively present to everyone. Even "among the nations" sin is fundamentally unbelief in Jesus Christ, action that does not "correspond" to Jesus Christ.[44] Yet unbelief is not the sheer absence of belief: the human being culpably "contradicts" and "opposes" Christ.[45] God created us with the capability of obedience, but we disobeyed.[46]

---

[41] *CD* IV.1, 16.   [42] *CD* IV.1, 17.   [43] *CD* IV.1, 42.

[44] "This Law [*scil.*, the law of faith] as now proclaimed is the truth which was objectively present to all nations from the creation of the world, standing before them in nature and history and speaking of the One from whom it came." *CD* IV.1, 37.

[45] *CD* IV.1, 61.

[46] "That for which God has made man capable and which He might expect of him is not forthcoming." *CD* IV.1, 126. Though he says it would be anachronistic to call Barth's view of human freedom "compatibilist" in a philosophical sense, Jesse Couenhoven has

Which brings us to Barth's view of the Fall and original sin. Human nature has not been corrupted by Adam, as though sin were our fate. No, the human being is the "one who poisons himself in his pride."[47] Yet Barth does not simply follow Pelagius. It is *not* the case that because nature is incorrupt, some of us are saved by obeying God while (most) of us disobey and need forgiveness. Our nature was not corrupted by Adam, but we *are* evil. Barth approvingly cites Kant in this connection:

[I]n relation to the transgression and therefore the corruption of man there is no time in which man is not a transgressor and therefore guiltless before God. To use the phrase of Kant, he lives by an "evil principle," with a "bias towards evil," in the power of a "radical evil" which shows itself virulent and active in his life, with which in some incomprehensible but actual way he accepts solidarity, with which he is not identical, but to which he commits himself and is committed.... He was always on that way and at that goal.... Because he himself as the subject of these activities is not a good tree, he cannot bring forth good fruit. Because his pride is radical and in principle, it is also total and universal and all-embracing, determining all his thoughts and words and works, his whole inner and hidden life, and his visible external movements and relationships. He is not just partly but altogether "flesh."[48]

We have not fallen from a state of original righteousness in time. We are *always* acting from an all-encompassing pride. Barth cites Kant in the course of making these claims. Why? What role does Kant's view play in Barth's account?

Certainly Barth maintains that culpable unbelief is universal, and, as we're about to see, Barth denies that unbelief is inherited. But Barth's own view of radical evil is different from Kant's in a crucial respect: for Kant, evil consists in the violation of a self-given moral law, whereas for Barth it

argued that Barth's operated with a "compatibilist conception" of human freedom. "Karl Barth's Conception(s) of Human and Divine Freedom(s)," in *Commanding Grace: Studies in Karl Barth's Ethics*, ed. Daniel L. Migliore (Grand Rapids, MI: Eerdmans, 2010), 239–55. Couenhoven doesn't discuss CD IV.1 §60.3. He may be right about Barth's views more broadly, but it is hard to see how Barth could have *consistently* been a compatibilist given what he says here. We will see Barth claim that Adam – who represents each one of us – was made good and capable of faithful obedience. We will see Barth sharply criticize Schleiermacher's compatibilism, suggesting that it opens the door for human beings to make excuses for their sins. "Will he [the human being who believes his sins are determined] not finally be able to reassure and console himself with the thought that secretly and at bottom his evil is a good, or the transition to it, that his sinning is imposed and posited and ordained by God[?]" CD IV.1, 32. And although true freedom is surely found only in Jesus Christ, for Barth, we will see him say, explicitly, that we sin "freely."

[47] CD IV.1, 135.   [48] CD IV.1, 136–7.

consists in the refusal to believe in, or conform one's life to, Jesus Christ. In light of this, we might say that Barth "christologized" radical evil: he kept (what he saw as) the core of the concept, while insisting that it can be properly understood only with reference to Jesus Christ.[49]

Barth then proposed that *"Erbsünde"* – the standard German term for *peccatum originale* – should be replaced with *"Ursünde."*[50] *Erbsünde* should be abandoned, because "there can be no doubt that the idea of a hereditary sin which has come to man by propagation is an extremely unfortunate and mistaken one."[51] *Ursünde*, by contrast, should be used to refer to

the voluntary and responsible life of every man – in a connexion with Adam that we have yet to show – which by virtue of the judicial sentence passed on it in and with his reconciliation with God is the sin of every man, the corruption which he brings on himself so that as the one who does so – and again in that connexion – he is necessarily and inevitably corrupt.[52]

The *Ursünde* (original sin) of the human being is the voluntary sin of every human being. This sin is depicted in Genesis 3, the story of Adam's Fall and Everyman. The Bible gives "the general title of Adam" to all human beings.[53] History "constantly re-enacts the little scene in the garden of Eden. There never was a golden age. There is no point in looking back to one. The first man was immediately the first sinner."[54] The biblical authors assumed that Adam was the historical parent of the

---

[49] For a treatment of christocentricity in Barth, see Marc Cortez, "What Does It Mean to Call Karl Barth a 'Christocentric Theologian?," *Scottish Journal of Theology* 60.2 (2007), 1–17.

[50] The English translation of *Erbsünde* is "hereditary sin." The English translation of *Ursünde* is "original sin."

[51] CD IV.1, 141. Barth argues as follows: "What I do as the one who receives an inheritance is something that I cannot refuse to do, since I am not asked concerning my willingness to accept it. It is only in a very loose sense that it can be regarded as my own act. It is my fate which I may acknowledge but for which I cannot acknowledge or regard myself responsible. And yet it is supposed to be my determination for evil, the corrupt disposition and inclination of my heart, the radical and total *curvitas* and *iniquitas* of my life, and I myself am supposed to be an evil tree merely because I am an heir of Adam. It is not surprising that when an effort is made to make the word 'heir' seriously, as has occasionally happened, the term 'sin" is necessarily dissolved. Conversely, when the term 'sin' is taken seriously, the term 'heir' is necessarily explained in a way which makes it quite unrecognisable, being openly or surreptitiously dissolved and replaced by other and more serious concepts. 'Hereditary sin' has a hopelessly naturalistic, deterministic and even fatalistic ring.... It is perhaps better to abandon altogether the idea of hereditary sin and to speak only of original sin [*Ursünde*] (the strict translation of *peccatum originale*)." CD IV.1, 142.

[52] CD IV.1, 142.   [53] CD IV.1, 149.   [54] CD IV.1, 149.

human race, but this was incidental to the story's theological import.[55] The story is not history but *saga*: "historical narration at the point where events are no longer susceptible as such of historical proof."[56] Our Adamic identity is our own fault. "No one has to be Adam. We are so freely and on our own responsibility."[57] As he puts it elsewhere, "[o]ur understanding of the enslaved will of sinful man has nothing whatever to do with determinism."[58] We are like Adam because we *act* as he did: "the successors of Adam are ... those who are represented in his person and *deed*."[59]

For Kant, evil is radical because every human being freely subordinates the moral law to self-love; for Barth, sin is radical because every human being – as represented by the saga of the Fall in Genesis 3 – refuses to believe in Christ. With Kant, Barth denies that Adam's descendants inherited his sin or corrupted nature. Those who reject Augustine's view of original sin will, of course, view this as an advantage of Barth's account. Those who simultaneously want to avoid Pelagianism will appreciate Barth's insistence that no one obeys the law unto salvation. Barth's is clearly a "modern" account of the doctrine in my stipulated sense: there is no theological significance to a historical Fall from original justice, because there wasn't one.

I am sympathetic to Barth: I agree that what is needed is an account of original sin that avoids the pitfalls of traditional Augustinianism and Pelagianism. But I have several concerns with his account. First, it is not clear that it includes infants or those with severe mental disabilities. One need not endorse the totality of Augustine's hamartiology to agree with him that the Gospel is for all human beings, from infants to the elderly. But if sin is reduced to the act of unbelief, then it seems that infants and the profoundly disabled are not in sin – and not yet in need of Jesus Christ. Indeed, this is a worry I have with the theological appropriation of Kant's account of radical evil more broadly. When sin is reduced to act or, better, when sin is reduced to the *volitions* of those with the use of free will – regardless of whether sin is held to be the lack of faithfulness to Jesus Christ, the violation of a self-given moral law, or the violation of a God-given natural law – infants and the severely mentally

---

[55] "Who is Adam? The great unknown who is the first parent of the race? There can be no doubt that this is how the biblical tradition intended that he should be seen and understood. But it is interested in him as such only for what he did." *CD* IV.1, 150.

[56] *CD* IV.1, 149.   [57] *CD* IV.1, 151.   [58] *CD* IV.2, 117.

[59] *CD* IV.1, 152, emphasis mine.

disabled are at least implicitly excluded. And if they are thought to have no part (yet) in God's providence, are they not at least implicitly dehumanized?[60]

That leads to a second, related worry about Barth's account: Does it provide an adequate explanation of the universality of culpable belief among adults? Recall that all sin is against *Christ*, not God qua author of nature. How can "pagans" (those who, outside Judaism and Christianity, haven't heard the gospel) be responsible for refusing to put their faith in, or conform their lives to, a man they've never heard of? At times, Barth seems to speak as though pagan culpability were grounded in the objective promulgation of the law of faith. If this is what Barth has in mind, however, it is hard to see how a merely objective presence of the law of faith is sufficient. If Sally, who is deaf, is working in her cubicle and her boss shouts from the common room, "Meet in the conference room in five," is she culpable if she misses the meeting? It seems obvious that she is not – unless she was informed via a method of communication intelligible to her. The "objective" presence of the announcement in the office is insufficient grounds for her culpability: "subjective" reception of the message must be possible.

Yet Barth emphatically denies that unbelief is a predetermined fate. It seems plausible, then, that he holds that all adults can have faith in Christ but that none of them do (at least not initially). But what grounds the claim that adults who have never heard the gospel *can* believe, or live lives of faithful obedience to Jesus Christ? If they did believe, would they be "anonymous Christians"? If so, then what difference, exactly, does the proclamation of the gospel make? The counterargument that gospel proclamation is how God, in his sovereignty, brings people to the obedience to the law of faith lands us on the other horn of the dilemma: those whom God has *not* sovereignly brought to the obedience of faith seem fated to unbelief.

One of the advantages of the hypothesis of the natural law is that it can explain pagan culpability without implying that every adult human being somehow has knowledge of Jesus Christ. *Pace* Barth, the traditional decision to prioritize hamartiology over Christology – that is, to acknowledge that human beings can violate the natural law without explicit

---

[60] If not explicitly: see Vandervelde, *Original Sin*, 263–4, for quotations from Vanneste to the effect that children have yet to become human.

knowledge of Jesus Christ – was not treated as though it were self-evident.[61] In fact, theologians such as Calvin and the Protestant scholastics (not to mention Catholic luminaries like Aquinas) offered theological arguments for this view. A common argument was that the natural law is necessary to explain pagan culpability for personal sin. If fallen human beings who have never heard the Gospel weren't – at least in an inchoate sense – able to understand God's commands, they wouldn't be responsible before God for disobeying them. Calvin et al. argued that this view was grounded in Paul: "[God's] eternal power and divine nature, invisible though they are, have been understood and seen through the things he had made. So they are without excuse" (Rom. 1:20). I am not claiming here that Calvin's (or any other theologian's) view of the natural law is correct. Yet a theological account of human responsibility *not* grounded in the natural law must find a way of responding to the concerns raised by those who have defended the natural law. It is not clear to me that Barth's account has done this.

FRIEDRICH SCHLEIERMACHER

Schleiermacher agreed with Kant that the meaning of the doctrines of the Fall and original sin does not depend on a historical change in humanity's relation to God. But his account of the doctrine was quite different from Kant's. Instead of reducing original sin to the universality of sinful volitions, Schleiermacher focused on humanity's communal solidarity in sin. We will focus on his account of original sin in the second edition of *The Christian Faith*, published in 1830.[62] This work, as B. A. Gerrish says, "traverses the entire territory of the inherited Protestant dogmatics," and its "main concern was to give an account of the distinctively Christian consciousness of sin and grace, the overall theme of the second part of the work."[63] I will begin with his treatment of the original perfection of the

---

[61] "What reason is there for that first belief that the doctrine of sin must precede Christology and therefore be worked out independently of it? The belief is a traditional one which has seldom been questioned but has usually been treated as more or less self-evident." *CD* IV.1, 32–3.

[62] Friedrich Schleiermacher, *The Christian Faith*, trans. H. R. Mackintosh and James S. Stewart (Berkeley: Apocryphile, 2011).

[63] B. A. Gerrish, "Schleiermacher, Friedrich Daniel Ernst," in *The Oxford Companion to Christian Thought*, ed. Adrian Hastings et al. (Oxford: Oxford University Press, 2000), 645.

world and humanity (§§57–61) and then turn to his account of sin in general (§§65–9) and original sin proper (§§70–2).

Schleiermacher denies that a lost paradisiacal state is relevant to Christian consciousness. "[T]he idea of a change in human nature entailed by the first sin of the first pair has no place among the propositions which rank as utterances of our Christian consciousness."[64] Even if God had created humanity without sin and mortality, it wouldn't follow that he hadn't also preordained death and evil.[65] This argument reveals Schleiermacher's determinism, discussed earlier in the work (§46) and confirmed in his treatment of God-consciousness in relation to sin and evil (§§81–5).[66] What relevance could original justice possibly have, if God had ordained the Fall? Schleiermacher reinterprets the "original perfection" of the world and humanity teleologically. The perfection of the world consists in the totality of finite existence's ability to work for the continuity of God-consciousness. The perfection of humanity consists in its ability to continually awaken God-consciousness (§§57–61). The development of God-consciousness does not develop uninhibited, however: it faces the obstacle of sin.

The Christian is conscious of sin as an antagonism between flesh and spirit. The pain we feel in this conflict is the consciousness of sin. Schleiermacher analyzes this conflict in §§65–9. Sin-consciousness develops with God-consciousness, for our flesh was with us from the earliest stages of development. Still, before God-consciousness, sin is better called the "germ" of sin.[67] (Only Jesus lacks consciousness of sin, and thus he alone

---

[64] Schleiermacher, *The Christian Faith*, §72.3, 298.

[65] "Even if we accepted absolutely the idea that apart from sin there would have been neither evil nor death, it would by no means follow from this that the earth must originally have been adapted to an enduring condition of sinlessness; evil and death may none the less have been preordained as certainly as God foreknew sin." Schleiermacher, *The Christian Faith*, §59.3, 243.

[66] "[W]e need have no misgiving in saying that God is also the Author of sin – of sin, however, only as related to redemption." Schleiermacher, *The Christian Faith*, §80.3, 328. Cf. §46.2, 174.

[67] "If our God-consciousness is not yet developed, there can be in us no resistance to it, but merely an independent activity of the flesh which, though in time it will quite naturally come to act as a resistance to the spirit, cannot at that stage be regarded as sin in the proper sense, but rather as the germ of sin." Schleiermacher, *The Christian Faith*, §67.1, 273. "[W]e become conscious also of sin as the God-consciousness awakes within us" (§67.1, 274). Schleiermacher goes so far as to say that "sin in general exists only in so far as there is consciousness of it" (§68.2, 277). It would be a mistake, though, to think that he denied sin before God-consciousness simpliciter, as we are about to see.

can exercise redemptive activity.[68]) We are also conscious of our sins having a source *outside* ourselves, in virtue of our dependence on communal life. This consciousness, in which sin is both received from without and present within, is the basis of Schleiermacher's rejection of accounts of original sin which veer exclusively toward the external or the internal. He argues that (what we are calling) realism makes sin far too internal, and that the legal theory makes sin far too external.[69] The theologian must do justice to our dual consciousness of sin as coming from within and without. This is the basis for the distinction between "original" and "actual" sin.[70]

In §70, Schleiermacher argues that the idea that human beings have sin "from the first" – that they have original sin – is in "perfect accord" with the view that the consciousness of God and sin are inextricably intertwined. If the awakened God-consciousness doesn't remove sin, how could we have been sinless before? The coexistence of sin and God-consciousness also implies that human beings in a sinful state prior to the awakening of God-consciousness are *utterly incapable* of any good, at least as far as Christian piety is concerned.[71] Schleiermacher is clear, though, that we retain our capacity to "appropriate redemption"[72] and perform "civil righteousness."[73] His conception of civil righteousness is

---

[68] "For since even our most perfect inner states still retain traces of sin (this is the testimony of the universal consciousness of mankind), then *he* alone to whom we do not ascribe that common consciousness of sin ... can exercise redeeming activity" (§68.3, 278–9).

[69] Theories "which most arbitrarily interpret God's command as a covenant made in the person of Adam with the entire human race, the legal consequences of violating which fall also on his posterity ... bring man's relation to God and God's imputation of sin under the category of a merely external legal relationship, a view which has had a most detrimental effect upon interpretation of the work of redemption" (§72.4, 301).

[70] Schleiermacher criticizes these terms for being misleading; they imply that original sin is not actual and therefore not real; while at the same time implying that original sin is "sin" univocally. He notes, however, that "if we would avoid breaking the historical continuity of doctrine, and causing fresh misconsiderations and misunderstandings, we shall have to carry out the charge by means of gradual adjustments" (§69, *Postscript*, 281).

[71] Schleiermacher, *The Christian Faith*, §70.1, 282–3.

[72] "Yet we must not magnify our congenital sinfulness to such an extent as would involve the denial of man's capacity to appropriate redemption, for that capacity is the very least that can be predicated of that disposition to the God-consciousness which is inherent in man's original perfection" (§70.2, 283).

[73] "Even within the sphere of voluntary action, however, thinkers have always taken care to confine the incapacity in question to what Christian piety regards as alone good in the strictest sense. This again takes for granted that there is a distinction of praiseworthy and blameworthy which is quite independent of a man's relationship to redemption; in fact, just as the unredeemed may have in themselves that which is commendable, so the redeemed are conscious of having acquired it without the aid of grace. Now this whole

thoroughly Augustinian: good deeds outside the sphere of redemption are nothing but so many manifestations of *amor sui*. Even the "spirit of patriotism," which Schleiermacher regards as civil righteousness's "highest purity and perfection,"

while capable of evoking the most consummate self-renunciation in the individual, is merely the self-love of the nation or the country as a composite person, and may be conjoined with animosity and injustice of all kinds towards those who are outside the group, unless the reverse is dictated by the group's own selfish interest or love of honour – and these, again, are but self-love. Hence the very best elements of this side of life, so far as they subsist independently of the power of the God-consciousness, can rank only as the mind, wisdom, and righteousness of the flesh.[74]

Even the soldier's sacrifice of life for country is only an expression of the self-love of the nation. How should we understand the origin and nature of this sin which antedates God-consciousness?

This brings us to the doctrine of original sin itself. Schleiermacher begins by describing the traditional doctrine tendentiously, claiming it often gives the impression that infants are so guilty that nothing they could do later in life could add to the horrendous guilt of original sin.[75] It is quite understandable, Schleiermacher observes, that some thinkers, when presented with the doctrine in this form, have rejected it and preferred to think of original sin merely as an evil. Some scholars, isolating this observation, assume that Schleiermacher is *endorsing* the view that original sin is only an evil, not a guilt. It is crucial, however, to keep reading.

The doctrine has this repugnant character only if we divorce it from actual sins. The link between original sin and actual sin is

not to be understood in the sense that original sin is not guilt until it breaks forth into actual sins, for the mere circumstance that there has been no opportunity for and no outward incentive to sin cannot enhance the spiritual status of man; it is to be understood rather as implying that in the individual original sin is the sufficient

---

phase of life may very appropriately be described as 'civil righteousness' – the expression taken in the broad sense" (§70.3, 284).

[74] Schleiermacher, *The Christian Faith*, §70.3, 284–5.

[75] "[I]n many theologians the doctrine of original sin appears to imply that the sinfulness innate in all men, just in so far as received from an external source, is yet in every case the individual's own guilt; a guilt indeed which involves eternal punishment as its due, so that the greatest possible accumulation of actual sins could add nothing to the penal desert which attaches to everyone on account of this so-called disease" (§71.1, 286).

ground of all actual sins, so that only something else outside of him, and not anything new within him, is needed for the generation of actual sin.[76]

The fact that infants are born without having actually committed sins does not make them innocent, does not enhance their "spiritual status," because "originated" original sin is the sufficient ground, in conjunction with environmental stimuli, to *become* an "originating" original sin when the infant grows up. One is reminded here of Kant's argument that acting in conformity to the law does not make one good if one is not incentivized by duty.

Schleiermacher clarifies, shortly after the foregoing quote, that there is no moral difference between originated and originating sins. "[T]his later sinfulness which has issued from the individual's own action is *one and the same* with that which was congenital in origin."[77] But he then backtracks, admitting that the difference between infants and adults is "not to be overlooked" and that it "probably has never been questioned" that infants are not sinners "in the same sense and in the same degree as those in whom actual sin has become permanent," especially regarding their "guilt."[78] But we shouldn't mistake the drift of his discussion, despite his hedging: infants have the same sin as their parents. What, exactly, is the nature of this sameness or unity? Is it numerical or specific? What are the different "degrees" of sin he speaks of, given that sin is really one and the same?

Considering the following quotation should help us grasp how Schleiermacher envisages the unity of sin. It contains his description of original sin as a corporate act (earlier, he claimed that original sin is "best represented as the corporate act and the corporate guilt of the human race"[79]).

Now if the sinfulness which is prior to all action operates in every individual through the sin and sinfulness of others, and if, again, it is transmitted by the voluntary actions of every individual to others and implanted within them, it must be something genuinely common to all. Whether, in fact, we regard it as guilt and deed or rather as a spirit and a state, it is in either case common to all; not something that pertains severally to each individual and exists in relation to him by himself, *but in each the work of all, and in all the work of each*; and only in this corporate character, indeed, can it be properly and fully understood. Hence the

[76] Schleiermacher, *The Christian Faith*, §71.1, 286, emphasis mine.
[77] Schleiermacher, *The Christian Faith*, §71.1, 287, emphasis mine.
[78] Schleiermacher, *The Christian Faith*, §71.1, 287.
[79] Schleiermacher, *The Christian Faith*, §71, p. 285.

doctrinal statements that deal with it are not to be regarded as utterances of the individual consciousness, which fall to be treated rather under the doctrine of actual sin, but are utterances of the corporate consciousness. *This solidarity means an interdependence of all places and all times in the respect we have in view.* The distinctive form of original sin in the individual, as regards its quality, is only a constituent part of the form it takes in the circle to which he immediately belongs, so that, though inexplicable when taken by itself, it points to the other parts as complementary to it. And this relationship runs through all gradations of community – families, clans, tribes, peoples, and races – so that the form of sinfulness in each of these points to that present in the forms as its complement; and the aggregate power of the flesh in its conflict with the spirit.[80]

The doctrinal statements concerning original sin, then, are utterances of the corporate consciousness. One inherits original sin, "the aggregate power of the flesh" running through all human communities, precisely as a member of a sinful community. The consciousness of the corporate character of original sin is comforting, for it comes with the corporate feeling of redemption. What does he mean by the statement that sin is "in each the work of all, in all the work of each"? Humanity was instituted in a state of sin; and the actual sins of our first parents, together with various causes from within the nature system, determine all the actual sins of subsequent human beings. This is why no individual sin can be considered in isolation from the whole; it was determined by previous sins, and it will in turn determine future human beings' sins.

Sin, Schleiermacher seems to imply, is *numerically* one; it is the corporate act of the human race. It is present in different degrees or, as Schleiermacher says, "different forms." But the different degrees or "forms" of sin are not numerically different members of the same species, as, say, in Thomas's metaphysics two different human beings agree in form but differ by virtue of their matter. No, for Schleiermacher, the sin in an infant must be considered in connection with *all previous, present, and subsequent* actual sins. Sin is "distributed among individuals in respect of place and time not equally and uniformly, but unequally" – yet this means no more than that "in one individual one type of sin is specially predominant and another less so, while in another individual the case is reversed."[81] "[A]ll actual sins must rank as equal not only in respect of their nature and character, but also of their origin; for every such sin is a manifestation of the universal sinfulness."[82]

---

[80] Schleiermacher, *The Christian Faith*, §71.2, 287–8.
[81] Schleiermacher, *The Christian Faith*, §73.2, 306.
[82] Schleiermacher, *The Christian Faith*, §74.1, 307.

Schleiermacher does not offer any analogies to explain the relation between sin itself and the different degrees of sin. Perhaps we could compare it to a soul and its body parts (assuming a Thomist account of their relation). As the one form of the human being, the soul, is in the brain and the foot, the one power of sin is in this human being and that human being, in the infant and in the murderer. Yet this analogy is misleading, at it might imply that we are only one person in the corporate act of sin. But Schleiermacher does not (as far as I can see) deny that we exist as individuals within the community, despite our union in the corporate act of sin.

There are several problems that follow from Schleiermacher's ambiguity regarding the unity of sin. Let's assume for the moment that, as I have suggested, he wants to claim that sin is numerically one. It seems that absurdities follow from this claim. First, it follows that everyone is equally guilty of the one corporate act of sin. This means, though, that children in ancient Rome are guilty for murders committed by modern humans, and vice versa. In short, it implies that everyone is equally guilty of everything, which is ridiculous. There are two points Schleiermacher could bring up in response.

We have already mentioned the first. Schleiermacher argued that the view that infants are guilty of original sin is problematic only if we separate original sin from actual sins. When one realizes that the infant will inevitably commit actual sins of her own and cause them in others, that she is, in a phrase, caught up in the community of sin, one will realize it is not absurd to consider her guilty. The second point Schleiermacher could bring up in response is one he makes a bit later. He argues that a deep-seated mistake in the Christian tradition is supposing that original sin is *punishable*. The link between our feelings of sin and redemption is broken "when the idea that original sin ought to be punished is thrust between the two." If our motive to avoid sin and find redemption were avoiding sense punishments (such as hellfire) and enjoying sensual pleasure (such as avoiding hellfire), then "one's motive for not willing the antagonism of the flesh, and for willing redemption, would then be merely the sensuous consequences of each, and here accordingly piety in the real sense fades out."[83] What does this have to do with my critique that it is absurd to consider everyone guilty of the same sin? Schleiermacher could argue that the only reason it seems absurd to consider infants guilty of

---

[83] Both from Schleiermacher, *The Christian Faith*, §72.4, 290–1.

horrendous crimes is because we are overly concerned with sensual punishments. But once we have realized that God does not mete out sense punishments for sin in infants, and it would be wrong for adult human beings to punish sin in infants, the problem disappears.

I would respond, though, that the question of whether original sin deserves punishment is a red herring. Even if sin (or at least the degree it takes in infants) does not deserve punishment, it is still absurd to claim that infants are guilty for the sins of their ancestors. We ought to speak truly about whether infants have guilt – and, assuming they do, what sort of guilt they have – regardless of whether they ought to be punished by God or anyone else. This leads to my response to Schleiermacher's first potential response, to the effect that the problem of the equality of guilt disappears when we consider the connection between original and actual sin. Let's grant that if determinism is true, the numerical unity of sin follows in the aforementioned sense. It seems to me that this would be a reason to reject determinism, not a reason to accept the thesis that everyone is guilty of everything – such that, to repeat, infants are guilty of crimes committed before their existence. For the claim that infants are guilty of crimes committed before their existence is obviously false, and determinism is not obviously true.

But perhaps Schleiermacher is not claiming that sin is numerically one in this strong sense. Perhaps the distinction between sin and the degrees of sin is comparable to the distinction between the human being and individual human beings in Platonism, such that there is a form of sin in which various sins participate to a greater or lesser extent. Thus infants participate in sin but not in the same degree as adults, and they are not guilty for the actions of their ancestors. If this were true, Schleiermacher would be much closer to the scholastics and the view that sin is predicated *secundum analogiam*. I cannot see, however, how this is compatible with his claim that there is ultimately only one act of sin or his claim that all sins rank as equal in nature, character, and origin.

Schleiermacher is wrestling with the same problems pertaining to the unity of sin that confronted Augustine. Recall that Augustine affirmed a radical unity in sin between Adam and his posterity without clarifying its precise mode. Recall also that Augustine was open to the idea of inheriting original *sins* from one's parents and grandparents. Schleiermacher has rejected the Augustinian view that nature is vitiated by sin; but he is deeply Augustinian in attempting to think through nature's radical unity in sin, in concupiscence. He also seems, with Augustine, to suggest that there are *peccata originalia*.

We saw Schleiermacher claim that the degrees of sin will vary not only from person to person but also from group to group and race to race ("families, clans, tribes, peoples, and races"). He also notes, a bit later, that different races and nations will experience evil in correspondence with their sin: for "every nation, and indeed of every social class in it, so far as it seems to stand by itself ... the measure of its sin will be also the measure of the evil that it suffers."[84] I am not sure what Schleiermacher means by this, given that sin is the one corporate act of humanity. If he means, however, that members of a given people group in the present are guilty of actions committed by members of the group in the past (and those in various outgroups are innocent), then I think we should reject his view.

Thomas and other medievals were right to affirm that personal guilt cannot be transmitted. I cannot defend this view at length here, but consider one unappealing consequence of believing in the possibility of inherited group guilt. It seems inevitable that if one group supposes another group has inherited sin in a particularly vile form or degree, the first group will *feel* the need for retributive justice. If the law of the land doesn't provide for it, they will feel the urge of a "natural law" to do "justice" themselves. Historical examples of the violent logic of group guilt, are, alas, easy to provide. How many Christians, for example, have attempted to justify violence against Jews on the supposition that the actions of a few Jews in the temple aristocracy have redounded to the entire Jewish people? After all, didn't the Jews declare, "His blood be on us and on our children" (Matt. 27:25)?[85]

Thomas's emphasis on individual responsibility is a helpful corrective here. "The sons of the Jews are guilty of the blood of Christ insofar as

---

[84] Schleiermacher, *The Christian Faith*, §77.1, 321.

[85] Thomas indicates that Augustine cites this verse as evidence of collective Jewish guilt in *De malo* q. 4, a. 8, arg. 9. For Augustine's preaching on the Jews, see Johannes van Oort, "Jews and Judaism in Augustine's *Sermones*," *Instrvmenta Patristica et Mediaevalia* 53 (2009), 213–65. Van Oort argues that Augustine's preaching downplays the role of the Romans in the Passion narrative; the Jews, and the Jews alone, are to blame. Augustine even adds certain accusations nowhere stated or implied in the biblical narrative: that the Jews watched the crucifixion with "cruel eyes" and "voluptuously" (p. 258). Van Oort argues that Augustine probably knew many Jews personally, but he does not address the question of whether Augustine considered *all* Jews to be guilty of deicide. Was deicide, in Augustine's mind, Judaism's original sin? Whether Augustine ever made this move explicitly or not, given the haziness of the concept of *peccata originalia*, it is easy to imagine later Augustinians making this move – that is, those who didn't join the medieval consensus in rejecting *peccata originalia* outright.

they imitate the evil of their parents by approving of it."[86] In other words, Jews are guilty for Christ's death just as Gentiles are: insofar as they approve of it. This is to *deny* that anyone is guilty for the death of Christ except the individual human beings who culpably contributed to his murder, and it is thus to deny that the Jews as a group are guilty of deicide. For to sinfully approve of a past deed is a distinct deed from the deed being approved. (Of course, we can speak in a broader sense of everyone killing Christ, insofar as Christ died for all sins; again, though, Jews and Gentiles both "killed Christ" in this sense, as they are both under sin.) I am not suggesting that Schleiermacher or Augustine claimed that Jews have inherited a special guilt for the killing of Christ. I am claiming that Thomas has the conceptual resources to clearly and consistently deny these sorts of odious claims, precisely because he denies that personal guilt can be transmitted.

Let's review. Sin, understood as concupiscence, the *amor sui*, is present in all infants except Jesus Christ; originated original sin inevitably breaks forth into actual sins. Original guilt is central to Schleiermacher's account. As the corporate act of humanity, the infant's sin cannot be separated from the totality of actual sins. Infants, however, don't yet have the same degree of sin as those whose originated original sin has broken forth into originating original sin. Schleiermacher decisively broke with the Augustinian tradition in separating original sin from original justice. He didn't hesitate to admit one clear consequence of this move: God is the author of sin, for the sake of redemption. Schleiermacher wrote before Darwin but in the midst of the rise of evolutionary thinking. The eventual success of evolutionary biology all but guaranteed that his views would be influential in late nineteenth and twentieth centuries.[87]

PIET SCHOONENBERG

Not everyone who concurred with his conclusion that a historical state of original justice is inessential to the doctrine of original sin, or that hamartiology should stress human solidarity in sin, accepted

---

[86] "[S]anguis Christi obligat filios Iudaeorum in quantum sunt imitatores paterne malitie ipsam approbando." *De malo* q. 4, a. 8, ad 9.

[87] For an account of liberal Christian responses to Darwin in which Schleiermacher features prominently, see Gary Dorrien, *The Making of American Liberal Theology: Imagining Progressive Religion, 1805–1900* (Louisville: Westminster John Knox Press, 2001), 314–18.

Schleiermacher's compatibilist account of freedom. A notable example is the Dutch Jesuit Piet Schoonenberg, whom Vandervelde calls the "pioneer" of the "situationalist" view of original sin. Schoonenberg, in effect, reconstructed a Schleiermacherian account of original sin that included a robust account of (an incompatiblist view of) free will.[88] Let's take a brief look at his account as articulated in his book *Man and Sin*.

We can begin with the third chapter of this book, "The Sin of the World." Schoonenberg claims that there are two ways of thinking about human responsibility in the Bible: the tribal (or communal) and the individual. An adequate theological account of original sin ought to take both the individual and communal aspects of responsibility seriously. The classical doctrine of original sin tends to neglect the communal aspect, insofar as it focuses on our relation to Adam.[89] For Schoonenberg, the goal is to understand both the communal and individual elements of sin together:

Hence it is good to examine how we must conceive that solidarity to make it intelligible. The sin of a community, ultimately the sin of the world, is more than the sum total of the individual sins considered without inner connection. On the other hand, what brings the sin of a community about is not that the guilt of one person simply passes to another person. That conflicts with the principle of personal responsibility. Hence, outside of the sins of the individuals there must be a link which connects the sins of one person with the sins of another, the sins of the father with those of the children. Can our reflection discover that other component of "the sin of the world"?[90]

What could the link between individual and communal sins be? To a degree, it may be punishment; we are sometimes punished for each other's sins (sometimes retributively, by God, at other times as the automatic

---

[88] Vandervelde, *Original Sin*, 58. Surprisingly, neither Kant nor Schleiermacher appear in the index of Vandervelde's study, and neither figure comes to the fore in Schoonenberg's *Man and Sin*.

[89] "Both Scripture and the statements of the magisterium of the church have emphasized human solidarity with respect to sin. The magisterium faced that theme in the dogma of original sin. Yet, as that dogma is generally presented, solidarity does not come much to the fore in it. It affirms a mysterious bond between each individual child and the first father of the race, while the sins of his own parents and of his environment and the great sinful decisions of past generations have no share in it. We wonder whether the dogma of original sin does not mean more." Schoonenberg, *Man and Sin*, 98.

[90] Schoonenberg, *Man and Sin*, 103.

effect of our sins). We also imitate each other's sins. But no one can truly cause another person to sin; this would destroy freedom.[91]

We can, however, influence each other, which is to say we can affect each other's *situation*. The link, then, between our sins must be thought of as this situation, or rather the person insofar as she is situated.

We are interested not in the situation but in the fact that the person is situated.... What matters ultimately as a component of the sin of the world is not a connecting link between personal sins (a link that would lie outside man and insofar as it lies outside man), but the fact that man himself is affected. The sin of the world as well as the historical sinfulness of a certain familial or cultural community – for example, anti-Semitism, colonialism – is a reality in man himself. In some it is a sinful self-determination, an action, and especially an attitude.[92]

Like Schleiermacher, Schoonenberg holds that the totality of previous sins, insofar as they affect this person, are part of this person's sin. The difference, though, is that while Schleiermacher held that sin was *one*, determined by previous originating sin and eventually growing into originating sin itself, Schoonenberg insists that the situation does not determine any particular act of sin.

[T]here is no contradiction to speak of a situated liberty. For we do not mean here that our freedom is determined by the situation so that it is forced from without to perform certain actions. That would indeed constitute a contradiction, since freedom means precisely not to be determined from without, but to determine oneself from within. (We have already remarked that God does not determine our freedom from without, but that, as the transcendent Cause, he is present *in* it and he gives it the power of determining itself.) What we mean is that our liberty is affected by its *field of action*, that the objects about which our liberty must decide are affected as are also the insights and the motives from which such decisions proceed. That these elements are affected and restricted does not contradict our freedom. The opposite is true; from the very first moment of its existence our freedom has never existed but as affected and restricted in its field of action, in its possible objects, in the insights and the motives presented to it; in fine, as a situated freedom.[93]

---

[91] "[N]obody can simply cause another person to sin ... even fathers cannot make their children sin. For the person can be driven to responsible acts proceeding from his freedom by nothing, not even another person." Schoonenberg, *Man and Sin*, 104. "All influences which pass from one free person to another free person as such, respecting the latter's freedom and appealing to it, may be lumped together under the term *situation*." Schoonenberg, *Man and Sin*, 104.

[92] Schoonenberg, *Man and Sin*, 105.   [93] Schoonenberg, *Man and Sin*, 105–6.

Schoonenberg goes on to depict two elements of the sin of the world – bad examples and obscured moral norms, which can lead to sins like "colonialism" or "war psychosis" – culminating in the killing of Christ.

In the final chapter of the book, Schoonenberg hypothesizes that original sin is the sin of the world.[94] Vandervelde's summary is helpful here: original sin is "the situational privation of sanctifying grace that renders every human being (analogously) guilty from the moment of birth."[95] Schoonenberg understood the privation in a basically Augustinian way. Original sin involves habitual self-love and precludes true love of others.[96] I have argued that this is not Thomas's way of understanding the effects of original sin. (And I will argue in Chapter 8 that Thomas had good reasons taking the position he did.) That point aside – which is not much stressed in *Man and Sin*, in any case – Schoonenberg's account, it seems to me, could be fruitfully synthesized with Thomas's perspective.[97] On Thomas's account, the material cause of original sin is undue habitually disordered concupiscence. One inherits this disorder, the impulses of which one has an obligation to resist upon reaching the age of reason. Why shouldn't the sinful situation – the totality of factors disposing us to sin, including sinful cultural norms, and so on – be considered concupiscence writ large? Just as one is not culpable for inheriting habitually disordered desires, one is not culpable for inheriting the sinful norms of one's society, at least insofar as they are inculcated in the pre-rational stages of childhood. But with free will comes the obligation to do good and flee from evil. In such a synthesis of Thomas and Schoonenberg, one's precise position on the moral status of concupiscence would apply, *mutatis mutandis*, to the moral status of the sinful situation. Granted that infants are not personally responsible for their disordered concupiscence,

---

[94] Schoonenberg is clear that his view is only a tentative hypothesis. *Man and Sin*, 179–80.

[95] Vandervelde, *Original Sin*, 147.   [96] Schoonenberg, *Man and Sin*, 71.

[97] One could argue that since Schoonenberg's ideas here derive (ultimately) from Schleiermacher, this synthesis would be of Thomas and Schleiermacher. But it seems to me that Schoonenberg's approach to freedom differentiates his account quite significantly from Schleiermacher's. From a Schleiermacherian point of view, Schoonenberg's non-deterministic approach is overly individualistic. Schleiermacher insisted that we cannot separate original sin from actual sin, in just this sense: the original sin of the infant will *generate* actual sins of necessity. If we claim that the infant, upon reaching the age of reason, needn't commit this or that personal sin, then we've broken the chain between originated and originating sin. From Schoonenberg's perspective, however, Schleiermacher's account has failed to maintain the delicate biblical balance between the individual and the communal weight of sin. In this respect Schoonenberg's account has much in common with Thomas's.

Thomists have disputed whether it is really part of original sin, or whether it is merely a consequence of the loss of sanctifying grace. My constructive proposal remains neutral on that question.

IAN MCFARLAND

Ian McFarland's *In Adam's Fall* is a robust defense of the doctrine of original sin. Among the book's many strengths are its helpful discussions of the doctrine's biblical sources and Christological implications, as well as its rich treatment of the theological accounts of the will in Augustine and Maximus the Confessor. Before developing his own account, McFarland critically engages what he calls the "Catholic view" of original sin, which "can be traced back to Anselm but receives more fulsome development in Aquinas."[98] It is worth discussing and responding to McFarland's criticisms, insofar as they bear on the parts of Thomas's account defended in this book.

The Catholic view, as McFarland describes it, is that original sin consists in the lack of a supernatural gift. This account, "while seeking to maintain sin's universality, nevertheless modifies the idea that postlapsarian humanity sins necessarily and is, correspondingly, born in a condition of estrangement from God."[99] This is closely related to the fact that original sin is seen not as resistance to God but as a privation.[100] Although McFarland claims that "[t]he logic behind this construal of original sin is clear and in many respects compelling" – due to the legitimacy of seeing submission to God as rooted in a supernatural gift – it nevertheless runs the risk of denying original sin:[101]

it is a noteworthy feature of Catholic teaching that original sin is not sin in the proper sense, but only analogically. At one level this affirmation can be seen as simply a means of characterizing the fact that for postlapsarian humanity original sin is "contracted" rather than "committed." At another, however, it tends to lend weight to the conclusion that original sin is not really sin at all, for although it is rightly described as an inclination or disposition to evil, it is not evil in itself.[102]

I agree with McFarland that accounts of the doctrine that reduce original sin to a mere disposition to sin are inadequate; as I argued in Chapter 2,

---

[98] McFarland, *In Adam's Fall*, 37.   [99] McFarland, *In Adam's Fall*, 36–7.
[100] "[T]he (negative) definition of original sin as privation implies that it is not in its essence a matter of (positive) resistance to God." McFarland, *In Adam's Fall*, 37.
[101] McFarland, *In Adam's Fall*, 37.   [102] McFarland, *In Adam's Fall*, 37–8.

one of the problems with this approach is that it leaves the link between original sin and the need for the gospel obscure (we are still disposed to sin after becoming Christians).

But for Thomas, sin is not merely the disposition to sin.[103] Although original sin includes a disposition to sin insofar as disordered concupiscence is its material cause, Thomas also affirms that it has a formal cause, the lack of justice in the will. When this lack is understood to be *of* sanctifying grace, it certainly is an evil: it brings about the damnation of the person. It's a *habitus*, yes, not a personally chosen act, but the *habitus* itself is an evil which estranges from God per se, not merely the disposition to future evil acts. I would argue, moreover, that Thomas received the idea that evil is a privation of the good, as opposed to an independent substance, *from* Augustine. Their disagreements, such as they were, focused on how to understand the privation involved in original sin.

Thomas did maintain that original sin is sin *secundum analogiam*. But why does this lend weight to the view that it isn't real sin? For McFarland, sin must involve genuine resistance to God. But why should we think this? Scripture doesn't give us an account of just what original sin is.[104] Granted, sin ordinarily does involve resistance to God; but why should we expect the "sin" in infants to be an ordinary sin? It seems to me that the denial that infants actively resist God is one of the major *advantages* of Thomas's perspective. It is far from clear – or at least it is far from clear to me – what it would *mean* for someone to genuinely or actively resist God from the womb. Or rather, it's far from clear what it would mean on the assumption that infants have not acted before they begin to exist in the womb, à la realist accounts of the doctrine. But McFarland is not defending infant preexistence. He may mean that infants develop in such a way that they will inevitably actively resist God, such that original sin is a *habitual* aversion from God.[105] In any case, he argues that we have good reasons to believe that infants resist God in some way: if original sin is not active resistance to God, then later sins generated by original sin will not involve active resistance to God either.[106] What if, however,

---

[103] McFarland says that the approach he describes receives "fulsome development in Aquinas," but I don't assume that he attributes all of these views to Aquinas.

[104] In Chapter 7, I discuss Rom. 5, which seems to suggest that different words are appropriate to describe the sins of infants and adults.

[105] In Chapter 8, I argue that there are good reasons to hold that infants are not habitually oriented to sinful self-love.

[106] "[I]f original sin is not itself genuine sin (viz., active resistance to God that merits condemnation), then it is hard to see how the various actual sins that it generates can

original sin itself does not involve active resistance to God, but later volitional sins ("mortal sins") do? What if mortal resistance to God is not generated by original sin but chosen by original sinners?

One final criticism McFarland offers of Aquinas's account of original sin is that "the idea that there are different degrees of deviation from God's will – so that those who commit actual sin acquire a level of (punishable) guilt that those afflicted only by original sin do not – undermines the Augustinian principle that all people stand equally in need of Christ."[107] As we saw in Chapter 1, Augustine maintained that condemned infants suffer lighter penalties in hell than adults. It doesn't seem that Thomas differs from Augustine simply because different people have different levels of punishable guilt. For Thomas, every human being deserves damnation, exclusion from the kingdom of heaven, from the first moment of her existence, and every human being thus equally needs the grace of Christ to avoid it. One is either damned or not. But this doesn't commit him to the *denial* that individual human beings, later in life, commit different sorts of sins. McFarland notes later in the book that we aren't all guilty of sin in the exact same sense: "the idea of a common human sinfulness – the core of the doctrine of original sin – no more requires that human beings be viewed as indistinguishable in God's sight than that the proclamation of a common salvation does. To say that all are equally sinners is not to imply that all are sinners in the same way."[108] Yet if we are not hamartiologically indistinguishable in God's sight, not all sinners in the same way, what is wrong with Thomas's view that infants are sinners in their own distinctive way?

I don't find McFarland's criticism of Thomas compelling, but it is an important one. If it were true that Thomas's account implicitly denied original sin, then I would agree that it should be rejected. Yet it seems to me that the habitual lack of grace is a real sin, because without grace the human being is separated from the knowledge and love of God we desire – in the deepest sense of the word *desire*, pertaining to that which perfects and fulfills and beatifies us – for all eternity. And what is "real" sin but separation from God? Infants are separated in a different way than adults: they haven't (yet) chosen to turn away from God. The child is called to a personal friendship with God that has not yet begun. And as I'll discuss

---

be counted as genuine either, since the congenital condition of debility under which they are committed would appear to constitute a mitigating circumstance of the highest order." McFarland, *In Adam's Fall*, 38–9.

[107] McFarland, *In Adam's Fall*, 38.   [108] McFarland, *In Adam's Fall*, 177.

further in Chapter 8, sanctifying grace just is what brings the human being into friendship with Jesus Christ. Precisely *because* "original sin, in its proper sense as a reflex of the gospel of Jesus Christ, is rightly used to emphasize God's gracious response to human need,"[109] Thomas's focus on that very need seems to look in the right direction.

Let's turn to McFarland's own proposal. He rejects, in principle, the task of explaining how his view of original sin relates to the origin of evil or sin. The job of the doctrine of original sin is not to provide an etiology of evil or sin: "the proper dogmatic function of original sin is limited to offering a *description of* rather than an *explanation for* the human condition apart from grace."[110] Central to McFarland's description is that the will of the original sinner does not desire God: "As created, the will is that feature of human nature by which human beings are freely (i.e., as self-conscious agents) empowered to desire God. When the will is damaged, therefore, its desire is no longer for God – and desire that is not oriented to God is by definition sinful."[111] "[F]or all human beings other than Christ, a damaged (but still inalienably good) nature is invariably correlated with a hypostasis that is congenitally sinful (and thus estranged from God)."[112] We cannot say that God has brought evil into being, or that the will is naturally sinful.[113]

McFarland holds that this is compatible with not affirming that Adam has caused original sin: "'Adam' can only be regarded as the first in a series of sinners and not as the unique 'cause' of subsequent human sin."[114] It is also compatible with not affirming that God has caused original sin.[115] How can we avoid the implication that God created us in sin without the doctrine of original justice, however? That is, don't we need at least a limited etiology of sin – God created us good, and we fell from that state – in order to avoid implying that God created us in sin? McFarland argues elsewhere that it is sufficient for the first human being to have been without sin, even if she wasn't created in original justice:

Clearly this position implies a historical "fall" that gave rise to this inherited perversion of the will (indeed, it implies that the first human being might be

---

[109] McFarland, *In Adam's Fall*, 48.   [110] McFarland, *In Adam's Fall*, 47.
[111] McFarland, *In Adam's Fall*, 183.   [112] McFarland, *In Adam's Fall*, 145–6.
[113] "[T]o say that the will is naturally or congenitally sinful is theologically illegitimate, because it would imply that God brings evil into being." McFarland, *In Adam's Fall*, 144–5.
[114] McFarland, *In Adam's Fall*, 160.
[115] "Doctrinally, Christians are committed to denying that God made them sinners." McFarland, *In Adam's Fall*, 131.

defined theologically as the first to have a fallen will, and thus the first to need saving). As human beings already bound up in this chain of inheritance, however, we can say nothing about what this prelapsarian state would have been like, or how a fall from that state would have occurred.[116]

The first human being, in a theological sense, is the first to have a fallen will and need salvation. The Fall was the first sin, but we can say nothing about the prelapsarian state.

It seems to me that even if it does not amount to a theodicy or defense, theology needs to give *some* account of the origin of original sin (even if the account is generic and doesn't decide between several, perhaps equally plausible, options). There are only a few logical possibilities. If original sin would not have been transmitted but for the sin or sins of the first human beings, then the original state of sinlessness plays the same theological role as the state of original justice (even without a literal Garden of Eden, and so forth); namely, it allows the clear affirmation that human beings, not God, brought about original sin. If original sin would have been transmitted *regardless* of whether the first human beings committed sin, then the source of originated original sin must lie elsewhere. One wouldn't necessarily need to argue that the source is God (perhaps "rebellious angels"[117] could be blamed). But if no non-human agent is to blame, and sinlessness couldn't have been passed on, then it seems we've implied that human beings are inevitably sinful, and God has created us sinful. I am not attributing this conclusion to McFarland – as we have seen, he rejects the view that God or human nature as such should be considered the source of sin – but I would contend that we need either to appeal to the possibility that sinlessness could have continued through the generations or to give a theological rationale for the view that God (or whatever we take to be sin's source) has brought about the state of original sin.

I will argue now that, from a broadly Thomist perspective, the view that God brings about a state of sinful self-love has unacceptable consequences. The critique is intended to apply to the accounts in this chapter – most clearly Schleiermacher's but also, fairly clearly, Schoonenberg's – that defend what we might call the "modern Augustinian" account of original sin. (It's not intended to apply to every possible

---

[116] Ian McFarland, "Original Sin," in *T&T Clark Companion to the Doctrine of Sin*, ed. Keith L. Johnson and David Lauber (New York: Bloomsbury T&T Clark, 2016), 312, n. 10.

[117] Loren T. Stuckenbruck, *The Myth of the Rebellious Angels* (Heidelberg: Mohr Siebeck, 2014).

account of the origin of sin in which God plays a prominent causal role.) These accounts are "modern" in the sense stipulated earlier, because they deny the theological relevance of a historical Fall. They are "Augustinian" because they affirm what is arguably the core of Augustine's account: original sin is concupiscence, understood as sinful self-love.

SIN AND THE WILL OF GOD

Thomas, as we have seen, asserts that God cannot cause sin but can cause natural evil. We haven't explored why Thomas made either of these claims. Why did Thomas claim that God can cause natural evil? The answer is fairly straightforward, once we understand that Thomas takes "evil" in a broad sense, such that it includes the "corruption" of any life form. For example, when a blade of grass withers and fades away, something "evil" has happened: the grass that previously existed has undergone "corruption" and now does not exist. The evil is evil with respect to *this* blade of grass, because it was good for this blade of grass to exist. But this blade's corruption is not necessarily evil for other beings: if a herbivore eats it, for example, this blade's corruption is the herbivore's nutrition, which is good for the herbivore. How exactly would one go about arguing that God cannot cause this kind of evil? Recall that God gave Adam and Eve plants to eat before the Fall (Gen. 1:29). If grass and various other plants are good (Gen. 1:11–12), then it seems we should say their destruction is evil. Thomas reasons that God can cause particular natural evils for the greater good of the universe. Sin is different. God does not and cannot will or cause sin, though he permits sin for the greater good. But why can't God will sin? If God can will natural evils for the sake of the greater good, why can't he will sinful evils for the sake of the greater good?

Thomas gives a consistent and, I would suggest, deceptively simple answer whenever he directly addresses this question. God cannot will or cause disorder (*deordinatio*) with respect to the ultimate end, and sin is disorder with respect to the ultimate end.[118] Thus the *Summa*, for

---

[118] Three places in which the same basic treatment is found are *Scriptum* II, d. 37, q. 2, a. 1; *De malo* q. 3, a. 1; *STh* I-II, q. 79, a. 1. "[P]eccati auctor Deus nullo modo dicendus est. Quod enim agit propter finem, non deficit a fine nisi propter defectum alicujus, vel suiipsius, vel alterius; et illud in quo invenitur defectus erit causa obliquationis a fine, sive sit ipsum principale agens, vel materia, vel instrumentum agentis, vel quidquid aliud; et ideo illud in quo nullo modo defectus cadere potest, non potest esse causa recessus a fine

example, states, "God cannot be the direct cause of sin, either in himself or in any other. This is because every sin is through recession from the order which is in himself to the end."[119] But what does Thomas mean by deordination? It is clear that he doesn't simply mean *any* estrangement from God, for human nature does not include grace. This is why, as we've seen, Thomas argues that God can cause a rational creature to exist without ordering it to the beatific vision. Thomas argues that a creature in such a state is not in sin, because the *deordinatio* (or "non-ordination") is not inherited from Adam's sinful will.

It is *not* simply the case, then, that God cannot cause sin because he cannot cause the creature to be averted from the ultimate end. So why does Thomas claim that God cannot cause sin because he cannot cause disorder with respect to the ultimate end? Consideration of the context of his claims, I contend, shows that the primary thing he has in mind is that God cannot cause mortal sin. This is understandable, given that, as we saw in our discussion of sin and analogy, Thomas claims that mortal sin is the *ratio propria* of the word "sin." God cannot cause originated original sin because it has an essential relation to mortal sin.[120] The best way to

---

in his quae ad finem ordinata sunt. *Cum igitur peccatum dicatur propter inordinationem a fine ad quem natura rationalis ordinata est,* non potest esse causa peccati Deus, in quo nullus defectus cadere potest; sed oportet quod peccatum causetur defectu illius agentis quod est possibile ad defectum, sicut est voluntas rationalis creaturae." *Scriptum* II d. 37, q. 2, a. 1, emphasis mine. "Peccatum enim prout nunc de peccato loquimur, consistit in auersione uoluntatis create ab ultimo fine. Impossibile est autem quod Deus faciat uoluntatem alicuius ab ultimo fine auerti, cum ipsemet sit ultimus finis." *De malo* q. 3, a. 1. We find this same assumption, more or less explicitly, in closely related contexts, such as whether God can will (*STh* I, q. 19, a. 9) or cause (*STh* I, q. 49, a. 2) evil in general. Often Thomas gives other arguments which are reducible to this fundamental argument. For example, he argues that God does not punish what he causes, but he punishes sin, therefore he doesn't cause it. But the reason he punishes sin is because it is culpable disorder with respect to the end; so the argument regarding punishment depends on the more fundamental argument regarding order to the end.

[119] "Deus autem non potest esse directe causa peccati vel sui vel alterius. Quia omne peccatum est per recessum ab ordine qui est in ipsum sicut in finem." *STh* I-II, q. 79, a. 1.

[120] What about venial sin? Here things are a bit thornier. Thomas thinks that, in reality, the disorder with respect to the ultimate end in every infant is caused by Adam. Moreover, Thomas denies that God in fact causes venial sins, which cause, in their own way, deordination with respect to the ultimate end (properly speaking they *dispose* to deordination). Here is the difficulty. If venial sins are only dispositions to a person's deordination, why couldn't God cause such actual dispositions, just as he could have caused the habit of disordered concupiscence? Thomas touches on the question of God's ability to cause venial sin in the *Scriptum*. He raises an objection arguing, in effect, that God can cause sin because God gives the sensual powers to human nature which cause

make this clear is to consider Thomas's answer to a slightly different question: whether God can will evil.

In *Summa theologiae* I, q. 19, a. 9, Thomas argues that God wills natural evil and not the evil of sin. First he argues that, strictly speaking, evil is not intended or willed, only good. Evil can be intended or willed *per accidens*. For example, a lion who kills a stag intends to eat (the good of nourishment); the death of the stag follows *per accidens*. An adulterer intends (let's say) the good of pleasure, not the infidelity per se. The condition for willing an evil accidentally is that the good attached to the evil is willed more than the good of which the evil is a privation. (The adulterer wills the good of pleasure more than the good of fidelity; if I hunt a stag for food I will the good of my nourishment more than the good of the stag's existence.) Thomas appeals to this principle as a justification for his claim that God cannot will sin:

> *God wills no good more than his own goodness.* He nevertheless wills some goods more than others. *Therefore* the evil of guilt, which causes disorder with respect to the divine good, God in no ways wills. But the evil of natural defect, or the evil of penalty, he does will. He does this by willing some good to which the evil is attached, as, by willing justice, he wills penalty; and by willing the order of nature to be saved, he wills that some things are naturally corrupted.[121]

God wills nothing more than his goodness; therefore, he cannot will sin, which involves disorder with respect to his goodness. Thomas's reasoning entails that the sin God cannot will is the sin in which something other than God is willed more than God. In other words, mortal sin. The natural evils and penalties which God does will, Thomas implies, are evils that can be ordered to God as ultimate end; the evil of mortal sin cannot be ordered to God as ultimate end. Why not? Because, by Thomas's

---

(venial) sin. Thomas replies, "concupiscibilis et irascibilis a Deo homini datae sunt, ita ut rationi subdantur. Unde si quis eis utatur secundum illum ordinem prout a Deo datae sunt, talis operationis Deus auctor erit, sed hoc peccatum esse non poterit. Si quis autem eis utatur praeter rationis ordinem, talis abusionis Deus auctor non erit, quia in hac peccatum est." *Scriptum* II, d. 37, q. 2, a. 1, ad 4. The reply, though, presupposes that Adam has caused the disorder. What would be the case if God created us directly with the principles of pure nature? Presumably, disordered movements of concupiscence would follow of necessity for many people. Would they count as sins?

[121] "*Nullum autem bonum Deus magis vult quam suam bonitatem*: vult tamen aliquod bonum magis quam aliud quoddam bonum. *Unde* malum culpae, quod privat ordinem ad bonum divinum, Deus nullo modo vult. Sed malum naturalis defectus, vel malum poenae vult, volendo aliquod bonum, cui coniungitur tale malum: sicut, volendo iustitiam, vult poenam; et volendo ordinem naturae servari, vult quaedam naturaliter corrumpi." *STh* I, q. 19, a. 9, emphasis mine.

lights, mortal sin just is willing a creature more than God; the one who sins mortally *ipso facto* wills a creaturely good as ultimate end. This is the key to Thomas's arguments concerning God as the cause of sin. Thomas is not claiming in *Summa theologiae* I–II, q. 79, a. 1, or the other aforementioned passages that God is obligated to create a creature in grace, ordered to the ultimate end; he is claiming that God cannot create a creature in mortal sin, ordered to another creature.

Thomas's reasoning here extends not only to discrete acts of mortal sin but also to the state of mortal sin itself. Thus God cannot create a creature habitually inclined to a created good as ultimate end either. For this would be for God to will the good to which the evil is attached – the existence of a creature in habitual mortal sin, a creature "hating" God, even if only subconsciously – more than the good of which the evil is a privation: the creature's love for God.

This strikes me as a strong objection to modern Augustinian accounts of original sin (i.e., accounts that state or imply that God creates human beings in a state in which they love creaturely goods more than God). It is absurd to claim that God concurs in the creature's sinful self-love. Not all modern Augustinian accounts are deterministic. But they all involve the claim that human beings are inevitably determined to love the creature over the creator. At most, humans have a choice among creaturely goods. They can love sex, or power, or even a good greater than themselves, such as the environmental good of the planet. They cannot love God. By implying or stating directly that God creates the creature in opposition to himself, modern Augustinianism implies that God hates God. Moreover, it also seems to veer toward an overly negative conception of human nature. For if human beings from the beginning – both as a species and as each individual in the species – have been ordered to the creature and not to God, in what sense does the gospel fulfill their deepest needs and desires?

This chapter has discussed the "modern" approach to the doctrine of original sin, in which a historical Fall is not held to be of theological significance. It seems to me that the examples discussed go a long way toward exhausting the logical space of the modern approach. Original sin may be the universality of sinful volitions. It may be part of human nature (such as self-love). Or it may be, in part or in whole, the sinful environment into which we are born. Although there is much to learn from the accounts we have discussed – for example, the salutary emphasis, beginning with Schleiermacher, on the need to pay careful attention to the ways in which human beings are sinfully situated by their communities – I have argued that they are ultimately inadequate. Holding that original sin is the universality of sinful volitions excludes infants and others from Christ's saving work. Holding that original sin is inevitable sinful self-love implies that human nature is intrinsically opposed to God. And holding that original sin is birth into a sinful world implies that Jesus was born in original sin. In sum, we do not yet have an adequate explanation of how the Fall could be removed from history. If this is true, then the challenges that evolutionary theory creates for the Fall are quite serious. For it is far from clear – given the state of the question in contemporary theology – how the concept of a historical Fall is compatible with mainstream evolutionary theory.

6

Original Sin and the Challenge of Evolution

Questions pertaining to human origins have loomed large in Christian responses to evolutionary theories. Nicolas Wiseman (1802–65), an erudite public intellectual created Cardinal in 1850, lectured on science and revealed religion at the Vatican in 1835. He argued that Lamarck's theory of evolution was inextricably linked with what would later be called "polygenesis": the view that different groups or races of human beings came into existence at separate places.[1] Wiseman thought this was bad science; he also declared – and his Roman audience surely would have agreed – that it was incompatible with the biblical account of creation, fall, and redemption.

The Word of God hath always considered mankind as descended from one parent, and the great mystery of redemption rests upon the belief that all men sinned in their common father. Suppose different and unconnected creations of men, and the deep mystery of original sin, and the glorious mystery of redemption, are blotted out from religion's book.[2]

---

[1] The word "polygenesis" is a compound first formed within English. The prefix "poly" is borrowed from the Greek πολυ and has the sense of "much" or "many." The noun "genesis" comes from the Latin *genesis* (and ultimately the Greek γένεσις), which means "origin." The etymological sense of the word is thus "many origins." The first attestation of the word found in the Oxford English Dictionary is 1863, in the context of linguistics; by 1871 it was being used in the context of ethnology to refer to the separate origins of human races. "Polygenesis, n." OED Online, June 2017 (Oxford University Press), www.oed.com/view/Entry/147150. Although it has fallen into desuetude in the scientific community, theologians have, somewhat awkwardly, continued to use the word to refer to any theory of origins that denies that all human beings have descended from a single ancestral couple.

[2] Nicolas Patrick Wiseman, *Twelve Lectures on the Connexion between Science and Revealed Religion* (London: Cox and Wyman, 1849), third lecture, 137. I learned of

Wiseman had in mind, of course, the traditional doctrine of original sin, according to which all human beings – with the exceptions of Adam, Eve, Jesus Christ, and, for many Christians, the Virgin Mary – contract sin from Adam at the first moment of their existence. If evolution is right, Wiseman argues, then the traditional doctrine is wrong. And if the traditional doctrine is wrong, Wiseman warns, then the Christian doctrine of redemption from sin is wrong too.

Many people have come to agree with Wiseman, to the effect that original sin is incompatible with evolution. Of course, the development of evolutionary theory since Wiseman's time has changed, in many respects, the nature of the apparent conflict between the Fall and evolution. This chapter engages three of the most important challenges contemporary evolutionary theory poses to the doctrines of the Fall and original sin. First is the problem of the continuous, gradual nature of evolutionary change. Even if we had been created in a state of original justice, it is hard to see how we could have fallen from it. The second problem stems from the complex legacy of our evolutionary history. It seems that evolution has selected for sinful behavior, implying that there was no state of original justice. The third is the problem of communal origins. If we haven't descended from a single ancestral pair, then either there are human beings who were not made sinners by Adam's disobedience, or we were created in sin. Neither of these options seems theologically acceptable.

The first two objections are aimed at all views of the Fall that involve inherited "corruption," that is, all views that involve something like the following "disease view of the Fall."[3] A human or humans sin. Therefore – without a miracle – if they reproduce, they necessarily pass on disordered desires to all their descendants. If they had not sinned, they would have necessarily passed on rightly ordered desires to the next generation. Each generation that refrained from sinning would have passed on rightly ordered desires. Regardless of whether one holds that humans inherit disordered desires and original sin, or only disordered desires, one faces the problems of gradual, continuous evolutionary change and the complex legacy of our evolutionary history. The third

---

Wiseman from David Livingstone's fascinating book, *Adam's Ancestors: Race, Religion, and the Politics of Human Origins* (Baltimore: Johns Hopkins University Press, 2008).

[3] The disease view of the Fall is similar to the disease view of original sin discussed in Chapters 1 and 2. But one does not need to believe in original sin to believe in a historical Fall.

objection, pertaining to communal origins, is aimed at original sin more broadly (including standard federalist and realist accounts of the doctrine). This chapter focuses on articulating the core problems; in Chapter 7, I offer a constructive response.

CONTINUOUS ORIGINS

The first challenge to the Fall comes from the "modern synthesis" of Darwin's theory of evolution by natural selection with Gregor Mendel's theory of inheritance.[4] In order to grapple with its theological implications, we need to discuss the basics of the modern synthesis (also known as the "synthetic theory" or "neo-Darwinism"). Synthetic theory is best understood in contrast to Jean-Baptiste Lamarck, who offered the first scientific theory of evolution. In his *Philosophie zoologique*, published in 1809, Lamarck proposed that evolution occurs through the inheritance of acquired characteristics.[5] Organisms behave in accordance with pressures exerted by their environments, and they pass on the traits they develop from their behavior. Darwin, by contrast, argued that variations are random with respect to the environment. Organisms with favorable heritable variations will survive and reproduce more successfully on average, leading over time to evolutionary change and the adaptation of populations to their environments. This is the theory of "natural selection."

Given that evolution is driven by natural selection, how are favorable variations passed on? Many biologists in Darwin's day assumed that offspring inherit the average of their parents' traits. This "blending" theory of inheritance does not cohere well with natural selection, however. Favorable mutations would be halved in each subsequent generation and eventually dissipate. Darwin never solved this problem. The Augustinian monk Gregor Mendel proposed a theory of inheritance through "particulate factors" – later known as "genes" – which would win widespread acceptance in the scientific community. Offspring inherit

---

[4] My comments on evolutionary theory throughout this chapter are indebted to Francisco J. Ayala and Camilo J. Cela-Conde, *Processes in Human Evolution: The Journey from Early Hominins to Neanderthals and Modern Humans* (Oxford: Oxford University Press, 2017).

[5] As Richard Burkhardt points out, the view that acquired traits are heritable was not original to Lamarck and was widely accepted throughout the eighteenth and nineteenth centuries, even by Darwin. "When the names were assigned to the theoretical positions, however, this detail was considered negligible." *The Spirit of System: Lamarck and Evolutionary Biology* (Cambridge, MA: Harvard University Press, 1995 [1977]), 2.

particulate factors from each parent, and the factors separate in the gametes (sex cells). Favorable variants can thus be maintained through the generations.

Geneticists in the 1920s and 1930s combined Mendel's account of particulate inheritance with Darwin's account of natural selection. This is the modern synthesis. By the 1940s, it was the consensus view among biologists. Many would say it still is. In recent years, however, debate has arisen *within* academic biology over whether the evolutionary mechanisms of the modern synthesis – which include not only natural selection but also genetic drift and recombination, gene flow, and founder effect – are sufficient. An "extended evolutionary synthesis" has been proposed to rectify the alleged shortcomings of the modern synthesis.[6] More on that shortly.

What challenge does the modern synthesis pose to the doctrine of the Fall? The Anglican philosophical theologian F. R. Tennant put it this way: "It is not easy to understand how one act of sin, however momentous, could serve to dislocate at once the whole nature of man."[7] Even if we grant that the first sin was a gross affront to God, it is far from clear how that action could have affected human nature at the biological level, such that sin or at least the disposition thereto would be passed on through the generations. Tennant was writing at the turn of the twentieth century, before the modern synthesis was adopted by the scientific community; the problem is equally (if not more) acute today. Yet there is a dearth of reflection on the problem among theologians who are both open to evolution and believe in a historical Fall. A quasi-Lamarckian view of inheritance is often assumed. A prominent philosopher-theologian recently argued, for example, that a hypothetical "neo-Augustine" would have no problem with evolutionary theory. Neo-Augustine could simply argue that the first human beings acquire vices which "become a part of their make-up – of their genetic structure if you will – to be inevitably

---

[6] For an introduction to the debate, see Kevin Laland, Gregory Wray, Hopi Hoekstra, et al., "Does Evolutionary Theory Need a Rethink?," *Nature* 514 (2014), 161–4. Advocates of the extended synthesis argue that the modern synthesis cannot account for how "physical development influences the generation of variation (developmental bias); how the environment directly shapes organisms' traits (plasticity); how organisms modify environments (niche construction); and how organisms transmit more than genes across generations (extra-genetic inheritance)" (p. 162). Defenders of the modern synthesis argue that it can take these phenomena into account.

[7] Tennant, *The Origin and Propagation of Sin*, 28; for a summary of the debate at the time, see "Note D: On the Heredity of Acquired Characters" (pp. 176–81).

handed down."[8] But this is not how we acquire traits, at least according to synthetic theory. The personal vices acquired by the first human beings would not be transmitted to all their descendants unless they had a genetic basis.[9] But if they had a genetic basis, then they were not acquired.

It is worth reformulating Tennant's intuition into an argument. In the argument that follows I'll use the phrase "strictly natural" to refer to traits which are passed on through the generations, in accordance with the disease view of the Fall. Here is an argument to the effect that contemporary evolutionary theory is incompatible with the Fall. The Fall is a volition whereby a human being loses the strictly natural trait of rightly ordered desires (first premise). Every strictly natural trait is transmitted through germline DNA (second premise). Therefore, the Fall is a volition that changes germline DNA. This is absurd, because the volition of a human being cannot change its germline DNA.

The first premise follows from the disease view of the Fall. The second premise arguably follows from mainstream biology. Traits that do not come from our environments (broadly construed, so as to include culture, nutrition, and so forth), free choices, or whatever immaterial parts we might have come from our DNA.[10] Thus if a trait were to be inseparably fixed to the human species, it would be transmitted through germline DNA. These premises seem to lead to the conclusion that the Fall would have altered human nature at the genetic level. But particular volitions do not change DNA – and thus the conclusion is absurd. Perhaps at one time it was reasonable to believe that an action corrupted our "seminal nature" (Augustine) or inculcated a transmissible "acquired vice" (Lamarck), but it is not today. Or so the argument goes. What might an advocate of the disease view say in response?

One might argue against the second premise as follows. Not all inherited traits come from germline DNA, contrary to synthetic theory. There has recently been a renewed interest in "soft inheritance," the inheritance of traits through non-genetic processes. The field of epigenetics, for example, studies changes in gene expression during organisms'

---

[8] John Rist, *Augustine Deformed: Love, Sin and Freedom in the Western Moral Tradition* (Cambridge: Cambridge University Press, 2014), 387.

[9] Of course, parents can have a bad influence on their children. But the particular vices of the first human beings were not inevitably handed down to all subsequent human beings, as evidenced by the diversity of human cultures and patterns of virtue and vice.

[10] This premise has nothing to do with "genetic determinism." One might think that the environment and free choice determine all the traits we care about and still accept this premise.

lifetimes and such changes which are transmitted from parents to children. Warren Burggren has helpfully distinguished intragenerational epigenetics – the study of epigenetic change within an individual's lifetime – from transgenerational epigenetics, "the inheritance of a modified phenotype from the prenatal generation without changes in genes or gene sequence."[11] An example of transgenerational epigenetics is that the offspring of fish who undergo hypoxia (the deprivation of oxygen) are sometimes born with thinner gills as a result.[12] Could the Fall have consisted in an epigenetic change? Given the current state of our knowledge, it is not clear that reinterpreting the Fall in epigenetic terms would be helpful. First, it is unclear whether transgenerational epigenetic changes last longer than a single generation in humans. It has been argued by Denis Alexander, among others, that this is unlikely.[13] But temporary changes are not strictly natural in the sense required by the disease view of the Fall, which requires that disordered desires persist in every generation. It is also unclear how a *volition* could bring about transgenerational epigenetic change.

One could also argue against the second premise by appealing to a preternatural power possessed by the first humans to transmit rightly ordered desires which has nothing to do with germline DNA.[14] If my reading of Thomas's view of original justice in Chapter 2 is broadly correct, then his mature thought is incompatible with the concept of intrinsic "preteradaptive gifts" (Austriaco's phrase), insofar as they are held to be distinct from sanctifying grace and perfectly regulate human desires. Moreover, even granting the possibility of preternatural justice, it is unclear how the hypothesis that the first humans had transmissible

---

[11] Warren Burggren, "Epigenetic Inheritance and Its Role in Evolutionary Biology: Reevaluation and New Perspectives," *Biology* 5.24 (2016), 2. This is opposed to intragenerational epigenetics, the "modification of gene expression through epigenetic marks (e.g., DNA methylation, covalent histone modification, microRNA action) that results in a modified phenotype, often considered at the molecular/cellular level, within an individual's lifespan" (p. 2).

[12] Burggren, "Epigenetic Inheritance and Its Role in Evolutionary Biology," 10.

[13] "[I]n mammals it is very unlikely that such long-term environmentally induced epialleles will ever be detected over more than a few generations for the simple reason that the great majority (though not all) of the epigenetic modifications gained during life are wiped from the genome during transmission of parental DNA to the next generation." Denis Alexander, *Genes, Determinism, God* (Cambridge: Cambridge University Press, 2017), 79.

[14] See Nicanor Pier Giorgio Austriaco, "A Theological Fittingness Argument for the Historicity of the Fall of *Homo sapiens*," *Nova et Vetera*, English edition, 13.3 (2015), 651–67.

preternatural powers that were forfeited by disobedience to God could be reconciled with contemporary genetics. What *were* these non-genetic, preternatural powers, and how were they to be transmitted? How could one act of disobedience bring it about that they were not?

COMPLEX ORIGINS

The previous argument against the Fall presupposed the possibility of a state of original justice. Even if the first humans had evolved with only good desires, it was difficult to explain how a single action could have reversed the course of evolutionary history and given the next generation of humans evil desires. We can now consider a second, independent objection to the Fall. This objection can grant for the sake of argument that the Fall is not in tension with natural selection. Even if one action *could* have corrupted human desire in principle, the fact is that at least some of the first humans inherited dispositions to sinful behavior from their non-human ancestors – not justice. This is because, as Richard Swinburne put it, "the desires which cause all the trouble are there in the monkeys and the apes as well. The desires are not caused in us by Adam's sin."[15] We can rephrase and extend this argument against original justice.

The doctrine of original justice requires that the first humans could have lived without the desire for sin (first premise). Evolutionary theory indicates that the hominid ancestors of the first humans had desires which – when they are in humans – are for sin (second premise). Therefore, the first humans could not have lived without the desire for sin, and the doctrine of original justice is false.

The first premise accords with the traditional view of original justice and the disease view of the Fall. The second premise neither affirms nor denies that non-human animals can sin or desire to sin. It claims that there are desires which, even if they are amoral in non-human beings, are ordered to sin in human beings. It also claims that the parents of the first humans had these desires.[16] What might they be? There are a wide variety of candidates; for the sake of space it will be convenient to nominate only

---

[15] Richard Swinburne, *Responsibility and Atonement* (Oxford: Oxford University Press, 1989), 143.
[16] I assume that there was a first generation of human beings. Given that human beings now exist but at one point did not, it seems that there must have been.

one: aggressive violence. By "aggressive" I mean "not undertaken in defense."[17] It should be uncontroversial, I take it, that the desire for aggressive violence in this stipulated sense is a desire for sin in humans. The results of several decades of biological research indicate that the hominid ancestors of the first humans were prone to aggressive violence.[18] To be sure, there is also a large body of recent research arguing that *cooperation* is a crucial feature of our evolutionary history. Sarah Coakley's 2012 Gifford Lectures call our attention to the recent "implosions" in evolutionary biology which focus on the evolutionary roots of cooperative and altruistic behavior, and she has recently co-edited a major volume on this theme.[19] Earlier generations of biologists may have overstressed the degree to which evolution has selected for selfishness and violence, implying that we have to work against the grain of our

[17] I will not attempt to define violence very precisely here. I take it that it means *at least* lethal violence, though I assume that there are other forms of violence which are sinful, at least when not undertaken in self-defense. Some Christians believe that all human violence is sinful. Though not all go that far, most Christians have believed that violent action not undertaken for defensive purposes is sinful. Thus regardless of whether unchosen desire for aggressive violence is sinful – that is, regardless of whether one needs to freely consent to a desire for or impulse to aggressive violence in order to be culpable for experiencing it – the desire is ordered to sin, such that *if* one consents to the desire, one is guilty of sin.

[18] The nature of early human violence is controversial. Some scholars, such as the anthropologist Douglas Fry, argue that war was not waged before the Holocene (though early humans did commit homicide and feud with each other). See *War, Peace, and Human Nature: The Convergence of Evolutionary and Cultural Views*, ed. Douglas P. Fry (Oxford: Oxford University Press, 2013). Archaeologists and biologists, such as Lawrence Keeley and Richard Wrangham, respectively, have argued that the evidence indicates that humans engaged in brutal warfare from the beginning. See *Chimpanzees and Human Evolution*, ed. Martin N. Muller, Richard W. Wrangham, and David R. Pilbeam (Cambridge, MA: Harvard University Press, 2017), and *Violence and Warfare among Hunter-Gatherers*, ed. Mark W. Allen and Terry L. Jones (Walnut Creek, CA: Left Coast Press, 2014). Important earlier works include Lawrence H. Keeley, *War before Civilization: The Myth of the Peaceful Savage* (Oxford: Oxford University Press, 1996), and Richard Wrangham and Dale Peterson, *Demonic Males: Apes and the Origins of Human Violence* (New York: Houghton Mifflin, 1996). In what follows, I focus on Wrangham and Peterson's *Demonic Males*, because it is a helpful introduction to salient biological research that should be accessible to theologians. However, even if the earliest humans were merely disposed to isolated acts of homicide, as opposed to warfare, the same problem for present purposes presents itself. Human desires or dispositions were not originally rightly ordered in the way that the classical view of the Fall assumed.

[19] *Evolution, Games, and God*, ed. Martin A. Nowak and Sarah Coakley (Cambridge, MA: Harvard University Press, 2013). For videos of the 2012 Gifford Lectures, see www.giffordlectures.org/lectures/sacrifice-regained-evolution-cooperation-and-god.

evolutionary history to foster cooperation.[20] But recent research, as Nowak and Coakley point out, has shown that cooperation and altruism are found in non-human animals such as bonobos. Given how closely related we are to bonobos, this research suggests that cooperation and altruistic behavior were found in human beings from the beginning.[21] Yet it does not seem that this research challenges the claim that violence played a role in our evolutionary history. Given the strict requirement of the doctrine of original justice – that the first humans could have lived without the desire for sin – the precise ratio of cooperative to violent behavior is not the issue. *Any* desire for aggressive violence among the first human beings would be incompatible with original justice. It may be worth briefly highlighting a summary of some salient literature.

According to Harvard biologist Richard Wrangham and author Dale Peterson, two crucial discoveries since the 1970s shed light on the origins of human violence. The first is that chimpanzees are far more violent than we had thought. In 1974, a researcher working with Jane Goodall's team at Gombe National Park in Tanzania observed a surprising event. A group of eight chimpanzees left their range and approached the territory of Kahama, another chimpanzee community. They found a member of the Kahama community named "Godi" eating alone. The eight chimpanzees initiated a vicious attack on Godi: they kicked, clawed, bit him and left him for dead. According to Wrangham and Peterson, this was the first time scientists had observed a lethal raid among chimpanzees.

The attack on Godi ... struck a momentous chord. This sort of thing wasn't supposed to happen among non-humans. Until the attack on Godi, scientists treated the remarkable violence of humanity as something uniquely ours. To be

---

[20] Or, at least, a typical effect of prominent popularizers has been that people have assumed that selfishness and violence were more central to our evolutionary history than they really were. Think of Richard Dawkins's bestselling book *The Selfish Gene*: many people who did not read the book probably assumed that science had proven we were genetically determined to be selfish. But, by 2016 at the latest, in the most recent edition of the book, Dawkins had retracted his earlier claim that "we are born selfish," arguing that it was a rhetorical flourish and that even the original edition emphasized cooperation. "Another good alternative to *The Selfish Gene* would have been *The Cooperative Gene*." Richard Dawkins, preface to the third edition of *The Selfish Gene* (Oxford: Oxford University Press, 2016 [1976]), x.

[21] Altruism is defined by Coakley as "a form of (costly) cooperation in which an individual is motivated by good will or love for another (or others)." Nowak and Coakley, *Evolution, Games, and God*, 5. Recent research indicates that humans are as closely related to bonobos as they are to chimpanzees. See Kay Prüfer et al., "The Bonobo Genome Compared with the Chimpanzee and Human Genomes," *Nature* 486 (2012), 527–32.

sure, everyone knew that many animal species kill; but usually that killing is directed toward other species, toward prey. Individual animals – often males in sexual competition – fight with others of their own species; but that sort of contest typically ends the moment one competitor gives up. Scientists thought that only humans deliberately sought out and killed members of their own species.[22]

The first discovery was how violent chimps are. The second discovery was how close to chimps *we* are. Scientists discovered in 1984 through DNA hybridization that humans are more closely related to chimpanzees than chimpanzees are to gorillas.[23] The last common ancestor of chimpanzees and humans existed around five million years ago, and since that time chimpanzees have changed very little. (They evolve "conservatively" because their habitat has remained stable.) What all this implies, Wrangham and Peterson argue, is that the investigation of chimpanzee behavior serves as a "time machine" that takes us back to the dawn of human history.[24] When we see aggressive violence in chimps, we see, in broad strokes, how the earliest humans would have behaved.

Interestingly, Wrangham and Peterson briefly venture into a discussion of the theological implications of their research. They claim that it has falsified the doctrine of original sin. "[W]e cloaked our own species' violence in culture and reason, two distinctly human attributes, and wondered what kind of original sin condemned us to this strange habit." We know now, though, that there was no fall from peace. We were always "deeply infused with the essence of that ancient forest brain."[25]

---

[22] Wrangham and Peterson, *Demonic Males*, 6–7.

[23] Charles G. Sibley and Jon E. Ahlquist, "The Phylogeny of the Hominoid Primates, as Indicated by DNA-DNA Hybridization," *Journal of Molecular Evolution* 20 (1984), 2–15. Wrangham and Peterson sum up the consensus *before* Sibley and Ahlquist's study as follows. "As for the three African ape species – gorillas, chimpanzees, and bonobos – well, a little common sense combined with some elementary anatomy would indicate that they were tightly associated in their own group.... Surely, so went the conventional thinking up to 1984, they were all each other's closest relatives, with humans as the special outsiders whose ancestors peeled off first." Wrangham and Peterson, *Demonic Males*, 38–9. "Sibley and Ahlquist took the two strands of DNA, zipped, heated ... and found that chimpanzees were more closely related to *humans* than they were to gorillas" (p. 40).

[24] "[T]he rainforest ape line has changed very little since these two species split around 8 to 10 million years ago. That means that our own rainforest ape ancestor, peeling away from the same line at 5 million years, came out of the chimpanzee-gorilla mold." Wrangham and Peterson, *Demonic Males*, 45. "[T]o be with modern chimpanzees in an African rainforest is to climb into a time machine. Stepping into the dappled world of these extraordinary apes we move back to glimpse our origins" (p. 47).

[25] Wrangham and Peterson, *Demonic Males*, 7, 62.

The belief that aggressive violence stemmed from a fall of some kind is no longer tenable: we have always been violent. This, at any rate, is their argument.

COMMUNAL ORIGINS

The third challenge to the doctrine of original sin comes from the hypothesis that human beings evolved as community of more than two people.[26] There is widespread agreement that contemporary humans are more closely related to chimpanzees and bonobos than any other living animals. The study of human evolution thus focuses on the "the lineage, or clade, comprising species more closely related to modern humans than to chimpanzees."[27] This lineage broke off from chimpanzees between five and eight million years ago.[28] *Homo sapiens* is the sole surviving species of this lineage. Uncontroversially, all living human beings are members of *H. sapiens*. But there is a great deal of debate over the boundaries of the genus *Homo* and the species *H. sapiens*:

Just what features of the cranium, jaws, dentition and the postcranial skeleton are specific to *H. sapiens*? For each morphological region, what are the "boundaries" of living *H. sapiens* variation? These are simple questions, to which one would have thought there would be ready answers. However, the concept of "modern humanness" has proved to be complex and difficult to express. Some researchers have made explicit suggestions that *H. sapiens* should be much more inclusive than just being limited to living and recent modern humans. For example, because they can see no obvious morphological discontinuity between *H. sapiens* and *H. erectus*, Wolpoff et al. (1994) have recommended that the boundary of *H. sapiens* be lowered to incorporate *H. erectus*, thus echoing a proposal made some time ago by Mayr (1950). This taxonomy has received little support, but at least the authors made an explicit statement about the scope of the morphology they were prepared to subsume into *H. sapiens*.[29]

There is also debate over the meaning of the terms "species" and "genus" and, among theologians, over the relation between the biological

---

[26] The word "communal," of course, can be used to refer to a pair of people. For present purposes, it refers to a group of more than two people. I am avoiding the word "polygenesis" in this context because it would probably be misleading. Cf. the first note of this chapter.

[27] Bernard Wood and Brian G. Richmond, "Human Evolution: Taxonomy and Paleobiology," *Journal of Anatomy* 196 (2000), 19.

[28] M. Ruvolo, "Genetic Diversity in Hominoid Primates," *Annual Review of Anthropology* 26 (1997), 515–40.

[29] Wood and Richmond, "Human Evolution," 49.

concepts *Homo* and *H. sapiens* and the proper sense of the word "human being" (more on these questions later). However one chooses to define – or *not* define – what it means to be human, there is widespread agreement among scientists that "the human lineage has not dipped below several thousand individuals for the last 3 million years or more – long before our lineage was even remotely close to what we would call "human.""[30] The lack of support for the view that the human population ever consisted of only two individuals is the first of our population problems.

Two models have dominated recent scientific discussion of human origins: "recent African origin" (RAO) and "multiregional evolution" (MRE). As the biological anthropologist John Relethford has noted, describing these models is "not a simple task," in large part due to widespread disagreement over how to define them.[31] While acknowledging that these labels "are frequently used to mean different things," Relethford offers lucid definitions of each model.[32]

The recent African origin model proposes that anatomically modern humans emerged in Africa roughly 200,000 years ago and then dispersed throughout the Old World, replacing preexisting archaic hominids with little or no admixture.... Implicit in many discussions of the recent African origin model is the idea that anatomically modern *Homo sapiens* are a separate species from archaic *Homo sapiens*. The origin of modern humans is, therefore, often seen as resulting from cladogenesis, the formation of a new lineage.[33]

The multiregional evolution model is not a specific model of modern human origins but rather a general model focusing on evolutionary process within a polytypic species.... Multiregional evolution views all hominid evolution since the origin of *Homo erectus* as taking place within a single evolutionary lineage. Multiregional evolution is a general evolutionary model that attempts to account for species-wide change while allowing for local and regional continuity. It is important to note that despite arguments to the contrary ..., multiregional evolution does not necessarily argue that the primary genetic input into any region of modern humans came from within the same geographic region. Other models are

---

[30] Venema and McKnight, *Adam and the Genome*, 55. Venema provides a helpful introduction to evolution in the first half of this book. In this context of his claim about the effective population size of the human lineage, he cites Albert Tenesa et al., "Recent Human Effective Population Size Estimated from Linkage Disequilibrium," *Genome Research* 17.4 (2007): 520–6.

[31] John H. Relethford, "Genetics of Modern Human Origins and Diversity," *Annual Review of Anthropology* 27 (1998), 2.

[32] Both from Relethford, "Genetics of Modern Human Origins and Diversity," 3.

[33] Relethford, "Genetics of Modern Human Origins and Diversity," 2.

also possible within the general multiregional framework, including major genetic changes originating within Africa and mixing, through gene flow, with non-African populations.[34]

The crucial claims of the recent African origin model, by Relethford's lights, are as follows. First, our origin – that is, the origin of "anatomically modern human beings" (AMHB), individuals falling within the range of anatomical variation of contemporary humans – is African because all human beings alive today descend from the first population of AMHB in Africa. Second, our origin is recent because AMHB evolved 200,000 years ago, later than archaic humans. Third, there is the sometimes-implicit idea that we were a new species, and thus did not significantly interbreed with other species in the genus *Homo*, such as Neandertals. If a new species did not evolve in Africa 200,000 years ago, it would arguably make no sense to speak of the origin of *our* species there and thus the model would have little to no explanatory power. On multiregional evolution, by contrast, AMHB were not a distinct species from archaic humans. Different human populations have existed as a single lineage – and thus actually or potentially interbred with each other – for some two million years, since *Homo erectus*. Human beings today do not descend exclusively from a recent African population; we may also descend from various archaic populations. MRE does not require that humanity originated on different continents; "African multi-regionalism" is the view that humanity originated in different parts of Africa.[35]

It seems that RAO enjoyed the support of most specialists from the late 1980s until quite recently.[36] The terms of the debate shifted with the publication of a draft sequence of the Neandertal genome in 2010. The most interesting conclusion of this research is that the genomes of con-temporary Eurasians (but not Africans) are between 1 and 4 percent

---

[34] Relethford, "Genetics of Modern Human Origins and Diversity," 3.

[35] Eleanor M. L. Scerri et al., "Did Our Species Evolve in Subdivided Populations across Africa, and Why Does It Matter?," *Trends in Ecology & Evolution* (in press), https://doi.org/10.1016/j.tree.2018.05.005.

[36] See Rebecca L. Cann, Mark Stoneking, and Allan C. Wilson, "Mitochondrial DNA and Human Evolution," *Nature* 325 (1987), 31–6. This influential article was widely interpreted as providing strong support for RAO. The authors hypothesized that "Africa is the likely source of the human mitochondrial gene pool" and supported the following view (now known as RAO): "the transformation of archaic to anatomically modern forms of *Homo sapiens* occurred first in Africa, about 100,000–140,000 years ago, and ... all present day humans are descendants of that African population" (p. 35).

Neandertal. The authors of the article discussed the implications of this conclusion for the human origins debate:

One model for modern human origins suggests that all present-day humans trace all their ancestry back to a small African population that expanded and replaced archaic forms of humans without admixture. Our analysis of the Neandertal genome may not be compatible with this view because Neandertals are on average closer to individuals in Eurasia than to individuals in Africa. Furthermore, individuals in Eurasia today carry regions in their genome that are closely related to those in Neandertals and distant from other present-day humans. The data suggest that between 1 and 4% of the genomes of people in Eurasia are derived from Neandertals. Thus, while the Neandertal genome presents a challenge to the simplest version of an "out-of-Africa" model for modern human origins, it continues to support the view that the vast majority of genetic variants that exist at appreciable frequencies outside Africa came from Africa with the spread of anatomically modern humans.[37]

The "simplest" version of RAO is challenged because significant interbreeding occurred between *Homo sapiens* and Neandertals; it is not the case that contemporary human beings descend exclusively from a recent African population. The debate was further complicated by research indicating that the DNA of another archaic group (the "Denisovans") is found in some contemporary Asians, especially Melanesians.[38]

This raises one of the controversial definitional issues mentioned at the outset of our discussion. To what extent does RAO depend on the denial of significant interbreeding between archaic and modern humans? Green et al.'s aforementioned comment to the effect that the *simplest* version of RAO is challenged by these data implies that a more complex version of RAO is still tenable.

Multiregionalists have disagreed. The paleoanthropologist John Hawks, for example, argued that the study of Green et al. rendered RAO untenable. "From now on, we are all multiregionalists trying to explain the out-of-Africa pattern."[39] It is not the simplest version of RAO that is challenged by the presence of Neandertal DNA in Eurasians; it is the RAO hypothesis itself. Most of our DNA comes from Africa, but that

---

[37] Richard E. Green et al., "A Draft Sequence of the Neandertal Genome," *Science* 328.5979 (2010), 721.

[38] David Reich et al., "Genetic History of an Archaic Hominin Group from Denisova Cave in Siberia," *Nature* 468.7327 (2010), 1053–60; Matthias Meyer et al., "A High-Coverage Genome Sequence from an Archaic Denisovan Individual," *Science* 338 (2012), 222–6.

[39] http://johnhawks.net/weblog/reviews/neandertals/neandertal_dna/neandertals-live-genome-sequencing-2010.html.

is not the point: if our anatomically modern ancestors interbred with archaic humans, then cladogenesis did *not* occur 200,000 years ago in Africa, and the hypothesis of a single lineage from *H. erectus* onward is supported. These claims arguably constitute the core of the MRE model. To get a better handle on the crux of the debate, it may be helpful to consider what leading multiregionalist Milford Wolpoff admits would falsify the model:

> multiregional evolution can easily be disproved if it can be shown that all of the ancestors of living humans at some discrete time in the Middle or Late Pleistocene lived in only one area of the world. If this were the case, then we should be able to trace the ancestry of every human genetic locus to a single population existing at some time in the past million years.[40]

If AMHE evolved in *one* region, then *multi*regionalism is false. This was always the basis of RAO: AMHB evolved in Africa, not multiple regions. Since the data support the hypothesis that we have both African and archaic ancestry, multiregionalists argue, MRE is the best model on offer.

Proponents of RAO, however, reject the way multiregionalists have tried to frame the debate. Chris Stringer, for example, argues that the Neandertal genome does not undermine RAO at all: "we are all out-of-Africanists who accept some multiregional contributions."[41] The central question is not whether we are exclusively of recent African origin. It is whether we are primarily of recent African origin. Since the archaic assimilation constitutes less than 10 percent of our genome, "'mostly out of Africa' is the appropriate designation and, for me, that is still RAO."[42] Others have argued that the data best support a model in between RAO and MRE. Fred Smith, for example, defends the "assimilation model" (AM). This model hypothesizes that AMHB did originate in Africa recently, but there was more "morphological continuity across the archaic-modern human boundary in several geographic regions of Eurasia" than RAO acknowledges.[43] David Reich has recently argued that the best model is a synthesis of MRE and RAO:

---

[40] Milford H. Wolpoff, John Hawks, and Rachel Caspari, "Multiregional, Not Multiple Origins," *American Journal of Physical Anthropology* 112 (2000), 131.

[41] Chris Stringer, "Why We Are Not All Multiregionalists Now," *Trends in Ecology & Evolution* 29.5 (2014), 251.

[42] Stringer, "Why We Are Not All Multiregionalists Now," 249.

[43] Fred H. Smith et al., "The Assimilation Model of Modern Human Origins in Light of Current Genetic and Genomic Knowledge," *Quaternary International* 450 (2017), 126.

[T]he out-of-Africa theory emphasizes the recent origin of the differences among present-day human populations, relative to the multimillion-year time depth of the human skeletal record. Yet the out-of-Africa argument is not entirely right either. We now have a synthesis, driven by the finding of gene flow between Neanderthals and modern humans based on ancient DNA. This affirms a "mostly out-of-Africa" theory.[44]

These debates clearly seem to hinge, at least in part, on what constitutes a species. MRE advocates typically use the biological species concept, which is standardly defined as follows. A species is "a group of organisms that can successfully interbreed and produce fertile offspring."[45] On the biological species concept, early AMHB and Neandertals belonged to the same species because they could interbreed and produce fertile offspring. RAO advocates, by contrast, typically emphasize the phenetic (or morphological) species concept, on which a species is a group of organisms that look alike. The degree of similitude necessary to ground a distinct species will depend on the judgment of scientists. Consider Stringer's observations:

[G]iven that interbreeding did occur between modern and archaic humans, out of Africa and perhaps within Africa too, does this mean that we should abandon the different species names and lump the fossils of the past million years or more as *H. sapiens*, as multiregionalists have suggested? If hybridisation events between the various lineages prove to have been widespread and significant in both time and space, we might have to do that, but I do not think that point has been reached yet. Personally, I have never equated the use of a separate species designation for Neanderthals (morphological species concept) with complete reproductive isolation from *H. sapiens* (biological species concept) and, in my view, there are still good scientific reasons to give populations that had long and (largely) separate evolutionary histories different names.[46]

In Stringer's view, the morphological differences between Neandertals and AMHB are significant enough to justify considering them as distinct species. If we lumped them together, the following oddities result: "we end up with a *H. sapiens* that is simultaneously characterised by a high and rounded skull; by no continuous brow ridge, and a strong continuous brow ridge; by a well-developed chin even in infants, and minimal chin

---

[44] David Reich, *Who We Are and How We Got Here: Ancient DNA and the New Science of the Human Past* (New York: Pantheon Books, 2018), 49–50.

[45] https://plato.stanford.edu/entries/species/. See also Elliott Sober's *Philosophy of Biology* (Boulder, CO: Westview Press, 2000), 156, for discussion of the biological species concept.

[46] Stringer, "Why We Are Not All Multiregionalists Now," 250.

development; by no suprainic fossa in adults, and a suprainiac fosa throughout ontogeny," and so on.[47] In his judgment, these differences are significant enough to divide AMHB and Neandertals into different species. Moreover, Stringer suggests that the offspring of AMHB and Neandertals were characterized by diminished fertility.[48]

In order to address the questions of whether or to what extent the doctrine of original sin is compatible with the foregoing hypotheses, we need to briefly discuss the relation between the species concepts deployed by biologists and the theological concept of the human being. I assume that human beings are made in the image of God. Non-human animals are not. Those with different theological or philosophical views of what the human being is can agree on this.[49] If a being is embodied and made in the image of God, then, in my view, she is a human being. If a being is embodied and not made in the image of God, then she is not a human being. Those with different views of what the image of God is can agree on this as well. I assume, moreover, that there are no partial human natures. A being either has a human nature or not. What follows from these assumptions, in conjunction with the theory of evolution, is that there once was a time when there were no human beings, and at a certain time human beings in the theological sense – embodied image-bearers – began to exist. This theological usage may or may not track with scientific usage.

Indeed, presumably it is different from the biological species concept, because, given common ancestry, the first embodied image-bearers descended from non-humans. Thus the parents of the first image-bearers would probably belong to the same species as their children from the point of view of biology, but they would belong to a different species as their children from the point of view of theology. We shouldn't confuse the epistemological question of whether we know when the first image-bearers began to exist with the ontological question of whether they did. It doesn't follow from the fact that we don't know when the first image-bearers began to exist that there were no first image-bearers. In what

---

[47] Stringer, "Why We Are Not All Multiregionalists Now," 250.

[48] "[W]hen modern humans and Neanderthals met and mixed, they were at the edge of biological incompatibility, such that there was reduced male fertility and rapid natural selection to remove the Neanderthal-derived variants that caused this sterility." Stringer, "Why We Are Not All Multiregionalists Now," 251.

[49] For example, those who hold that the human being is essentially a soul and those who, by contrast, hold that the human being is essentially a soul–body compound.

follows, when I speak of the "human being" without qualification, I mean to speak of the embodied image-bearer.

Let's take stock. The following claims are widely agreed on in the scientific community. All human beings alive today receive most of their DNA from a population in Africa some 200,000 years ago. All human beings alive today descend from a population of no fewer than 6,000. Europeans have some Neandertal DNA, and Asians have some Neandertal and some Denisovan DNA. The question of when the first human beings lived, by contrast, is contested. We could identify them with *Homo erectus*, some two million years ago. Dennis Bonnette has defended this view on the basis of *H. erectus*'s Achulean industry, which he argues evinces rationality.[50] Alternatively, we could follow the tendency of biologists and identify human beings with anatomically modern *H. sapiens*, some 200,000 years ago. It has also been suggested that the first humans began to exist only 50,000 years ago, corresponding with the advent of "behavioral modernity."[51] Proposed dates for the origin of humanity, then, range from roughly two million to fifty thousand years ago. Just as there is no agreement on when the first human beings began to exist, there is no consensus on *where* they began to exist. Some argue that RAO has been falsified and MRE vindicated, others argue that the most plausible hypothesis is a synthesis of both.

A related but arguably distinct question concerns the identity of Adam and Eve. Denis Alexander has recently suggested that they were Neolithic farmers but not the first human beings.[52] The view that there were human beings on Earth before Adam and Eve is known as "pre-Adamism." The story of Adam and Eve features prominently in Genesis, according to the pre-Adamite view, because they were the first human beings elected for fellowship with God. Of course, if one takes Adam and Eve to be symbolic figures, or definite descriptions of the first humans, then questions of pre-Adamites are otiose. For Adam qua symbol would equally symbolize the first man as much as any other, and Adam qua definite descriptor would pick out only the first man, even if he lived long before the development of horticulture. In the latter case, one could maintain that the early chapters of Genesis retroject aspects of postexilic culture into the

---

[50] Dennis Bonnette, *Origin of the Human Species*, 3rd ed. (Ave Maria, FL: Sapientia Press, 2014).

[51] Denis O. Lamoureux, "Beyond Original Sin: Is a Theological Paradigm Shift Inevitable?," *Perspectives on Science and Christian Faith* 67.1 (2015), 43.

[52] Denis Alexander, *Creation or Evolution? Do We Have to Choose?* (Oxford: Monarch Books, 2014).

narrative of ancient human origins. Naturally these exegetical questions are complex – and important in their own right – but they need not detain us here.

We are now in a position to consider the major challenges the hypothesis of communal origins presents to the doctrine of original sin. The first challenge is this. If we originated as a group of more than two people, then one of two absurd consequences follows. Either there were sinless human beings *post lapsum*, or God is the author of sin.

It is absurd to claim that there are sinless postlapsarian human beings. If the doctrine of original sin is found in Scripture, surely it is found in Rom. 5:12–21, which teaches that the transgression of Adam brought sin, death, and condemnation to all human beings. If, after Adam's sin, there were sinless human beings, then Paul's teaching is false. One might respond that Adam's sin *eventually* spread to all of humanity (such that everyone alive today was born in sin) and that until then, other human beings, like Eve, sinned of their own volition. But this is to no avail: Paul is clear. Human beings receive their sin from Adam. If one holds that part of postlapsarian humanity does not, one might as well plump for Pelagius.

Alternatively, one might argue that a communal origin is compatible with Adam bringing sin to all. One could argue, for example, that sin came to Adam's contemporaries who didn't descend from him on the basis of his act, so long as they lived in a close-knit community.[53] But this won't do either. A condition sine qua non of receiving sin from Adam is descending from him. This is true on all the classic models of the Fall. On realism, humanity needs to preexist in Adam so as to sin in or with him; on federalism, humanity needs to receive a corrupt nature as the basis for God's imputation of Adam's act; on disease theory, original sin is defined

---

[53] This hypothesis has been formulated by Catholic and (evangelical) Protestant authors. "[I]t is at least conceivable that after the special creation of Eve, which established the first human pair as God's viceregents and clinched the fact that there is no natural bridge from animal to man, God may have now conferred his image on Adam's collaterals, to bring them into the same realm of being. Adam's 'federal' headship of humanity extended, if that was the case, outwards to his contemporaries as well as onwards to his offspring, and his disobedience disinherited both alike." Derek Kidner, *Genesis: An Introduction and Commentary* (Downers Grove, IL: InterVarsity Press, 2008 [1967]), 32. "Polygenism, therefore, allows us to imagine a hominization area where those beings that originated mankind formed a genuine biological and historical unit, achieved through a genuinely possible personal communication process. Such a regional limitation of the hominization area which made a real original unity of man's origins possible in the history of mankind would still be scientifically acceptable if we believe that mankind was prepared by a very *old* special line in the development of evolution." Karl Rahner, "Evolution and Original Sin," in *Concilium* 26, trans. Johannes Metz (New York: Paulist Press, 1967), 68.

as sin inherited from Adam. If God simply *made* otherwise innocent, sinless human beings into sinners because of Adam's sin, then clearly he is the author of their sin. And that is absurd.

The second challenge follows from the hypothesis of multiregionalism. On MRE, humans originated in different parts of Africa or even different continents. Even granting for the sake of argument that Adam could have represented his contemporaries in sin in a small tribe, it is hard to see how Adam could have represented people who didn't know him at all. MRE also poses a challenge to prominent accounts of original sin that deny a historical Fall, à la Schleiermacher. If original sin is the unity of the human community in sin – "In each the work of all, in all the work of each" – then it seems we need to share a common origin.[54]

It has occasionally been argued that a form of monogenesis is compatible with evolution. Kenneth Kemp, for example, proposes a distinction between theological human beings (i.e., rational animals called to the beatific vision) and merely biological human beings (non-rational animals who can interbreed with theological human beings).[55] On this basis, he argues that a modified form of monogenesis is still possible even in light of mainstream genetics. This is because the children of the first theological human beings could have interbred with various non-rational human beings.[56] It is possible that we have all descended ultimately from two theological human beings, from whom we have contracted original sin, while simultaneously descending from a population of at least thousands of merely biological humans. Let us assume that Kemp's proposal is compatible with mainstream genetics.[57] It seems to create several theological problems. Why didn't God elevate us as a group, if evolution had prepared an entire population for human existence? Similarly, why wouldn't God have created a population of theological human beings large enough for them to avoid widespread interbreeding with non-

---

[54] Cf. Rahner's argument against "polyphylism," which corresponds roughly to MRE: "We should not let ourselves slip into a kind of polyphylism, rejected by most anthropologists on scientific grounds; otherwise the biotype in which hominization (even a polygenetic hominization) took place would be divided into (biologically and humanly) completely disparate and independent areas." Rahner, "Evolution and Original Sin," 67. Even after accepting "polygenesis" (i.e., as he used the term, simply the view that we have not all descended from a single pair), Rahner continued to reject polyphylism because it would rupture the unity of the human community.

[55] Kemp, "Science, Theology, and Monogenesis."

[56] This interbreeding may not have been permitted by God.

[57] S. Joshua Swamidass, "The Overlooked Science of Genealogical Ancestry," *Perspectives on Science and Christian Faith* 70.1 (2018), 19–35.

humans? It seems that it would be better, if at all possible, to construct a doctrine of original sin that doesn't rely on the scenarios invoked by Kemp's proposal.

It is hard to see how our continuous, complex, and communal origins are compatible with the doctrine of original sin. It is also hard to see how mainstream evolutionary theory is compatible with a disease view of the Fall (which non-disease views of original sin often rely on to explain our disordered desires or "concupiscence"). Moreover, it seems that either God is responsible for original sin, or Paul's teaching that humanity has been in a state of sin since Adam's Fall is false. I will argue in the next chapter, however, that Thomas's account of original sin can be reconstructed in such a way as to respond to these challenges, without falling into the pitfalls of the modern accounts discussed in Chapter 5.

7

Original Sin

In dialogue with Thomas Aquinas, the evolutionary theory discussed in Chapter 6, and biblical scholarship, this chapter offers a new perspective on the doctrine of original sin. The account I am developing here presupposes the cogency of at least one of the objections raised in Chapters 2 and 4. Recall that Chapter 2 argued that Thomas's developing view of original justice created a major problem for his view of original sin. Either original justice is preternatural, in which case it is not removed when the person receives sanctifying grace, or original justice is supernatural, and it is not possible for Adam to transmit an effectual disposition to it. Neither of these alternatives is acceptable. Recall, moreover, that Chapter 4 argued that partial voluntareity – a phrase I used to describe Thomas's view that original sin is voluntary in the infant, "*voluntarium voluntate alterius*" – is a confused concept and does nothing to explain the inheritance of guilt. The moral quality of a habit cannot depend on the moral quality of its efficient cause. If either of these criticisms is on target, then Thomas's view must at least be rethought, if not rejected tout court. This is because both impinge on his account of what original sin is. For Thomas, original sin is the lack of due original justice, and the "debt" or *ratio culpae* is the infant's partially voluntary failure to receive original justice from Adam's sinful will.

Why then do we need Thomas's view at all? Let me explain what I take to be his distinctive contribution to the doctrine. To do that, it is necessary to say a few words about his view of evil. Thomas, indebted directly to Augustine, held that all evils are privations. Yet because evil is the privation *of* a subject – it cannot exist on its own – we can speak "positively" of the being of which the evil is a privation, or "negatively" of the privation itself.[1] For example, if a sprinter suffers a knee injury, we say that she lacks her sprinting ability (negatively). But if we want to know the precise extent of her injury we need to know what she can still do (positively). Perhaps she can still jog, if the injury is minor; perhaps she tore her ACL and can only limp. Accordingly, when we consider the habit of original sin formally, we can consider it negatively, insofar as it is a privation, or positively, insofar as we consider its subject, the infant's soul. I contend that Thomas advanced the doctrine in both of these respects.

Let's first consider his treatment of original sin qua privation. Anselm had defined original sin as the lack of due justice, and Thomas agreed, insofar as he argued that the lack of original justice is original sin's formal component. "In original sin, deordination from the end is formal."[2] Thomas's distinctive contribution to the doctrine of original sin qua privation is his hypothesis that the privation is formally of a supernatural gift. I defend the view that original sin is the privation of a supernatural gift in Chapter 8. For now, suffice it to note a couple of its major benefits. It allows us to deny that grace is exacted by human nature and to affirm that human beings are born in need of the transforming grace of the gospel. Moreover, it doesn't entail that human nature is corrupted in the strict sense, a view which has many absurd consequences. If original sin is the privation of human nature in the strict sense, if it *deprives* human beings of their nature, then it is unclear how postlapsarian human beings continue to exist. Thomas's robust commitment to the continued existence of human beings led him to address the *subject* of original sin in a new way as well.

The broadly Augustinian tradition held that the subject of original sin was oriented to self-love. Thomas demurred. Why? Remember that, although human nature without grace is not sinful per se, human nature deprived of grace by Adam's sin is sinful; thus, the object of the fallen human being's telos is, materially, the same as the "purely natural" human being's telos. If, then, Thomas had said that the fallen human being is ordered to sinful self-love (or any other sin), he would have been committed to the view that the human being is ordered to sin *as such*.

---

[1] Thomas puts it crisply in the *De malo*: "malum uno modo potest intelligi id quod est subiectum mali, et hoc aliquid est: alio modo potest intelligi ipsum malum, et hoc non est aliquid, sed est ipsa priuatio alicuius particularis boni." Q. 1, a. 1, *corpus*.

[2] "[I]n peccato originali ... deordinatio a fine sit ibi sicut formale." *Scriptum* II, d. 30, q. 1, a. 3, *corpus*.

For Thomas, this is an absurd conclusion, because (inter alia) it implies that our true happiness does not lie in God. (I discuss this point further in Chapter 8.) Nor can it be the case that we have *no* end. As Gilson argued, in line with Thomas, the very nature of existence requires acting for an ultimate end. "[T]o be (*esse*) is to act (*agere*), and to act is to tend (*tendere*) to an end wherein achieved being may ultimately rest."[3] What, then, is the end of human nature, if not sin or nothing? Daringly, Thomas argued that the answer is *God*. The formal cause of original sin, considered in the infant as its subject, is the natural orientation to nature's author. This orientation is, as we have seen, separable from the preter- and supernatural gifts: it is one of the *propria* that follow from the *principia naturae*; one cannot begin existence as a rational creature without it. To be is to be in act. The creative act of the almighty God is required for the limited act of the finite creature. Through Jesus Christ, and through the Holy Spirit, the Father makes all things for himself. From all this, Thomas argues, it follows that to be from God is to be for God.

The embodied spiritual creature is called to participation in the inner life of God, but its natural act of existence is insufficient to efficaciously pursue that end. By nature, material beings tend to dissolution and corruption. In order to enter into the personal relationship with God that makes us "participants of the divine nature" (2 Pet. 1:4) and leads us to eternal life, we need the supernatural gift of the Holy Spirit. Without him, we cannot be born again, or enter the kingdom of heaven: our default destination is eternal separation from God in hell.

The contribution of Thomas's account, in sum, is its suggestion that original sin involves the lack of sanctifying grace in the human being. Its limitation is the implication that the infant's lack of grace is sinful if and only Adam failed to sexually transmit it. My proposal is, in one respect, very simple. Leave the limitation, take the contribution. A new Thomist view of original sin follows from this proposal. Here are the two core claims of the new Thomist view. Original sin is the lack of sanctifying grace in the human being, and the human being with original sin retains human nature. In the rest of this chapter and the next, I unpack this proposal's salient implications. Let me begin with a few preliminary clarifications.

I am not arguing that we should abandon Thomas's doctrine of original guilt and keep his doctrine of original sin. Thomas argues that the

---

[3] Etienne Gilson, *Being and Some Philosophers* (Toronto: Pontifical Institute of Medieval Studies, 1952 [1949]), 186. Cf. *STh* I-II, q. 1, a. 1, ad 1.

former is essential to the latter. I am arguing that his views of human nature and grace imply that he didn't need to ground original sin in partial voluntareity. Nor am I denying original guilt, construed as God's judgment (more on this shortly). For now, suffice it to say that though the person lacking grace is oriented to God, she cannot have friendship with God in this life or enjoy the beatific vision in the kingdom of heaven in the next. Moreover, the person in original sin is mortal and has habitually disordered desires. I intend to remain neutral on the question of whether habitually disordered desire is part of original sin or the consequence of original sin. This is because, or so I will argue in Chapter 8, one's answer to this question has more to with one's view of justification than sin.

My account does not straightforwardly fit into the typology of models heretofore discussed. Neither the category of disease nor the category of judgment does heavy-duty explanatory work. Insofar as sins and diseases are both bad, they are comparable, and illuminating analogies can be drawn between them. "They who are whole have no need of the physician, but they that are sick" (Mark 2:17). But original sin is not a disease, properly speaking, because human nature neither includes nor transmits grace. Original sin is not a "real" participation in an action committed before infants are born. Insofar as God judges the sin that is *in* the infant, original sin is imputed to the infant. This divine imputation is not an extra decision beyond seeing the human being without grace. Original sin is not, as Thomas had it, partially voluntary. It is involuntary, both in the sense that the human being with original sin has not chosen anything and in the sense that no sinful action of any other agent is part of the *ratio* of the infant's own sin. It is not a modern account in the sense stipulated earlier, because the new Thomist view is logically compatible with multiple perspectives on the importance of the historical Fall. I will explain what I mean by this in the next section, which responds to the challenges posed by evolutionary theory in Chapter 6.

ORIGINAL SIN AND EVOLUTION

The primary aim of this book is to propose and defend the new Thomist view of (originated) original sin, which is logically separable from originating original sin. I argue in this section, however, that the new Thomist view of original sin is also logically compatible with a new Thomist view of the Fall that is not in tension with – or at least does not contradict – mainstream evolutionary theory. The objections raised in the previous chapter, however, *do* seem to create insurmountable problems for disease theories of the Fall and original sin. Thus the logical separability of the new Thomist view of original sin from the new Thomist view of the Fall should not be a reason for theologians who believe in a historical Fall to reject my proposed view of original sin. The fact that the new Thomist view of original sin is compatible with a view of the Fall that is itself compatible with evolutionary theory ought to be seen as an advantage of the new Thomist view of original sin. I also argue, however, that the new Thomist view of original sin should be attractive to theologians who reject a historical Fall. This is because it does not entail the absurd consequences that follow from the modern accounts discussed in Chapter 5. My argument, in short, is that the new Thomist perspective on original sin should be attractive to a wide variety of theologians interested in the dialogue between theology and evolutionary theory.

Before responding to the challenges from evolutionary theory discussed in the previous chapter, I will briefly describe the new Thomist view of the Fall. Here are its core claims. The first humans sin. Therefore – sans miracle – if they reproduce, they necessarily pass on mortality and disordered desires to all their descendants, to whom God does not immediately give sanctifying grace. If they had not sinned, God would have given sanctifying grace to their children. If their children obeyed, their grandchildren would have been born in the same grace, and so on. On this account, the first humans were given supernatural grace, but that grace was withheld from later generations. Subsequent humans begin to exist with only human nature and as a result have disordered desires. This account of the Fall, when combined with my view of original sin, does not imply that God imputes Adam's act to his posterity: original sin is *ex hypothesi* the infant's own lack of grace. It is to say that God instituted a contingent condition of humanity's remaining unfallen: obedience. This would not change Adam's absolute inability to have sexually transmitted grace.

I will address the objections from the previous chapter in order. First is the objection from continuous origins, or natural selection. The new Thomist view of the Fall does not claim that our DNA has been corrupted or altered. The Fall is not the loss of a "strictly natural" trait in the aforementioned sense, a trait that was to be transmitted throughout the generations. We do not need to appeal to the hypothetical possibility of the first human beings sexually transmitting righteousness; we need only to appeal to the hypothetical possibility that God would have continued to bestow the gift of sanctifying grace, the gift of divine friendship. I assume that natural selection is not in tension with the view that the earliest human beings enjoyed friendship with God, or that subsequent generations could have enjoyed this friendship as well.

Second is the objection from complex origins, including the tendency to aggressive violence. The new Thomist view of the Fall is compatible with two different ways of responding to the objection from original violence. The first option (option "A") is this. The first humans were created in sanctifying grace which restrained all their disordered desires, including the desire for aggressive violence. The second option (option "B") is this. The first humans were created in sanctifying grace that did not restrain all their naturally disordered desires. The grace was sufficient to give them free will to resist these desires, however. They might have been tempted to commit violent actions, for example, but they could have refrained from actual violence. Option A is more traditional but arguably open to the aforementioned objection that it stands in tension with evolutionary theory. Option B is easier to square with evolution but arguably open to the aforementioned objection that evil is built into creation.

Whether one picks A or B will relate both to one's view of the nature of sin and to one's view of evolution. First, the nature of sin. Recall that Anselm argued that disordered concupiscence (roughly speaking, habitually disordered desires) is not sinful, that sin is *only* in the rational will. Alternatively, in dialogue with Augustine, other theologians have argued that disordered concupiscence itself is sinful. If one thinks that disordered concupiscence is sinful, then option B implies that the first humans were created in sin, despite the fact that they were also created in sanctifying grace. If one takes a broadly Anselmian view, which denies that disordered concupiscence is intrinsically sinful, one could maintain that the first human beings had disordered desires *without* sin, so long as they had sanctifying grace. In either case, the new Thomist view denies that the Fall affected the DNA of the first humans. It is thus compatible with the story Wrangham and Peterson tell of our pre-human history. Without grace, at least some of us are inclined to aggression. But it is compatible with other stories as well, should our picture of our pre-human origins need to be adjusted.

There are objections that can be raised against this response. One could argue that this appeal to a supernatural gift at the dawn of history carries a whiff of fundamentalism. Even if this hypothesis is not formulated on scientific grounds, doesn't it involve rejecting a plausible scientific hypothesis – the first humans were disposed to violence because their ancestors were – on the basis of the Bible? Isn't this the same sort of argumentation used to defend the special creation of species against evolution in general? Alternatively, one could argue that it would be unfitting for God to use evolution to create (at least the bodies of) the first human beings if he intended to cancel out the effects of that evolution from the beginning. Why not guide evolution to select for the properties the first human beings were always intended to have? If that was impossible or undesirable – though it is hard to see *why* it would be impossible for an omnipotent God and hard to see why it would be undesirable on the supposition that God intended us to have these dispositions – why not simply create human beings from the dust, as classical Christian theology has it? I do not have space to address these questions in any depth here. But the first objection to a supernatural gift, if cogent, does not prove that B is "fundamentalist," only A. For B does not require rejecting any scientific hypothesis. The second objection, regarding the goals of evolution in the context of providence, is more difficult. I do not have anything more to say about it here, except that it is a theological objection, and my goal here has only been to show that there is an account of the Fall compatible with mainstream evolutionary theory.

The final objections were raised on the basis of communal origins. If humanity evolved as a group of more than two, then it seems that one of two unacceptable consequences follows: either there were sinless human beings post lapsum or God is the author of sin. Moreover, on MRE, even views of original sin that don't rely on a historical Fall (such as Schleiermacher's) seem to be falsified, for there is no single community of sin. In what follows I offer two possible responses to these challenges that are compatible with the new Thomist view of original sin. The first appeals to the new Thomist view of the Fall, and the second does not involve a historical Fall.

It seems that the claim that "either there were sinless human beings post lapsum or God is the author of sin" is a false dilemma. Consider the possibility that a single large group (or multiple groups) of human beings is created in grace, including one human named "Adam." If Adam obeys, the next generation of humanity will receive grace, whether they descend from him or not. Suppose that everyone freely sins except for Adam, and then Adam sins. In this scenario, humanity originated as a large community (or series of communities), and there are no sinless human beings post lapsum.[4] God did not make otherwise innocent human beings into sinners

---

[4] A similar scenario is sketched by Karl Rahner, "Original Sin," in *Sacramentum Mundi: An Encyclopedia of Theology*, v. 4, ed. Karl Rahner et al. (London: Burns and Oates, 1969), 328–34.

because Adam sinned: the first generation all sinned freely, just as in the traditional view Eve sinned freely before Adam sinned, without prejudice to Paul's claim that Adam brought sin, death, and condemnation to the many. But what about the next generation? How do they contract sin? Isn't God's decision to withhold grace from them the cause of their sin, if *ex hypothesi* sin is the lack of grace?

Not necessarily. If human beings have the power to transmit human nature – in the strict sense, such that they can be the principal cause of their children's existence – then they can be the principal cause of their own personal sins as well as the original sin of their posterity. This scenario does not require "traducianism" – the view that the human being's soul consists of a part or parts of at least one of her parents' souls – because it doesn't require holding that souls are fissiparous. It only requires that humans have the power to bring it about that their children have souls (a view that has been called "generationism"). If we combine the new Thomist view of the Fall and original sin, a generationist account of the transmission of the soul, and the hypothesis of communal origins, then the following scenario is possible. The first human beings are created in grace. They sin and forfeit grace, and as a result they transmit sinful human nature to the next generation. God does not cause personal sin or original sin. Of course, Thomas himself held that only God can be the principal cause of the human soul. Following Peter Lombard, he also argued that traducianism is a heresy (although as we noted, the Lombard relied on a pseudo-Augustinian text to make this point). If one agrees with Thomas that God must infuse the soul directly, it seems hard to avoid the implication God is causally involved in the transmission of original sin. Perhaps one could argue that even if God infuses souls without sanctifying grace, he is not the true cause of original sin because he *would* have given grace had Adam not sinned.

Alternatively, one could defend the new Thomist view of original sin without appeal to a historical Fall. The absurd consequences that follow from the modern accounts criticized in Chapter 5 don't follow from the new Thomist view of original sin. Unlike the hypothesis of radical evil, infants and those with severe disabilities have original sin and are thus included in God's saving work. And unlike modern Augustinianism, the new Thomist view of original sin does not involve the view that God creates creatures in sinful self-love. God can create a human being with only the principles of nature and what follows from them. Such a creature is oriented to God, not sinful self-love. But she needs grace to be saved. This, on my view, just is what it means to be in a state of original sin.

Thomas's argument that God cannot cause (mortal) sin does not apply. God wills the good of the infant in original sin more than the good of which the evil is a privation, the infant's graced love for God. The evil attached to the good of the infant in original sin, namely, lacking grace, does not involve loving a creature more than God; thus the evil can be ordered by God to God. If God wills an infant to be in original sin instead of being in grace, God wills a lesser good instead of a greater good. This is unproblematic. God frequently wills lesser particular goods to exist over greater particular goods: for example, every time God creates a stone instead of a bird. In sum, God could create a human being in original sin, because the sinful infant does not love the creature more than God.

Is the lack of grace in the human being really a privation? Doesn't the concept of "privation" presuppose a prior good which has been privated, corrupted, lost? How could there be a privation in the infant if she never could have had grace to begin with? In other words, how could there be a privation of a good if there is no moral obligation for the good to be present? In my view, the debt of sin is the natural failure of the infant. Natural evils in general don't need to stem from an agent who has failed to fulfill a moral obligation; God, as we've seen, can cause natural evils. This doesn't make them any less evil: it is no less evil for a blade of grass to be corrupted on the basis of God's good action than it is for it to be corrupted on the basis of some sinful action. Natural evil is the absence of a perfection in the perfectible subject; for an infant to lack grace is to lack a perfection; this lack is an evil for her regardless of its source. This is not "Manichaeism," for the infant's evil is not essential; she is evil precisely as she is called to the deifying love of God, not qua creature or qua embodied. The new Thomist view is in line with Thomas's fundamental principles, despite its departure from him on the particular point regarding God's ability to bring about original sin. God can create the creature without immediately bestowing the principle of deification, called to grace but not yet in grace. This would be to create the creature in original sin.

Nevertheless, one might object that Scripture teaches that God has not created humanity in sin. And even presupposing the metaphysical *possibility* of God's creating human beings in original sin, the doctrine of creation more broadly requires us to affirm that the first human beings were created good, indeed very good – and thus not in sin. If one sympathetic to my view of original sin holds this, then she will need to adopt the new Thomist view of the Fall as well. Admittedly, however, those who insist both that God directly infuses the soul and that God cannot be causally involved in the transmission of sin may not be able to adopt my proposal.

I have argued that the new Thomist view of original sin is compatible with mainstream evolutionary theory. Moreover, it does not require the view that God brings about opposition to himself ("mortal" sin), or denying that infants have sin. I take it that these are advantages of the proposal. Another advantage of the new Thomist view, I would suggest, is that it is open to a number of interdisciplinary conversations in evolutionary ethics. It's worth briefly raising a question, by way of conclusion to this section, of how it might relate to questions of altruism, cooperation, and grace. There is no need, in my view, to deny that postlapsarian humans are capable of love and altruism, or to reduce postlapsarian motivation to selfishness. It would be problematic, however, to identify natural altruism with charity or supernatural grace. Adam Willows has proposed that the evolutionary disposition to cooperate with other human beings should be *identified* with charity.[5] But from a Thomist perspective, this won't work, because grace and charity are supernatural gifts. Our discussion suggests another possible way forward. Might Aquinas's concept of natural love be used to describe evolved altruistic behavior? Might it allow us to receive the insights of the new evolutionary emphasis on cooperation without giving up the uniqueness of the Christian concept of charity? More work would be needed to develop this idea. In any case, we are now in a position to discuss my proposal's relation to biblical teaching.

ORIGINAL SIN AND HOLY SCRIPTURE

The focus of this study has been on what lies "ahead" of the biblical text: both the history of theological reflection on (inter alia) Genesis 3 and Romans 5, as well as reflection on what this history might mean today. Ultimately, however, the theory developed in this book stands or falls with its comportment, or lack thereof, with the canonical witness of Christian Scripture. This section takes as a case study the locus classicus of the doctrine (Rom. 5:12–21) and suggests that its hamartiological implications are at least compatible (and perhaps consonant) with the

[5] Adam M. Willows, "Natural Love: Aquinas, Evolution and Charity," *The Heythrop Journal* (June 2017), https://doi.org/10.1111/heyj.12665. Cf. Williams, *Doing without Adam and Eve*, 158. From a non-Thomist perspective, Williams also proposes that charity can arise through nature.

new Thomist perspective. I argue that this passage implies that sin is universal, that the doctrine of original sin follows from the universality of sin, and that no particular theory of original sin is entailed by this passage. Before beginning, it may be helpful to say a word about what lies *behind* the text.

It may be helpful, that is, to begin with a few brief remarks about Jewish views of sin. Many scholars would agree with the following claims of E. P. Sanders: "In Judaism sin is uniformly transgression."[6] "[T]he Rabbis did not have a doctrine of original sin or of the essential sinfulness of each man in the Christian sense."[7] By Sanders's lights, Palestinian Judaism from c. 200 BC to AD 200 held a uniform conception of sin: it consists solely in transgression of divine law. Yet a growing body of literature, including for example the work of Miriam Brand and Rosen-Zivi on Second Temple and Rabbinic perspectives on evil, respectively, challenges the idea that Jewish hamartiology was monolithic.[8]

Take, for example, Brand's interpretation of prayers from the Hodayot, a collection of hymns from Qumran. Here are two salient passages:

Yet I am a creature of clay and (a thing) kneaded with water, a foundation of shame and a spring of impurity, a furnace of iniquity, and a structure of sin, a spirit of error, and a perverted being, without understanding, and terrified by righteous judgments. What could I say that is not known, or what could I declare that has not been told? (1QH^a IX.23b–25)[9]

"What is one born of woman amid all your [gre]at fearful acts? He is a thing constructed of dust and kneaded with water. Sin[ful gui]lt is his foundation, obscene shame, and a so[urce of im]purity. And a perverted spirit rules him" (1QH^a V.31b–33).[10] Brand comments, "The speaker does not claim that he is guilty of particular sins. Rather, as a member of humanity, he shares in its lowly and sinful state."[11] "[T]he speaker in

---

[6] E. P. Sanders, *Paul and Palestinian Judaism* (Philadelphia: Fortress Press, 1977), 546.

[7] Sanders, *Paul and Palestinian Judaism*, 114.

[8] Miryam Brand, *Evil within and Without: The Source of Sin and Its Nature as Portrayed in Second Temple Literature* (Vandenhoeck & Ruprecht, 2013); Ishay Rosen-Zivi, *Demonic Desires: Yetzer Hara and the Problem of Evil in Late Antiquity* (Philadelphia: University of Pennsylvania Press, 2011). Cf. also Nicholas A. Meyer, *Adam's Dust and Adam's Glory in the Hodayot and the Letters of Paul: Rethinking Anthropogony and Theology* (Leiden: Brill, 2016).

[9] Citation from Brand, *Evil within and Without*, 62.

[10] Citation from Brand, *Evil within and Without*, 62.

[11] Brand, *Evil within and Without*, 61.

Hodayot is intrinsically sinful because of his human status as a 'creature of clay.'"[12] Of course, the speaker does not think that human existence is *essentially* sinful (such that it could not be purified by God). "The speaker yearns for, and benefits from, purification from the *state* of sinfulness he suffers from as a result of his humanity. It is clear that only God can effect this purification."[13] Did the Covenanters predicate "sin" of infants? Given that they thought *everyone* outside their sect was damned, and that human nature is intrinsically sinful, it would hardly be surprising if they did.[14]

The book of Ben Sira (written originally in Hebrew c. 200–175 BC), by contrast, does understand sin solely as transgression. God hates sin and is not responsible for it. Sin is the free transgression of a divine command. "God from the beginning created humankind and placed him in the hand of his *yēṣer*. If you wish you will keep (his) commandment and understanding to do his will" (Sir. 15:14–15). The *yetzer* in this context is not the Rabbinic *yetzer hara* (on which more shortly); it is rather "a neutral capacity that enables the human being to make a moral choice."[15] There is a universal desire for sin (Sir. 17:31), but "[h]e who keeps the law gains mastery over the object of his thought" (Sir. 21:11).

In these texts, neither the Qumran Covenanters nor Ben Sira claimed that Adam's or Eve's sin changed the spiritual condition of humanity. This reflected a general trend of Second Temple thought, but there were exceptions. 4 Ezra and 2 Baruch are notable. The author of 4 Ezra (c. AD 81–96) assumes that all, or almost all, human beings have an "evil heart."[16] Adam's heart was evil *ab initio*, and Torah does not extirpate it: "Yet you did not take away from them their evil heart, so that the Torah might bring forth fruit in them. For the first Adam, burdened with an evil heart, transgressed was overcome, as were also all who were descended from him" (4 Ezra 3:20–1). The interpretation of these verses has been a matter of contention: Brand's view is that the text comes close to implying that God made the evil heart in Adam.[17] Despite the fact that sin is equated with action and not the heart itself, the text does not seem to presuppose that sinful actions can be avoided. "In none of these

---

[12] Brand, *Evil within and Without*, 61. [13] Brand, *Evil within and Without*, 61-2.

[14] "One of the most basic views of the Qumran community was that all outside the sect were damned." Sanders, *Paul and Palestinian Judaism*, 318.

[15] Brand, *Evil within and Without*, 101.

[16] Brand, *Evil within and Without*, 130. Noah, Abraham, Isaac, Jacob, and David appear to be exceptions.

[17] Brand, *Evil within and Without*, 130.

examples, however, is sinfulness a condition that exists independently of one's actual sins. The evil heart is expressed in the desire to sin; the inevitable sins that follow demonstrate the sinfulness of humankind."[18] In 2 Baruch, Adam brings death to subsequent human beings but not sin.

> For though Adam sinned first and brought untimely death upon all, also those who were born from him have prepared for himself the coming torment. And also, each one of them has chosen for himself glories to come. For truly he who believes will receive reward.... So Adam is not the cause, except only for his own soul. But each of us has been the Adam of his own soul. (2 Bar. 54:15–16; 19)

Much more could be said about all this, but for now it is sufficient to note that there are a wide variety of perspectives on sin in Second Temple thought. Some texts conceptualize sin as following from the human condition, others from the misuse of free will, or being outside the scope of divine election. Still others, which we have not focused on, highlight the role of demons. The emphasis on the demonic seemed to increase after the destruction of the Temple: "the rabbinic (evil) *yetzer* is a sophisticated antinomian enticer, struggling to trap humans."[19] "[I]t is not a cosmic being but a fully internalized entity that resides inside the human heart."[20] Let's turn to another Jewish author, who did more than anyone to shape the Christian understanding of sin: the Apostle Paul.

I will focus on the locus classicus of the doctrine of original sin: Rom. 5:12–21. Rivers of ink have been spilled on this pregnant passage. Paul proclaims the sin, death, and condemnation of humanity in connection with Adam; the analogy (and disanalogy) between Adam's sin and subsequent sins; the grace, life, and justification of humanity in connection with Jesus Christ; and the similarity yet ever-greater difference between the sin of Adam and the gift of Christ. Needless to say, a full treatment of these themes would constitute the better part of a systematic theology. For present purposes, it will be enough to sketch a reading of its hamartiological implications. In what follows I bracket the question of the historicity of Adam and Eve.

Let's begin by briefly noting this passage's context in Romans. Paul has already established several crucial arguments. First, as he argues in Rom. 3:9, Jews and Gentiles are both under sin. "Jews and Greeks are both under sin" (*ioudaious te kai hellēnas pantas hyph hamartian einai*). What is the "sin" under which Jews and Gentiles exist? There has been a

---

[18] Brand, *Evil within and Without*, 133.   [19] Rosen-Zivi, *Demonic Desires*, 6.
[20] Rosen-Zivi, *Demonic Desires*, 7.

major debate between the so-called apocalyptic and existential schools of New Testament scholarship on this point, which we'll return to in a moment.[21] Some would have us translate the word in the upper case: humans are under Sin, a demonic or quasi-demonic entity. While granting that sin may also be Sin, it seems that at this point in the letter it means *at least* "sins" – that is, the sinful actions of both Jew and Gentile. Paul himself was at pains to emphasize that Jew and Gentile alike are *without excuse*; if sin were reducible to cosmic powers, an excuse would be ready-to-hand. Gentiles are "without excuse" (*anapologētous*) for their bad behavior because God's power and divine nature have been understood through creation (Rom. 1:20). Jews are without excuse (*anapologētous*) because, "[t]hough gifted with a superior understanding whereby he can agree with Paul's indictment of the pagan, nevertheless the Jew is just as guilty for the pagan for another reason: he does not do what his superior moral understanding bids him to do."[22] Despite the great benefits of being Jewish (Rom. 3:1–2), they are equal to the Gentiles *quantum ad statum peccati*. Paul's second major argument is that Jews and Gentiles are united in salvation. Jesus Christ died for Jews and Gentiles when they were sinners (Rom. 5:8). They were thereby reconciled to God *when* they were his enemies (Rom. 5:10). In Christ, we are "justified by his blood" and "will be saved through him from the wrath of God" (Rom. 5:9). We now look forward to being "saved in his [Christ's] life" (Rom. 5:10).

The discussion until Rom. 5:12–21 focuses on Jews and Gentiles *as groups*. The claims about Jewish and Gentile sins "are not meant to be diagnoses of the condition of each and every individual."[23] For one thing, the focus is on morally responsible adults, not infants or those with severe mental disabilities. Moreover, many have argued that the groups Paul does speak of are not indicted as though *every* one of their members has committed the sins that pertain to the group. For example, Paul's point in Rom. 2:17–24 – "if you call yourself a Jew and rely on the law and boast of your relation to God" – is not that everyone in the Jewish community has boasted of their relation to God. The same goes, *mutatis mutandis*, for the sins of the Gentiles listed in Romans 1. If all this is true, then it seems that there is no clear affirmation of the universality of sin, in the strict

[21] See Matthew Croasmun, *The Emergence of Sin: The Cosmic Tyrant in Romans* (Oxford: Oxford University Press, 2017), for a helpful review of this debate.

[22] Fitzmyer, *Romans*, 299.

[23] Timothy G. Gombis, "Paul," in the *T&T Clark Companion to the Doctrine of Sin*, ed. Keith L. Johnson and David Lauber (New York: T&T Clark, 2016), 109.

sense, in Rom. 1–5:11. Sin is universal in the strict sense only if the doctrine of original sin is true, that is, only if "sin" is predicable of each and every human being – with the usual exceptions – from the first moment of their existence.

Let's turn to Rom. 5:12–21. We have seen verse 12 cited throughout this study. Here is the NRSV's translation: "Therefore, just as sin came into the world through one man, and death came through sin, and so death spread to all because all have sinned." It is difficult to know which of Paul's previous claims is the basis of "therefore" (*dia toutou*). Cranfield's judgment, that Paul has the argument of "5:1–11 as a whole" in mind, seems likely. Verses 1–11 affirmed that those who have been justified by the blood of Christ have peace, and no longer enmity, with God. This truth, Paul goes on to argue in verses 12–21, "does not stand by itself: it means that something has been accomplished by Christ which is as universal in its effectiveness as was the sin of the first man."[24] Most scholars agree that verse 12 is an anacoluthon, because "just as" begins a comparison that is left incomplete.[25]

Now what does it mean to say that "sin came into the world through one man"? Sin entered the world through Adam's act of transgression.[26] It seems that Paul uses the word "*hamartia*" here to refer to more than that single transgression, for the *hamartia* that entered the world is the *hamartia* that reigned in death (v. 21). It would be hard to defend the view that *hamartia* means anything less than all acts of transgression, and it

---

[24] Both from C. E. B. Cranfield, *A Critical and Exegetical Commentary on the Epistle to the Romans*, vol. 1 (Edinburgh: T&T Clark, 1975), 271.

[25] That is, most agree that it is left incomplete at least in its immediate context, because in v. 13 Paul abruptly turns to a discussion of sin and law. It has been argued that the comparison begun is finished in v. 18 (see Robert Jewett, *Romans: A Commentary* [Minneapolis, MN: Fortress, 2007], 373). Though as Fitzmyer argues, "the comparison is not smoothly worked out." Fitzmyer, *Romans*, 406. He thinks that if Paul had completed the comparison, it would have gone something like this: "so through Christ came uprightness (and with it life eternal)" (p. 406). However, it seems to me that a strict comparison would run more like this: "Justice came into the world through one man, and life through justice, and thus life came to all because all did justice." Though scholars often assume this anacoluthon is a result of Paul's frenetic writing style, it may well be full of theological significance. This is chiefly because life does not come to the many *because* the many do justice, whereas death does come to the many because the many sin (or perhaps sin comes to the many because the many die). The difference between the disobedience of Adam and the obedience of Christ does not simply lie in the fact that Christ's work is *good* and Adam's *bad*, but in the *power* of God in Christ to save, which would have in any case saved Adam.

[26] That Adam is the "one man" in v. 12 – who is also mentioned multiple times in vv. 15–21 – is clear from v. 14 ("death reigned from Adam").

may well mean more. Scholars associated with the apocalyptic reading of Paul have argued that *hamartia* in 5:12 is not only the sine qua non of subsequent human sin and suffering at the hands of demons – which of course is a standard view in the Christian tradition – but is itself a cosmic force of some kind. I say "of some kind" advisedly, for it is not clear what the (n)ontological status of this force is supposed to be. At least, it is not clear to me. Beverly Gaventa, for example, warns against trivializing Paul's "frequent use of Sin (*hamartia*) as the subject of a verb"; we should not dismiss it "as only a literary device."[27] Yet she also insists that "[t]o speak of Sin as a power is not to claim to peer into Paul's mind and see there the existence of a literal character by the name of Sin."[28] Satan is shorthand for Sin, but Sin is not Satan.[29] Martinus de Boer says that sin and grace are "warring orbs of power," that "the direction of Paul's argument" is "to hypostatize death as a quasi-angelic, cosmological power."[30] Presumably what goes for death goes, *mutatis mutandis*, for sin, and Sin and Death are both held to be *quasi*-angelic powers. But what is a quasi-angelic power? We are not told.

I agree that restricting *hamartia* to discrete acts of transgression runs the risk of trivializing it. Indeed it would be perfectly compatible with the account I am developing if Paul referred simultaneously to evil cosmic forces, unjust social systems, concupiscent human dispositions, and more; in short, he may refer to each and every thing which is rightly labeled with the word "sin." The crucial question at hand is whether *hamartia* is predicable of infants. If it is, then as far as I'm concerned, the doctrine of original sin is true. Considering Paul's account of *death* lights the way toward an answer.

"And death through sin." The first consequence of Adam's sin is that death (*thanatos*) entered the world. What did Paul mean by *thanatos*? Broadly speaking, three possibilities have been proposed. First is physical death, or mortality. Second is spiritual death, the "death" of the soul that follows from the act of sin. Third is the eternal death of damnation. Of course, it could also be some combination of these three. For present purposes, the most important question is whether Paul *at least* means

---

[27] Beverly Roberts Gaventa, *Our Mother Saint Paul* (Louisville: Westminster John Knox Press, 2007), 127, 134.

[28] Gaventa, *Our Mother Saint Paul*, 134.

[29] "Satan is more than adequate as a shorthand reference to the anti-God powers, prominent among whom is Sin itself." Gaventa, *Our Mother Saint Paul*, 133.

[30] Martinus C. de Boer, *The Defeat of Death: Apocalyptic Eschatology in 1 Corinthians 15 and Romans 5* (Sheffield: JSOT Press, 1988), 139.

physical death, for reasons which will become clear when we get to verses 13–14. For now let's turn to the second half of verse 12.

"And so death spread to all because all have sinned (*kai houtōs eis pantas anthrōpous ho thanatos diēlthen eph' hō pantes hēmarton*)." The second half of Rom. 5:12 is very difficult to understand. This is because it is difficult to know what precisely Paul meant by "*eph' hō*." The Old Latin Bible and Vulgate read "*in quo*" (in whom), and as a result Western readers for more than a millennium thought Paul had clearly said that "all sinned in Adam." There is a scholarly consensus to the effect that this is a mistranslation. The most common translation in English is "because" (NRSV) or a synonym like "since" (CEB). Joseph Fitzmyer argues forcefully, however, that it should be rendered "with the result that" or "so that," such that *eph' hō* is "the equivalent of consecutive conj. *hōste*."[31] The sense of the phrase is that physical death spread to all human beings and somehow resulted in human beings sinning. Fitzmyer assumes that adults are in view; the idea is that mortality is linked with the free sins of adults. Many scholars who opt for "because" agree, though they would reverse the causal priority; the personal sins of adults bring about death.

It is not clear to me, however, how this makes sense of verses 13–14: "sin was indeed in the world before the law, but sin is not reckoned when there is no law. Yet death exercised dominion from Adam to Moses, even over those whose sins were not like the transgression of Adam, who is a type of the one who was to come." It seems clear that the "sin" that was in the world before the law, unreckoned (v. 13), is the sin that is not in the likeness of the transgression of Adam (v. 14). How could there be sin without law, or sin unlike Adam's transgression? Recent commentators have typically either charged Paul with incoherence (because the concept of sin makes sense only if there is a violation of a law) or argued that Paul is thinking of sins which, because they did not violate clear-cut divine commandments, were not as grave as Adam's. Thus Cranfield argues that these verses refer to those who, "while they had indeed sinned and were punished for their sin, had not sinned after the likeness of Adam's transgression, that is, by disobeying a clear and definite divine commandment such as Adam had (Gen. 2:17) and Israel was subsequently to have in the law."[32] He denies that Paul had infants (or, presumably, the severely

---

[31] Fitzmyer, *Romans*, 416. He discusses eleven possible translations on pp. 413–17.

[32] Cranfield, *A Critical and Exegetical Commentary on the Epistle to the Romans*, 1: 283. "Paul does not mean that it [sin] is not registered in the sense of being charged to men's account, reckoned against them, imputed; for the fact that men died during this period of

mentally impaired) in mind in this passage: "those who die in infancy are a special and exceptional case, and Paul must surely be assumed to be thinking in terms of adults."[33] Dunn concurs: "the meaning here is clear enough – 'who did not sin in just the way that Adam transgressed' ... There is no thought of children who die in infancy here."[34]

Surely more needs to be said on this score. First, the dominion of *thanatos* in verse 14 seems to refer to our mortal condition as well as – to borrow Heidegger's use of the term – our *demise*, the event of dying. Evidently, infants are mortal and, tragically, die all too often. Obviously, however, one needn't have every human being *in mind* as a distinct individual to speak *about* all human beings. For example, if with Aristotle we say that "the human being is a rational animal," we obviously don't need to have every human being "in mind" in order to refer, categorically, to every single human being. And we might, as we say this, *think* about adults we are familiar with, without in any way restricting the range of the proposition *to* those adults we happen to be picturing. This seems fairly straightforward. One might argue that this is beside the point, because Paul didn't intend to speak of infants; he excluded them. But why should we think that? He says that death reigned, and he obviously would have known that infants are mortal and die (given the high infant mortality rates at the time, he probably would have been *more* aware of this than those of us living in the modern West). So even if he didn't have infants in mind, he may well have included them implicitly in his universal statement.

---

the law's absence (v. 13) shows clearly enough that in this sense their sin was indeed registered. [*ouk ellogeitai*] must be understood in a relative sense: only in comparison with what takes place when the law is present can it be said that in the law's absence, sin [*ouk ellogeitai*]. Those who lived without the law were certainly not 'innocent sinners' – they were to blame for what they were and what they did. But, in comparison with the state of affairs which has obtained since the advent of the law sin may be said to have been, in the law's absence, 'not registered,' since it was not the fully apparent, sharply defined thing, which it became in its presence. It is only in the presence of the law, only in Israel and in the Church, that the full seriousness of sin is visible and the responsibility of the sinner stripped of every extenuating circumstance" (1: 282).

33 Cranfield, *A Critical and Exegetical Commentary on the Epistle to the Romans*, vol. 1, 279.

34 James D. G. Dunn, *Romans 1–8* (Dallas: Word Books, 1988), 276. Dunn argues that it is somewhat mysterious why Paul didn't appeal, as he did earlier, to the fact that "those outside the law have a knowledge of God and of his will in terms of which they will be judged (see on 2:14), or by arguing that the law itself was already known in whole or in part already in the garden (see on 7:7). That he chooses not to do so, when he was prepared to take up such ideas elsewhere in the same letter, must be significant (cf. Zeller). What the significance is, however, remains unclear" (p. 275).

If he did, then it seems that the doctrine of original sin is true. If death came to all because all sinned, and infants are mortal, then infants must have sin. If sin came to all because all died (i.e., were mortal), then it still follows that infants have sin, because all infants are mortal. Whether one wants to call this the *sensus plenior* of the text, because Paul wasn't consciously focused on infants, or whether one thinks it is the *sensus literalus* because Paul's statements evidently imply that death and sin are universal, it seems that the doctrine of original sin is found here. Not having sinned (*mē hamartēsantas*) in the likeness of Adam's transgression, not having violated a divine command of their own volition, infants have nevertheless sinned. They have begun to exist outside Jesus Christ. They have died in Adam.

A consideration of the rest of the passage seems to bear out the view that Paul is affirming the universality of sin, but it does not, I would submit, tell us precisely what grounds the nature of this universality. That is, he does not give us a specific account or theory of original sin, though he does give us a generic doctrine of it. On the other hand, I would argue that the *drift* of Paul's discussion tends toward an analogical, rather than a univocal, concept of sin. This is the case both because he speaks of dissimilitude between Adam's sin and the sins of at least some of us and because the language he uses to describe Adam's action is distinct from the language he (arguably) uses to speak of sin universally. Consider verses 17–19, where Paul affirms that the trespass of Adam brings sin, death, and condemnation to the rest of humanity:

If, because of the one man's trespass, death exercised dominion through that one, much more surely will those who receive the abundance of grace and the free gift of righteousness exercise dominion in life through the one man, Jesus Christ. Therefore just as one man's trespass led to condemnation for all, so one man's act of righteousness leads to justification and life for all. For just as by the one man's disobedience the many were made sinners, so by the one man's obedience the many will be made righteous.[35]

Note that Paul does not state that every human being has committed a "transgression" (*parabaseōs*), "trespass" (*paraptōma*), or act of "disobedience" (*parakoēs*). Each of these words is used to describe Adam's sin; none of them is used in a way that implicitly applies to every human being. By contrast, sin, death, and condemnation are arguably predicated at least implicitly of all human beings. Death came to all, because all

---

[35] Rom. 5:17–19.

sinned (v. 12); one sin brought condemnation for all (vv. 16, 18); the many were made sinners (*hamartōloi katestathēsan hoi polloi*, v. 19); sin reigned in death (v. 21). Of course, Paul holds that a significant number of human beings (perhaps all) who *can* transgress, trespass, and disobey *have* transgressed, trespassed, and disobeyed. Christ's gift came after "many trespasses" (*pollōn paraptōmatōn*, v. 16). But there is no direct evidence from this passage that every human being, including every infant, has trespassed, or has had an act of trespass imputed against her, or has inherited guilt for Adam's disobedience, or has participated in Adam's transgression in a realist sense. If anything, the language here suggests the opposite. Perhaps Paul uses *hamartia* generically because everyone has sin, while not using words that describe Adam's act of sin generically precisely because he does not want to imply that every human has violated a divine command of her own volition. Moreover, Paul maintained earlier in the letter that Jews and Gentiles are without excuse. But if the Gentiles were habitual idolaters *ab initio* they would seem to have a very good excuse for their behavior, namely, that it had been generated by Adam and Eve.

On the new Thomist view, infants begin a sinful act of being in the first moment of their existence, but they have not chosen to disobey God. They are condemned for this sin, insofar as God sees that they will perish and be justly excluded from his presence forever if they do not come to love Jesus Christ. That is how I would understand original guilt. But one man's act of righteousness leads to justification and life for all, Paul says explicitly. It is difficult – to say the least – to reconcile this with the affirmation of the actual damnation of human beings irrespective of their personal sin.

It seems to me, in conclusion, that there are a number of theological advantages to adopting the new Thomist view of original sin. It allows us to respond to the major challenges from evolutionary biology. It does so, moreover, without entailing that God has brought about God-hatred, and it is compatible with a certain construal of original righteousness, one which focuses on the relation of friendship with God to which we are graciously invited. It also dovetails nicely with Paul's claim that sin is universal, not simply the result of discrete volitions. Moreover, it does not require claiming that infants are sinners in just the same way that adults are, or that God arbitrarily decided to hold infants personally accountable for Adam's act, or that sin is a sexually transmitted disease.

On a different note, another potential benefit, it seems to me, is that the new Thomist view could be fruitfully read in conversation with a prominent strand of feminist theology. In an influential article first published in 1960, Valerie Saiving criticized what she saw as the predominant hamartiology of the Western tradition: "identify[ing] sin with self-assertion and love with selflessness."[36] This account of sin and love is pernicious, she argued, because women tend more to self-abnegation than pride. The church's stress on humility served to reinforce unjust social structures. Saiving called for a balanced approach that recognizes that not all human beings tend to sin in the same way. A large literature has developed in feminist theology discussing, developing, and at times contesting Saiving's thesis. Rebekah Miles, for example, has argued that Saiving's account should not be restricted to women but extended, in effect, to all the oppressed.[37] Thomas, as I say, could be an interesting dialogue partner here. One of the ethical implications of his view of nature and sin is that not every human being is born in a state of pride. We are born in sin, but the sin is the lack of original righteousness. If this dialogue were to be pursued, attention would need to be given to Thomas's account of the virtue of magnanimity, which is roughly the virtue corresponding to the ordered pursuit of one's own excellence (*STh* II-II, q. 129), as well as the vice of pusillanimity (*STh* II-II, q. 133), in which one fails to pursue one's own excellence to a sufficient degree. Of course, even if one agrees that my account has the advantages I'm suggesting, one could object that it creates serious problems that outweigh these advantages.

[36] Valerie Saiving, "The Human Situation: A Feminine View," in *Womanspirit Rising: A Feminist Reader in Religion*, ed. Carol P. Christ and Judith Plaskow (New York: HarperCollins, 1992 [originally published in 1960 in *The Journal of Religion*]), 26.

[37] Rebekah Miles, "Valerie Saiving Reconsidered," *Journal of Feminist Studies in Religion* 28.1 (Spring 2012), 79–86.

8

A Response to Some Objections

This chapter endeavors to raise – and respond to – the most likely and serious objections to my account. (At least, the ones I have not already engaged at least implicitly. For example, I have already dealt with salient aspects of original sin's relation to Scripture. And the reader who has stayed with me from Chapter 1 has seen me try to head off some important objections – for example, that Thomas's view is an implicit denial of original sin – throughout the book.) It may seem that the new Thomist view falls into "Manichaeism" or "Jansenism." Alternatively, non-Thomists of various stripes may wonder whether it is *rigidly* Thomist: for example, would accepting my proposal entail accepting a Thomist view of sanctifying grace or justification? Relatedly, my view may seem to be an instance of "Semipelagianism." Others may grant my argument in what follows that neither Thomas's account nor my proposed reconstruction should be pigeonholed into those heretical categories. They may also grant that those who are opposed to other parts of Thomas's thought could, in many cases, adopt a Thomist view of original sin. Yet they may still object. And it is with one such objection that I will begin. Although in a sense it is less serious than many of the objections just mentioned – it is not the claim that my view is a heresy – it is more urgent that I respond to it. For if the reader accepts it, she will have grounds to reject *every* possible permutation of Thomas's account out of hand.

The objection is this. The new Thomist view implies a rejection of the *nouvelle théologie* and a recrudescence of "two-tier Thomism." This term is typically used to refer to a system of theology in which human nature (the bottom tier) exists on its own, with no need or even desire for grace (the top tier). Henri de Lubac famously argued that this system began in the sixteenth century as a reaction against the Protestant attempt to revive Augustine's teaching on nature, grace, and sin. Cajetan and other Catholic scholastics argued that Protestants wrongly implied that grace was due to humanity. In reality (it was argued), God could have created a state of pure nature, without sin and without grace – indeed, without even an implicit *desire* for grace. Nature only desires the proportional, connatural end within its power. For de Lubac, the hypothesis of pure nature was understandable – he even admits that it was the best response to Protestantism that could have been given at the time – but it was deeply problematic. Taken seriously, pushed to its logical conclusions, it implies that grace is alien to human beings. This implication has many disastrous results; perhaps the worst is that it muddles the logic of evangelism. The Augustinian tradition prayed and proclaimed, "Our hearts shall be restless until they rest in thee"; the early modern scholastics added the pointless and ultimately pernicious distinction, "Well, yes, but you could just as well have rested in the connatural knowledge of the Supreme Being, if that is what God had offered you." I begin by arguing that this objection is wrongheaded. In fact, my reading of Thomas's hamartiology is deeply congruous with a *nouvelle* perspective on desire.

THE INDIVIDUAL DISTINCTION

Let us begin with the question of nature and grace. The first question we need to address is whether we should distinguish nature from grace in the first place. In accordance with the unpopularity of two-tier Thomism, many contemporary theologians assume the whole enterprise of dividing up the bits of creation that belong to grace from those that belong to nature is deeply problematic. Shouldn't we attribute everything to God's grace?

The first thing I would say in response to this objection is the following. With Thomas, I understand "nature" as "the grace of creation"; all creatures exist because of God's gracious decision to create and sustain them. It is not as though "nature" designates an autonomous sphere of creaturely activity apart from God. Because "nature" is a type of "grace," I certainly have no interest in criticizing theologians, preachers, or other Christians for speaking of everything in creation as flowing from God's grace. Why then draw this potentially misleading distinction? Wouldn't it be safer to simply ascribe everything to the grace of God?

Many critics of the nature/grace distinction argue that the Thomist view, to the effect that "nature" is the "grace of creation," is worse than confusing. John Milbank has argued that it is *idolatrous*.[1] Milbank starkly argues that everything is gracious and, equally starkly, denies that grace presupposes anything – not even the grace of creation.[2] Let's investigate the reasons he offers for this claim.

Milbank's first argument against distinguishing nature from grace is that it undermines the distinction between creature and creator. In order to distinguish nature from grace, he argues, one must presuppose that there is a sphere of creation that is not a gift in the first place. This presupposition is false – and dangerously so. It implies that God is in debt to his creatures, and this leads directly to conceptual idolatry. A God who could be in debt to his creatures is an anthropomorphic God, a God subject to the univocal application of the creaturely categories of gift and debt.[3] But God is not subjected to the univocal application of these categories; he transcends them. What we should say, instead, is that beings created by God have been freely created, period. Their existence is gratuitous, full stop. It is a gift to exist and a gift to advance by grace to the beatific vision; neither is owed by God to the creature.

Milbank thus argues that nothing is presupposed by grace. "Grace, like the act of creation, presupposes *nothing* – not even Creation (since God *could* have made an immediately beatified angel); hence it cannot be gratuitous in relation to a contrasting necessity or a recipient existing independently of its reception."[4] Milbank's assertion that there is no realm of nature or creation presupposed by grace is the conclusion of the aforementioned argument, though the parenthetical comment

---

[1] Milbank does not, as far as I'm aware, ascribe this view to Thomas.

[2] John Milbank, *The Suspended Middle: Henri de Lubac and the Renewed Split in Modern Catholic Theology* (Grand Rapids, MI: Eerdmans, 2014 [2005]). Milbank claims to represent the authentic thought of Henri de Lubac, but we will not be concerned with the historical accuracy of that claim here.

[3] "In the realm of the ontological difference, of the creative emergence of *entia* from *esse*, gratuity arises before necessity or obligation and does not even require this contrast in order to be comprehensible. The creature as creature is not the recipient of a gift; it is itself this gift. The same consideration applies to a spiritual creature: as spirit he does not receive a gift; he is this gift of spirit." "It follows that where grace is thought of as an extrinsic superaddition and as *requiring* the contrasting notion of the non-grace of pure nature, then it is covertly subordinated to an idolatrous and impossible common medium between nature and grace, just as God thought of as a mere *ens* is covertly subordinated to a univocal *esse* shared between him and creatures." Both from Milbank, *The Suspended Middle*, 48, 50.

[4] Milbank, *The Suspended Middle*, 50.

concerning the beatified angel seems to be a distinct argument for the same conclusion: grace cannot presuppose creation because God can create an immediately beatified angel.

The first thing to say in response to Milbank is that the *debitum naturae* can be (and often has been) used analogically, just like the language of gift. Take, for example, the "debt of nature" as it is used by Thomas himself. Thomas often uses this phrase to refer to what a thing is owed if it is to be a certain kind of thing.[5] The debt of nature corresponds, roughly, to the distinctively Thomist sense of the word "nature" discussed in Chapter 3: the principles of nature and that which flows from them. As Guy Mansini puts it, "[w]hat is owed, we might say, belongs to the thing, and what belongs to a thing is a sort of part of the thing."[6] A triangle is "owed" three sides if it is to be a triangle and not a square, for example. A rational creature is "owed" a body if it is to be a human being and not an angel.[7] And so forth.

I will use the phrase "debt of nature" in two senses, one communal, one individual. The phrase "individual debt of human nature" I define as follows: it is what a given human being has *ab initio* by virtue of human nature and what follows from human nature necessarily (on the assumption she has not been given grace or any preternatural gift). In other

---

[5] Cf. *STh* I-II, q. 111, a. 1, ad 2. See also *STh* I, q. 21, a. 1, ad 3, where Thomas responds to, in effect, the same objection Milbank poses: God is no creature's debtor. Thomas replies that God can owe a debt of justice in two ways. First, he owes it to himself to manifest his goodness and wisdom in creation. Second, he owes it to the creature to possess the sorts of things that are ordered to the creature by nature. "Debitum etiam est alicui rei creatae, quod habeat id quod ad ipsam ordinatur: sicut homini, quod habeat manus, et quod ei alia animalia serviant. Et sic etiam Deus operatur iustitiam, quando dat unicuique quod ei debetur secundum rationem suae naturae et conditionis." What precisely does Thomas think is included in the debt of human nature? He gives two examples here: that non-human animals serve the human being and that the human being has hands. One of the problems with Thomas's definition is that it doesn't distinguish between the sorts of things that belong to human nature as such from the sorts of things that belong to human nature due to the arrangements of providence (which presumably could have been otherwise). Another difficulty is that Thomas doesn't distinguish what follows *normally* from human nature from what follows of *necessity* from human nature. Presumably, Thomas thinks that having hands normally but not necessarily follows from human nature (i.e., presumably he doesn't think someone born without hands is not a human being). But clearly some things do follow of necessity in his view. Thomas may draw these sorts of distinctions elsewhere. But, in any case, I will be drawing them in this chapter.

[6] Guy Mansini, "Lonergan on the Natural Desire in the Light of Feingold," *Nova et Vetera*, English edition, 5.1 (2007), 196, apropos of Thomas Aquinas, *In librum beati Dionysii de Divinis Nominibus expositio* IV, lect. 9, n. 406.

[7] Or, at least, a human being is owed some sort of relation to a corporeal body – perhaps a relation of perfectibility – that an angel is not.

words, the individual debt of nature refers to the minimum conditions of beginning to exist as a human being. It is not equivalent to the essence of the human being, though a human being without grace has a human essence. The essence of the human being, as I understand it, is the basic mode of human existence, and every human being – with or without grace, hypostatically united to the Word or not hypostatically united to the Word – exists with a human essence.[8]

Even this cursory look at the concept should make it clear that "debt" in the debt of nature is not the same as "debt" in the field of exchange. If John owes Jane $20 and fails to pay her back in an appropriate amount of time, he has done something wrong. If God creates a square circle, or a human without a body, he hasn't done anything at all, because these aren't the sorts of things that can be done. If God decides to create nothing at all, no wrong is done, because no human being is owed existence.

The debt of nature is a way of talking about the structures of created being. There is an analogy between human and divine debts. Just as I am obligated to pay back my financial debts, on the supposition that I have incurred them, God is "obligated" to pay the creature its debt of nature, on the supposition he has chosen to create it. Once we've understood what the phrase means, the grounds of Milbank's objection disappear. It is not idolatrous to believe that some creatures exist in this way, others in that way. Neither is it idolatrous to suppose that, if God wants to create a creature existing in this way, he must give it a mode of existence by which it exists in this way. (One could, I suppose, argue that it is idolatrous to deny what Plantinga somewhere called "universal possibilism" – the view, sometimes ascribed to Descartes, that God is not bound by the law of non-contradiction. On this view, God could create four-sided triangles and other such things. I do not think, though, that is idolatrous to deny universal possibilism.)

What about Milbank's other argument, that grace's presupposition of nature is ruled out by the fact that God can create an immediately beatified angel? This argument is a non sequitur. The fact that a quality of a thing can come into existence simultaneously with that thing does not prove that the quality presupposes nothing. God could create an immediately hirsute human being; this doesn't prove that no one is bald. It

---

[8] My view of essence is indebted to Sarah Borden Sharkey and, by extension, Norris Clarke; see her "How Can Being Be Limited?: W. Norris Clarke on Thomas's 'Limitation of Act by Potency,'" *The Saint Anselm Journal* 7.1 (2009), 1–19.

doesn't prove, in other words, that hairy humans do not have human bodies on which hair can grow or not. To say that grace presupposes (the debt of) nature is only to say that grace presupposes a potentially receptive subject; it is not to say anything about the chronological order in which grace is received.

Having argued that distinguishing nature from grace is not idolatrous, I would argue, furthermore, that several deeply problematic consequences follow with respect to our existence *in uia* if they are not distinguished. If grace does not presuppose nature, then either human beings now do not exist (having lost their original grace, there is no presupposed postlapsarian nature to remain) or they do not need grace (having retained their original grace). But the former is false, because human beings do exist. The latter is also false, because human beings need grace. If one replies that we exist now by one grace but stand in need of another grace, my point has been conceded. For the grace by which we now exist is what I mean by "nature" or the synonymous phrase "creation's grace." One can disagree about what the precise properties of the *gratia naturae* are – one might deny that corrupt nature involves an orientation to God, for example, holding with baroque Thomism that *natura corrupta* is habitually idolatrous. Or one could hold, with Calvin – or at least one prominent reading of Calvin – that fallen nature does evil only of its own power but often receives extra, common graces to do ordinary good things. Or one could hold, on another reading of Calvin, that fallen existence is shot through with common grace.[9] Regardless, there is a mode of fallen existence which is called to a higher, sanctified existence.

But what should we say to theologians who envisage the debt of nature differently from both Milbank (who rejects the concept altogether) and myself? Some – we mentioned this view briefly at the end of Chapter 2 – would argue that the debt of nature is not "what a given human being has *ab initio* by virtue of human nature and what follows from human nature necessarily (on the assumption she has not been given grace or any preternatural gift)." We should instead (these theologians would argue) understand the debt of nature as what belongs to the first human beings *ab initio* by virtue of human nature and what follows from human nature necessarily. There is no need to add the qualifier "without grace," for

---

[9] For a reading of Calvin that stresses common grace, see Paul Helm's "Pure Nature and Common Grace," in his *Calvin at the Centre* (Oxford: Oxford University Press, 2010), 308–39. For the possibility of pagan good works, see *Institutio* II.3.3–4, where Calvin claims God dispenses common grace beyond the bounds of the elect.

there is no need to distinguish the natural orientation to God from supernatural charity. Charity is the natural relation of the human being to God. The first human beings had it, then lost it for themselves and their children, and it is restored by the grace of the gospel.

My position is this. Grace (as well as faith, hope, and love) is supernatural, in this sense; it is not part of the individual debt of human nature.[10] As I argued in Chapter 6, God can create human beings without it. I suggested in Chapter 2 that theologians who accept a soteriology of deification should think of grace as supernatural; now I will offer a couple of arguments for this conclusion which don't depend, as far as I can see, on one's view of deification.

First, there is the following problem with thinking of grace or charity as natural. It's far from clear how nature could have been corrupted in the first place. Say, for example, that Adam and Eve loved God with a natural charity. It's easy enough to see that they lost this gift for themselves when they sinned. But if this love is part of the debt of nature, how could it fail to be present in their children? The problem is especially acute if God must directly create the soul. If this is the case, then God must decide what the basic orientation of the soul is. If he creates the soul without charity, then we've run into the problem from Chapter 5: God has negated himself by creating the creature hating himself. But even if humans can transmit human nature, it's still difficult to see how (assuming that Adam and Eve successfully reproduce and thereby cause a new soul to exist) their child's soul could fail to have charity. For presumably natural reproduction, if it is successful, terminates in an offspring with the same nature as her parents. But charity is, on this hypothesis, part of the debt of human nature, something that every human being must have at the beginning of her existence. It seems, then, either that Adam and Eve would have failed to reproduce or that their children would have charity.

There is another problem with thinking of charity as natural. How could Adam and Eve cause their children to be in a habitual state of God-hatred? It seems that hating God must involve a personal action, prioritizing a created good more than God and breaking some divine command. But the infant hasn't done this in the first moment of her existence. Since she has original sin and thus cannot have grace or charity, it seems we need to posit a third alternative between God-hatred and charity; this is the role played by the natural orientation to God.

---

[10] I don't deny that there are other senses in which grace could rightly be called "natural" – for example, in the Scotist sense that it perfects human nature.

There is a third problem with thinking of grace as natural. If grace were natural, it would not be a gift to human beings. I share the scholastic intuition that grace must be a gift to humanity. What Milbank points out – even if grace were part of the debt of human nature, creation itself would be gratuitous – is true. This, however, is not the issue. The question is whether grace is a gift *to* the human being or the same gift *as* human being.[11] It's important not only that grace presupposes nature; it's important that a supernatural grace presupposes nature, such that the first gift, nature, is creatable.

I have argued that supernatural grace presupposes nature, that grace is not part of the individual debt of human nature. The next question is: What, if anything, does God owe the human community?

THE COMMUNAL DISTINCTION

Two-tier Thomism still has defenders (who would undoubtedly protest that the sketch in the introduction of this chapter is a caricature). Indeed, it has arguably been in the midst of a renaissance for the last decade or so.[12] And for readers sympathetic to two-tier Thomism – or rather, as I will call it from now on, "baroque Thomism" – the problem with my account of original sin will seem somewhat different. Even if these readers aren't inclined to think my account is a straightforward instance of Pelagianism or Manichaeism, nevertheless, by equating humanity's moral

---

[11] For an argument on behalf of the nature/grace distinction along roughly the same lines as the one I'm giving here – that is, an argument to the effect that grace must be a gift to human nature, not included within nature itself – see Karl Rahner, "Concerning the Relationship between Nature and Grace," trans. Cornelius Ernst, in *Theological Investigations*, v. 1 (Baltimore: Helicon, 1961), 297–317. The core of this essay was originally published as Karl Rahner, "Eine Antwort," *Orientierung* 14 (1950), 141–5. It was, as David Coffey notes, Rahner's "intervention" in the debate inaugurated by de Lubac's *Surnaturel*, a work which (at least) appeared to, à la Milbank, deny that the scholastic nature/grace distinction was legitimate. David Coffey, "The Whole Rahner on the Supernatural Existential," *Theological Studies* 65 (2004), 95. Rahner himself assumed a fairly *sharp* nature/grace distinction. He assumed, with Cajetan, that nature itself does not even desire grace. Sympathetic to the problem de Lubac observed regarding the "extrinsicism" of such a model, Rahner then posited a "supernatural existential," a divine gift which orients the person to grace but is distinct from grace. Critics have charged that there can be no such distinction, and that Rahner implicitly denied original sin. Coffey's article defends the view that the supernatural existential is distinct from sanctifying grace.

[12] For evidence of the renewed interest in baroque Thomism, see the symposium on the work of Lawrence Feingold in the English edition of *Nova et Vetera*, vol. 5 (2007).

ability in corrupt nature with humanity's natural moral ability simpliciter, it may seem that I have Jansenistically denied nature's integrity.

The problem, for these readers, is not distinguishing nature from grace; that is all well and good. The problem is, rather, that the individual distinction is insufficient; we also need to distinguish nature from grace on the communal level. That is to say, it must be the case not only that individual human beings can exist without grace; the human species as a community must have been able to exist without grace and without sin, in a state of pure nature. Nature must have, as Reinhard Hütter puts it, its own "relative integrity."[13] If pure nature were impossible, then grace would no longer be gratuitous, a free gift to human nature; it would come with nature automatically.[14] But for the new Thomist view, sin is clearly part of the individual debt of nature in our stipulated sense of the phrase: sin follows from being human without grace or preternatural gifts. It implies that sin follows from the principles of human nature and thus renders a state of pure nature impossible, shattering, as it were, nature's integrity.

Before responding to this objection, it's important to say more about just what a state of pure nature would consist in. I argued in Chapter 4 that Thomas himself did hold that such a state was within divine power but that its inhabitants would be just as morally weak as human beings in corrupt nature. Later Thomists came to think that pure nature would be stronger morally than nature is now (leading to widespread confusion

---

[13] "[T]he relative integrity of the principle (or the order) of nature is the necessary condition for the possibility of differentiating properly between the realities of creation, creation *sub conditione peccati*, and redemption. Failing to do so would inevitably lead to deficient theological positions, such as doctrines denying sin's impact on human nature, or doctrines defending the essential corruption (allegedly due to original sin) or the essential transmutation (presumably due to deification) of human nature." Reinhard Hütter, "*Desiderium Naturale Visionis Dei – Est autem duplex hominis beatitudo sive felicitas*: Some Observations about Lawrence Feingold's and John Milbank's Recent Interventions in the Debate over the Natural Desire to See God," *Nova et Vetera*, English edition, 5.1 (2007), 102. Hütter doesn't discuss original sin in depth, but he seems to assume the consensus reading of Aquinas I argued against in Chapter 4. "Moreover, it is indeed important to emphasize that for Aquinas human nature under the condition of sin in the present order of providence is emphatically not to be understood as the result of a fall into some state of 'pure nature.' Rather, original sin has affected human nature in such a way that in the present order of providence, after the loss of original justice, human nature is wounded" (p. 101).

[14] Cf. the well-known statement of Pius XII in *Humani Generis*. "Others destroy the gratuity of the supernatural order, since God, they say, cannot create intellectual beings without ordering and calling them to the beatific vision" (DH 3891).

concerning the effects of original sin). Despite this difference, there are significant similarities between the conception of the state of pure nature in Thomas and later Thomism. The first point of agreement regards the basic definition of pure nature. Pure nature is a way things could have been – a "possible world," if you like – in which human beings are created without sin (though with the capability of sinning), without grace or preternatural gifts, and without the vocation to the beatific vision.

Once we've understood this general definition of pure nature in conjunction with Thomas's view of the effects of original sin, a problem quickly arises. Thomas's own view also seems to compromise nature's integrity. Though by Thomas's lights God can create human beings without grace and without sin, nature is so weak – it inevitably involves death and, for those who reach the age of reason, at least venial sin – that it appears ludicrous to suggest that God could have left humanity in it. One could even argue that it would have been *unjust* for God to leave us in nature. Since God is just (not to mention merciful), Thomas's view of nature can't be correct. Either pure nature is impossible or Thomas's account of it needs to be tweaked in order to render its counterfactual possibility plausible.

The reasons Thomas's account and my account seem to compromise nature's integrity are slightly different. My account seems to render pure nature logically impossible regardless of one's view of divine mercy and wisdom, whereas Thomas's account implies that nature has an *exigency* for grace (on the supposition that God's justice is incompatible with leaving us to sin and death). The objection though, is the same: in both cases pure nature is impossible, and the gratuity of grace is destroyed.

In order to respond, we need to delve deeper into the concept of pure nature. A preliminary question we need to ask is this: assuming that pure nature is possible, what gives us the right to speculate about what it would be like? What gives us the right, that is, to say anything more than that it's a state initially without sin or grace? Our knowledge of divine providence is limited even in the actual world; what could we possibly say with confidence about a hypothetical providential order? We just mentioned that the objection to Thomas's view could be framed in terms of God's justice: it would be unjust for God to leave humanity in sin and death. The assumption at the heart of pure nature speculation, then, is that we have some cognizance, albeit analogical, of God's justice in providence. Just as there is the "individual debt of nature," so too there is what I will call a "communal debt of nature": what God must give, in consideration of at least his justice, to at least some members of the human species.[15]

The first (and least controversial) part of the communal debt involves a suitable environment. For example, God owes it to his own justice not to create the entire human species "twenty leagues beneath the sea," as one recent defender of pure nature put it.[16] Other necessary conditions include food, water, human beings with whom to socialize, reproduce, and so forth (the details – can we know whether human beings would be gendered in the way we are, for example? – are irrelevant for our purposes). God may not provide for every individual in the species; we know all too well that in the actual world God permits many untimely deaths. Yet arguably God could not create a world where everyone dies an untimely death. Notice that the logic pertaining to the communal debt of nature differs from that pertaining to the individual debt of nature. The individual debt of nature concerns the nature of the human being and the sorts of things that follow therefrom. The communal debt of nature takes God's justice into account. Taking our cue from Long's example, if we try to conceive, or succeed in conceiving, the whole human species beginning to exist underwater, despite the fact that each human being has everything belonging to her vis-à-vis the individual debt of nature – a soul, a body, and so forth – the species (arguably) does not have as a group what follows from the communal debt, what God must give it with respect to his own justice.[17]

Neither Thomas, nor any Thomist I am aware of, claimed that God could have created humanity without an appropriate environment. Controversy begins when we ask what humanity's relationship to God is in pure nature. Two questions are vital. Does God owe humanity the opportunity for an everlasting embodied existence? Does God owe humanity the ability to avoid all sin?

---

[15] Just as in the case of the individual debt, this assumes God has chosen to create and to create humanity.

[16] Steven A. Long, *Natura Pura: On the Recovery of Nature in the Doctrine of Grace* (New York: Fordham University Press, 2010), 58.

[17] I think we can at least try to conceive (or "imagine") the human species beginning to exist underwater, even if it turns out to be the case that God cannot create the human species underwater. One could argue, though, that if God cannot do this, then it is strictly speaking or "metaphysically" impossible; and, since the metaphysically impossible is inconceivable, it follows that no one can really conceive it. But even if this is true, we can try to conceive it.

It's hard to know how Thomas would have answered these questions. Death follows from the principles of nature. The implication would seem to be – though Thomas never makes this point explicitly as far as I know – that if God were to create the whole species in pure nature every human being would die, and every human being's soul would eternally subsist in (at best) a limbo-like state. Moreover, at least venial sin follows from the habitually disordered concupiscence that follows from the principles of nature, and thus those who reached the age of reason would inevitably venially sin. These two points – the inevitability of death and sin in nature – seem to have underlain Thomas's view that human beings would have been created in vain (*frustra et vane*) if they were not, as a group, able to reach their ultimate end, the beatific vision (*De malo* q. 5, a. 1, ad 1). Jesus is the cure for nature's sickness.

Things are complicated, however, by Thomas's shifting view of original justice. We saw in Chapter 2 that the early Thomas held that natural original justice – a graceless "preternatural" state involving immortality, freedom from concupiscence, and subjection to God – was possible. Presumably (though once again I don't know that Thomas ever explicitly made this point) if God could have left us in a state of pure nature, he also could have left us in a state of preternature. Presumably the goal of such a state would be the stable, everlasting contemplation of the creator. One could imagine various possibilities in a preternatural state: perhaps the first human beings would maintain allegiance to God, perhaps they would sin. In the latter case there are various possibilities corresponding roughly to God's postlapsarian options in this order of providence: perhaps God would forgive them but penalize them with death before resurrecting them (as Thomas says God does with us), or perhaps he would do something else, such as not forgive them at all. The complication, however, is that Thomas eventually came to think that grace is required for justice: according to this logic there is no natural original justice and no possible preternatural state. For the mature Thomas, then, it's either nature *or* grace.[18]

---

[18] Technically, Thomas's principles imply a third, bizarre possibility. God could create human beings who, with respect to their intrinsic being, are in "pure nature" – with only the principles of nature and that which follows therefrom. But God could bind their habitual concupiscence such that disordered impulses never arise, as he did with Mary before the incarnation. As we noted earlier, Mary's concupiscence was habitually disordered even after she received sanctifying grace but was bound such that she would have no actual movements of disordered concupiscence. This was an exceptional case precisely because Thomas thinks God ordinarily gives things forms by which to act. Now,

Certainly a tremendous amount of ink has been spilled on the question of what precisely Thomas said or implied about the possibility of a purely natural state, and one could raise various objections to my quick overview (even presupposing that my view of original justice and sin is broadly correct). One could argue that Thomas actually implies that although immortality doesn't follow from the principles of nature, he nonetheless holds that the dignity of the soul somehow demands the gift of immortality.[19] Or one could argue that the aforementioned reference to *De malo*, which states that nature would be vain without the beatific vision, implies only that pure nature would be less fitting than grace. None of this is decisive for present purposes, however. To sum up, Thomas's speculation about pure nature was minimal. He seemed to say that it was within divine power. In any case, for Thomas, the integrity of nature doesn't entail that pure nature would be a wonderful world, only that, at most, it would be a world.

Baroque Thomism would deepen the debt of nature by answering the question of whether sin and death are found in pure nature differently from Thomas. To understand the difference, it may be helpful to consider the following definition of pure nature from Lawrence Feingold, a contemporary representative of the baroque commentary tradition:

> The "state of pure nature" is normally understood by Scholastic theologians to refer to a state in which God would give to man only what belongs to or follows from the constitutive principles of human nature, together with those aids of God's providence that are due to human nature so that it may reach its proportionate and connatural final end.[20]

the view that all of humanity would be intrinsically in a natural state, while bound by a preternatural vise, so to speak, would imply that God had not given human beings a form by which they could be subjected to him but instead *did the subjecting himself*, from the outside, as it were. As far as I can see, though, there's nothing about Thomas's mature view of original justice that rules out *this* sort of "preternatural state" as a middle ground between pure nature and sanctifying grace. (It seems, by the way, that Garrigou-Lagrange's view of pure nature, with his deterministic view of human freedom, amounts to something like this third scenario: God gives enough *esse* to at least some human beings such that they avoid sin, despite the fact that they do not have the perfectly ordered concupiscence which only sanctifying grace can provide. This is probably why he was able to recognize the shift in Thomas's view of original justice but didn't think it entailed any major consequences with respect to the doctrine of pure nature.)

[19] "Hoc autem providentia divina disposuit propter dignitatem animae rationalis, quae cum naturaliter sit incorruptibilis, *debebatur* sibi incorruptibile corpus." *Super Rom*, c. 5, *lectio* 3, emphasis mine.

[20] Feingold, *The Natural Desire to See God According to St. Thomas and His Interpreters*, 224. See also Andrew Dean Swafford's description of the debt of nature along baroque

Feingold's definition seems to imply that it would be unjust for God to leave humanity in sin and death. God must give the human species the ability to reach its connatural end: a stable, unending contemplation of the creator. It may be reached after dying and a so-called natural resurrection, or perhaps human beings never would have died in the first place. Feingold himself didn't discuss concupiscence in any depth, but his definition seems to imply that he held that God must give the human species the ability to pursue the connatural end over time by regulating its concupiscence.

For later Thomists, God owes the human species an everlasting embodied existence as well as regulated concupiscence. Concupiscence may not be perfectly rightly ordered as it would be in original justice, but it needs to be regulated to such a degree that human beings can suppress it and reach their connatural end. In a word, what was preternatural for Thomas became purely natural for baroque Thomism.

We are now in a position to return to the objection with which we began this section. I do think that the new Thomist view is incompatible with the standard definition of the state of pure nature. This is because, to repeat, sin follows from being human without grace, and pure nature is generally defined as a state in which human beings are created without sin, without grace, and without preternatural gifts. I would argue, however, that if one's real concern is not so much affirming the possibility of the state of pure nature thus defined but rather avoiding the view that nature contains an exigency for grace, then one can accept the new Thomist view. This is because the question of the exigency for grace depends on one's view of the relation of God's power to his justice. With that said, I will now lay out a few different positions concerning the state of pure nature that are available to one who accepts the new Thomist view of original sin.

The first option is this. God is free to create human beings with only what belongs to them by virtue of the individual debt of nature, in conjunction with a suitable environment. Human beings will have the orientation to God, original sin, and disordered concupiscence. The connatural end will either be embodied or disembodied contemplation of

---

Thomist lines: "the *debitum naturae* stipulates that some things are in fact *due* to the creature on account of the creature's nature or essence. God's justice to the creature entails that He provides whatever is necessary for a given creature to reach its *natural* end." Andrew Dean Swafford, *Nature and Grace: A New Approach to Thomistic Ressourcement* (Eugene, OR: Wipf & Stock, 2014), 10, emphasis his. Swafford assumes the baroque view of original sin (p. 131 and passim).

God – and it may be the case that virtually no one reaches it, on account of falling into sin.

The second option is this. God owes it to his justice to provide not only a suitable environment but also the ability of human beings to avoid all personal sin, such that a significant number of them will reach the connatural end, a contemplation of the creator. This ability to avoid sin would stem from the preternatural regulation of concupiscence and justice in the rational will. This option, then, is incompatible with Thomas's mature view of original justice. However, because original sin is the lack of grace, even human beings who avoided all personal sin and reached a stable contemplation of God would have original sin.

The first option is close to Thomas's own view; the second is closer to the baroque Thomist perspective. But both of these options deny nature's exigency for grace. They are thus compatible with a "state of pure nature" in a broader sense of the phrase, in which it refers to a way things could have been in which human beings pursue God without grace. We can expand the options by considering different views of divine power. The next two options are non-Thomist accounts of divine power, conjoined with the new Thomist account of original sin.

The third option is this. God always does the very best.[21] On this view he owes it to himself – by virtue of his intrinsic perfection, let's say, or perhaps his infinite mercy – to offer grace. Perhaps he offers grace only to some. Or perhaps God owes it to his mercy to offer grace to every single human being. On this account, the communal debt has been greatly extended, yet the individual debt hasn't been extended at all. It would still be the case, that is, that every human person has her existence from outside herself; it would still be the case that every human person has a nature which receives the grace of God from God. Nature would have an exigency for grace, on this view, in the sense that it would be impossible for humanity to have existed without the offer of grace. But the exigency would flow from God's mercy alone, not human nature.

The fourth option is this. God's power extends to anything not entailing a logical contradiction. There is, let's say, no communal debt of nature whatsoever. God could create human beings without a suitable environment; he could create some human beings in one instant and

---

[21] This is Abelard's view, according to William J. Courtenay, "The Dialectic of Omnipotence in the High and Late Middle Ages," in *Divine Omniscience and Omnipotence in Medieval Philosophy: Islamic, Jewish, and Christian Perspectives* ed. Tamar Rudavsky (Boston: D. Reidel, 1995), 246.

annihilate them the next, and so forth. As long as one admits that there is an individual debt of nature which includes the orientation to God but not grace, that is, assuming that it would be absolutely impossible for God to create a human being without at least the orientation to God, this view of divine power is compatible with the new Thomist view of original sin.

Options three and four are intended to represent logical extremes (or views approaching the logical extremes, at least) of divine power. I think that if my view is compatible with these extremes, it is compatible with views in between them. For example, maybe God doesn't need to do the best, but he needs to do more than act in accordance with strict justice; perhaps he needs to act in accordance with mercy and there are many merciful options. One view which *is* required by the new Thomist account is that there is an individual debt of nature. If there isn't, perhaps because there are no necessary features of human existence, then original sin would need to be thought of in a different way.

Let's sum up the arguments of this section and the previous one. My view of original sin only requires an individual debt of nature which includes the orientation to God. Rational creatures are intrinsically unable to reach the beatific vision and kingdom of God of their own power. Our existence is not in our power, nor is our rebirth in Jesus Christ. Whatever one makes of the possibility of existence without the beatific vision, one could, in principle, agree that sin is the lack of grace.

SANCTIFYING GRACE

Another objection to Thomist accounts of original sin could be raised along the following lines. Grace is not a created reality. Thus original sin cannot be understood as the lack of a grace that, when present, perfects the person. As God's favor toward his creatures, grace is uncreated. Even on the supposition that nature, the grace of creation, and grace, the supernatural, deifying gift to the creature, should be somehow distinguished, it arguably does not follow that grace should be thought of as a creaturely possession, a supernatural substance in its own right.

This objection could be formulated from a Protestant perspective. For example, as Alister McGrath argues in his widely used textbook on the Reformation, "[d]uring the Middle Ages, grace tended to be understood as a supernatural substance, infused by God into the human soul in order to facilitate redemption."[22] Protestants rediscovered the biblical sense of the word "grace," which simply means unmerited favor. This had revolutionary consequences for the doctrine of justification. "It is the idea of grace as the unmerited favour of God which underlies the doctrine of justification by faith."[23] Grace is God's unmerited favor. Once this is understood, we no longer need to worry about earning our own justifying grace. The objection, then, is that the view that grace is a created reality is part and parcel of the Catholic system of works righteousness.

I will postpone discussion of justification until the next section. The same conclusion – grace is not a created reality – could be defended from an Orthodox perspective, though for different reasons from the ones just given. Bruce Marshall summarizes this objection in the following way.

But, the [Orthodox objection to Aquinas] runs, this "grace" remains wholly a created reality, and therefore incapable of sustaining a genuine notion of deification. Interposed between God and the human being, Thomas's idea depersonalizes and reifies grace, and keeps God at a distance. Deprived of direct contact with the persons of the Trinity – and especially with the Holy Spirit, who is supposed to be the immediate agent of deification – we are conformed not to God, but merely to a creature. "Created grace" leaves us not with deification, but with a sort of creaturification.[24]

If grace were merely a created reality in us, then we could not be deified. Admittedly (the objection might continue), aspects of our creaturely existence are intrinsically changed over time in the Christian life; our love for God and enemy grows, and so forth. What we need at the deepest level, though, is not to become better and better people – to be "creaturified" in Marshall's sense – what we need is literal *contact* with God through his divine energies.

In response to these objections I will first argue that a Thomist view of grace does not preclude deification and does not imply that grace is a substance. To make this case, I will unpack some of the basics of Thomas's view of sanctifying grace (*gratia gratum faciens*). The part I will defend is this: sanctifying grace, after the incarnation of Jesus Christ, is the transforming, indwelling presence of the triune God in the human person that enables her to live for Jesus Christ.

---

[22] Alister McGrath, *Reformation Thought: An Introduction* (Malden, MA: Blackwell, 1999 [1988]), 103.
[23] McGrath, *Reformation Thought*, 103.   [24] Marshall, "*Ex Occidente Lux?*," 28.

We can begin with the first article of question 110 of the *Prima secundae*, "the essence of the grace of God,"[25] which deals directly with the question at hand. Is grace something in the human soul? Thomas begins, characteristically, by paying close attention to how grace is used in ordinary language. Thomas notes that we tend to speak of grace in three ways: as love, as gift, and as thanks. As an example of the first mode of usage, Thomas gives the phrase, "the solider has the grace of the king, that is, the king looks on him favorably" (*iste miles habet gratiam regis, idest, rex habet eum gratum*). A similar phrase in contemporary English is "to be in someone's good graces." Grace in this first sense, then, is a love or favor one has for another. Second, we speak of grace in relation to freely given gifts. The phrase Thomas gives as example – "*hanc gratiam facio tibi*" – has no word-for-word parallel in English, but the same basic idea could be conveyed by speaking of a "gracious gift" or, less pleonastically, "gift." Third, we speak of grace in relation to thanksgiving for a gift. Thomas's Latin example – "*agere gratias beneficiorum*" – has close English parallels; in English we "say grace" and are "grateful" for gifts.

Thomas claims that the primary sense of these uses is the first: grace as love.[26] This is because the second sense, grace as gift, presupposes love. To give a gift requires a motive, and as the motive cannot be the repayment of a debt, the motive is love. The third use, grace as thanksgiving, follows from the second, as one is grateful to the giver for her gift. The theological senses of the word "grace" mirror ordinary language. Grace primarily signifies God's love for his creatures, and it also signifies the gift given to the creature as a result of this love. In the following quotation Thomas explains these two basic theological senses of the word "grace" (though he first subdistinguishes two senses of God's love for his creatures):

God's love for the creature can be considered in different ways. First, there is his common love, by which he "loves all things that are," as Sap. 11[:25] says. This is the love by which he gives created things the act of being. Second, there is his special love, by which he draws the creature above the condition of its nature, to participation in the divine good. And according to this love he is said to love something simpliciter. It is by this love that God absolutely wills the eternal good, himself, to the creature. Thus when the human being is said to have the grace of God, something supernatural in the human being, from God, is signified. And yet

---

[25] *STh* I-II, q. 110, *prooemium*. The following quotes are from a. 1 of this question.

[26] "Quorum trium secundum dependet ex primo: ex amore enim quo aliquis alium gratum habet, procedit quod aliquid ei gratis impendat. Ex secundo autem procedit tertium: quia ex beneficiis gratis exhibitis gratiarum actio consurgit." *STh* I-II, q. 110, a. 1.

the grace of God can also refer to the eternal love of God itself. An example of this is when we speak of the grace of predestination (by which God graciously – not from merits – elects or predestines some of us), we are speaking of God's own love. As it is said in Eph 1[:5–6], "he predestined us as adopted sons to the praise of his glorious grace."[27]

God's own love is not a different reality from God himself, but we can consider it in two ways. We can first consider it as it is common to all creatures: God loves every creature by giving it being, existence. God's special love, by which he gives himself in an absolute sense, is reserved for rational creatures. He draws human beings above the condition of their mortal, weak, sin-disposed nature and gives them a share of his own life. This is the basis for Thomas's affirmation that grace is something in the creature and not only God's favor toward the creature considered in God. Indeed, we cannot coherently restrict our consideration of God's love for us to God's inner life, precisely because it is by that very love that he has given us a share of his life.

Given that Thomas thinks that the first, primary sense of the word "grace" refers to grace as it exists in the giver, we can say that Thomas acknowledges that grace is primarily uncreated. But the effect of this grace in us, the new birth by which God's predestination takes place, is also called "grace." Grace is something we receive, then, but what exactly is it? Thomas argues in the next article (*STh* I-II, q. 110, a. 2) that grace is that by which the human being is called a new creation. Christians are "created in Christ Jesus for good works" (Eph. 2:10); grace is the principle of Christian living and working and being. But before we discuss this further, let me briefly discuss a point which Thomas assumes throughout the treatise on grace.

If a human being is created anew as Ephesians claims, she must exist before and after the new creation. This passage is not talking about the annihilation of one human being and the creation of a numerically

---

[27] "[D]ifferens consideratur dilectio Dei ad creaturam. Una quidem communis, secundum quam diligit omnia quae sunt, ut dicitur *Sap*. XI; secundum quam esse naturale rebus creatis largitur. Alia autem est dilectio specialis, secundum quam trahit creaturam rationalem supra conditionem naturae, ad participationem divini boni. Et secundum hanc dilectionem dicitur aliquem diligere simpliciter: quia secundum hanc dilectionem vult Deus simpliciter creaturae bonum aeternum, quod est ipse. Sic igitur per hoc quod dicitur homo gratiam Dei habere, significatur quiddam supernaturale in homine a Deo proveniens. Quandoque tamen gratia Dei dicitur ipsa aeterna Dei dilectio: secundum quod dicitur etiam gratia praedestinationis, inquantum Deus gratuito, et non ex meritis, aliquos praedestinavit sive elegit; dicitur enim ad *Ephes*. I, praedestinavit nos in adoptionem filiorum, in laudem gloriae gratiae suae." *STh* I-II, q. 110, a. 1.

different human being; otherwise, the whole sense of the passage would be lost. It would make no sense, for example, to exhort the Christian to remember her time as a Gentile sinner, far off from Christ, in contrast to her new existence in Jesus Christ (Eph. 2:11–13), if she never had been a sinner in the first place. If a brand-new human being inhabiting the body of someone who used to exist as a sinner but now ceases to exist (or at least ceases to exist in that body) were exhorted to remember her time as a sinner, then one of two things would follow. Either she would not understand the exhortation at all (*what sins have I committed?*) or, exhibiting what psychologists call "false memory syndrome," she would suppose that the sinful life of the previous inhabitant of her body was her own. But surely Ephesians exhorts the reader to remember her *own* time as a sinner, far off from Christ. The new creation in Christ is a radical change. But it is the change of a human being.

What then is grace in the new Christian, the grace by which she is born again and lives in Christ? In his treatment of the divine missions earlier in the *Summa*, Thomas argued that grace is the indwelling presence of the Trinity. But what could it mean for the Trinity to dwell in the creature, if, as God, he is omnipresent by nature? Although God is omnipresent by "essence, power, and presence," insofar as he gives being to all things, has power over all things, and knows all things, he can begin to exist in a new way in his creature by grace (*STh* I, q. 8, a. 3). The Father sends the Son and the Spirit to us; we are united to the Spirit especially by charity and to the Son especially by the faith that leads to charity (*STh* I, q. 43, a. 5, ad 2). The whole Trinity lives in the person by grace, but it is the Son and Spirit who are said to be "sent," as Thomas thinks a divine person must proceed from another and begin to exist somewhere in a new way in order to be sent.[28]

Having said that grace is that by which the whole Trinity lives in us and that the Son and Spirit are sent by the Father, I will speak of sanctifying grace as the gift of the Holy Spirit.[29] The Holy Spirit doesn't move from one location to another; but he is given by the Father, with the Son, "to live in her [the creature] as in his temple."[30] Can we say anything

---

[28] "[P]er gratiam gratum facientem tota Trinitas inhabitat mentem, secundum illud Ioan. XIV, *ad eum veniemus, et mansionem apud eum faciemus.* Mitti autem Personam divinam ad aliquem per invisibilem gratiam, significat novum modum inhabitandi illius personae, et originem eius ab alia." *STh* I, q. 43, a. 5.

[29] "[S]piritui Sancto, inquantum procedit ut Amor, competit esse sanctificationis donum." *STh* I, q. 43, a. 7.

[30] "habitare in ea sicut in templo suo." *STh* I, q. 43, a. 1.

more about sanctifying grace, then, other than that it is the principle of the Christian life, the gift of the Holy Spirit by which we love God in charity?

Thomas argues that we can. Sanctifying grace, insofar as it signifies the indwelling presence of the Holy Spirit in us, is a habitual gift in the soul:

> God infuses a habitual gift of grace into the soul. This is because it would be unfitting for him to provide less for creatures whom he loves in order for them to acquire the supernatural good, than creatures he loves in order for them to acquire the natural good. Now consider that God not only moves natural creatures to natural actions; he gives them forms and powers which are the principles of their actions, by which they are inclined to move. The motions of creatures thus moved by God are connatural and easy. As Sap. VII says, "he disposes all things sweetly." Much more, therefore, does God infuse supernatural forms or qualities into those creatures whom he moves to the eternal supernatural good, so that they can pursue it sweetly and promptly. And thus the gift of grace is a quality in the soul.[31]

Grace, insofar as it refers to the gift of the Holy Spirit as received by the human person, is a habitual gift infused by God into the soul. It is that by which the human person moves toward her supernatural good – the beatific vision in the kingdom of heaven. Ontologically, it is a quality of the person, a type of accident, rather than a substance in its own right. It is that by which we are "constituted in new being, from nothing (that is, not from merits). As Eph. 2:10 says, we are 'created in Jesus Christ for good works.'"[32] Grace constitutes us as new creatures to do good works in Christ.

Two things can now be said in response to the aforementioned objections. First, for Thomas, grace is not a substance but an accident. (This is probably one reason why he doesn't speak of "created grace" very often: substances, not accidents, are properly speaking said to be created.) McGrath's narrative, according to which the scholastic conception of

---

[31] "[H]abituale donum a Deo animae infunditur. Et hoc ideo, quia non est conveniens quod Deus minus provideat his quos diligit ad supernaturale bonum habendum, quam creaturis quas diligit ad bonum naturale habendum. Creaturis autem naturalibus sic providet ut non solum moveat eas ad actus naturales, sed etiam largiatur eis formas et virtutes quasdam, quae sunt principia actuum, ut secundum seipsas inclinentur ad huiusmodi motus. Et sic motus quibus a Deo moventur, fiunt creaturis connaturales et faciles; secundum illud *Sap.* VIII: *Et disponit omnia suaviter.* Multo igitur magis illis quos movet ad consequendum bonum supernaturale aeternum, infundit aliquas formas seu qualitates supernaturales, secundum quas suaviter et prompte ab ipso moveantur ad bonum aeternum consequendum. Et sic donum gratiae qualitas quaedam est." *STh* I-II, q. 110, a. 2.

[32] "[I]n novo esse constituuntur, ex nihilo, idest non ex meritis; secundum illud ad *Ephes.* 2 [:10], creati in Christo Iesu in operibus bonis." *STh* I-II, q. 110, a. 2, ad 3.

grace as a substance led to a misunderstanding of justification, cannot be quite right. Neither Thomas nor any scholastic I am aware of taught that grace was a substance. In the second place, for Thomas, grace just is the divinely appointed means of deification. It is not something that stands in between us and God; it is God's own Spirit in us, leading us to deeper and deeper communion with himself. As Marshall puts it, "[g]race deifies not because it lacks any created reality, but because of the kind of created reality grace is." Grace is that created reality which conforms us to God. "We are not conformed *to* the created habit of grace, touching it instead of God; rather this grace is our conformity itself."[33]

What else, exactly, could grace be? Assuming, as I am, that the Holy Spirit is omnipresent, the Christian union with God will need to take place through some change in the Christian. Could we be united to God through something that is neither creature nor creator, a "divine energy" of some sort? Space precludes in-depth discussion of this question. But even if we grant that the existence of a genuine tertium quid between creature and creator is possible, it seems that such energy would not be able to explain our union with God. For on the assumption that grace is not an intrinsic change in us but the indwelling of some energy, we will be united not to God but to this energy. The same thing applies, *mutatis mutandis*, if the energy is itself a creature.

ORIGINAL SIN AND JUSTIFICATION

Is it possible for theologians who disagree with Aquinas on other soteriological issues to adopt his account of original sin? Put differently, does one need to buy into Thomas's entire "system" – in which sanctifying grace justifies us, allows us to merit further grace, and can be forfeited by our mortal sin – in order to accept his view of original sin?[34] Here, as a case study, I'll focus on the doctrine of justification (with a couple of side remarks on merit). In order to avoid a long historical digression, I will

---

[33] Both from Marshall, "*Ex Occidente Lux?* Aquinas and Eastern Orthodox Theology," 29.

[34] See *STh* I-II, q. 113–14 for Thomas's treatment of justification and merit. This discussion in the *Summa* should be read in conjunction with Thomas's Pauline commentaries. For a discussion of the neglected forensic aspects of Aquinas's account of justification which come through clearly in his commentary on Romans, see Bruce D. Marshall, "*Beatus vir*: Aquinas, Romans 4, and the Role of 'Reckoning' in Justification," in *Reading Romans with Saint Thomas Aquinas*, ed. Matthew Levering and Michael Dauphinais (Washington, DC: Catholic University of America Press, 2012), 216–38.

simply ask whether Thomas's view of original sin can be synthesized with the following (logically) extreme view of justification. Sanctifying grace transforms the person; justification is a purely forensic, irrevocable legal status. (Perhaps justification consists in God's forgiveness or non-imputation of sin; perhaps it is the imputation of Christ's active or passive righteousness; perhaps something else.) Let's say that the person is initially justified and sanctified simultaneously; that is, a person receives sanctifying grace (faith, hope, charity) and justification in the same moment. Sanctification and justification are separable in following sense. Having been justified and sanctified, a person can later fail to love God (*ipso facto* forfeiting her sanctifying grace) without losing her justification.

It might seem that the prospects of synthesizing Thomas's view of original sin with the foregoing view are bleak. From the foregoing perspective, Thomas's view that grace is justifying is confused from the outset; justification is a juridical status freely bestowed by God and cannot be forfeited by our own failings. Moreover, one might want to claim, progress in sanctification is itself gratuitous and thus is not properly speaking merited (cf. Rom. 4:4–5). Given that the job of a doctrine of original sin is to explain the infant's need for the grace of the gospel, such disagreement over the nature of gospel grace seems to render agreement on original sin impossible. For Thomists who think that sanctifying grace is (the beginning of) justification, original sin can be the lack of sanctifying grace. But for theologians who think that justification is forensic, original sin will likewise need to be fundamentally forensic; and, moreover, the sanctifying grace we need is of a fundamentally different type – namely, the grace that orients us to God but doesn't enable merit.

I'm inclined to think, however, that such disagreements over justification and merit are just that: disagreements over justification and merit. I'm inclined to think, to be more precise, that they entail only *minor* differences with respect to original sin itself, however important they may be in themselves. For consider a few of the points that can still be, theoretically at least, agreed on: (1) original justice is not logically necessary for original sin because the principles of human nature and orientation to God are present in the person with original sin; (2) original sin consists only in the need for the grace of the gospel; (3) personal guilt cannot be transmitted; (4) infants have not acted before they begin to exist in the womb.

Admittedly, with respect to (2), there will be a difference in what precisely the grace of the gospel is thought to be: Is it sanctifying grace, or is it sanctifying grace conjoined with juridical justifying grace? And it is true that there are differences in what precisely sanctifying grace enables: Does it enable the condign merit of further grace, or not? Whether or not these differences are significant with respect to original sin is a judgment call. In my judgment, they are not very significant due to the aforementioned points of agreement.

In general, it seems to me that the precise sorts of things that sanctifying grace enables – beyond the previous sketch of the abiding presence of the Holy Spirit that orients us to beatitude – are proper accidents of grace. General agreement about the essence of a thing is compatible with specific disagreement about its proper accidents. For example, theologians may agree that the human being is essentially a rational animal and disagree over whether a desire for the beatific vision follows from having a rational nature as such, whether the soul can subsist after death, and so forth. Likewise, theologians could agree that original sin is essentially the lack of sanctifying grace but disagree concerning sanctifying grace's proper accidents (thus implicitly disagreeing about original sin's proper accidents), such as whether it enables the condign merit of further grace, whether it is really or only logically distinct from charity, and so forth.

PELAGIANISM

The next objection is this: the Thomist view of original sin is Pelagian and should be rejected. Now it's clear that Thomas accepted *some* Pelagian beliefs rejected by Augustine. As we mentioned earlier, Thomas, along with Anselm and many other medievals, agreed with the Pelagians that our sexual intercourse *in uia* is not necessarily tainted by sin. Yet agreement with the Pelagians against Augustine does not necessarily make one a Pelagian. For example, many (if not virtually all) contemporary theologians deny that infants who die without water baptism are *ipso facto* damned. But surely not all of these theologians are "Pelagians" in any problematic sense. I would submit that Thomas, though he affirmed certain teachings of Pelagius, should not be considered a Pelagian. This is principally because Thomas affirmed that infants have a damning original sin and robustly denied that human beings can fulfill the natural law (and *a fortiori* the commands of Jesus Christ) without the supernatural grace of the Holy Spirit.

The objection can easily be nuanced, however. The Thomist view of original sin should be rejected because it is "Semipelagian." Now what exactly is "Semipelagianism" supposed to be? As Irena Backus and Aza

Goudriaan have recently argued in an excellent article, this term stemmed from neither the Molinist controversy of the 1590s nor the 1577 *Formula of Concord*; its first attestation is found in Theodore Beza's 1556 annotations to the New Testament.[35] Beza links Semipelagianism to sundry affirmations of contemporary Catholics. He associates it with, inter alia, the following views: concupiscence in the person with sanctifying grace is not sinful; the fallen will retains some orientation to the good; we must cooperate with grace in order for it to be effectual; we need to prepare for grace to receive grace; justification is our own and not Christ's; salvation is partly due to God and partly due to our effort. In short, Beza held that Roman Catholic theological anthropology and soteriology was Semipelagian. Catholics didn't necessarily deny original sin outright, but they nevertheless overestimated postlapsarian moral ability. Catholic writers, beginning with Nicholas Sander(s) in 1571, first applied the term "Semipelagian" to the Massilians; it would eventually be used in a wide variety of disputes, including the Molinist and Jansenist controversies.[36]

I've already avowed this book's neutrality with respect to the sinfulness of concupiscence, grace's justifying and merit-enabling character, and now let me add the question of cooperation with grace. Does the charge of Semipelagianism have any teeth, then, with respect to the core Thomist view I am defending? It seems that there are three possible ways it might, pertaining, respectively, to the goodness of human nature, the merit of the first grace, and the natural love of God.

---

[35] "The earliest use of the terms 'Semipelagianism' and 'semipelagian' can be traced back to Theodore Beza and his anti-Catholic polemics. Beza uses the terms without once adverting to their 'Massilian' fifth-century context, although it is quite clear that the terms are of interest to him as indication of a mitigated or subtle form of 'Pelagianism,' itself a major and instantly recognisable heresy." "Theoretically, the possibility that the term had multiple inventors, independent of one another, cannot be ruled out entirely. In the realm of historical probability, however, a *Begriffsgeschichte* that starts with Beza has a high degree of plausibility." Irena Backus and Aza Goudriaan, "'Semipelagianism': The Origins of the Term and Its Passage into the History of Heresy," *The Journal of Ecclesiastical History* 65.1 (2014), 35, 45; see 35–40 for Beza's use of the term.

[36] Backus and Goudriaan, "'Semipelagianism': The Origins of the Term and Its Passage into the History of Heresy," 42. As this article observes, though, Augustine himself "sharply distinguished the Massilians (*Massilienses*), as he called them, from the Pelagians, the chief difference between the two being that the Massilians believed in original sin and that they thought that men's wills were actually anticipated by God's grace. Moreover, in contrast with the Pelagians, the Massilians did not think that human will unaided by grace could do anything good.... The debates with the Massilians, it is important to note, focused on justification. The issue of original sin did not enter into them, in contrast with the Pelagian quarrel" (pp. 27–8).

First, one might argue that at least part of Semipelagianism is the affirmation that some goodness is present in the human being with original sin. Since Thomism affirms this, it is Semipelagian. Yet I would argue that if this were true, then Augustine himself would have been a Semipelagian. He consistently taught that evil is the privation of the good in a subject which, insofar as it is, is good. And infants with original sin still exist, which is why they can be evil and guilty. A definition of Semipelagianism which counts Augustine as a Semipelagian is surely unhelpful.

Now this objection could be sharpened: it pertains to Semipelagianism to affirm that the *will* retains an orientation to the good, that there is still freedom between good and evil (Rom. 14:23). I would respond that there is nothing problematic with thinking that human beings do various good things without sanctifying grace but with nature, creation's grace: solve math problems, build bridges, and so forth. At the same time, there is another sense in which it is legitimate to speak of nature as utterly sinful: the whole person is called to a higher life in grace. Given that the whole person is reoriented by grace to love the triune God, we can say that the whole person who does not love the triune God is sinful.

Perhaps the view that the human being with original sin can merit the reception of grace is Semipelagian. This is widely considered to be a part of Semipelagianism. The Council of Orange, as we briefly discussed in Chapter 1, holds that God's grace comes to us by grace, not works. It's well known that the medievals distinguished *meritum de congruo* from *meritum de condigno*. Roughly, the distinction is between rewards which are earned properly speaking and rewards which exceed what is earned. No prominent medieval theologian as far as I know (and certainly not Thomas) affirmed that human beings in original sin can condignly merit grace. But some medieval theologians – possibly including, as we mentioned in Chapter 4, Thomas in the *Scriptum* – held that one could congruously merit the first grace. If this is true, then the early Thomas was (let's grant *arguendo*) a Semipelagian. However, a consideration of the concept of *de congruo* merit – a human being "merits" X because God has graciously deigned to order one's action to the reception of X – shows that whether one affirms or denies a congruous merit of the first grace is independent of whether one affirms or denies a Thomist view of original sin. For example, if one holds with Thomas that the natural orientation to God remains in the person with original sin, one can easily deny – as Thomas himself arguably denied in his maturity – that God has freely chosen to reward those who do what is in themselves by nature with grace. Conversely, one could (in theory) adopt a more Augustinian view of original sin and *affirm* that those who do what is in themselves are rewarded with grace. The issues are logically independent, and I am not affirming a congruous merit of the first grace. This objection doesn't refute the new Thomist view of original sin.

The most plausible formulation of the objection is that Thomism's affirmation of the natural orientation to God in the person with original sin is Semipelagian. This is obviously essential to the Thomist view of original sin; indeed, I've suggested that it's precisely what distinguishes Thomas's view of original sin from Augustine's. But Thomas's innovation seems to have led him into a major problem. As the Council of Orange concludes:

> To love God (*diligere Deum*) is completely a gift of God. He who, not being loved, grants that he may be loved. While not being pleasing, we have been loved, so that there might be produced in us something by which we might please. For the Spirit of the Father and the Son, whom we love with the Father and the Son, has poured forth charity (*caritatem*) into our hearts.[37]

This canon, drawing on Augustine's homilies on John, clearly implies that the person born in original sin does not love God. Only later, when the Holy Spirit is poured into our hearts, do we love God. One might be tempted to argue that Thomism contradicts this canon because the orientation to God is tantamount to the love of God.

It seems to me, though, that Orange's denial that we are able to love God (*diligere Deum*) should be understood as a denial that we have charity (*caritatem*). This is because loving God is identified with the love of God poured out by the Holy Spirit into our hearts, by which we love the Trinity. But neither Thomas nor I have suggested that charity is present in the person with original sin. Given that Thomas does not affirm what this canon condemns, there's no contradiction between his view and the Council of Orange. But just what is this natural orientation to God? Can it coherently be distinguished from charity?

THE ORIENTATION TO GOD

Here I discuss what it means for the human person with original sin to be oriented to God. In brief: it means that, from the first moment of her existence, she is moving ultimately toward some kind of dim

---

[37] Can. 25 (DH 395), translation slightly modified.

contemplation and love of God, distinct from the beatific vision. It does not entail that any human person will avoid sin and succeed in reaching such a state of natural contemplation. It does not entail, even, that anyone will consciously contemplate or love God by nature. I will begin by describing a few salient aspects of Thomas's teleology. Since I am putting it to constructive use, I will freely draw on various works, chiefly the *Summa contra Gentiles*, without attempting to compare them. I do not have space to defend these teleological assumptions from various metaphysical objections, though I think that, in many cases, they are plausible. I will only describe them.

Written sometime between 1259 and 1265, the intended audience of Thomas's early *Summa* is uncertain, but its internal structure is clear.[38] The first book treats God's internal operation. The second discusses God's external operation, the freely chosen emanation of creation. It remains for book III to treat the perfection of God as he is the end of all things, directing what has come from him back to himself. Because anything produced by an agent is directed to its proper end by that agent, God directs the things he has made to their proper end. Each of the things produced through the will of an agent is directed to an end by the agent. For the proper object of the will is the good which is the end. As a result, things which proceed from will must be directed to some end. Moreover, each thing achieves its ultimate end through its own action which must be directed to the end by him who gives things the principles through which they act.[39]

Everything created by God is ruled by God, and thus is directed to its proper end by God. The providential direction to the proper end is not added onto things; it takes place through the nature of things, through their proper operations. As a result, the rule of God is different in different creatures, according to their diverse natures and operations.[40] Thus go Thomas's introductory comments. He then spends the next twenty-three chapters discussing teleology in general. In chapter 2, Thomas argues that every agent acts for a definite and ultimate end. Subrational and even inanimate beings act for a definite and ultimate end.

---

[38] For a discussion of its dating, purpose, plan, and content, see Torrell, *Saint Thomas Aquinas: The Person and His Work*, 98–111.

[39] *Summa contra Gentiles* (Rome: Typis Riccardi Garroni) [hereafter, *ScG*] III, c. 1, 3.22–5.

[40] "Huius vero regiminis effectus in diversis apparet diversimode, secundum differentiam naturarum." *ScG* III, c. 1, 3.1–3.

The end is what an agent tends toward. The end is either external to the agent (e.g., when a human being shoots an arrow at a target or builds a house) or internal (the end of understanding is the action of understanding itself). Thomas gives several arguments in this chapter on behalf of the conclusion that every agent must seek a definite end, the termination of its action. Here is the first. If there were no end to the action of an agent, there would be no terminus for it to tend toward, and thus it would tend to infinity. But it is impossible to proceed to infinity, and nothing is moved toward what cannot be reached. Thus, no agent could even begin to act without an end.[41] In the next chapter, Thomas fleshes out the character of the definite end that agents necessarily act toward. Because agents tend toward what is appropriate to them in light of their natural power, and whatever is appropriate to a thing is its good, agents necessarily act for some good.[42] The good provides a terminus for the appetite. But the end is that in which the appetite finds its rest, and thus agents must be acting for some good. In chapter 16, Thomas connects the two preceding points (every agent acts for an end; every agent acts for a good). The end of everything is its distinctive good. "If every agent acts for the good, as was discussed earlier, it follows that the end of every being is its good."[43]

In one sense, every agent's end, perfection, and good is God. The production of any agent is for that agent. Thus all creatures are made for God by God; all creatures are directed to God by God. Every agent has its own proper perfection and good. In reaching this good, the agent has come closer to God – though is still infinitely removed from him – because of a likeness between its finite good and God's infinite good. Book I argued that God is goodness itself, that the goodness of created being is possible only through participation in the goodness of God. The actualization of a creature's potency to achieve perfection is an increase in

---

[41] Aquinas, *Summa contra Gentiles*, III, c. 2, 5.3–9.

[42] "Inde enim manifestum est omne agens agere propter finem, quia quodlibet agens tendit ad aliquod determinatum. Id autem ad quod agens determinate tendit, oportet esse conveniens ei: non enim tenderet in ipsum nisi propter aliquam convenientiam ad ipsum. Quod autem est conveniens alicui, est ei bonum. Ergo omne agens agit propter bonum." *ScG* III, c. 3, 9.3–10.

[43] "Si autem omne agens agit propter bonum, ut supra probatum est, sequitur ulterius quod cuiuslibet entis bonum sit finis. Omne enim ens ordinatur in finem per suam actionem: oportet enim quod vel ipsa actio sit finis; vel actionis finis est etiam finis agentis. Quod est eius bonum." *ScG* III, c. 16, 38.1–7.

participation in the being of God, its attainment of God. "God is the end of things ... in the sense that he is reached (*acquiritur*) by things."[44]

What does it mean to say that God is "reached" or "acquired" or "attained" by his creatures? Generically speaking, the sense in which every creature can "reach" God is *very* thin. Thomas discusses it at some length in chapters 19–21; here I'll simply note the most important point: the creature "reaches" God by virtue of the fact that it exists. God is existence itself (*ipsum esse subsistens*); every creature who exists – and, as we've seen, thereby acts for an end which is its good – thereby participates in existence, has in part what God has in full.

This, to repeat, is the generic sense in which creatures reach God. Given that creatures exist in different ways in accordance with their different natures, the mode of reaching God will vary from creature to creature. Before we ask what this means for infants, let's sum up the discussion so far. Every being acts for an ultimate end, either as already possessing it or as seeking it. God is always already in possession of his ultimate end (himself); other beings pursue various proximate ends en route to their ultimate end. Every being "has" God as its ultimate end, though different beings seek God in different ways, in accordance with their different natures.

We saw in Chapter 4 that Thomas speaks of beings' pursuit of their natural ends in terms of *love* (though this language isn't prominent in the beginning of *ScG* III). I will use the word "love" generally to refer to a being's pursuit of its goodness. For beings who don't have freedom, there is no possibility of turning away from God as end; these beings always, of necessity, love God as much as they can. The rational, that is, spiritual creature is the only creature who can refuse to love God. And this, Thomas holds, can happen only through a deficient act of freedom, a mortal sin. As we have already discussed, in mortal sin a spiritual creature swerves away from God and pursues some other creature as if it were its ultimate end.

What does this mean for infants? They do not have the use of reason or freedom; they thus do not have the ability to actively contemplate and love God. If things go well for them in this life, they eventually will; otherwise, they will in the next life. The infant's love for God, then, is analogous to subrational beings' love for God: it is not initially conscious, not chosen through an act of will, not grasped through an intellective

---

[44] "Relinquitur igitur quod Deus sit finis rerum ... quia ipse rebus acquiritur." *ScG* III, c. 18, 42.14–18.

process. It is given with nature. I am not denying that infants are rational beings. I am claiming only that in the earlier stages of development they do not have the ability to actively exercise all of the capacities that, if things go well for them in this life, they will have, the capacities that, if they die before exercising them, they will be perfected by having in the next life. By contrast, if non-human animals were given freedom, reason, and ultimately grace (whether in this life or the next), they would not be perfected but destroyed, changed into a new sort of being.

To say that infants initially love God on a par with other subrational creatures raises the question of what happens when they are able to actively exercise their natural spiritual capacities. There are two options: either they die before they act freely or they eventually reach the age of reason *in uia*. The basic question is the same, though: What is it that the infant is moving toward of her own power when she begins to exist? That is to ask, what is her natural end? Before we can even begin to answer this question, we need to more sharply distinguish a few senses of the word "end" (*finis*).

The first distinction is between the end qua "thing" (*res*) and the end qua "use" (*usus*) of the thing. This distinction appears throughout Thomas's works. It was implicit in our discussion of the *Summa contra Gentiles* a moment ago. It appears explicitly in (for example) *STh* I-II q. 2, a. 7, where Thomas discusses whether beatitude is something "in" the soul. It is as far as "use" goes; it isn't as far as "thing" goes. God is the "thing" humans aim at in desiring happiness; the "use" of God is their contemplation of him. Another way of thinking about this distinction is in terms of the object of an activity and the activity itself. Beatitude will involve contemplation of God: God is the object of the contemplation, contemplation the activity itself.

In the second place, there is the distinction (see *STh* I-II, q. 1, a. 7) between beatitude, the ultimate end that truly perfects us (the end *secundum rationem ultimi finis*), and any end that is not beatitude that is actually sought, regardless of whether it is the perfective end, regardless, that is, of whether it is that in which the concept of the ultimate end is found (*id in quo finis ultimi ratio invenitur*). Creatures in grace but not yet confirmed in beatitude are moving toward God as the perfective end. Creatures who have mortally sinned are moving toward some creature.[45] There are many different ends that are actually sought, many different

---

[45] All creatures seek (or have found) "happiness" (*secundum communem rationem beatitudinis* [*STh* I-II, q. 5, a. 8]); that is, they are all moving toward something as an

"for-the-sake-of-whiches," that is, many different things in which human beings can place their ultimate end. Many of them are creaturely goods: pleasure, honor, and so on.

But there is a further distinction among non-ultimate ends. Not all of them are creaturely goods. God, insofar as he is sought as the natural end, is himself a non-ultimate end. The human being in original sin seeks God with her natural power. As I suggested earlier, Thomas doesn't discuss this distinction in questions 1–5 of the *Prima secundae* because he is principally concerned with the action of creatures who have the use of reason. Since (as we argued) he thinks all creatures with the use of reason are in grace or mortal sin, he didn't need to discuss the natural end in that context. If Thomas had written the *Summa*'s eschatology, he presumably would have made this distinction again, just as he actually did in the mature *De malo* (cf. *De veritate* q. 14, a. 2; *STh* I, q. 62, a. 1).

There is, then, a natural end within the creature's power and a supernatural end that is not.[46] Precisely what this natural end consists in for Thomas has been the subject of tremendous debate.[47] It's clear that the object or *res* of the end is God and not a creature; it's unclear what precisely the activity or *usus* of the subject who obtains this end will consist in. One of the chief difficulties concerns the question of the natural desire for the supernatural end. If a person reaches the natural end, will she be fully satisfied by it? Or will she desire to be given the supernatural beatific vision? If her desires are not fully satisfied by the so-called natural end, is it really an end after all? Different texts in Thomas's *corpus* can be

---

ultimate end which they take to be their good, whether or not it really is their good. In other words, something that satisfies their will.

[46] It may be worth noting another, Scotist distinction between the natural and the supernatural. An end may be supernatural in the sense that it cannot be acquired by natural power and yet "natural" in the sense that it perfects the nature. I don't deny that the beatific vision is the natural end in the sense of perfecting the spiritual creature. In any case, when I call grace and the beatific vision "supernatural" I mean that they are beyond the spiritual creature's natural power. When I speak of the "natural end" I am speaking of an end which consists in the sort of knowledge and love of God that is, in principle, within the creature's natural power. See the first question of Duns Scotus's prologue to the *Ordinatio*, concerning the necessity of revealed doctrine. For a helpful discussion of Scotus's views on this question, see Allan B. Wolter, "Duns Scotus on the Natural Desire for the Supernatural," in *The Philosophical Theology of John Duns Scotus*, ed. Marilyn McCord Adams (Ithaca, NY: Cornell University Press, 1990), 125–47.

[47] Lawrence Feingold's *The Natural Desire to See God According to St. Thomas and His Interpreters* helpfully traces the history of Thomistic commentators' views on the question. My comments on Cajetan and general impression of the baroque commentators are indebted to Feingold.

adduced to support different views. On the one hand, there are places where he seems to affirm that the rational creature naturally desires to know the essence of everything that it knows exists (cf. *ScG* III, c. 50). On the other hand, there are places Thomas seems to say that knowledge of and desire for the supernatural end utterly exceeds natural power (once again *De veritate* q. 14, a. 2, is pertinent). Moreover, given his mature doctrine of limbo, Thomas seems to say that in *reality* there are infants who are at rest in the natural contemplation and love of God. It's not surprising, then, that there have been a variety of later Thomist perspectives on this issue.

The traditional Thomist position is found in Cajetan, or at least the standard reading of Cajetan. There is no desire for grace or the beatific vision. The reason is because natural desires are proportioned to natural powers. The human being neither knows nor desires anything by nature beyond the contemplation of the creator. Once this contemplation is achieved, she can rest everlastingly in it. She retains the obediential potency for the supernatural, but, being nescient of that potency, it does not have a negative effect on her.

The other option is to affirm that there is a natural desire for the beatific vision. There are then many different ways of explaining this desire. One way is along the lines of what Feingold calls the "scholastic consensus." The desire for the beatific vision is, properly speaking, elicited by knowledge of the existence of the creator. *Pace* Cajetan, every spiritual creature desires to know fully what she knows partially, brightly what she knows dimly. She thus cannot fully rest in her natural end. She perhaps hasn't lost all hope, but she "lives on in desire." But even within this consensus, there are a great variety of opinions as to how sad or happy she will be, corresponding to the nature of the elicited desire. Some have argued that she would not know that the beatific vision is possible, only that it is fitting. Thus the desire would be a wish (*velleity*); she would desire it on the condition that it is possible, not knowing whether it is possible. Others argue that it is demonstrably possible. As such, it seems the desire would be stronger, perhaps unconditional, and she would be sadder without it.

It seems to me that these traditional Thomist options are compatible with the new Thomist view of original sin. It also seems that there are non-Thomist positions of natural desire compatible with a Thomist view of original sin. Take Scotus, for example. In keeping with his view that the beatific vision is natural qua perfecting, he holds that there is a natural desire for the beatific vision insofar as the soul without the vision stands in a relation of perfectibility to it. As Wolter puts it, "an *appetitus naturalis* is simply an ontological relationship between any faculty (or the soul) and that which perfects it."[48] Whether or not this is the best way to think of natural desire, I don't see any contradiction between this view and the affirmation that sin is the lack of grace. The view that natural desire is fundamentally the same as habitual sanctifying grace is, it seems, incompatible with Thomism.

For theologians who do not affirm limbo or the need to ground the gratuity of grace in God's ability to have created a state of pure nature, it may be the case that not only do no human beings achieve the natural end in this world; it may be the case that God would never leave a human being with only her natural end in *any* world. But the importance of the natural end remains, because it is what human beings are actually directed to in the real world for as long as they are only in original sin. The question remains, then. What happens in this world when infants with original sin reach the age of reason? There are several possible answers. The first is Thomas's own solution, discussed in Chapter 4. Grace intervenes, and everyone is quickly divided up into two groups: those pursuing God in grace and those in mortal sin. A second option would be to accept the possibility that some people, of their own natural power, avoid mortal sin. In order to avoid contradicting Paul, one could distinguish mortal from venial sin. Everyone commits venial sins (which don't orient the person to the creature), not everyone sins mortally. Since fulfillment of the natural law requires the avoidance of all sin simpliciter, no one can fulfill the natural law. A third option would be to hold that human beings are "radically evil": every human who reaches the age of reason freely sins mortally.

I have argued that my proposed revision of Thomas's account of original sin does not require the absurd consequences that, prima facie, it might seem to entail. It is compatible with a variety of views on the possibility of a state of human nature without sanctifying grace, the natural desire for God, and justification and merit. My account does require what I have called "the individual distinction" between human nature and sanctifying grace, as well as the affirmation that the human being retains the natural orientation to God. There are, of course, other objections that could be raised. They will have to be discussed elsewhere, because our time here is almost over.

[48] Wolter, "Duns Scotus on the Natural Desire for the Supernatural," 140.

Conclusion

Many people today believe that the doctrine of original sin is pernicious, antibiblical, irrational, and opposed to the deliverances of the scientific community. A significant number of Christians share at least some of these concerns or objections, while at the same time believing that the doctrine is part of their faith. In constructive and critical dialogue with the most important accounts of original sin in the history of theology, this book has sought to respond to these concerns (focusing on those raised by evolution). Here I review the major arguments of the book and suggest a few directions for future research.

In the course of developing my own interpretation of the doctrine, I discussed several aspects of its history. Against the common assumption that Augustine invented original sin, I suggested that its roots lie in Paul's teaching that sin and death are intertwined. By the fourth century, a number of Christians believed that "sin" should normally be predicated of infants. Augustine proffered a powerful interpretation of the doctrine that relied heavily on the hypothesis that humanity was, or was in, Adam. His account was crying out for clarification, given the ambiguity of that crucial claim. Medieval theologians asked, "How *could* we have been united with Adam?" Theories proliferated. Was it because we acted in him, as Anselm argued? Was it because God judged us together with him, as Abelard claimed? Or was it because our body was part of his body, as Peter Lombard stated?

Our discussion of these figures was intended to prepare for the book's primary historical contribution, a close reading (and evaluation) of Thomas's account of original sin. We took into consideration his longest treatments of the doctrine, in the *Scriptum* and *De malo*, and I argued that they shed light on the semantics of *"natura"* in the *Summa theologiae*. Original sin is a privation of the gift of grace, not nature. We are in Adam because we are outside Christ. The Spirit leads us beyond merely human existence to a deified participation in the inner life of the Holy Trinity. I argued that Thomas's mature thought implied that original justice couldn't have been sexually transmitted, and that, even if it could have, it would not affect the culpability of infants who inherit the lack of justice. (These are two key reasons I gave for modifying Thomas's account in Chapter 7.)

Future research might ask how Thomas's doctrine of original sin relates to other interesting aspects of his theological anthropology. How might, for example, his view of the desire for God relate to his account of the Fall? I remained neutral after discussing the basics of this question in Chapter 8. A more in-depth study of the links between Thomas's hamartiology and account of the desire for God might prove to have interesting implications for our understanding of the latter.

In the second half of the book, I proposed that Thomas's thought can help light the way toward a solution to a modern problem. How should we understand the doctrine of original sin in light of evolution? There are three major challenges that evolution poses to the doctrine. There is the problem of our "continuous" or gradual origins. It does not make sense, in light of gradual evolution by natural selection, to affirm that a single action "corrupted" human nature. There is the problem of the "complexity" of our origins: human beings are not naturally disposed to only good actions. Finally, there is the problem of our "communal" origins – the indication of population genetics that humanity first evolved in at least one fairly large group. I discussed important modern accounts of the doctrine of original sin – some of which are able to respond adequately to the challenge of evolution – but, despite their advantages and in some cases brilliance, I found them theologically wanting.

I proposed a new version of Thomas's account of original sin that has major theological advantages in its own right and can respond to the challenge of evolution. Original sin is the lack of sanctifying grace, human nature's need for friendship with Jesus Christ. This view does not involve the claim that human nature or DNA has been corrupted. It is open to the hypothesis that evolution has selected for both good and evil behaviors. And it does not depend on humanity's descent from a single ancestral pair, or even a single ancestral group. This view does not involve the claim that Adam's personal guilt is transmitted to infants or reduce sin to volition.

One clear direction for future research is a broader consideration of Scripture and original sin. I engaged Romans 5 and its implications for originated original sin, but the scope of the study precluded discussion of the *locus classicus* of the Fall and originating original sin: Genesis 3. How should we understand Genesis, the Fall, and other biblical texts that bear on origins and hamartiology? Other directions for research would involve thinking through the systematic connection between original sin and other doctrines in more depth – the doctrine of the atonement, for example. It strikes me that my proposed theory of original sin is compatible with a variety of theories of the atonement, as long as they are open – as Thomas was – to the possibility that Christ died for different kinds of sins, sins which correspond to degrees of culpability and, indeed, in the case of infants, no personal guilt at all.

We began this study with the story of Tess's sorrow over Sorrow. She represents the grief of parents who believed the children they had lost were lost to God. This sorrow is the natural result of one prominent theory of original sin. However, on the theory developed in this book, the sin that should be predicated of infants signifies the lack of the due sanctifying grace of the Holy Spirit. To say that a child is born in sin is thus not to say that she is hated or rejected by Jesus. It is rather to say that she has a *vocation* to know and love Jesus. The doctrine of original sin means that every human being, even the littlest, is called to the knowledge and love of Christ, for it is "to such as these that the kingdom of heaven belongs" (Matt. 19:14).

Select Bibliography

PRIMARY SOURCES

Abelard, Peter. *Commentaria in epistolam Pauli ad Romanos*. Ed. Eligius Buytaert (CCCM 11). Turnhout, 1969.

Anselm of Canterbury. *Cur deus homo. Opera Omnia*, vol. 2. Ed. Franciscus Salesius Schmitt. Rome, 1940.

De conceptu virginali et de originali peccato. Opera Omnia, vol. 2. Ed. Franciscus Salesius Schmitt. Rome, 1940.

Aquinas, Thomas. *Compendium theologiae*: S. Thomae Aquinatis doctoris angelici *Opera Omnia iussu Leonis XIII*, vol. 42, cura et studio Fratrum Praedicatorum. Rome, 1979.

Quaestiones disputatae de anima: S. Thomae Aquinatis doctoris angelici *Opera Omnia iussu Leonis XIII*, vol. 45, cura et studio Fratrum Praedicatorum. Rome, 1996. [*De anima*]

Quaestiones disputatae de malo: S. Thomae Aquinatis doctoris angelici *Opera Omnia iussu Leonis XIII*, vol. 23, cura et studio Fratrum Praedicatorum. Rome, 1982. [*De malo*]

Quaestiones disputatae de veritate: S. Thomae Aquinatis doctoris angelici *Opera Omnia iussu Leonis XIII*, vol. 22, 3/1: qq. 21–29, cura et studio Fratrum Praedicatorum. Rome, 1973. [*De veritate*]

Scriptum super Libros Sententiarum magistri Petri Lombardi episcopi Parisiensis, vol. 2. Ed. Pierre Mandonnet. Paris, 1929. [*Scriptum*]

Summa theologiae: S. Thomae Aquinatis doctoris angelici *Opera Omnia iussu Leonis XIII*, vols. 4–12, cura et studio Fratrum Praedicatorum. Rome, 1888–1906. [*STh*]

Super Epistolas S. Pauli Lectura. Turin: Marietti, 1953.

Augustine of Hippo. *De civitate Dei libri XXII*. Ed. B. Dombart and A. Kalb (CCL 47–8). Turnhout, 1955.

Cajetan, Thomas de Vio. *Commentaria in Summa theologiae*. S. Thomae Aquinatis doctoris angelici *Opera Omnia iussu Leonis XIII*, vol. 7, cura et studio Fratrum Praedicatorum. Rome, 1892.

Gregory of Nyssa. *De infantibus praemature abreptis*; Gregorii Nysseni ΓΡΗΓΟΡ-ΙΟΥ ΕΠΙΣΚΟΠΟΥ ΝΥΣΣΗΣ ΠΡΟΣ ΙΕΠΙΟΝ ΠΕΡΙ ΤΩΝ ΠΡΟ ΩΠΑΣ ΑΝΑΡΠΑΖΟΜΕ-ΝΩΝ ΝΗΠΙΩΝ. *Opera Dogmatica Minora*, vol 3. Ed. Hadwiga Horner. Leiden, 1987.

Lombard, Peter. *Sententiae in IV libris distinctae*, 2 vols. Ed. Ignatius Brady (SpicBon 4/5). Grottaferrata, 1971/81.

OTHER SOURCES

Alexander, Denis. *Creation or Evolution? Do We Have to Choose?* Oxford: Monarch Books, 2014.

Genes, Determinism, God. Cambridge: Cambridge University Press, 2017.

Altaner, Berthold. *Patrologie*. Freiburg: Herder, 1958.

Anderson, Gary A. "*Necessarium Adae Peccatum*: The Problem of Original Sin." In *Sin, Death, and the Devil*, ed. Carl E. Braaten and Robert W. Jenson, 22–44. Grand Rapids, MI: Eerdmans, 2000.

Augustine. *The City of God against the Pagans*. Trans. R. W. Dyson. Cambridge: Cambridge University Press, 1998.

The Works of Saint Augustine: A New Translation for the 21st Century. Hyde Park, NY: New City Press, 1990.

Austriaco, Nicanor Pier Giorgio. "A Theological Fittingness Argument for the Historicity of the Fall of *Homo sapiens*." *Nova et Vetera* 13 (2015): 651–67.

Austriaco, Nicanor Pier Giorgio, James Brent, Thomas Davenport, and John Baptist Ku, eds. *Thomistic Evolution: A Catholic Approach to Understanding Evolution in the Light of Faith*. Providence, RI: Cluny Media, 2016.

Ayala, Francisco J., and Camilo J. Cela-Conde. *Processes in Human Evolution: The Journey from Early Hominins to Neanderthals and Modern Humans*. Oxford: Oxford University Press, 2017.

Babcock, William S. "Augustine on Sin and Moral Agency." *The Journal of Religious Ethics* 16 (1988): 28–55.

Backus, Irena, and Aza Goudriaan. "'Semipelagianism': The Origins of the Term and Its Passage into the History of Heresy." *The Journal of Ecclesiastical History* 65.1 (2014): 25–46.

Bagby, Stephen. *Sin in Origen's Commentary on Romans*. Lanham, MD: Lexington, 2018.

Barth, Karl. *Church Dogmatics*. Ed. G. W. Bromiley and T. F. Torrance. Trans. G. W. Bromiley. London: T&T Clark; New York: Continuum, 2009.

Bartmann, Bernhard. *Lehrbuch der Dogmatik*, vol. 1. Freiburg: Herder, 1932.

Beatrice, Pier Franco. *The Transmission of Sin: Augustine and the Pre-Augustinian Sources*. Trans. Adam Kamesar. Oxford: Oxford University Press, 2013.

Beiting, Christopher. "The Idea of Limbo in Thomas Aquinas." *The Thomist* 62 (1998): 217–44.

Berry, R. J., and T. A. Noble, eds. *Darwin, Creation and the Fall: Theological Challenges*. Nottingham: Apollos, 2009.

Billings, J. Todd. *Calvin, Participation, and the Gift: The Activity of Believers in Union with Christ*. Oxford: Oxford University Press, 2007.

Blankenhorn, Bernhard. "The Instrumental Causality of the Sacraments: Thomas Aquinas and Louis-Marie Chauvet." *Nova et Vetera*, English edition, 4.2 (2006): 255–94.

Blocher, Henri. *Original Sin: Illuminating the Riddle*. Grand Rapids, MI: Eerdmans, 1997.

Bonino, Serge-Thomas. "La théorie des limbes et le mystère du surnaturel chez saint Thomas d'Aquin." *Revue Thomiste* 101 (2001): 131–66.

Bonner, Gerald. *St. Augustine of Hippo: Life and Controversies*. Norwich: Canterbury Press, 1986.

Bonnette, Dennis. *Origin of the Human Species*, 3rd ed. Ave Maria, FL: Sapientia Press, 2014.

Bouillard, Henri. *Conversion et grâce chez s. Thomas d'Aquin*. Paris: Aubier, 1944.

Bowlin, John. "Nature's Grace: Aquinas and Wittgenstein on Natural Law and Moral Knowledge." In *Grammar and Grace: Reformulations of Aquinas and Wittgenstein*, ed. Jeffrey Stout and Robert MacSwain, 154–74. London: SCM, 2004.

Boyce, James. *Born Bad: Original Sin and the Making of the Western World*. Berkeley: Counterpoint, 2015.

Bradley, Denis J. M. *Aquinas on the Twofold Human Good: Reason and Human Happiness in Aquinas's Moral Science*. Washington, DC: Catholic University of America Press, 1999.

Brand, Miryam. *Evil within and Without: The Source of Sin and Its Nature as Portrayed in Second Temple Literature*. Göttingen: Vandenhoeck & Ruprecht, 2013.

Brower, Jeffrey E. "Anselm on Ethics." In *The Cambridge Companion to Anselm*, ed. Brian Davies and Brian Leftow, 222–57. Cambridge: Cambridge University Press, 2004.

Brown, Peter. *Augustine of Hippo: A Biography*. Berkeley: University of California Press, 1967.

——— "Pelagius and His Supporters: Aims and Environment." *Journal of Theological Studies*, New Series, 19.1 (1968): 93–114.

Burggren, Warren. "Epigenetic Inheritance and Its Role in Evolutionary Biology: Re-evaluation and New Perspectives." *Biology* 5.24 (2016): 1–22.

Burkhardt, Richard. *The Spirit of System: Lamarck and Evolutionary Biology*. Cambridge, MA: Harvard University Press, 1995 [1977].

Calvin, John. *Commentaries on the Last Four Books of Moses, Arranged in the Form of a Harmony*. Vol. 1. Trans. Charles Bingham. Grand Rapids, MI: CCEL, 1852.

——— *Institutionis Christianae Religionis*. Ed. F. G. Tholuck. Berolini, 1834.

Cann, Rebecca L., Mark Stoneking, and Allan C. Wilson. "Mitochondrial DNA and Human Evolution." *Nature* 325 (1987): 31–6.

Cavanaugh, William T., and James K. A., Smith, eds. *Evolution and the Fall*. Grand Rapids, MI: Eerdmans, 2017.

Clarke, Norris. "Person, Being, and St. Thomas." *Communio* 19 (1992): 601–18.

Coffey, David. "The Whole Rahner on the Supernatural Existential." *Theological Studies* 65 (2004): 95–118.

Collins, R. "Evolution and Original Sin." In *Perspectives on an Evolving Creation*, ed. K. B. Miller, 469–501. Grand Rapids, MI: Eerdmans, 2003.

Colish, Marcia L. *Peter Lombard*. Leiden: E. J. Brill, 1994.

Cortez, Marc. "What Does It Mean to Call Karl Barth a 'Christocentric Theologian'?" *Scottish Journal of Theology* 60.2 (2007): 1–17.

Couenhoven, Jesse. "Karl Barth's Conception(s) of Human and Divine Freedom (s)." In *Commanding Grace: Studies in Karl Barth's Ethics*, ed. Daniel L. Migliore, 239–55. Grand Rapids, MI: Eerdmans, 2010.

"St. Augustine's Doctrine of Original Sin." *Augustinian Studies* 36.2 (2005): 359–96.

Stricken by Sin, Cured by Christ: Agency, Necessity, and Culpability in Augustinian Theology. Oxford: Oxford University Press, 2013.

Courtneay, William J. "The Dialectic of Omnipotence in the High and Late Middle Ages." In *Divine Omniscience and Omnipotence in Medieval Philosophy: Islamic, Jewish, and Christian Perspectives*, ed. Tamar Rudavsky, 243–69. Boston: D. Reidel, 1995.

Cranfield, C. E. B. *A Critical and Exegetical Commentary on the Epistle to the Romans*, vol. 1. Edinburgh: T&T Clark, 1975.

Cress, Donald A. "Augustine's Privation Account of Evil." *Augustinian Studies* 20 (1989): 105–23.

Crisp, Oliver D. *An American Augustinian: Sin and Salvation in the Dogmatic Theology of William G. T. Shedd*. Milton Keynes: Paternoster, 2007.

Jonathan Edwards and the Metaphysics of Sin. Aldershot: Ashgate, 2005.

"On Original Sin." *International Journal of Systematic Theology* 17.3 (2015): 252–66.

Croasmun, Matthew. *The Emergence of Sin: The Cosmic Tyrant in Romans*. Oxford: Oxford University Press, 2017.

Cross, Richard. *Duns Scotus*. Oxford: Oxford University Press, 1999.

Crouzel, Henri. *Origen: The Life and Times of the First Great Theologian*. Trans. A. S. Worrall. San Francisco: Harper & Row, 1989.

Cunningham, Conor. *Darwin's Pious Idea: Why the Ultra-Darwinists and Creationists Both Get It Wrong*. Grand Rapids, MI: Eerdmans, 2010.

Dabrowski, Wieslaw. "La dottrina sul peccato originale nei commenti di san Thommaso d'Aquino alle lettere di san Paolo Apostolo." *Angelicum* 83 (2006): 557–629.

Davies, Brian. "Introduction" to *On Evil*. Translation of Thomas Aquinas's *De malo* by Richard Regan. Oxford: Oxford University Press, 2003.

Thomas Aquinas's *Summa Contra Gentiles*: A Guide and Commentary. Oxford: Oxford University Press, 2016.

Davis, William A., Jr. "The Rape of Tess: Hardy, English Law, and the Case for Sexual Assault." *Nineteenth-Century Literature* 52.2 (1997): 221–31.

Dawkins, Richard. *The Selfish Gene*. Oxford: Oxford University Press, 2016 [1976].

De Boer, Martinus C. *The Defeat of Death: Apocalyptic Eschatology in 1 Corinthians 15 and Romans 5*. Sheffield: JSOT Press, 1988.

De Letter, P. "Original Sin, Privation of Original Justice." *The Thomist* 17 (1954): 469–509.

De Lubac, Henri. *Augustinisme et théologie moderne*. Paris: Les Éditions du Cerf, 2008.

Decosimo, David. *Ethics as a Work of Charity: Thomas Aquinas and Pagan Virtue*. Stanford: Stanford University Press, 2014.

Denlinger, Adam C. *Omnes in Adam ex pacto Dei*: Ambrogio Catarino's Doctrine of Covenantal Solidarity and Its Influence on Post-Reformation Reformed Theologians. Göttingen: Vandenhoeck & Roprecht, 2011.

Denzinger, Heinrich. *Enchiridion Symbolorum: A Compendium of Creeds, Definitions, and Declarations of the Catholic Church*, 43rd ed. Ed. Peter Hünnerman. San Francisco: Ignatius Press, 2012.

Dewan, Lawrence. "Natural Law and the First Act of Freedom: Maritain Revisited." In *Wisdom, Law, and Virtue: Essays in Thomistic Ethics*, 221–42. New York: Fordham University Press, 2008.

Di Noia, J. A. "Not 'Born Bad': The Catholic Truth about Original Sin in a Thomistic Perspective." *The Thomist* 81.3 (2017): 345–59.

DiCenso, James J. *Kant's Religion within the Boundaries of Mere Reason: A Commentary*. Cambridge: Cambridge University Press, 2012.

Dole, Andrew. *Schleiermacher on Religion and the Natural Order*. Oxford: Oxford University Press, 2010.

Domning, Daryl P., and Monika K. Hellwig. *Original Selfishness: Original Sin and Evil in Light of Evolution*. Burlington, VT: Ashgate, 2006.

Dorrien, Gary. *The Making of American Liberal Theology: Imagining Progressive Religion, 1805–1900*. Louisville: Westminster John Knox Press, 2001.

Downing, Andrew. "Sin and Its Relevance to Human Nature in the *Summa Theologiae*." *The Heythrop Journal* 50 (2009): 793–805.

Drecoll, Volker Henning. *Die Entstehung der Gnadenlehre Augustins*. Tübingen: Mohr Siebeck, 1999.

Dubarle, André-Marie. *Le Péché originel. Écriture et tradition*. Paris: Cerf, 1999. "La Pluralité des péchés héréditaires dans la tradition augustinienne." *Revue des etudes augustiniennes* 2 (1957): 113–36.

Duffy, Stephen J. "Our Hearts of Darkness: Original Sin Revisited." *Theological Studies* 49 (1988): 597–622.

Dunn, James D. G. *Romans 1–8*. Dallas: Word Books, 1988.

Dupont, Anthony. "Original Sin in Tertullian and Cyprian: Conceptual Presence and Pre-Augustinian Content?" *Revue d'études augustiniennes et patristiques* 63 (2017): 1–29.

Ereshefsky, Marc, "Species." In *The Stanford Encyclopedia of Philosophy* (Fall 2017 edition), ed. Edward N. Zalta. https://plato.stanford.edu/archives/fall2017/entries/species/.

Espenberger, Johanes. *Elemente der Erbsünde nach Augustin und der Frühscholastik*. Mainz: Verlag von Kirchheim, 1905.

Evans, G. R. *Augustine on Evil*. Cambridge: Cambridge University Press, 1982.

Feingold, Lawrence. *The Natural Desire to See God According to St. Thomas and His Interpreters*. Naples, FL: Sapientia Press, 2010.

Firestone, Chris L., and Nathan Jacobs. *In Defense of Kant's Religion*. Blooming-ton: Indiana University Press, 2008.

Fitzmyer, Joseph A. *Romans: A New Translation with Introduction and Commentary*. New York: Doubleday, 1993.

Fitzpatrick, Edmund J. *The Sin of Adam in the Writings of Saint Thomas Aquinas*. Mundelein: Saint Mary of the Lake Seminary, 1950.

Frediksen, Paula. *Sin: The Early History of an Idea*. Princeton: Princeton University Press, 2012.

Gagnebet, M.-Rosaire. "L'amour naturel de Dieu chez saint Thomas et ses contemporains (II)." *Revue Thomiste* 49 (1949): 31–102.

Garrigou-Lagrange, Réginald. *De Deo Trino et Creatore: Commentarius in Summam Theologicam S. Thomae (Ia q. xxvii–cxix)*. Taurini: Marietti and Descleé de Brouwer, 1943.

"La mortification et les suites du péché original." *La vie spirituelle* 12 (1925): 17–31.

"Utrum gratia sanctificans fuerit in Adamo dos naturae an donum personae tantum." *Angelicum* 2 (1925): 133–44.

Gaudel, A. "Péché originel." In *Dictionnaire de Théologie Catholique* 12 (1933): 275–606.

Gaventa, Beverly Roberts. *Our Mother Saint Paul*. Louisville: Westminster John Knox Press, 2007.

Gavrilyuk, Paul L. "The Retrieval of Deification: How a Once-Despised Archaism Became an Ecumenical Desideratum." *Modern Theology* 25.4 (2009): 647–59.

George, Marie I. "Aquinas on Intelligent Extra-Terrestrial Life." *The Thomist* 65 (2001): 239–58.

Gerrish, B. A. "Schleiermacher, Friedrich Daniel Ernst." In *The Oxford Companion to Christian Thought*, ed. Adrian Hastings, Alistair Mason, and Hugh Pyper, 644–6. Oxford: Oxford University Press, 2000.

Givens, Terryl L. *When Souls Had Wings: Pre-mortal Existence in Western Thought*. Oxford: Oxford University Press, 2010.

Goethe, Johann Wolfgang von. *Goethes Briefe*, 4 vols. Hamburg: Christian Wegner Verlag, 1964.

Gombis, Timothy G. "Paul." In the *T&T Clark Companion to the Doctrine of Sin*, ed. Keith L. Johnson and David Lauber, 97–110. New York: T&T Clark, 2016.

Green, Richard E., et al. "A Draft Sequence of the Neandertal Genome." *Science* 328.5979 (2010): 710–22.

Grimm, Stephen R. "Kant's Argument for Radical Evil." *European Journal of Philosophy* 10.2 (2002): 160–77.

Grisez, Germain. "The True Ultimate End of Human Beings: The Kingdom, Not God Alone." *Theological Studies* 69 (2008): 38–61.

The Way of the Lord Jesus, vol. 1: Christian Moral Principles. Chicago: Franciscan Herald Press, 1983.

Gross, Julius. *Geschichte des Erbsündendogmas: Ein Beitrag zur Geschichte des Problems vom Ursprung des Übels*. 4 vols. München: Ernst Reinhardt, 1960–72.

Hall, Peter, ed. *The Harmony of the Protestant Confessions: Exhibiting the Faith of the Churches of Christ, Reformed after the Pure and Holy Doctrine of the Gospel, throughout Europe*. London: John F. Shaw, 1842.

Hardy, Thomas. *Tess of the d'Urbervilles: A Pure Woman*. London: Folio Society, 1991.

Hare, John. *The Moral Gap: Kantian Ethics, Human Limits and God's Assistance*. Oxford: Clarendon, 1996.

Haught, John F. *God after Darwin: A Theology of Evolution*, 2nd ed. Boulder: Westview Press, 2008.

Helm, Paul. *Calvin at the Centre*. Oxford: Oxford University Press, 2010.

Henrici, Peter. "The Philosophers and Original Sin." *Communio* 18 (1991): 489–501.

Hervé, J. M. *Manuale theologiae dogmaticae*. Vol 2. Paris: Berche et Pagis, 1935.

Hick, John. *Evil and the God of Love*. New York: Palgrave Macmillan, 2010.

Hiestand, Gerald. "A More Modest Adam: An Exploration of Irenaeus' Anthropology in Light of the Darwinian Account of Pre-Fall Death." *Bulletin of Ecclesial Theology* 5.1 (2018): 55–72.

Hochschild, Joshua P. The Semantics of Analogy: Rereading Cajetan's *De Nominum Analogia*. Notre Dame: University of Notre Dame Press, 2010.

Holte, Ragnar. *Béatitude et sagesse: Saint Augustin et le problème de la fin de l'homme dans la philosophie ancienne*. Paris: Études augustiniennes, 1962.

Houck, Daniel W. "*Natura Humana Relicta est Christo*: Thomas Aquinas on the Effects of Original Sin." *Archa Verbi* 13 (2016): 68–102.

"Original Sin in Abelard's Commentary on Romans." In *Being Saved: Explorations in Soteriology and Human Ontology*, ed. Marc Cortez, Joshua Farris, and S. Mark Hamilton, 54–67. London: SCM Press, 2018.

Hudson, Hud. *The Fall and Hypertime*. Oxford: Oxford University Press, 2014.

Hütter, Reinhard. "*Desiderium Naturale Visionis Dei – Est autem duplex hominis beatitudo sive felicitas*: Some Observations about Lawrence Feingold's and John Milbank's Recent Interventions in the Debate over the Natural Desire to See God." *Nova et Vetera*, English edition, 5.1 (2007): 81–132.

Janz, Denis R. *Luther and Late Medieval Thomism*. Waterloo: Wilfrid Laurier University Press, 1982.

Jewett, Robert. *Romans: A Commentary*. Minneapolis, MN: Fortress, 2007.

Johnson, Mark F. "Augustine and Aquinas on Original Sin: Doctrine, Authority, and Pedagogy." In *Aquinas the Augustinian*, ed. M. Dauphinais, B. David, and M. Levering, 145–58. Washington, DC: Catholic University of America Press, 2007.

"St Thomas and the 'Law of Sin.'" *Recherches de théologie et philosophie médiévale* 67 (2000): 80–95.

Kant, Immanuel. *Lectures on Religion*. In *Religion and Rational Theology*, ed. and trans. Allen Wood and George di Giovanni. Cambridge: Cambridge University Press, 1996.

Metaphysics of Morals. In *Practical Philosophy*, ed. and trans. Mary J. Gregor. Cambridge: Cambridge University Press, 1996.

Religion within the Limits of Reason Alone. Trans. Theodore M. Green and Hoyt H. Hudson. New York: Harper and Brothers, 1960.

Kaup, Julian. "Die Begründung des Schuldcharakters der Erbsünde bei Thomas von Aquin und ihre Kritik durch Johannes Peckham und Petrus Johannis Olivi." In *Wahrheit und Verkündigung: Michael Schmaus zum 70. Geburtstag*, vol. 1, ed. L. Scheffczyk, W. Dettloff, and Richard Heinzmann, 851–76. München: Schöningh, 1967.

Kemp, Kenneth W. "Science, Theology, and Monogenesis." *American Catholic Philosophical Quarterly* 85 (2011): 217–36.

Kidner, Derek. *Genesis: An Introduction and Commentary*. Downers Grove, IL: InterVarsity Press, 2008 [1967].

Kleffman, Tom. *Die Erbsündenlehre in sprachtheologischem Horizont: Eine Interpretation Augustins, Luthers und Hamanns*. Tübingen: J. C. B. Mohr (Paul Siebeck), 1994.

Klima, Gyula. "The Medieval Problem of Universals." In *The Stanford Encyclopedia of Philosophy* (Fall 2013 edition), ed. Edward N. Zalta. http://plato.stanford.edu/entries/universals-medieval/, accessed January 10, 2016.

Kors, J. B. *La Justice primitive et le péché originel d'après S. Thomas*. Paris: Bibliothèque Thomiste, 1922.

Korsmeyer, Jerry D. *Evolution and Eden: Balancing Original Sin and Contemporary Science*. New York: Paulist Press, 1998.

Köster, Henrich M. *Urstand, Fall und Erbsünde in der Scholastik*. Freiburg: Herder, 1979.

Labourdette, M. M. *Le Péché originel et les origines de l'homme*. Paris: Alsatia, 1953.

Laland, Kevin, Gregory Wray, Hopi Hoekstra, et al. "Does Evolutionary Theory Need a Rethink?" *Nature* 514 (2014): 161–4.

Lamoureux, Denis O. "Beyond Original Sin: Is a Theological Paradigm Shift Inevitable?" *Perspectives on Science and Christian Faith* 67.1 (2015): 35–49.

Lawler, M. G. "Grace and Free Will in Justification." *The Thomist* 35 (1971): 601–30.

Levering, Matthew. *Engaging the Doctrine of Creation: Cosmos, Creatures, and the Wise and Good Creator*. Grand Rapids, MI: Baker Academic, 2017.

Livingstone, David. *Adam's Ancestors: Race, Religion, and the Politics of Human Origins*. Baltimore: Johns Hopkins University Press, 2008.

Lockett, Leslie. *Anglo-Saxon Psychologies in the Vernacular and Latin Traditions*. Toronto: University of Toronto Press, 2011.

Lombardo, Nicholas. *The Logic of Desire: Aquinas on Emotion*. Washington, DC: Catholic University of America Press, 2011.

Lonergan, Bernard. *Grace and Freedom: Operative Grace in the Thought of St. Thomas Aquinas*. Toronto: University of Toronto Press, 2000.

Long, Steven A. *Natura Pura: On the Recovery of Nature in the Doctrine of Grace*. New York: Fordham University Press, 2010.

Lottin, D. Odon. "Le péché originel chez Albert le Grand, Bonaventure et Thomas d'Aquin." *Recherches de Théologie ancienne et médiévale* 12 (1940): 275–328.

Psychologie et morale aux XIIe et XIIIe siècles, Tom. IV: Problèmes de morale, troisième partie. Louvain, 1954.

Lyonnet, S. "Le Péché Originel et l'exégèse de Rom. 5, 12–14." *Recherches de science religieuse* 44 (1956): 63–84.

Madueme, Hans. "'The Most Vulnerable Part of the Whole Christian Account': Original Sin and Modern Science." In *Adam, the Fall, and Original Sin: Theological, Biblical, and Scientific Perspectives*, ed. Hans Madueme and Michael Reeves, 225–49. Grand Rapids, MI: Baker Academic, 2014.

Magrath, Oswin. "St. Thomas's Theory of Original Sin." *The Thomist* 16.2 (1953): 161–89.

Mahoney, Jack. *Christianity in Evolution: An Exploration.* Washington, DC: Georgetown University Press, 2011.

Mansini, Guy. "Lonergan on the Natural Desire in the Light of Feingold." *Nova et Vetera*, English edition, 5.1 (2007): 185–98.

Marenbon, John. *The Philosophy of Peter Abelard.* Cambridge: Cambridge University Press, 1997.

Marshall, Bruce D. "Aquinas as Postliberal Theologian." *The Thomist* 53.3 (1989): 353–402.

"*Beatus vir*: Aquinas, Romans 4, and the Role of 'Reckoning' in Justification." In *Reading Romans with Saint Thomas Aquinas*, ed. Matthew Levering and Michael Dauphinais, 216–38. Washington, DC: Catholic University of America Press, 2012.

"Christ the End of Analogy." In *The Analogy of Being: Invention of the Antichrist or the Wisdom of God?*, ed. Thomas Joseph White, 280–313. Grand Rapids, MI: Eerdmans, 2011.

"Debt, Punishment, and Payment: A Meditation on the Cross, in Light of St. Anselm." *Nova et Vetera*, English edition, 9.1 (2011): 163–81.

"*Ex Occidente Lux?* Aquinas and Eastern Orthodox Theology." *Modern Theology* 20.1 (2004): 23–50.

"Faith and Reason Reconsidered: Aquinas and Luther on Deciding What Is True." *The Thomist* 63.1 (1999): 1–48.

"Justification as Declaration and Deification." *International Journal of Systematic Theology* 4.1 (2002): 3–28.

"Look on the Faith of Your Church: Mary's Assent and the Task of Theology." *Nova et Vetera*, English edition, 13.2 (2015): 419–39.

"*Quod Scit Una Uetula*: Aquinas on the Nature of Theology." In *The Theology of Thomas Aquinas*, ed. Joseph Wawrykow and Rik Van Nieuwenhove, 1–35. Notre Dame: University of Notre Dame Press, 2005.

"Religion and Election: Aquinas on Natural Law, Judaism, and Salvation in Christ." *Nova et Vetera*, English edition, 14.1 (2016): 61–125.

Trinity and Truth. Cambridge: Cambridge University Press, 2000.

Martin, R. M. "La doctrina sobre el pecado original en la Summa contra Gentiles." *La Ciencia Tomista* 10 (1915): 389–400.

"La question du péché originel dans Saint Anselme." *Revue des sciences philosophiques et théologiques* 5 (1911): 735–48.

Mausbach, Joseph. *Die Ethik des Heilegen Augustinus.* Vol 2. Freiburg: Herdersche Verlagshandlung, 1909.

McCabe, Hebert. *God Still Matters.* London: Continuum, 2005 [2002].

McCormack, Bruce L. "Karl Barth's Version of an 'Analogy of Being': A Dialectical No and Yes to Roman Catholicism." In *The Analogy of Being: Invention of the Antichrist or the Wisdom of God?*, ed. Thomas Joseph White, 88–144. Grand Rapids, MI: Eerdmans, 2011.

McDermott, Timothy. "Original Sin, I & II." *New Blackfriars* 49 January–February (1968).

McFadyen, Alistair. *Bound to Sin: Abuse, Holocaust and the Christian Doctrine of Sin*. Cambridge: Cambridge University Press, 2000.

McFarland, Ian A. *In Adam's Fall: A Meditation on the Christian Doctrine of Original Sin*. West Sussex: Wiley-Blackwell, 2010.

"Original Sin." In *T&T Clark Companion to the Doctrine of Sin*, ed. Keith L. Johnson and David Lauber, 303–18. New York: Bloomsbury T&T Clark, 2016.

McGrath, Alister E. *Reformation Thought: An Introduction*. Malden, MA: Blackwell, 1999.

Merlin, Nicolas. *Saint Augustin et les dogmes de péché originel et de la grâce*. Paris: Librairie Letouzey, 1931.

Mews, Constant J. *Abelard and Heloise*. Oxford: Oxford University Press, 2005.

Meyer, Matthias, et al. "A High-Coverage Genome Sequence from an Archaic Denisovan Individual," *Science* 338 (2012): 222–6.

Meyer, Nicholas A. *Adam's Dust and Adam's Glory in the Hodayot and the Letters of Paul: Rethinking Anthropogony and Theology*. Leiden: Brill, 2016.

Milbank, John. *The Suspended Middle: Henri de Lubac and the Renewed Split in Modern Catholic Theology*. Grand Rapids, MI: Eerdmans, 2014.

Miles, Rebekah. "Valerie Saiving Reconsidered." *Journal of Feminist Studies in Religion* 28.1 (Spring 2012): 79–86.

Miller, Eddis N. *Kant's "Religion within the Boundaries of Mere Reason": A Reader's Guide*. New York: Bloomsbury, 2015.

Mohler, Albert R., Jr. "The New Shape of the Debate." *Southern Seminary Magazine* (Winter 2011): 22–6.

Mulchahey, M. Michèle. *"First the Bow Is Bent in Study …": Dominican Education before 1350*. Toronto: Pontifical Institute of Mediaeval Studies, 1998.

Mulhall, Stephen. *Philosophical Myths of the Fall*. Princeton: Princeton University Press, 2005.

Nisula, Timo. *Augustine and the Functions of Concupiscence*. Boston: Brill, 2012.

Noll, Mark. "Charles Hodge." In *Reading Romans through the Centuries: From the Early Church to Karl Barth*, ed. Jeffrey Greenman and Timothy Larsen, 169–86. Grand Rapids, MI: Brazos, 2005.

Nowak, Martin A., and Sarah Coakley, eds. *Evolution, Games, and God*. Cambridge, MA: Harvard University Press, 2013.

O'Brien, T. C. "Fallen Nature." In appendix 9 to vol. 26 of the Summa theologiae *Ia2æ*, ed. T. C. O'Brien, 154–61. New York: McGraw-Hill, 1965.

O'Donovan, Oliver. *The Problem of Self-Love in Augustine*. London: Yale University Press, 1980.

Oliva, Adriano. "La contemplation des philosophes selon Thomas d'Aquin." *Revue des sciences philosophiques et théologiques* 96 (2012): 585–662.

O'Meara, Thomas. *Thomas Aquinas, Theologian*. Notre Dame: University of Notre Dame Press, 1997.

Osborne, Thomas M. *Love of Self and Love of God in Thirteenth-Century Ethics*. Notre Dame: University of Notre Dame Press, 2005.

Otto, S. A. "'Felix Culpa.' The Doctrine of Original Sin as Doctrine of Hope in Aquinas's *Summa contra Gentiles*." *The Heythrop Journal* 50 (2009): 781–92.

Palmquist, Stephen R. *Comprehensive Commentary on Kant's Religion within the Bounds of Bare Reason*. West Sussex: Wiley-Blackwell, 2016.

Pasternack, Lawrence R. *Kant on Religion within the Boundaries of Mere Reason*. London: Routledge, 2014.

Pelagius. *Commentary on St. Paul's Epistle to the Romans*. Trans. Theodore de Bruyn. Oxford: Clarendon Press, 1993.

Pesch, Otto Hermann. *Theologie der Rechtfertigung bei Martin Luther und Thomas von Aquin: Versuch eines systematisch-theologischen Dialogs*. Mainz: M. Grünewald, 1967.

"Der Urstand des Menschen. Eine Erkundung bei Thomas von Aquin." *Münchener Theologische Zeitschrift* 63 (2012): 134–44.

Peterson, Gregory. "Falling Up: Evolution and Original Sin." In *Evolution and Ethics: Human Morality in Biological and Religious Perspective*, ed. Phillip Clayton and Jeffrey Schloss, 273–86. Grand Rapids, MI: Eerdmans, 2004.

Portalié, Eugène. *A Guide to the Thought of Saint Augustine*. Trans. Ralph J. Bastian. Chicago: Henry Regnery, 1960.

Rahner, Karl. "Concerning the Relationship between Nature and Grace," in *Theological Investigations*, vol. 1. Trans. Cornelius Ernst, 297–317. Baltimore: Helicon, 1961.

"Evolution and Original Sin." In *Concilium* 26, trans. Johannes Metz, 61–73. New York: Paulist Press, 1967.

"Original Sin." In *Sacramentum Mundi: An Encyclopedia of Theology*, vol. 4, ed. Karl Rahner et al., 328–34. London: Burns and Oates, 1969.

Ramírez, Jacobus. *De vitiis et peccatis, In I-II Summae theologiae Divi Thomae expositio*. Salamanca: San Esteban, 1990.

Rea, Michael C. "The Metaphysics of Original Sin." In *Persons: Human and Divine*, ed. Peter van Inwagen and Dean Zimmerman, 319–56. Oxford: Oxford University Press, 2007.

Redding, John P. *The Influence of St. Augustine on the Doctrine of the II Council of Orange Concerning Original Sin*. Washington, DC: Catholic University of America Press, 1939.

Reich, David. *Who We Are and How We Got Here: Ancient DNA and the New Science of the Human Past*. New York: Pantheon Books, 2018.

Relethford, John H. "Genetics of Modern Human Origins and Diversity." *Annual Review of Anthropology* 27 (1998): 1–23.

Resnick, Irven M. "Introduction: Odo of Tournai." In *On Original Sin and a Disputation with the Jew, Leo, Concerning the Advent of Christ, the Son of God*. Trans. Irven M. Resnick. Philadelphia: University of Pennsylvania Press, 1994.

Reynolds, Philip Lyndon. *Food & the Body: Some Peculiar Questions in High Medieval Theology*. Leiden: Brill, 1999.

Rigby, Paul. "Original Sin." In *Augustine through the Ages: An Encyclopedia*, ed. A. Fitzgerald, 607–14. Grand Rapids, MI: Eerdmans, 1999.

Original Sin in Augustine's Confessions. Ottawa: University of Ottawa Press, 1987.

Rist, John M. *Augustine Deformed: Love, Sin and Freedom in the Western Moral Tradition*. Cambridge: Cambridge University Press, 2014.

Rondet, Henri. *Le Péché originel dans la tradition patristique et théologique*. Paris: Librairie Fayard, 1967.

Rosemann, Philipp W. *Peter Lombard*. Oxford: Oxford University Press, 2004.

Rosen-Zivi, Ishay. *Demonic Desires: Yetzer Hara and the Problem of Evil in Late Antiquity*. Philadelphia: University of Pennsylvania Press, 2011.

Rosenberg, Stanley P., Michael Burdett, Michael Lloyd, and Benno van den Toren, eds. *Finding Ourselves after Darwin*. Grand Rapids, MI: Baker Academic, 2018.

Sage, Athanase. "Le péché originel dans la pensée de saint Augustin, de 412 à 430." *Revue des études augustiniennes* 13 (1969): 211–48.

Saiving, Valerie. "The Human Situation: A Feminine View." In *Womanspirit Rising: A Feminist Reader in Religion*, ed. Carol P. Christ and Judith Plaskow, 25–42. New York: HarperCollins, 1992.

Sanders, E. P. *Paul and Palestinian Judaism*. Philadelphia: Fortress Press, 1977.

Savage, Minot Judson. *The Religion of Evolution*. Boston: Lockwood, Brooks, 1881.

Schenk, Richard. "Analogy as the *discrimen naturae et gratiae*: Thomism and Ecumenical Learning." In *The Analogy of Being: Invention of the Antichrist or the Wisdom of God?*, ed. Thomas Joseph White, 172–91. Grand Rapids, MI: Eerdmans, 2011.

Schleiermacher, Friedrich. *The Christian Faith*. Trans. H. R. Mackintosh and James S. Stewart. Berkeley: Apocryphile, 2011.

Schönborn, Christoph. "Die kirchliche Erbsündenlehre im Umriss." In *Zur kirchlichen Erbsündenlehre. Stellungnahmen zu einer brennenden Frage*, ed. Christoph Schönborn, 69–102. Einsiedeln: Johannes Verlag, 1991.

Schoonenberg, Piet. *Der Macht der Zonde*. L.C.G. Malmberg: Hertogenbosch, 1962.

Man and Sin: A Theological View. Trans. J. Donceel. Notre Dame: University of Notre Dame Press, 1965.

Schubert, Anselm. *Das Ende der Sünde: Anthropologie und Erbsünde zwischen Reformation und Aufklärung*. Göttingen: Vandenhoeck & Ruprecht, 2002.

Shanley, Brian. "Aquinas on Pagan Virtue." *The Thomist* 63 (1999): 553–77.

Sharkey, Sarah Borden. "How Can Being Be Limited?: W. Norris Clarke on Thomas's 'Limitation of Act by Potency.'" *The Saint Anselm Journal* 7.1 (2009): 1–19.

Siewerth, Gustav. *Die christliche Erbsündelehre: Entwickelt auf Grund der Theologie des Heiligen Thomas von Aquin*. Einsiedeln: Johannes Verlag, 1964.

Smith, James K. A. "Lost in Translation? On the Secularization of the Fall." In *The Devil Reads Derrida: And Other Essays on the University, Church, Politics, and the Arts*, 62–7. Grand Rapids, MI: Eerdmans, 2009.

Sober, Elliott. *Philosophy of Biology*. Boulder, CO: Westview Press, 2000.

Southern, R. W. *Saint Anselm: A Portrait in a Landscape*. Cambridge: Cambridge University Press, 1990.

Southgate, Christopher. *The Groaning of Creation: God, Evolution, and the Problem of Evil*. Louisville: Westminster John Knox, 2008.

Staffner, Hans. "Die Lehre des hl. Augustinus über das Wesen der Erbsünde." *Zeitschrift für Katholische Theologie* 79 (1957): 385–416.

Stringer, Chris. "Why We Are Not All Multiregionalists Now." *Trends in Ecology & Evolution* 29.5 (2014): 248–51.

Suchoki, Marjorie Hewitt. *The Fall to Violence: Original Sin in Relational Theology*. New York: Continuum, 1994.

Swafford, Andrew Dean. *Nature and Grace: A New Approach to Thomistic Ressourcement*. Eugene, OR: Wipf & Stock, 2014.

Swamidass, Joshua S. "The Overlooked Science of Genealogical Ancestry." *Perspectives on Science and Christian Faith* 70.1 (2018): 9–35.

Swinburne, Richard. *Responsibility and Atonement*. Oxford: Oxford University Press, 1989.

Te Velde, Rudi. "Evil, Sin, and Death: Thomas Aquinas on Original Sin." In *The Theology of Thomas Aquinas*, ed. R. van Nieuwenhove and J. Wawrykow, 143–66. Notre Dame: University of Notre Dame Press, 2005.

Tennant, F. R. *The Concept of Sin*. Cambridge: Cambridge University Press, 1912.

The Origin and Propagation of Sin, 2nd ed. Cambridge: Cambridge University Press, 1906.

The Sources of the Doctrine of the Fall and Original Sin. Cambridge: Cambridge University Press, 1903.

Torrell, Jean-Pierre. *Initiation à saint Thomas d'Aquin: Sa personne et son oeuvre*. Fribourg: Les Éditions du Cerf, 2002.

"Nature et grâce chez Thomas d'Aquin." *Revue Thomiste* 101 (2001): 167–202.

St. Thomas Aquinas, vol. 1: The Person and His Work. Trans. Robert Royal. Washington, DC: Catholic University of America Press, 2005.

Trooster, S. G. M. *Evolution and the Doctrine of Original Sin*. Trans. John A. Ter Haar. Glen Rock: Newman Press, 1968.

Tschipke, Theophil. *L'humanité du Christ comme instrument de salut de la divinité*. Fribourg: Academic Press, 2003.

Van den Toren, Benno. "Human Evolution and a Cultural Evolution of Original Sin." *Perspectives on Science and Christian Faith* 68.1 (2016): 12–21.

Van Oort, Johannes. "Jews and Judaism in Augustine's *Sermones*." *Instrvmenta Patristica et Mediaevalia* 53 (2009): 213–65.

Van Roo, William A. *Grace and Original Justice According to St. Thomas*. Rome: Gregorian University Press, 1955.

Vandervelde, George. *Original Sin: Two Major Trends in Contemporary Catholic Reinterpretation*. Washington, DC: University Press of America, 1981.

Vanneste, A. *Het dogma van de erfzonde: Zinloze mythe of openbaring van een grondstruktuur van het menselijk bestaan?* Tielt: Lannoo, 1969.

Le dogme du péché originel. Louvain: Nauwelaerts, 1971.

Venema, Denis R., and Scot McKnight. *Adam and the Genome: Reading Scripture after Genetic Science*. Grand Rapids, MI: Brazos Press, 2017.

Verriele, A. *Le Surnaturel en nous et le péché originel*. Paris: Bloud et Gay, 1932.

Vollert, Cyril. *The Doctrine of Hervaeus Natalis on Primitive Justice and Original Sin: As Developed in the Controversy on Original Sin during the Early Decades 14th Century*. Rome: Gregorian University Press, 1947.

"Saint Thomas on Sanctifying Grace and Original Justice: A Comparative Study of a Recent Controversy." *Theological Studies* 2 (1941): 369–87.

Walsh, Liam G. "Thomas Aquinas, the Doctrine of Original Sin, and the Dogma of the Immaculate Conception." In *Studying Mary: Reflections on the Virgin Mary in Anglican and Roman Catholic Theology and Devotion*, ed. Adelbert Denaux and Nicholas Sagovsky, 110–30. London: T&T Clark, 2007.

Walton, John H. *The Lost World of Adam and Eve: Genesis 2–3 and the Human Origins Debate*. Downers Grove, IL: InterVarsity Press, 2015.

Wawrykow, Joseph. *God's Grace and Human Action: "Merit" in the Theology of Thomas Aquinas*. Notre Dame: University of Notre Dame Press, 1995.

Weberburger, Richard. "'Limbus Puerorum.' Zur Enstehung eines theologischen Begriffes." *Recherches de théologie ancienne et médiévale* 55 (1968): 83–133.

Webster, John. "'The Firmest Grasp of the Real': Barth on Original Sin." *Toronto Journal of Theology* 4.1 (1988): 19–29.

Weingart, Richard E. *The Logic of Divine Love: A Critical Analysis of the Soteriology of Peter Abailard*. Oxford: Oxford University Press, 1970.

Weir, D. A. *The Origins of the Federal Theology in Sixteenth-Century Reformation Thought*. Oxford: Clarendon Press, 1990.

Whitehead, A. N. *Process and Reality: An Essay in Cosmology*. New York: Free Press, 1979.

Wiley, Tatha. *Original Sin: Origins, Developments, Contemporary Meanings*. New York: Paulist Press, 2002.

Williams, A. N. *The Ground of Union: Deification in Aquinas and Palamas*. New York: Oxford University Press, 1999.

Williams, N. P. *The Ideas of the Fall and of Original Sin: A Historical and Critical Study*. London: Longman, Green, 1927.

Williams, Patricia A. *Doing without Adam and Eve: Sociobiology and Original Sin*. Minneapolis, MN: Fortress Press, 2001.

Willows, Adam M. "Natural Love: Aquinas, Evolution and Charity." *The Heythrop Journal* (June 2017): 1–11. https://doi.org/10.1111/heyj.12665.

Wiseman, Nicolas Patrick. *Twelve Lectures on the Connexion between Science and Revealed Religion*. London: Cox and Wyman, 1849.

Wolpoff, Milford H., John Hawks, and Rachel Casparai. "Multiregional, Not Multiple Origins." *American Journal of Physical Anthropology* 112 (2000): 129–36.

Wolter, Allan B. "Duns Scotus on the Natural Desire for the Supernatural." In *The Philosophical Theology of John Duns Scotus*, ed. Marilyn McCord Adams, 125–47. Ithaca, NY: Cornell University Press, 1990.

Wood, Allen. *Kant's Ethical Thought*. New York: Cambridge University Press, 1999.

Wrangham, Richard, and Dale Peterson. *Demonic Males: Apes and the Origins of Human Violence*. New York: Houghton Mifflin, 1996.

Yarnold, Edward. *The Theology of Original Sin*. Hales Corner: Clergy Book Service, 1971.

Index

For EU product safety concerns, contact us at Calle de José Abascal, 56–1°, 28003 Madrid, Spain or eugpsr@cambridge.org.

www.ingramcontent.com/pod-product-compliance
Lightning Source LLC
Chambersburg PA
CBHW030033110325
23303CB00002B/75